THE PAPERS OF ULYSSES S. GRANT

U. S. Grant
Bvt. 2ᵈ Lt. 4ᵗʰ Infy.

THE PAPERS OF

ULYSSES S. GRANT

Volume 1 : 1837–1861

Edited by

John Y. Simon

———

SOUTHERN ILLINOIS UNIVERSITY PRESS

CARBONDALE AND EDWARDSVILLE

FEFFER & SIMONS, INC.

LONDON AND AMSTERDAM

To Major General Ulysses S. Grant 3rd

Contents

Foreword

BY RALPH G. NEWMAN

The Civil War centennial was welcomed with mixed emotions. Some greeted it as an opportunity to commemorate the deeds of a war a century earlier which had caused much death and misery but had established the principles of full freedom in these United States. Others cringed at the prospect of celebration rather than commemoration, of re-enactment of battles, of tourist promotions, and of other activities of doubtful taste, many of which seemed more concerned with reward and riches than with respect and remembrance.

The states of Ohio, Illinois, and New York had all served with honor in the fight to preserve the Union. The dedication and valor of the sons of these states had contributed in a major way to the ultimate victory. Among the heroes were some of the most distinguished names in American history—Lincoln, Logan, McPherson, Schofield, Sheridan, Sherman, Sickles, Wadsworth, and others. And there was the great hero whom they shared—Grant. Ulysses S. Grant belonged to the three states: Ohio, where he was born; Illinois, where he rose to greatness; and New York, where he spent his last years and was buried.

Early in the Civil War centennial, representatives of the three states agreed that some joint project which would pay tribute to the memory of General Grant would be proper and desirable. On May 3, 1962, the late Robert S. Harper, secretary of the Ohio Civil War Centennial Commission, brought together some of the members of the Civil War centennial commissions of Ohio, Illinois, and New York to discuss ways in which the centennial could lead to an increased understanding and appreciation of the Union commander and Eighteenth President. The meeting was held in Columbus, Ohio, and the participants were Robert S. Harper and Erwin C. Zepp of Ohio, Ralph G. Newman and J. W. Scott of Illinois, and Carl Haverlin of New York. Also present for part of the meeting was Allan Nevins, chairman of the United States Civil War Centennial Commission, who had been a resident of New York, but had recently moved to California, and E. B. Long of Illinois, director of research for Bruce Catton. Mr. Haverlin proposed that the three commissions sponsor the collecting, editing, and publication of the collected works of Ulysses S. Grant— a suggestion that was unanimously adopted by the conferees.

The first action taken by the three state commissions was the formation of the Ulysses S. Grant Association with a charter from the State of Illinois as a not-for-profit corporation. At a meeting held in Chicago, officers and directors were elected, and an editorial board headed by Allan Nevins was selected. Funds for the beginning of the project were supplied by the three commissions. John Y. Simon, a native Illinoisan with a Ph.D. in history from Harvard, then a member of the history faculty of Ohio State University, was employed as executive director of the association and editor of the collected works. On September 1, 1962, the Ulysses S. Grant Association began work in Columbus, in offices supplied by the Ohio Historical Society.

Immediately after the initial suggestion for the project, Ralph G. Newman and Erwin C. Zepp, representing the three commissions, called on Major General Ulysses S. Grant 3rd at his home in Clinton, New York, to obtain his consent for the undertaking involving his grandfather's writings. He was most gracious in his endorsement of the idea and offered to make available much important material in his control and in addition agreed to suggest that other members of the Grant family cooperate with the editorial and publication plan.

In 1964, the approaching end of the Civil War centennial and the exhaustion of available funds from the Ohio and New York commissions made it necessary for the association to seek a working arrangement that would assure the project the continuity and support necessary for its successful completion. Dr. Delyte W. Morris, president of Southern Illinois University, on behalf of his institution, expressed an interest in the venture and arranged for a meeting of members of his faculty and representatives of the association. The project was enthusiastically accepted, and arrangements were made for an immediate transfer of all work and headquarters to Carbondale, Illinois, where facilities were provided in the Morris Library of Southern Illinois University. In addition, the Southern Illinois University Press made a commitment to publish the work when completed.

The National Historical Publications Commission was approached for financial aid, and the request met with success. In addition, Dr. Oliver Wendell Holmes, director of the commission, agreed to serve as a member of the editorial board of the Ulysses S. Grant Association. The involvement of the commission has been much more than the providing of much needed finances to supplement the commitment from Southern Illinois University. It has also, through its director and staff, helped to make material in the National Archives available for this enterprise.

Eighty years ago, as he completed his *Memoirs*, General Grant wrote, "I feel that we are on the eve of a new era, when there is to be great harmony between the Federal and the Confederate. I cannot stay to be a living witness to the correctness of this prophecy, but I feel it within me that it is to be so. The universally kind feeling expressed for me at a time when it was supposed that each day would prove my last, seemed to me the beginning of the answer to 'Let us have peace.' " It is in this spirit and with this hope that the Ulysses S. Grant Association proudly presents this first volume of what we believe will be a noble series and a distinguished contribution to the study of our past and of the life and times of a remarkable American.

Preface

BY BRUCE CATTON

———

Most men who saw U. S. Grant during the Civil War felt that there was something mysterious about him. He looked so much like a completely ordinary man, and what he did was so definitely out of the ordinary, that it seemed as if he must have profound depths that were never visible from the surface. Even Sherman, who knew him as well as anybody did, once remarked that he did not understand Grant and did not believe Grant understood himself. In general, people simply agreed with Abraham Lincoln's admiring comment, "Wherever he is, things move!"

This was baffling, because the quality in him that made things move seemed to be beyond analysis. There was one officer, however, who saw a good deal of Grant at Chattanooga in the early winter of 1864, who believed the general's success was chiefly due to "his fine common sense and the faculty he possesses in a wonderful degree of making himself understood."

That is perhaps as good a judgment as any. Common sense, to be sure, is actually such an uncommon trait that nobody is ever quite able to define it, but the interesting thing about the Chattanooga officer's finding is the balance of the sentence—the reference to Grant's uncommon ability to make himself understood.

No one can read the letters herewith presented without agreeing that U. S. Grant was one of the most articulate of all American soldiers. He knew how to present exactly what was on his mind. Whether he was writing to his wife, explaining what was happening to him and what he wanted to do next, or composing an order that would set armies marching and lead to great battles, he was always lucid. You never have to re-read one of his letters to find out what he was driving at. No matter what he was talking about, he always made himself understood. That there were things he did not write about at all—that he had a certain reticence that kept him, at times, from revealing what was going on inside his head—was of course as true of him as it is likely to be of anyone else. But what he does say is never in the least foggy. The message always comes through. One of Grant's unlooked-for assets was a simple mastery of the art of composing clear English prose.

To study his wartime telegrams and dispatches is to see what a great help this was to him as a soldier. His subordinates always knew what he had on his mind and what they were expected to do, and although things often went wrong with Grant's campaign and battle plans the things that went wrong seldom went that way because the commanding general had not made himself understood. Anyone who ploughs through the unending stream of documents in the *Official Records* comes sooner or later to the point where he can recognize a Grant letter without waiting to see the signature: it gets to the point, avoids unnecessary verbiage, and tells the recipient exactly what the recipient needs to know. Nothing could be more direct, for instance, than two short sentences in the letter Grant gave to General George Gordon Meade, commander of the Army of the Potomac, telling Meade what he was supposed to do when the 1864 campaign began: "Lee's army will be your objective point. Wherever Lee goes, there you will go also."

All of this sort of thing, to be sure, is primarily of interest to the student of military affairs. What is more to the point here is the way the supposedly taciturn Grant continually reveals himself in his more personal letters, especially in the letters he sent before the war to Mrs. Grant. These letters show a Grant who is not at all like the man who became a legend—hard, self-contained, unimaginative, stolid. On the contrary they present an intensely warm, deeply emotional man who poured out his heart in as revealing a series of compositions as any biographer could hope to see. Reading them, one forgets about the great general who was going to come on stage a few years later and sees only a lonely young officer, beset by a variety of misfortunes, relying desperately on the love of a wife from whom he was separated by most of the width of a continent.

In other words, they show a man very much in love, and almost

unendurably lonely. In his letters from the West Coast, Grant is forever sending kisses, telling his wife how he has dreamed of her and the
children, asking eagerly for the smallest bits of information about how
the children are growing and learning, and in every line showing as
vividly as a man can show that this long separation from his family was
more of a load than he knew how to carry.

Perhaps a word of explanation is in order here.

During the early 1850's Grant was a first lieutenant of infantry,
stationed far up on the West Coast at the very height of the Gold Rush.
The Gold Rush needs to be mentioned because it had driven prices and
wages in the Far West up out of sight; as a result, Grant's pay and
allowances as an officer were desperately strained to provide for his
own living and still send money home to his family. (He remarked at
this time that the pay of an army captain would not hire a cook.) To
have his family join him, at such a post as Fort Vancouver, as an officer
would do under ordinary circumstances, was simply out of the question.
It would cost much more than he could possibly afford.

So along with his work as an army officer Grant was trying
desperately to raise extra money. He did all sorts of things, applying
himself industriously, and saw all of them fail. He rented land and did
some farming on the side, raising potatoes: a venture that would have
been profitable, food prices in San Francisco being so high, except that
a Columbia River flood destroyed most of the crop. With some other
officers he had one hundred tons of ice cut from the river and sent down
to San Francisco by schooner—an excellent idea, but headwinds
delayed the vessel so long that by the time it docked, huge cargoes of
ice had come down from Alaska and the market collapsed. He bought
hogs and sent them off to what looked like a rising market, only to lose
several hundred dollars when other operators got in ahead of him. He
and other officers invested money in a combined rooming house and
billiard room in San Francisco, which was full of unattached males; but
the agent hired to operate the establishment absconded with the funds,
and Grant's circle lost everything.

After a couple of years of this Grant had had it, and by the spring of
1854 the loneliness and frustration were too much for him; and we
find him writing to Mrs. Grant that he wanted to resign and trust to
Providence "and my own exertions" that he could make a living back
in the Middle West as a civilian family man. But this was a chancy
prospect, at best. The army had been his life, he was not sure that he

could make a living on the outside, and *"poverty, poverty* begins to stare me in the face, and then I think what would I do if you and our little ones should want for the necessaries of life."

It was a tough outlook, but Grant confessed that "I do not feel as if it was possible to endure this separation much longer." So at last, on April 11, 1854, we find this letter from Grant to the adjutant general of the army. "I very respectfully tender my resignation of my commission as an officer of the Army, and request that it may take effect from the 31st July next." The ill luck that pursued Grant so relentlessly in the Far West followed him back East. He started a new career as a farmer in Missouri, but he was desperately cramped by lack of capital. His father, a canny Yankee type named Jesse Grant, was a prosperous tanner and merchant, and it seems clear that he could have extended more of a helping hand than he did. In the winter of 1857 Grant sent to Jesse a letter that makes painful reading. He needed a thousand dollars that he did not have, and he wrote to his father in these words. "It is always usual for parents to give their children assistince in begining life (and I am only begining, though thirty five years of age, nearly) and what I ask is not much. I do not ask you to give me anything. But what I do ask is that you lend, or borrow for, me Five hundred dollars, for two years, with interest at 10 pr. cent payable anually, or semmi anually if you choose, and with this if I do not go on prosperously I shall ask no more from you."

Clearly enough, in the period just before the Civil War, Grant sank close to rock bottom. How he established himself, at last, as a clerk in his father's store in Galena, Illinois, supporting his family acceptably but apparently having no prospect whatever of rising in the world, is part of a story that lies beyond the immediate compass of these volumes. The letters do provide the background for an understanding of it.

They provide, of course, more than that. They show one of America's great soldiers being hammered into shape during the years before his great moment of opportunity. A character was built in that time, and the process is revealed to us in these letters. To read them is to learn more about the great Civil War general than any military analysis can show. The qualities that made Grant a master of war may still be more than slightly mysterious, as Sherman believed, but the qualities that first made him master of himself come through clearly. What came afterward was built on them.

Preface

BY ALLAN NEVINS

IT IS no accident that many of the great captains of history —Miltiades, the victor of Marathon; Gustavus Adolphus, the Lion of the North; Wellington—united political and military careers as did Ulysses S. Grant. The qualities of mind and will that they displayed on tented fields were deemed to entitle them to civil leadership. The popular supposition that Wellington was made prime minister and Grant elected President as marks of gratitude for Waterloo and Appomattox is largely erroneous. They were elevated because they had shown traits of decision, determination, and tenacity that the trials of peace demanded no less than those of war. The fact that the problems of peace and war are entirely different seemed irrelevant to those who made Wellington prime minister in 1828 and those who elected Grant forty years later. Eventually admirers of both men found that the differences can be tremendous. Wellington had to shutter his house against a mob, and Grant to endure vitriolic denunciation. But faith in the abiding value of the traits both had brought to a wartime crisis persisted.

Like Washington, Grant had a history that for a quarter-century was largely the history of his country. His name came before the nation with rolls of thunder; during four years the thunder of guns, and then thunderous cheers for a war hero, a President, an ex-President turned globe-traveller, and an aspirant for a third term. The result was the creation of a unique image; to many Americans not unlike what a Kitchener and an Asquith rolled into one would have been in Great Britain later. It is usual to emphasize the dichotomy of Grant's life, and the contrast between the impressive military career and the disappointing political record; separate books have been published on each, as if the central figures were different men. Yet they were the same Grant, and the careers had a strong bond.

They were bound together by the fact that they rested upon the same basis: Grant's character. He gained his place in the American pantheon not by intellectual power, not by brilliance, cleverness, or agile skill, and not by gifts of personality; he gained it by character. Between Belmont and Spotsylvania he placed before the country the image of a quietly masterful general, exercising command without hesitancy; a resolute and combative leader, unflinching under any strain; a captain as simple and direct as Hannibal or Cromwell. He carried this image into the White House. Even when his countrymen learned that his simplicity could be naïveté, that his directness could be clumsiness in political situations where finesse and tact were essential, and that reliance upon bad subordinates could be as harmful in government as in battle, their faith in his character remained.

Of course many will read the rich materials in these volumes for the light they throw upon events and men; but many will also study them for their revelation of character, a character unique and fascinating. Nobody ever thought Grant a man of genius, or even of the flashes of inspiration that Stonewall Jackson repeatedly brought to his tasks. He lacked the Olympian harmony and majesty of personality that Robert E. Lee possessed. His mind gave little evidence of the subtleties and nuances of thought that often lurked behind Lincoln's firm logic, and he had none of the eloquence and poetry that come out in Lincoln's best papers from the Second Annual Message and the J. C. Conkling letter down to the Second Inaugural. Never mind, said Americans; he had saved the Union by his unconditional-surrender nerve, his fight-it-out-on-this-line-if-it-takes-all-summer tenacity, his attack-Hood-at-once aggressiveness. He saw his goals plainly even if he oversimplified the road; he moved to them with clearheaded if rough vigor. He gives us a coarse-grained Administration, men said; he makes queer blunders; nevertheless, we confide in him.

As we study his life we have a curious sense of some deep inner force at work. Sherman, remarking that he never understood Grant and believed he never understood himself, felt this. From cadet days he went through humiliation after humiliation. Yet in his trials then and in great crises afterward he appeared to find strength in this hidden inner force. His aide Adam Badeau remarked the fact, stating that, when he asked Grant to explain the reasoning behind a major decision, Grant in a puzzled way would say the decision had just sprung up and possessed him. From inner depths came his tremendous fortitude. The State of Illinois treasures a pawn ticket showing how, in the sad, shabby years of his ante-bellum struggles in Missouri, he pledged his watch to give his family Christmas money. This was 1857; eleven years later the penniless owner, whose heroism on his Hard-scrabble farm excelled that he had exhibited as a young officer at Monterey, was a conqueror and President-elect! His fortitude had triumphed.

The core of his character remained the same. No matter how harshly beleaguered by dire circumstances and hostile men, he never faltered. Did he and Sherman blunder at Shiloh in lack of preparation and vigilance? He would push into the second day's battle that re-deemed the first. Was Henry Wager Halleck taking steps to suspend him from command and planning to ruin him? He would carry on. Were hostile editors and Senators of power and implacable temper dividing his party at the end of his first term to bring him down in humiliation? In blunders and missteps, as in sure moves and triumphs, he remained Grant, simple, determined, undefeatable.

Other traits of character, too, will give his letters an enduring interest for many readers, when details of engagements, political struggles, and diplomacy concern only the specialist. They come out in his *Memoirs* and his dispatches in the *Official Records*, but most of all in his personal epistles. The magnanimity shown in his treatment of subordinates, and in his courteous mode of receiving Lee's surrender, is recurrent. His modesty is engaging. In a time of strutting brigadiers the general-in-chief despised epaulets and slipped into obscure seats in public, as when he turned up in Willard's Hotel to get his high com-mission from Lincoln. His imperturbability was another fundamental trait. When, in speaking of Sherman, he wrote Stanton, "What a splendid general he is!" he came as near emotion as his reserve allowed. As Mark Twain would put it, he never slopped over. When Mrs. Grant visited the army, only a very sharp-eyed observer caught them holding hands in their tent. One of the distinctions of this collection is that when completed it will give us a large array of hitherto un-known correspondence with wife, father, and children, showing how warm of heart Grant really was.

Under fire, whether political or military, this same imperturbability was unfailing. At North Anna, where he sat under a tree writing dispatches as shells hurled fragments about him, a Wisconsin soldier repeated the familiar saying: "Ulysses doesn't scare worth a damn." Sherman defined his coolness more fully. "I am a damn sight smarter man than Grant," he told James Harrison Wilson. "I know a great deal more about war, military history, strategy, and grand tactics than he does; I know more about organization, supply . . . and about every-thing else." But, he added, in one essential Grant beat him and all the world. "He don't care a damn for what the enemy does out of his sight . . . He issues his orders and does his level best to carry them out." Generosity was another marked characteristic. He never forgot a friend, and to the men who had befriended him when he was poor, unregarded, and ill-treated he was often all too generous—for some of them later betrayed him and the country.

And Grant's truthfulness seems always to have been conspicuous. His taciturnity (reinforced by prudence) sometimes kept him from tell-ing the whole truth, as in his brief and opaque report upon Shiloh. But Hamilton Fish, who was at his elbow during eight years, declared him the most truthful man he had ever known. He certainly had no skill in self-serving equivocation, in the political and diplomatic art that Fish knew so well, of chipping the cube of truth to make it roll.

Not least important among Grant's virtues, to those who read the past in the light of today, was his strong humanitarian concern for the former slaves, the neglected and woebegone Negroes. As he moved south to take Vicksburg and east to hold Jackson, his forces liberated hundreds of thousands of slaves, many of them the victims of con-scienceless abuse. His letters on this problem breathe a constructive compassion. His appointment of a Dartmouth-trained educator, John Eaton, to organize the freedmen's camps in the Mississippi Valley, was supported by measures to furnish schooling and employment as well as food and shelter; and his papers on the subject are among the most creditable Union documents of the time.

A catalogue of virtues tends to dullness, and too many who have written on Grant have done so in fulsome vein. He would have been far less interesting had he not possessed his share of human shortcomings, and some of his frailties appear in his letters. We know he did drink at times, and here John A. Rawlins had to constitute himself (as records show) a vigilant guardian; though it is probably true that, as General Charles King argues, a very little liquor would flush Grant's fair complexion and thicken his never glib tongue. Generous-hearted as he was, he could occasionally conceive real hatred of a man. His correspondence would do something to prove the fact even if other evidence were wanting. If he did not detest John A. McClernand, his temporary rival on the Vicksburg front, he came close to it—feeling perhaps also a little jealous apprehension. If he did not hate Charles Sumner, he came still closer. A record exists of Grant shaking his fist one night at Sumner's closed window—but then haters of Sumner, with good cause, were legion. Men will never forget Grant's crisp remark when told that the pompously egotistical Senator did not believe in the Bible. "No," ejaculated the President, "he did not write it." Yet Grant usually kept his temper admirably. He furnished as few instances of anger as Washington, the one best-remembered being his hot outburst when he saw a brutal teamster beating a horse over the head.

Usually deliberate and cool, Grant could nevertheless, as his papers show, be at times indiscreetly impetuous. Once his impatient impetuousity—if there was anything he loathed it was failure to execute commands—led him to direct the replacement of George H. Thomas just before the battle of Nashville, an order happily stopped in the nick of time. If his nearly singlehanded attempt to effect the annexation of Santo Domingo was not one of the most impetuous strokes in the history of our foreign relations, it comes near that bad eminence. His motives were good, and he offered some valid arguments, but this whole chapter of diplomacy was deplorable—and it was all his own.

While Grant could not be termed an inordinately ambitious man, in this collection of his letters and other papers we can find evidence of how strongly ambition grew upon him. He approached the Presidency with initial reluctance. It seems plain that, keeping his own counsel so that even his wife did not know his feeling, he did not make a decision to seek the office until his complete breach with Andrew Johnson made any other decision impossible. When he first entered the political world he felt it alien, excessively complicated, and in many respects highly distasteful. His shyness was more evident than ever, and his reticence more marked. These qualities combined with his military habit of mind, his belief that important Republican chiefs ought to be staff aides rather than independent associates, to lead him into some of his worst errors. His initial Cabinet had immediately to be reorganized because he had not sought the advice of men who could have told him that his first choice for the Treasury, A. T. Stewart, was legally ineligible, that it was an error to name two members (Hoar and Boutwell) from Massachusetts, that the Philadelphian Adolph E. Borie did not wish to be head of the Navy, and so on. Other mistakes of similar origin followed.

A leader of such positive traits, and such enigmatic ways, combining great powers and great deficiencies, and holding eminent positions through one of the stormiest of quarter centuries, was sure to be involved in controversy after controversy. In few segments of our national history have the problems faced been more numerous, more complex, or more bizarre. From the very beginning of his political involvements, uncertainty and dissension ruled. Grant's position in 1864 demands study on two fronts. He was fighting his last great military campaign in a determined way that, while it brought victory steadily nearer, did it at such cost in life and anguish that popular resentment boiled ominously near the explosion point. At the same time he was beset by great dissatisfied elements in the Republican Party that, disliking Lincoln, fearing his Reconstruction views, and believing defeat at the polls almost certain, urged the general to step forward as Presidential candidate. Against such folly he was happily adamant. Then in the assassination of Lincoln the nation lost the one man who might have managed the Pandora's box of troubles that the war had opened.

Reconstruction; foreign affairs; the management of national finance when the Panic of 1873 and ensuing Depression made inflation or deflation an issue of the most painful nature; and the reduction or elimination of an omnipresent mass of corruption—these were the four main heads of the hydra with which Grant had to grapple. No era except that just before the Civil War was so full of varied antagonisms. In no era was the record of Congress, the chief state governments North and South, the city administrations, and large-scale business more deplorable. On each of the four great subjects named Grant had to take an unequivocal stand, and on each his policies and acts inevitably provoked dissent, disgust, resentment, and rejection, as well as scattered assent and bursts of applause. That eventually he piloted the country, however uncertainly at times, through the choppy waves, was something of a miracle. It is indeed high time that we had his full writings to help us study his work, and the storm-tossed course of the government.

In Reconstruction Grant bowed to the Radicals in Congress and to military views of the situation; after all, he was an unflinching believer in discipline. He bowed, as most historians have agreed, too completely, but that the Southern whites behaved very badly is equally clear. In foreign affairs he fortunately had—after the Dominican fiasco —the sagacity, experience, and dignified moderation of Hamilton Fish, a man of his own calm, to guide him. In finance he took his boldest decision alone and unaided: a veto of an inflationary bloating of the paper currency, urged by his Secretary of the Treasury and the Senate Finance Committee, but clearly fraught with possible disaster. In dealing with the great waves of corruption that swept over business and banking, over state capitols and city halls, and into parts of the national government, he hardly showed the moral rigor of a Theodore Roosevelt, though he did accomplish something. "Let no guilty man escape," he said when the Whiskey Ring was exposed, but his close friend Orville Babcock did escape. So did scores of others, many after confessing guilt, and his dishonest Secretary of War somehow got out of the government without the dismissal he merited.

All this is a bizarre and many-hued tale, and we are fortunate that now we shall have papers for its more complete and doubtless more interesting exploration. These papers will permit a full rehearsal of the story, how through it all Grant retained the respect of his closest associates, and not only the regard but the affection of the general public. To millions he was still the Grant they had once worshipped, and as the Hayes Administration drew to its exemplary but colorless end, a widespread demand arose for his reinstatement in power. He was ready, unfortunately, to yield to it, and Mrs. Grant, as James G. Blaine and Adam Badeau tell us, was still more eager to resume residence in the White House. The acclaim that Grant had met on his tour of the world, itself a fascinating story that can now be told with many new values, had increased the prestige of the soldier-President. To be sure, it was largely acclaim for the republic whose united strength he had helped maintain, and which in time would use that strength for the support of liberty, freedom, and concord throughout the democratic sphere. But it was partly acclaim for the general whose modesty, courtesy, and geniality enhanced his dignity and made friends everywhere. As the long tour ended, happily, the third term movement collapsed.

The last and in some respects most appealing chapter of Grant's life was not to be written upon a renewal of his life in the White House.

It was to be written around his heroic stand at Mount McGregor against the pain and weakness of mortal illness, a stand which revealed again to even the most critical of Americans his true heroism. Whispering when he could no longer speak, he dictated for the support of his now impoverished family, and the enlightenment of coming generations of Americans, the two volumes of memoirs that stand as one of his most remarkable achievements. This is a tale, too, on which we shall now have fresh light, and the new information will help contribute a last fitting touch to the record of an indomitable American hero.

Acknowledgments

═══

Inquiries for Grant material have been made in every state and many foreign countries. Institutional and private owners of Grant documents are identified in the text. Literally hundreds of people have assisted the Grant Association in assembling more than 30,000 relevant documents. Listed below are some of the people to whom the officers of the Grant Association are especially grateful.

V. L. Bedsole, Louisiana State University Library; Robert Brubaker, Illinois State Historical Library; Henry Cadwalader, Historical Society of Pennsylvania; Herbert Cahoon, Pierpont Morgan Library; Henry J. Caren, Ohio Historical Society; Alexander P. Clark, Princeton University Library; Meredith Colket, Western Reserve Historical Society; Joan Corbett, National Historical Publications Commission; Dennis M. Corrigan, Illinois State Archives; Robert Cupp, Ohio Historical Society; John Wells Davidson, Papers of Woodrow Wilson; Clive E. Driver, Philip H. & A. S. W. Rosenbach Foundation; Kenneth W. Duckett, Southern Illinois University Archives; Lloyd A. Dunlap, Library of Congress; Sherrod East, National Archives; Elaine Everly, National Historical Publications Commission; H. B. Fant, National Historical Publications Commission; Margaret Flint, Illinois State Historical Library; Sallie Folden, Southern Illinois University Press; Ulysses S. Grant IV, San Diego, Calif.; Josephine Harper, State Historical Society of Wisconsin; Arthur B. Hayes, Cleveland, Ohio; Robert W. Hill, New York Public Library; David W. Hirst, Papers of Woodrow Wilson; Donald Holmes, Library of Congress; William T. Hutchinson, Papers of James Madison; Victor Jacobs, Dayton, Ohio; George R. Jones, Chicago, Ill.; Russell W. Jones, Jr., Illinois State Archives; Helene Levene, Civil War Centennial Commission of Illinois; Helen Mangold, Henry E. Huntington Library and Art Gallery; Watt Marchman, Rutherford B. Hayes Library; Elizabeth Martin, Ohio Historical Society; Ralph McCombs, Ohio Civil War Centennial Commission; Ralph E. McCoy, Southern Illinois University Libraries; Mary Lynn McCree, Civil War Centennial Commission of Illinois; R. Gerald McMurtry, Lincoln National Life Foundation; Haskell M. Monroe, Jr., Papers of Jefferson Davis; Archie Motley, Chicago Historical Society; C. Percy Powell, Library of Congress; Harold Rath, Southern Illinois University Libraries; Stephen T. Riley, Massachusetts Historical Society; James Rodabaugh, Ohio Historical Society; Fred Shelley, National Historical Publications Commission; Paul Spence, Illinois State Historical Library; Vernon Sternberg, Southern Illinois University Press; Wayne C. Temple, Illinois State Archives; Karl Trever, Washington, D.C.; Bernard Wax, Illinois State Historical Library; James M. Wells, Newberry Library.

The maps were drawn by Barbara Long. Material for this volume has been typed by Kathryn Overturf, secretary for the Grant Association, and by Harriet Simon, related by marriage to the project.

The Grant Association has received major financial support from Southern Illinois University, the National Historical Publications Commission, the Civil War Centennial Commission of Illinois, the Ohio Civil War Centennial Commission, the New York Civil War Centennial Commission, the Illinois State Historical Society, Bruce Catton, and Major General Ulysses S. Grant 3rd. Other funds have come from the Sons of Union Veterans of the Civil War (and its Massachusetts chapter), the Civil War Centennial Association, and the Civil War Round Table of Chicago.

Introduction

BY JOHN Y. SIMON

⸻

T̲HE LITERARY QUALITIES of Grant's *Memoirs* have often been praised while little attention has been given to his other writings. The chief reason has been that they were generally unavailable in printed form and difficult to locate in manuscript. As recently as the 1930's one historian concluded that Grant "wrote as little as possible," and "there is no considerable collection of his manuscripts."[1] Biographer William B. Hesseltine complained of "the almost complete lack of Grant manuscripts."[2] Now, however, the Grant Association has material for at least a dozen volumes of his papers.

Grant seems to have made no effort to preserve his private correspondence. Because of his professional military training, his Civil War headquarters records[3] were carefully organized and comprehensive. In the White House, however, no such careful records were kept; in fact, much correspondence was left behind. Some of it became part of the collection of his successor, Rutherford B. Hayes, and four letterbooks remained in the White House until transferred to the Library of Congress in 1921. Although Grant told his fiancée, Julia Dent, that he was saving her letters, they have not been found, and there is no indication that he saved personal correspondence at any other time. Grant ruefully admitted that "the only place I ever found in my life to put a paper so as to find it again was either in a side coat-pocket or the hands of a clerk or secretary more careful than myself."[4]

---

1. Frederic Logan Paxson in *DAB*, VII, 501.
2. William B. Hesseltine, *Ulysses S. Grant: Politician* (New York, 1935), p. vii.
3. Grant's Civil War headquarters records will be discussed in the next volume.
4. *Personal Memoirs of U. S. Grant* (New York, 1885–86), I, 233.

It is not surprising that only two slim volumes[5] have been devoted exclusively to Grant's private correspondence.

In recent years, however, a great quantity of new material has become available. Many Grant letters in private hands or owned by dealers have been acquired by libraries. The Library of Congress, which had sought since 1904 to build a Grant collection, received between 1953 and 1960 from Major General Ulysses S. Grant 3rd his grandfather's headquarters records in 111 volumes and the letters written by Grant to his wife.[6]

In addition, Grant material has become more accessible. Many of the great manuscript collections in all parts of the country are now available on microfilm. Great improvements in photocopying techniques make it possible to collect dependable texts from remote places. A number of new guides, most notably the *National Union Catalog of Manuscript Collections*, have brought to light materials generally unknown. The National Historical Publications Commission, established by the federal government to promote and support documentary editions of the papers of leading Americans, has made available the rich resources of the National Archives and Library of Congress.

The final factor which has made a comprehensive edition of Grant possible is a new interest in the man himself. Henry Adams, in his *Education*, had made Grant a symbol of post-Civil War America. "The progress of evolution from President Washington to President Grant," he concluded, "was alone evidence enough to upset Darwin."[7] An elaborated version of Henry Adams could be found in *Meet General Grant*, a 1928 biography by William E. Woodward, who overcame his own admiration of Grant through an appreciation of a market in which debunking was popular.[8] As Woodward traced Grant's rise from "the bottom of his pit, a forlorn figure," in Galena to "a complacent bourgeois" in New York, Grant became the scapegoat for an entire generation.[9]

In 1950, with the publication of *Captain Sam Grant* by Lloyd Lewis, the tide began to turn. Lewis carried his biography to Grant's

5. James Grant Wilson, ed., *General Grant's Letters to a Friend, 1861–1880* (New York, 1897); Jesse Grant Cramer, ed., *Letters of Ulysses S. Grant to his Father and his Youngest Sister, 1857–78* (New York, 1912).

6. Library of Congress, *Index to the Ulysses S. Grant Papers* (Washington, 1965), pp. v–vi.

7. *The Education of Henry Adams* (Boston and New York, 1918), p. 266.

8. See William E. Woodward, *The Gift of Life* (New York, 1947).

9. *Meet General Grant* (New York, 1928), pp. 136, 477.

entrance into the Civil War and revealed a man of greater intelligence and sensitivity than was generally known. Analyses of Grant's generalship by authors like K. P. Williams and Bruce Catton have made it clear that his victories were due to more than luck and larger armies. By the time the Grant Association was organized in 1962 there was more interest in Grant and more controversy concerning his role in American history than at any time since his death. Certainly a documentary record of Grant's own words was already long overdue. Orme W. Phelps of Claremont Men's College had already assembled texts of some Grant letters and this collection provided a nucleus for the Grant Association.

Major General Ulysses S. Grant 3rd and his sister, Mme. Julia Cantacuzene, generously gave permission to the Grant Association to print the text of all letters of their grandfather and helped to locate valuable family papers. The Grant Association gathered photoduplicates of anything in Grant's hand, addressed to him, or containing significant information about him, and indexed each item with multicopy cards. Present plans call for the publication of the Grant Papers in five series: (1) the prewar period (1837–1861); (2) the Civil War and Reconstruction (1861–1868); (3) the political years (1868–1880); (4) the last years (1880–1885); (5) additional volumes containing Grant interviews and an annotated edition of the *Memoirs*.

The first of these series is complete in the present volume. Much of the documentary record of the first thirty-nine years of Grant's life has vanished; what remains is especially valuable both because of its rarity and the inadequacy of other sources concerning Grant for this period. The bulk of the letters (109) are written to Julia Dent Grant and are fairly evenly divided between the periods before and after their marriage in 1848. Since only 6 letters from Grant to Mrs. Grant have been found outside the Grant family collection in the Library of Congress, it appears likely that Mrs. Grant maintained a fairly complete collection of the letters she received. Julia Dent wrote Grant on June 10, 1846, that she had 25 of his letters; this is exactly the number for the period now in the Library of Congress.[10]

Most of the other Grant letters owe their existence to the record-keeping procedures of the army. No letter from Grant to his parents or brothers and sisters is known to survive written before the mid-1850's, and earlier letters may well have been lost when the Grant

10. See letter of July 2, 1846.

family moved from Bethel, Ohio, to Covington, Ky., in 1855. Other surviving Grant letters owe their existence to good fortune and are widely scattered. We can feel no confidence that all of these have been located for inclusion in this volume, but hope that strays will be called to our attention for use in a supplement to *The Papers of Ulysses S. Grant.*

At least 80 per cent of the text has never before been printed and most has been unavailable in any form. Every significant Grant document is printed in full and all others are incorporated in a calendar at the back of this volume. Items in the calendar include routine letters and documents, letters to Grant with no known reply, and material for which no reliable text is available. Editorial insertions in the text have been held to a minimum so that the printed page follows the manuscript document as closely as possible. None of Grant's spelling, grammar, or punctuation has been altered. Notes provide additional information on persons, places, and events mentioned in the text. In some places an absence of annotation stands as a mute confession of ignorance on the part of the editor.

In many cases Grant has served as his own editor. In writing to Julia he rarely forgot what he had written previously or omitted crucial background information on matters he discussed. When a letter from Mexico had a new dateline, he customarily explained his move from a previous location. Often his writing material was limited to a single sheet of paper folded once to form four surfaces, the fourth reserved for use as an envelope; although some of the earlier letters have sections written on the envelope and across the first page of the letter, Grant soon learned to fit a complete message to the available paper with no omissions or waste space. Grant mastered the formal style and limited vocabulary of official military correspondence with considerable skill to produce letters remarkable alike for brevity and clarity. With an instinctive grasp of the weight and significance of words, he produced letters which clearly reveal his patterns of thought in dealing with the subject at hand.

Of the hitherto printed sources of information about Grant's life before the Civil War, the most important is, of course, *Personal Memoirs of U. S. Grant* (1885–86). Prepared during the last year of Grant's life, much of it written while he was dying of cancer, the *Memoirs* cover his early life with equanimity and candor. Grant has never lacked biographers, though few have added much new material. Before 1900 there were 91 published biographies of Grant, nearly equalling the 110 Lincoln biographies.[11] Three Grant biographies are outstanding for their treatment of the early years. Albert D. Richardson's *A Personal History of Ulysses S. Grant* (1868) was the work of an enterprising journalist with good connections among some of Grant's closest friends. Hamlin Garland's *Ulysses S. Grant* (1898) originated as a serial in *McClure's Magazine*. Garland made a careful search for people who had known Grant well, and while many of the reminiscences he collected for the early years have the defects of long-range memory, they still shed a dim light on questions otherwise completely dark. Lloyd Lewis in *Captain Sam Grant* (1950) provides the best modern synthesis of Grant's life before the Civil War and has a useful bibliography. The only biography of Julia Dent Grant, *The General's Wife* (1959) by Ishbel Ross, is based on some material unavailable to Lewis.

No source, however, can surpass in value what Grant himself recorded at the time in his official and private correspondence. Like many well-known Americans, Grant has often suffered at the hands of those who prefer symbolic significance to historical accuracy. Much of his life, the early years particularly, has become encrusted with myth, some of which will always remain in the absence of reliable documentation. Other myths, however, will vanish once Grant speaks for himself.

11. The figures were established by counting biographical accounts of more than 50 pages in Jay Monaghan, *Lincoln Bibliography, 1839–1939* (Springfield, Ill., 1945), and doing the same with the Grant bibliography now being prepared by the Grant Association.

Editorial Procedure

========

1. *Editorial Insertions*

A.   Words or letters in roman type within brackets represent editorial reconstruction of parts of manuscripts torn, mutilated, or illegible.

B.   [. . .] or [— — —] within brackets represent lost material which cannot be reconstructed. The number of dots represents the approximate number of lost letters; dashes represent lost words.

C.   Words in *italic* type within brackets represent material such as dates which were not part of the original manuscript.

D.   Numbered notes marking passages crossed out of letters from USG to Julia Dent Grant represent material deleted by Mrs. Grant in later years. It is the wish of her descendants that this material remain unprinted. In some early letters the deleted material contains unfavorable reactions to the Mexican people; in later letters the omissions involve minor personal matters. In neither case are the deletions extensive.

E.   Material crossed out by USG is indicated by ~~cancelled type~~.

F.   Material raised in manuscript, as "4th," has been brought in line, as "4th."

2. *Symbols Used to Describe Manuscripts*

AD	Autograph Document
ADS	Autograph Document Signed
ADf	Autograph Draft
ADfS	Autograph Draft Signed
AL	Autograph Letter

ALS   Autograph Letter Signed
D   Document
DS   Document Signed
Df   Draft
DfS   Draft Signed
LS   Letter Signed

3. Military Terms and Abbreviations

Act.   Acting
Adjt.   Adjutant
AG   Adjutant General
AGO   Adjutant General's Office
Art.   Artillery
Asst.   Assistant
Bvt.   Brevet
Brig.   Brigadier
Capt.   Captain
Cav.   Cavalry
Col.   Colonel
Gen.   General
Hd. Qrs.   Headquarters
Inf.   Infantry
Lt.   Lieutenant
Maj.   Major
Q. M.   Quartermaster
Regt.   Regiment or regimental
USMA   United States Military Academy, West Point, N.Y.
Vols.   Volunteers

4. Short Titles and Abbreviations

ABPC   *American Book-Price Current* (New York, 1895—)
CG   *Congressional Globe* Numbers following represent
               the Congress, session, and page.
J. G. Cramer   Jesse Grant Cramer, ed., *Letters of Ulysses S. Grant
               to his Father and his Youngest Sister*, 1857–78 (New
               York and London, 1912)

DAB   *Dictionary of American Biography* (New York, 1928–36)

Garland   Hamlin Garland, *Ulysses S. Grant: His Life and Character* (New York, 1898)

HED   *House Executive Documents*

HMD   *House Miscellaneous Documents*

HRC   *House Reports of Committees* Numbers following HED, HMD, or HRC represent the number of the Congress, the session, and the document.

Lewis   Lloyd Lewis, *Captain Sam Grant* (Boston, 1950)

Memoirs   *Personal Memoirs of U. S. Grant* (New York, 1885–86), 2 vols.

Richardson   Albert Deane Richardson, *A Personal History of Ulysses S. Grant* (Hartford, Conn., 1868)

SED   *Senate Executive Documents*

SMD   *Senate Miscellaneous Documents*

SRC   *Senate Reports of Committees* Numbers following *SED, SMD, SRC* represent the number of the Congress, the session, and the document.

USGA Newsletter   *Ulysses S. Grant Association Newsletter*

5. Location Symbols

CSmH   Henry E. Huntington Library, San Marino, Calif.

CU-B   Bancroft Library, University of California, Berkeley, Calif.

DLC   Library of Congress, Washington, D.C.

DNA   National Archives, Washington, D.C. Additional numbers identify record groups.

I-ar   Illinois State Archives, Springfield, Ill.

ICarbS   Southern Illinois University, Carbondale, Ill.

ICHi   Chicago Historical Society, Chicago, Ill.

ICN   Newberry Library, Chicago, Ill.

IHi   Illinois State Historical Library, Springfield, Ill.

InU   Indiana University, Bloomington, Ind.

KHi   Kansas State Historical Society, Topeka, Kan.

MHi   Massachusetts Historical Society, Boston, Mass.

MiD   Detroit Public Library, Detroit, Mich.

MoSHi	Missouri Historical Society, St. Louis, Mo.
NjP	Princeton University, Princeton, N.J.
NjR	Rutgers University, New Brunswick, N.J.
NN	New York Public Library, New York, N.Y.
OHi	Ohio Historical Society, Columbus, Ohio.
OrHi	Oregon Historical Society, Portland, Ore.
PHi	Historical Society of Pennsylvania, Philadelphia, Pa.
PPRF	Rosenbach Foundation, Philadelphia, Pa.
USG 3	Maj. Gen. Ulysses S. Grant 3rd, Clinton, N.Y.
USMA	United States Military Academy Library, West Point, N.Y.

Chronology

1822, APRIL 27. Birth of a son, later named Hiram Ulysses Grant, to tanner Jesse Root Grant (Jan. 23, 1794–June 29, 1873) and Hannah Simpson Grant (Nov. 23, 1798–May 11, 1883) at Point Pleasant, Clermont County, Ohio.

1823, AUTUMN. The Grant family moved to Georgetown, Brown County, Ohio.

1836, AUTUMN, to 1837, SPRING. USG attended the Maysville Seminary at Maysville, Ky.

1838, AUTUMN, to 1839, SPRING. USG attended the Presbyterian Academy at Ripley, Ohio.

1839, MARCH 22. USG appointed to USMA, West Point, N.Y.
MAY 29. USG arrived at West Point.

1843, JUNE. USG graduated from USMA.
SEPT. 30. Bvt. 2nd Lt. USG reported for duty to Jefferson Barracks near St. Louis, Mo.

1844, MAY. USG proposed marriage to Julia Dent.
JUNE 3. USG reported at Camp Salubrity near Natchitoches, La.

1845, AUG. The 4th Inf. sailed from New Orleans to Corpus Christi, Tex. USG promoted to 2nd lt. (Sept. 30).

1846, APRIL 24. A Mexican declaration of war followed the march of
Gen. Zachary Taylor's army (including USG) across disputed
territory.
MAY 8. Battle of Palo Alto, now located in Tex.
MAY 9. Battle of Resaca de la Palma, now located in Tex.
MAY 18. Occupation of Matamoros, Mexico.
SEPT. 24. Surrender of Monterey negotiated.

1847, MARCH 27. Surrender of Vera Cruz negotiated.
APRIL 18. Battle of Cerro Gordo.
SEPT. 8. Battle of Molino del Rey.
SEPT. 13. Storming of Chapultepec, battles at San Cosmé and
Belén Garitas, leading to capture of Mexico City.
SEPT. 16. USG promoted to 1st lt. Brevet rank as 1st lt. and
capt. dated from Sept. 8 and Sept. 13.

1848, MAY 30. Completion of the Treaty of Guadalupe Hidalgo which
ended the Mexican War.
JULY 23. USG landed at Pascagoula, Miss.
AUG. 22. Marriage of USG and Julia Dent in St. Louis.
NOV. 17. USG reported at Detroit, and was reassigned to duty
at Madison Barracks, Sackets Harbor, N.Y.

1849, APRIL 18. USG reported at Detroit after transfer from Sackets
Harbor.

1850, MAY 30. Birth of Frederick Dent Grant, the Grants' first child.

1851, JUNE 12. USG arrived at Sackets Harbor following transfer from
Detroit.

1852, JULY 5. Departure from New York of USG and the 4th Inf.
bound for the Pacific Coast.
JULY 22. Birth of Ulysses S. Grant, Jr., the Grants' second child.
SEPT. 20. Arrival of USG at Columbia Barracks (later Fort Vancouver), Oregon (later Washington) Territory.

1853, AUG. 5. USG promoted to capt.

1854, JAN. 5. USG reported for duty at Fort Humboldt, Calif.
APRIL 11. USG wrote his resignation from the army.
SUMMER. USG rejoined his family at White Haven, outside
St. Louis, Mo.

1855, SUMMER. USG moved from White Haven to Wish-ton-wish,
the farm of Lewis Dent on the Dent estate.
JULY 4. Birth of Ellen Grant, the Grants' third child.

1856, SUMMER. USG moved from Wish-ton-wish to Hardscrabble,
the home he built on part of the Dent estate given to his wife by
her father.

1858, FEB. 6. Birth of Jesse Root Grant, Jr., fourth and last of the
Grant children.

1860, SPRING. USG moved to Galena, Ill., and began work in his
father's leather goods store.

1861, APRIL 12. Fort Sumter attacked.

The Papers of Ulysses S. Grant

1837–1861

Enlistment

I, Cadet U. S. Grant, of the State of Ohio, aged seventeen years and two months, do hereby engage, with the consent of my guardian, to serve in the Army of the United States for eight years, unless sooner discharged by the proper authority. And I, Cadet U. S. Grant, do hereby pledge my word of honor as a gentleman, that I will faithfully observe the Rules and Articles of War, the Regulations for the Military Academy; and that I will in like manner, observe and obey the orders of the President of the United States, and the orders of the officers appointed over me, according to the rules and discipline of War.

Subscribed to at West Point, N.Y., this 14th day of September eighteen hundred and thirty nine, in presence of G G Waggaman

Adjt.   U S Grant

DS, USMA. Only the signature is by USG. 1st Lt. George G. Waggaman of Va., USMA 1835, was appointed assistant instructor of inf. tactics at USMA on Aug. 29, 1837, and adjt. on Feb. 17, 1839.

The chain of events which took USG to USMA began when G. Bartlett Bailey, son of Dr. George Bailey of Georgetown, Ohio, received an appointment to USMA in 1837 through Congressman Thomas L. Hamer. Young Bailey encountered academic difficulties before the year was out. Renominated by Hamer, Bailey reentered in July, 1838, but resigned in three months. Dr. and Mrs. Bailey tried to keep their son's resignation secret, but Jesse Root Grant found it out and approached his friend, Senator Thomas Morris, for an appointment for his son, Ulysses. Jesse Grant learned from Morris that an appointment would have to come through Congressman Hamer.

Jesse Grant and Thomas Hamer were close personal and political friends from the time Grant moved to Georgetown in 1823 until the election of 1832. Hamer and his former law preceptor, Thomas Morris, were opposing candidates for Congress, with Jesse Grant supporting Morris. At the end of considerable newspaper warfare, Jesse Grant publicly renounced Hamer's friendship. "Mr. Hamer would do well to try to remove the beam from his own eye, before he picks the mote from his neighbor's—to brush away the glaring inconsistencies, that hung about his own political character, before he attempts to condemn others— and finally, to wash his hands, and purify his heart, from gross deceit, before he attempts to accuse others of acting hypocritically. Mr. Hamer's course here, is but a verification of the sayings, of many of his acquaintances.—That he would at any time sacrifice a tried personal friend, to buy over two enemies, who will answer present purpose:—That he cares not who sinks so as he swims—and that he is alike faithless in his political principles, and his personal attachments. Mr. Hamer's personal friendship, never was held in very high estimation, by many who are well acquainted with him. And I can assure him, he is at perfect liberty, to withdraw it from me, (as he certainly will) whenever it suits his interest." Georgetown, Ohio, *The Castigator*, Sept. 25, 1832.

On Feb. 19, 1839, however, Jesse Grant wrote to Hamer. "Dear Sir, In consequence of a remark from Mr Morris while [here] last fall, I [was induced] to apply to the War Department through him for a cadet appointment for my Son H. Ulysses—A letter this evening recd from the department informs me that you only are entitled to the nomination, & that your consent will be necessary to enable him to obtain the appointment I have thought it advisable to consult you on the subject. And if you have no other person in view for the appointment, & feel willing to consent to the appointment of Ulysses, you will please signafy that consent to the department. When I last wrote to Mr. Morris, I refered him to you to recommend the young man if that were necessary Respectfully yours, Jesse R Grant" ALS, MHi.

On March 1, 1839, Col. Joseph G. Totten, chief engineer, addressed a circular to various congressmen, including Hamer, entitled to make appointments to USMA. Hamer, a lame-duck, had to send in a nomination by March 4 or forfeit his privilege. DNA, RG 94, Letters Sent, USMA.

Hamer's nominee had been named Hiram Ulysses Grant after a family conference. Jesse Grant favored the name "Ulysses," used it always in speaking to or of his son, and made it the common name for the boy in Georgetown. Hamer had been asked for an appointment for "H. Ulysses," but the appointment named U. S. Grant. Although Hamer apparently took the middle initial "S" from the mother's maiden name of Simpson, the appointment was not made in that name and USG never acknowledged it as a middle name.

While preparing to leave for USMA, Hiram Ulysses Grant decided to reverse his first two names. When he arrived at West Point, he registered at Roe's Hotel as U. H. Grant and signed the adjutant's record at USMA on May 29, 1839, as Ulysses Hiram Grant. Since he had been appointed as U. S. Grant, however, USMA officials used this name for four years while the cadet continued to sign personal material as Ulysses (or U.) H. Grant. Upon graduation, however, Ulysses S. Grant was adopted as the standard name.

To R. McKinstry Griffith

———

Military Academy
West Point N.Y.
Sept. 22d 1839

DEAR COZ.

I was just thinking that you would be right glad to hear from one of your relations who is so far away as I am so, I have put asaid my Algebra and French and am going to tell you a long story about this prettiest of places West Point. So far as it regards natural attractions it is decidedly the most beautiful place that I have ever seen; here are hills and dales, rocks and river; all pleasant to look upon. From the window near I can see the Hudson; that far famed, that beautiful river with its bosom studded with hundreds of snow ~~white~~ sails. Again if I look another way I can see Fort Putnan frowning far above; a stern monument of a sterner age which seems placed there on purpose to tell us of the glorious deeds of our fathers and to bid us remember *their* sufferings—to follow their examples. In short this is the best of all places—the *place* of all *places* for an institution like this. I have not told you *half* its attractions. here is the house Washington used to live in—there Kosisuseko[1] used to walk and think of *his* country and of *ours*. Over the river we are shown the duelling house of Arnold, that *base* and *heartless* traiter *to* his country and his God. I do love the *place*. it seems as though I could live here ferever if my friends would only come too. You might search the wide world over and then not find a better. Now all this sounds nice, very nice, "what a happy fellow you are" you will say, but I am not one to show fals colers the brightest side of the picture. So I will tell you about a few of the *drawbacks*. First, I slept for two months upon one single pair of blankets, now this sounds romantic and you may think it very easy. but I tell you what coz, it is *tremendeus hard*. suppose you try it by way of experiment for a night or two. I am pretty shure that you would be perfectly satisfied that is no easy matter. but glad am I these things are over. we are now in our quarters. I have a spleanded bed and get along very well. Our pay is nomonally about twenty eight dollars a month. but we never see one cent of it. if we want any thing from a shoestring to a coat we must go to the commandant of the post and get an order fer it or we cannot have it. We have tremendous long and hard lessons to get in both French and Algebra. I study hard and hope to get along so as to pass the examination in January. this examination is a hard one they say, but I am not frightened *yet*. If I am successful here you will not see me fer two long years. it seems a long while to me. but time passes off very fast. it seems but a few days since I came here. it is because every hour has it duty which must be performed. On the whole I like the place very much. so much that I would not go away on any account. The fact is if a man graduates here he safe fer life. let him go where he will. There is much to dislike but more to like. I mean to study hard and stay if it be possible. if I cannot—very well—the world is wide. I have now been here about four months and have not seen a single familier face or *spoken* to a single lady. I wish some of the pretty girles of Bethel were here just so I might look at them. but fudge! confound the girles. I have seen great men plenty of them. let us see. Gen Scott. M. Van Buren. Sec. of War and Navy. Washington Irving[2] and lots of other big bugs. If I were to come home now with my uniform on. they way you would laugh at my appearance would be curious. My pants sit as tight to my skin as the bark to a tree and if I do not walk *military*. that is if I bend over quickly or run. they are very apt to crack with a report as loud as a pistol. my coat must always be buttoned up tight to the chin. it is made of sheeps grey cloth all covered with big round buttens. it makes me look very singulir. If you were to see me at a distance. the first question you would ask would be. "is that a Fish or an animal"? You must give my very best love and respects to all my friends particulaly you[r] brothers. Uncle Ross & Sam'l Simpson.[3] You must also write me a long. long letter in reply to this and till me about evry thing and every body including yourself. If you happen to see my folks just till them that I am happy, *alive* and *kicking*.

I am truly your cousin
and obedand servant

McKinstrey Griffith   U. H. GRANT

N.B. In coming on I stopped five days in Philidelpha[4] with my friends they are all well. Tell Grandmother Simpson that they always have expected to see here before. but have almost given up the idea now. they hope to hear from her often. U. H. GRANT

My very best respects to Grandmother Simpson. I think often her, I put this on the margen so that you may remember it better. I want you to show this letter and all others that I may write to you, to her

I am going to write to some of my friends in Philadelphia soon when they answer I shall write you again to tell you about them &c. &c. remember and write me very soon fer I want to here much

I came near forgetting to tell you about our demerit or "black marks" They give a man one of these "black marks" for almost nothing and if he gets 200 a year they dismiss him. To show how easy one can get these a man by the name of *Grant*[5] of this state got *eight* of these "marks" fer not going to Church today. he was also put under arrest so he cannot leave his room perhaps fer a month, all this fer not going to Church. We are not only obliged to go to church but must *march* there by companys. This is not exactly republican. It is an Episcopal Church

Contrary to the prediction of you and rest of my Bethel friends I have not yet been the least *homesick* no! I would not go home on any account whatever. When I come home in two years (if I live) they way I shall astonish you *natives* will be *curious*. I hope you wont take me for a Babboon

Carl Sandburg, *Lincoln Collector: The Story of Oliver R. Barrett's Great Private Collection* (New York, 1949), pp. 300–303. The four final paragraphs are written on margins. A facsimile of the last nine lines and closing (303) does not agree precisely with the printed text. Griffith, however, supplied the text in *The National Republican*, Aug. 9, 1885, with which there is general agreement. R. McKinstry Griffith was the son of James Griffith, a blacksmith, and Mary Simpson Griffith, sister of Hannah Simpson Grant, USG's mother.

1. Tadeusz Kosciuszko, Polish nationalist and col. of engineers during the American Revolution, supervised the construction of fortifications at West Point from March, 1778, to June, 1780.
2. Bvt. Maj. Gen. Winfield Scott, President Martin Van Buren, Secretary of War Joel Roberts Poinsett, Secretary of the Navy James Kirke Paulding, and author Washington Irving.
3. James Ross, married to Ann Simpson (sister of USG's mother), was

uncle to both USG and McKinstry Griffith, as was Samuel Simpson, a younger brother of USG's mother.

4. "I stopped five days in Philadelphia, saw about every street in the city, attended the theatre, visited Girard College (which was then in course of construction), and got reprimanded from home afterwards for dallying by the way so long." *Memoirs*, I, 38.

5. Cadet Elihu Grant of N.Y., did not graduate.

To Col. Joseph Totten

Military Academy, West Point, N.Y.
March 20, 1840

TO COL. TOTTEN, CHIEF ENGINEER.

As my parents have not received, from the War Department, any reports relitive to me, I think it my duty to inform you of it. I presume that there is some mistake on the subject—that my reports have been sent to the State of New York—to the Guardian of Cadet E Grant, who has lately left the Academy, instead of to Georgetown—Brown County, Ohio, where my parents reside.

Yours very respectfully,
CADET U. H GRANT

Copy, Isabella Stewart Gardner Museum, Boston, Mass. Col. Joseph Gilbert Totten, USMA 1805, as chief engineer was responsible for the reporting of grades.

Jesse Grant moved from Georgetown to Bethel when he entered a partnership with E. A. Collins, a tanner of Bethel, under which Jesse Grant was to expand the tannery in Bethel while Collins sold the products in Galena, Ill. Edward Chauncey Marshall, *The Ancestry of General Grant and their Contemporaries* (New York, 1869), p. 68. On March 9, 1840, Jesse Grant had written to the Secretary of War requesting that quarterly reports be sent to him at Bethel, Ohio. Listed in DNA, RG 107, Registers of Letters Received, but not found. Jesse Grant's letter was answered by Col. Totten on March 19, 1840. "The Secretary of War has referred to this Department your letter of the 9th Inst, and in answer I have to inform you that the standing of your Son as a member of the 4th Class was not ascertained until the examination in January last, when the original of which the enclosed is a duplicate was directed to you at George Town, Ohio. Conduct Reports for September, October, & Novr were directed to the same place. So soon as the Report for February is received an extract from it will be sent you." Copy, DNA, RG 94, Letters Sent, USMA.

Jesse Grant wrote directly to Col. Totten on Aug. 15, 1840. "In answer to my note to the Secretary of War of the 9th of March, I recd your prompt & satisfactory answer of the 19th of the same month, enclosing an 'Extract from the Class & Conduct Reports of the *Military Academy*' &c Since that time the 'Reports' have been regularly rec.d until Apl inclusive—But the Reports of May, June & July have not been rec.d. As I feel anxious to see the official Reports of the standing of my Son—Cadet Grant, and being encouraged by the prompt attention paid to my other note, I have been induced to trouble you again with a notice of their failure—The report of the June Examination I am particularly anxious to see. If you have in your Department an extra copy of 'The Rules & Regulations of the Military Academy,' you will confer a favor by sending me a copy." ALS, DNA, RG 94, Correspondence, USMA. On Aug. 21, 1840, the letter was answered by Capt. Frederic Augustus Smith. "Your letter of the 15th Inst has been received, and in answer I have the honor to inform you that there is no Circular issued of the standing of the Cadets in May, June, July or August. A register of the Officers & Cadets of the M Academy, this day received from West Point, is sent herewith, which will furnish the standing of your Son as arranged at the General examination June last. You will be supplied with the report of the standing of your Son for September, the moment it is received from West Point, which will be in October." Copy, DNA, RG 94, Letters Sent, USMA.

On Sept. 7, 1841, Jesse Grant wrote to Col. Totten that he had not received a report of the June examinations. ALS, DNA, RG 77, Letters Received. On Sept. 16, 1841, 1st Lt. George L. Welcker forwarded this report. Copy, DNA, RG 94, Letters Sent, USMA.

To Capt. Charles F. Smith

———

[*July 13, 1840*]

TO CAPT. C. F. SMITH.

SIR:

Agreeable to your request I submit the following statement relative to the difficulty between Cadets Hammond & Taylor at evening parade on the 10th instant. When the command "right dress" was given, Mr Hammond ordered (if I remember right) the left of the centre to dress up and at the same time ordered Mr Taylor personally to dress up which command did not appear to be obeyed, then Cadet Hammond repeated the command to Cadet Taylor in a very loud & harsh manner, at which Taylor seemed to take offense and called Cadet Hammond by several bad names, such as a d——n little t——d and other names quite as vulgar, and said if he caught Cadet Hammond out of ranks or if Cadet H. spoke to him in such a manner out of ranks—I do not remember which—he would kick him. These are the principal circumstances that I rember, not expecting to have been called upon to make a statement of them.

By Cadet U. H Grant

Copy, DNA, RG 94, ACP 4754/1885; another copy, USMA. Capt. Charles Ferguson Smith, commandant of cadets and instructor of infantry tactics at USMA, later served as gen. under USG from Sept., 1861, until his death on April 25, 1862.

On Aug. 11, 1840, Maj. Richard Delafield of N.Y., USMA 1818, superintendent of USMA, wrote to Col. Joseph G. Totten requesting that Cadet J. G. Taylor be dismissed from USMA. Delafield enclosed twenty-six documents concerning the matter including the USG statement. The trouble between Cadet Taylor and Cadet Richard P. Hammond of Pa., USMA 1841, began at morning parade on July 10, 1840, when Hammond, as cadet lt., reprimanded Taylor for delay in obeying an order. When Taylor began to mutter, Hammond ordered "stop talking in ranks." At evening parade that same day the incident described by USG occurred. The cadet statements agree that Taylor directed considerable abuse at Hammond. Four days later when Hammond reported the incident Taylor replied that "the provocation given by the reporting cadet merited more from me, than mere cursing him; which is the only way that I returned his overbearing and insolent behavior." Taylor was placed in arrest on July 21, 1840, and ordered to remain in the guard tent. He repeatedly left the guard tent, however, and sent a note to Superintendent Delafield asking quick action on his case since "it is immaterial to J. G. T. how soon he is dismissed as he is sincerely anxious of leaving the post." When Delafield ordered Taylor to his home and gave him the money for his transportation, Taylor charged that the sum was inadequate and threatened to have a defamatory account of Delafield published in the *New York Herald*. Delafield's request to Totten for Taylor's dismissal was favorably endorsed by Totten and approved by Secretary of War Joel Roberts Poinsett. The documents are in DNA, RG 94, USMA, Superintendent of the Academy, Letters Received.

To Carey and Hart

_____

U.S. Military Academy West Point March 31st/43

MESSRS CAREY & HART

SIRS

Within inclosed you will find $2.00, the cost of the illustrated editions of "Charles O'Malley" and "Harry Lorrequer." These works will be sent to ~~the~~ my address at this Post office.

Yours &c

To Messrs Carey & Hart   CADET. U. H. GRANT

ALS, PPRF. Charles Lever (1806–72), an Irish novelist, wrote *Charles O'Malley, the Irish Dragoon,* and *The Confessions of Harry Lorrequer,* comic novels of military life in the period of the Napoleonic Wars. "Much of the time [at West Point], I am sorry to say, was devoted to novels, but not those of a trashy sort. I read all of Bulwer's then published, Cooper's, Marryat's, Scott's, Washington Irving's works, Lever's, and many others that I do not now remember." *Memoirs,* I, 39. Carey and Hart was a Philadelphia publishing firm.

To Carey and Hart

_____

U.S. Military. Academy. West Point, April 8th/43

MESSRS. CAREY & HART

SIRS

Last Saturday (April 1st) I sent a letter to your direction, containing $2.00 the cost of the illustrated editions of "Charles O'Malley" and "Harry Lorrequer." As I have not yet received these works I suppose that that you have not yet received my letter. If you have I would desire you to send me the works as soon as possible.

Yours &c
ULYSSES. H. GRANT

To Messrs Carey & Hart   Cadet. U S. M. A.

ALS, IHi. See preceding letter.

Boycott Notice

We, the undersigned, do hereby agree that we will purchase nothing from John DeWitt after this date, except what we have already ordered, or whatever is absolutely necessary, the reason being supposed manifest to every one.

JOHN H. GRELAUD,	J. JONES REYNOLDS,
C. J. COUTS,	L. NEILL,
ISAAC F. QUINBY,	JOHN PRESTON JOHNSTONE,
N. ELTING,	J. J. PECK,
R. S. RIPLEY,	H. R. SELDON,
GEORGE STEVENS,	A. CROZET,
G. DESHON,	F. GARDNER,
F. T. DENT,	L. B. WOOD,
HENRY F. CLARKE,	T. L. CHADBOURNE,
J. H. POTTER,	E. HOWE,
R. HAZLITT,	S. G. FRENCH,
HENRY M. JUDAH,	J. C. MC FERREN,
W. K. VAN BOKKELEN,	RUFUS INGALLS,
GEORGE C. MC CLELLAND,	W. B. FRANKLIN,
U. H. GRANT,	JOSEPH ASFORDD.
C. G. MERCHANT,	

West Point, April 15, 1843.

Samuel G. French, *Two Wars: An Autobiography* (Nashville, 1901), p. 16. All signers were members of USMA class of 1843 except Joseph Asfordd, who has not been identified. John DeWitt was post sutler. In a letter to Isaac F. Quinby, Sept. 16, 1889, Rufus Ingalls says: "Did we not cut old DeWitt because he caused some of us to be reported?" *Ibid.*, pp. 16–17.

Painting by Cadet U. S. Grant. *Courtesy George Washington University Library.*

USG studied drawing at USMA while in the third class, 1840–41, and the second class, 1841–42. The third class studied topographical and anatomical drawing; the second class studied landscape drawing and apparently its entire work consisted of copying other drawings. Classes met each weekday afternoon for two hours. *The Centennial of the United States Military Academy at West Point, New York.*, HMD, 58–2–789, I, 294–5. Robert Walter Weir, teacher of drawing since 1834, had studied in Italy, 1824–27. From 1836 to 1840 he painted "The Embarkation of the Pilgrims" for the rotunda of the Capitol at Washington, D.C. *DAB*, XIX, 612–3. Weir's assistant, 2nd Lt. Richard Somers Smith of Pa., USMA 1834, later became a professor at Brooklyn Collegiate and Polytechnic Institute, president of Girard College, and professor at the United States Naval Academy. *Ibid.*, XVII, 334–5.

Painting by Cadet U. S. Grant. *Courtesy United States Military Academy.*

USG presented one of his cadet paintings to Kate Lowe, daughter of John Lowe
of Batavia, Ohio. See letter of June 26, 1846; William Conant Church, *Ulysses S.
Grant and the Period of National Preservation and Reconstruction* (New York and
London, 1897), p. 19. *Garland*, pp. 47–48 (a reproduction of this water color
follows p. 48). One of the pictures in the Chicago Historical Society was presented
by USG to his cadet classmate Norman Elting. See letters of July 28, 1844,
May 20, 1849; Norman Elting to Franklin H. Tinker, Nov. 7, 1886, ICHi. The
painting now owned by the United States Military Academy was given by USG
to Secretary of the Navy Adolph E. Borie. George W. Childs, *Recollections of
General Grant* (Philadelphia, 1890), pp. 6–7. An additional cadet drawing by
USG is owned by the Ohio Historical Society.

Water Color by Cadet U. S. Grant. *Courtesy Chicago Historical Society.*

Drawing by Cadet U. S. Grant. *Courtesy Library of Congress.*

Water Color by Cadet U. S. Grant. *Courtesy Library of Congress.*

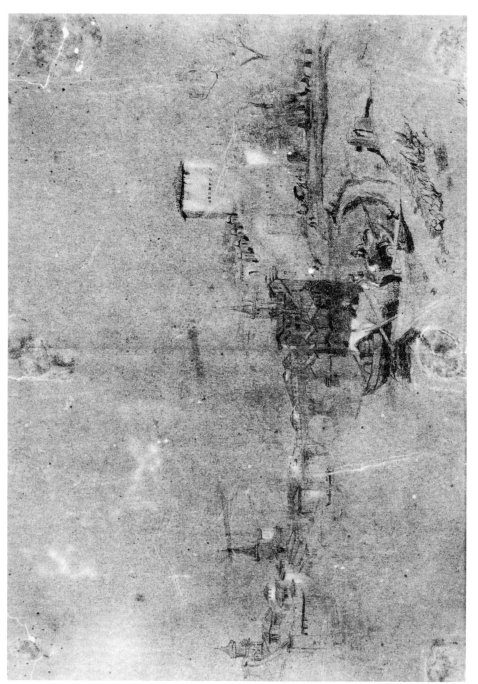

Drawing by Cadet U. S. Grant. *Courtesy Library of Congress.*

Drawing by Cadet U. S. Grant. *Courtesy Chicago Historical Society*.

Drawing by Cadet U. S. Grant. *Courtesy Mme. Julia Cantacuzene*.

U. S. Military Academy, West Point April 8ᵗʰ/43

Messrs Carey & Hart

Sirs

Last Saturday (April 1ˢᵗ) I sent a letter to your direction, containing $2.00 the cost of the illustrated editions of "Charles O'Malley" and "Harry Lorrequer." As I have not yet received these works I suppose that that you have not yet received my letter. If you have I would desire you to send me the works as soon as possible.

Yours &c

U S lysses H. Grant
Cadet. U S M A.

Messrs Carey & Hart

Letter written by Cadet U.S. Grant in 1843. *Courtesy Illinois State Historical Library.*

Dialectic Society Certificate

DIALECTIC SOCIETY,
UNITED STATES MILITARY ACADEMY.

Be it known that James Allen Hardie of the State of New York is entitled to all the rights and privileges of an honorary member of the Dialectic Society.

In Testimony of which we have caused to be hereunto affixed the seal of the Society and the signatures of our President and Secretary.

U. H. GRANT,
 President.   Dated at the Hall of the Society,
W. S. HANCOCK,   West Point, June 20, 1843.
 Secretary.

Garland, p. 46. Last recorded at Stan. V. Henkels Sale, Nov. 22, 1932. James Allen Hardie of N.Y., USMA 1843, served with the Army of the Potomac during the Civil War and became inspector gen., March 24, 1864. Winfield Scott Hancock of Pa., USMA 1844, was maj. gen. of vols. during the Civil War and 1880 Democratic candidate for President.

Oath of Office

I, Ulysses S. Grant, APPOINTED A Bvt. Second Lieut. IN THE ARMY OF THE UNITED STATES, DO SOLEMNLY SWEAR, OR AFFIRM, THAT I WILL BEAR TRUE ALLEGIANCE TO THE UNITED STATES OF AMERICA, AND THAT I WILL SERVE THEM HONESTLY AND FAITHFULLY AGAINST ALL THEIR ENEMIES OR OPPOSERS WHATSOEVER;

AND OBSERVE AND OBEY THE ORDERS OF THE PRESIDENT OF THE UNITED STATES, AND THE ORDERS OF THE OFFICERS APPOINTED OVER ME, ACCORDING TO THE RULES AND ARTICLES FOR THE GOVERNMENT OF THE ARMIES OF THE UNITED STATES.

ULYSSES S. GRANT

SWORN TO AND SUBSCRIBED BEFORE ME, AT my offices—THIS 28th DAY OF July 1843
John Quinlan JUSTICE OF THE PEACE. Clermont County. O.

DS, DNA, RG 94, ACP 4754/1885.

To Adjutant General's Office

Bethel Clermont Co. Ohio
July 31st/43

ADJUTANT GENERAL'S OFFICE
SIRS

"Gen. Orders No 42" have been rec'd and this is to notify that I accept the appointment therein confered. My berth place is Point Pleasant Clermont Co Ohio, & I was appointed from Ohio.

I have the honor to be &c
U. S. GRANT
4th Inf.

ALS, DNA, RG 94, ACP 4754/1885. Received Aug. 7, 1843. In accordance with normal procedure for USMA graduates, USG was commissioned a bvt. 2nd lt. He was assigned to duty with the 4th Inf. at Jefferson Barracks, Mo., a few miles south of St. Louis. General accounts of the 4th Inf. and Jefferson Barracks are William H. Powell, *A History of the Organization and Movements of the Fourth Regiment of Infantry* . . . (Washington, 1871), and Henry W. Webb, "The Story of Jefferson Barracks," *New Mexico Historical Review*, XXI, 3 (July, 1946), 185–208.

To Bvt. Brig. Gen. Roger Jones

————

Jefferson Barracks Mo.
Nov. 17th 1843

SIR

I have the honor to apply for a transfer from the 4th Infantry to the Dragoons.

I am encouraged to make application for a transfer to that arm of service which was my first choice on leaving the Military Academy, from the fact that there is, at this time, no one of the graduates of the same class with myself holding appointments in this arm, and that there is one less number of Bvts in the Reg. for which I apply than in the 4th Inf.

Very Respectfully Your Obt. Svt.
U S GRANT
Bvt. 2nd Lt. 4th Inf.

R. Jones
Adj. Gen.

ALS, Mrs. Walter Love, Flint, Mich. On Dec. 12, 1843, Bvt. Brig. Gen. Roger Jones of Va., replied to both USG and Bvt. 2nd Lt. Robert Hazlitt of Ohio, USMA 1843 (see following letter). "In reply to your application to be transferred to the Regiment of Dragoons, you are informed that, due regard to the interest of the general service, will not justify the exchange you propose." DNA, RG 94, AGO, Selected Letters Sent.

To Julia Dent

————

Camp Salubrity
Near Nachitoches Louisiana
June 4th 1844

MY DEAR JULIA

I have at length arrived here with the most pleasing recollections of the short leave of absence which ~~accom~~ prevented my accompanying my Regiment; and as well, with the consequences of the leave.[1] I arrived here on Monday the 3d Ins; I believe just the day that I told you I thought I should arrive. My journey to N. Orleans was a pleasant one, on a pleasant boat, with pleasant passengers and officers, but was marked with no incident worth relating, except that as we approached the South the Musquetoes become troublesome, and by the time I left N. Orleans my hands and face bore the strongest testamony of their numbers and magnitude.—I spent something over a day in N. Orleans, and its being a tolerably large place, and my Bump of Acquisitiveness prompting me on to see as much of the place as possible, the result was that I went over the town just fast enough to see nothing as I went, stoped long enough at a time to find out nothing atall and at the end found found myself perfectly tired out. But I saw enough to convince me that a very pleasant season might be passed there; and if I *cant* get back to *Jeff. Bks* again will make no objections to the contemplated change which sends me there. But I am not disposed to give up a known good for an untried one, and as I *know* the climate &c. (&c. meaning much more than what precedes it) about St. Louis suits me well, I will by no means fail to take up with any offer which will take me back.—My journey up the Red River was not so pleasant as the other. The boat was quite small and considerably crouded with passengers, and they not of the most pleasant sort; a number of them being what are usually called *Black Legs* or Gamblers; and some of them with very cut throat appearances. There was some of them that I should very much dislike to meet unarmed, and in a retired place, their knowing I had a hundred dollars about me. Likely I judge harshly. The monotony of the Journey though was somewhat broken by the great difference in the appearance of the Red River country and anything else I had ever seen. The first hundred miles looks like a little deep and winding canal finding its way through a forest so thickly set, and of such heavy foliage that the eye cannot penetrate. The country is low and flat and overflown to the first limbs of the trees. Aligators and other revolting looking things occupy the swamps in thousands; and no doubt the very few people who live there shake with the ague all Summer. As far up the river as where we are the land is high and healthy, but too poor to bear any thing but one vast pine forest. Since Mr. Hazlitt[2] wrote to you our Encampment has been moved to a much more pleasant and higher situation. We are on the top of a high ridge, with about the best spring of water in Louisiana runing near. There is nothing but pine woods surrounding us and they infested to an inormaus degree with Ticks, Red bugs, and a little creeping thing looking like a Lizard, that I dont know the name of. This last vermin is singularly partial to society, and become so very intimate and sociable on a short acquaintance as to visit our tents, crawl into our beds &c. &c. Tis said they are very innocent but I dont like the looks of th[em].—Nearly the first person I met here was Hazlitt, [or] Sly Bob, with one of those Stage driver's round top wool hats and a round jacket, trying to take the heat as comfortably as possible. He drew me into his tent; which by the way is a little linen affair just like your Fishing tent, with the ground covered with Pine leaves for a floore. It took me one day to answer his questions, and you may rest assured that a number of them were about Ellen and yourself together with the rest of the family.[3] When you write to him tell him how Clarra is comeing on.—Since I first set down to write we have had a hard shower and I can tell you my tent is a poor protection. The rain run through in streams. But I will have a shed built in a few days then I will do better. You have been to Camp Meeting, and know just how the people cook, and sleep, and live there? Our life here is just about the same. Hazlitt probably told you all about how we live here. While I think of it he sends his love to you and Ellen and the rest of the family, and to Wrenshall Dent's family.[4] Mine must go to the same.—

I was detained a day longer in St. Louis than I expected and to make time pleasantly pass away I called on Joe Shurlds[5] and had a long talk of three or four hours, about—about!—let me see: What was the subject? I believe it was the usual topic.

Nothing in particular, but matters generally. She pretends to have made a great discovery. Can you concieve what it was?

Julia! I cannot express the regrets that I feel at having to leave Jeff. Bks. at the time that I did. I was just learning how to enjoy the place and the *Society*, at least a part of it. Blank ————

——— ——— ——— ——— ——— ——— ——— ———

——— ——— ——— ——— ——— ——— ——— ———

——— ——— ——— ——— ——— ——— Read these blank lines just as I intend them and they will express more than words.—You must not forget to write soon and what to seal with. Until I hear from you I shall be,—I dont know what I was going to say—but I recon it was your most humble [. . . . .] and Obt. Friend.

                               ULYSSES S GRANT

Miss Julia Dent
Gravois Mo.

P.S. Did you get the Magazines I sent you, one from Memphis the other from N. Orleans?   usg

ALS, DLC-USG, postmarked Natchitoches, June 7, 1844.

    1. USG was absent with leave from May 1 until May 20, 1844, with orders to report back to Jefferson Barracks. 4th Inf. Return, May, 1844, DNA, RG 94. He returned to Jefferson Barracks even though he knew his regiment had left for La. *Memoirs*, I, 48. From there he left for Camp Salubrity, after first proposing to Julia.
    Camp Salubrity, three miles from Natchitoches, had been established on May 24 to relieve overcrowding at Fort Jesup, twenty-five miles southwest of Natchitoches, the major military post in the area. See J. Fair Hardin, "Fort Jesup, Fort Selden, Camp Sabine, Camp Salubrity, V," *Louisiana Historical Quarterly*, 17, 1 (Jan., 1934), 139–68. Troops were stationed in the area as a result of negotiations for the annexation of the Republic of Texas to the United States. The treaty of annexation promised U.S. military and naval protection in the southwest as a safeguard against Mexican attack. Although the treaty was rejected by the Senate on June 8, President John Tyler left troops in the area while urging Congress to accept the annexation treaty by joint resolution.
    2. Bvt. 2nd Lt. Robert Hazlitt, USMA 1843. An Ohioan, USMA classmate, and officer of the 4th Inf., Hazlitt was USG's close friend until his death in the battle of Monterey, Sept. 21, 1846.
    3. Frederick Dent and Ellen Bray Wrenshall Dent had eight children: John C., George Wrenshall, Frederick Tracy, Lewis, Julia Boggs, Ellen Wrenshall (Nellie), Mary, and Emily Marbury (Emma).

4. George Wrenshall Dent (see note 3) had married Mary Isabella Shurlds on Oct. 14, 1841.

5. Probably Eliza Margaret Perry Shurlds, who had gone to school with Julia Dent and whose sister had married George Wrenshall Dent.

To Mrs. George B. Bailey

———

Camp Salubrity
Near Nachitoches Louisiana
June 6th 1844

MRS. BAILEY

My journey fortunately is at an end, and agreeably to your request, and my own pleasure, I hasten to notify you of my safe arrival here   It always affords me pleasure to write to old acquaintances, and much more to hear from them, so I would be pleased if the correspondence would not stop here. As long as my letters are answered, if agreeable to you I will continue to write.—

My trip to this place "forty days journey in the wilderness" was marked with no incident, Save one, worth relating and that one is *laughable curious, important, surprising* &c. &c. but I cant tell it now. It is for the present a secret,[1] but I will tell it to you some time. You must not guess what it is for you will go wrong. On my route I called arroune by the way of St Louis and Jefferson Barrack where I spent four or five days very pleasantly among my newly made acquaintances   From St Louis to N Orleans I had a very pleasant trip on a large and splendid boat, with pleasant passengers and not much crouded. As we approached the South the sun become sensibly warmer, and the Musquetoes desidedly more numerous   By the time we got to N Orleans my hands and face bore the strongest evidence of the number and size of this insect in a Southern climate   I was but one day

in Orleans which was spent in runing over the city just fast
enough to tire myself out and get but little good of my visit   But
from what I saw I think it would be a pleasant place to live,
and it is now contemplated that my Regiment will go in that
neighborhood in case Texas should not be anexed to the U States,
but in case of the anexation we will probably have to go much
farther West than we are now. Probably to the Rio Colorado.
From N. Orleans to Nachitoches I had the bad fortune to travel
on a small boat considerably crouded, through a hot country,
with gambling going on day and night. Some of the passengers
had very cut throat appearances. From Nachitoches I had to
walk (or pay an extravigant price for a conveyance) three miles
through the hotest sun I think I ever felt   I found my Regiment
Camping out in small linen tents on the top of a high Sandy ridge
and in the midst of a pine forest   The great elevation of our
situation and the fact that one of the best springs of water in the
state puts out here are the only recommendations the place has.
We are about three miles from any place, there is no conveyance
to take us from on place to another and evry thing is so high
that we cant afford to keep a horse or other conveyance of ~~there~~
our own. I could walk myself but for the intensity of the heat.
As for lodgings I have a small tent that the rain runs through as
it would through a seive. For a bedstead I have four short pine
sticks set upright and plank runing from the two at one end to
the other. For chairs I use my trunk and bed, and as to a floor
we have no such a luxury yet. Our meals are cooked in the woods
by servants that know no more about culinary matters than I do
myself. But with all these disadvantages my appetite is becoming
extravigant. I would like to have our old West Point board
again that you may have heard so much about. As for the troublesome insects of creation they abound here. The swamps are full
of Aligators, and the wood full of Red bugs and ticks; insects
the you are not trouble with in Ohio, but are the plague of this
country. They crawl entirely unde the skin when they git on a
person and it is impossible to keep them off.—So much for
Camp Salubrity.—I should be happy to get an answer to this as

early as possible; and if nothing more, a Post Script from the Young ladies. Ladies are always so much better at giving the news than others, and then there is nothing doing or said about Georgetown that I would not like to hear. They could tell me of all the weddings &c. &c. that are talked of. Give my love to evry body in Georgetown.

LT. U S GRANT
4th Infantry

To Mrs. G. B. Bailey
Georgetown Ohio

P. S. I give my title in signing this not because I wish people to know what it is, but because I want to get an answer to this and put it there that a letter may be directed so as to get to me

Facsimile in Frank A. Burr, *A New, Original and Authentic Record of the Life and Deeds of General U. S. Grant* . . . (Cleveland: 1885), pp. 93–99. Mrs. Bailey, wife of Dr. George B. Bailey, lived across the street from the Grants in Georgetown. Her sons were playmates of USG, and the departure of Bartlett Bailey from West Point provided a vacancy for USG.

1. The secret is his engagement to Julia Dent, described in *Memoirs*, I, 48–51.

To Julia Dent

———

Camp Salubrity La.
Near Nachitoches
July 28th 1844

MY DEAR JULIA.

Mr. Higgins[1] has just arrived from Jefferson Barracks and brings word that he saw you well on the 4th Inst. He delivered your message and says that he promised to bring some letters from you but supposes that you expected him out at your house

to recieve them. You can hardly immagine how acceptable your
message was but when I found that I might have expected a
letter from you by his calling for it, I took the Blues (You told
me that you had experienced the same complaint) so badly that
I could resort to no other means of expelling the dire feeling
than by writing to My *Dear Julia*. It has been but few days
since I wrote to you but I must write again. Be as punctual in
writing to me Julia and then I will be compensated in a slight
degree,—nothing could fully compensate—for your absence.—
In my mind I am constantly turning over plans to get back to
Missouri, and until today there has been strong grounds for
hoping that the whole of the 4th Regiment would be ordered
back there; but that hope is blasted now. Orders have arrive
from Washington City that no troops on the frontier will be
removed. Fred's[2] Regiment as well as mine will have to remain.
Mexico has appropriated four millions of dollars for the purpose
of raising an Army of thirty thousand men for the re-conquering
of Texas, and we are to remain here to preserve neutrality
between the United States and the belligerent parties. Who
knows but Fred. and me may have something to do yet? though
it may be something short of the conquest of Mexico, or the over-
powering of some other big country. Would you not be glad to
hear of something of the kind after the difficulty was all over and
we were safely out ~~of the difficulty~~? I think there is no danger
however, from any present causes, of anything of the kind taking
place. Fred. and me are doomed to stay safe and quietly in the
woods for some time yet. I may be able to get to the same post
with Fred. by transfering with Lt. Elting[3]   I have written to
Towson on the subject. If I should get there Fred. and me will
be great friends as we always have been, and no doubt will spend
many pleasant hours together talking over the pleasant times
both of us have spent on the Gravois. No doubt your brother will
have many pleasant things to relate of the place, and to me they
will be doubly interesting because Julia Dent is there. Many a
pleasant hour have I spent at Camp Salubrity thinking over my
last visit to Mo. and its results. Never before was I satisfied that

my love for you was returned, but you then assured me that it was. Does Mrs. Dent know of the engagement between us? I believe from Freds letter that he half suspects it, though he mentions nothing of the kind. I would be perfectly willing that he should be acquainted with the fact though of course, would not tell him myself.—Mr. Higgins gives us an account of the Barbecue on the Gravois the 4th of July. ~~Billy Long kept whisky to sell in one corner, and Miss Lucy entertained the gentle[men] is his account.~~ No doubt Miss Fanny Morrison[4] was in all her glory with her returned intended! Does Fanny call out to see you often? What does she say about me? What is the reason I cant be there myself to hear? evry body els is going. Col. Garland, Captain Morris & Capt. Barber are just starting, and in a few days Capt. Morrison[5] will be off.—Julia write to me soon and give a long account of how you pass your time. No doubt it is much more pleasantly spent than mine in the hot pine woods of Louisiana. Hazlitt and me visit each other, at our linen Mansions about three times per day, and our calls are so unfashionable that the three calls lasts from morning until bed time. The subjects of our conversations are usually Missour[i]   Turn over and commence reading the cross lines on the first page.

To Miss Julia Dent.   Yours most Constantly U S GRANT and the people of Missouri—Miss J. & E Dent[6] in particular and our future prospects and plans. We have big plans laid for visiting Mixico and Texas this winter and Missouri too soon. Sometimes we get to talking about your house I almost immagine myself there. While speaking of Mr. Hazlitt let me tell you that he has just left my tent and the last words he said was for me to be sure and give you and Ellen, and the rest of the family his very best love. He says that he expects a partnership letter from you two.—I wish Julia that you and Ellen could be here for one hour to see our mode of living. When any body calls to see me we have very cozily to take our seats side by side on the bed for I have no chair. If I could only be in your parlor an hour per day what a recreation it would be. Since I arrived here it has been so very hot that I but seldom go out of Camp. Once I was over at Fort Jesup and saw Mr. Jarvis.[7] Tell Ellen that he fell a good deal more than half in love with her. He seemed very anxious to know what word she had sent him by me. Has Miss Fanny ever tried to convince you *since,* that she is in possession of all my secrets and knows just who I love best? Dont you think it strange that a young lady will talk so. I am affraid that you will find difficulty in reading the crossed lines. I will therefore conclude on the page left for directing the letter. u.s.g.

Julia I would not presume so much as to send this letter without having recieved an answer to either of my others if Mr. Higgins had not mentioned that you told him you had rec'd letters from Mr Hazlitt and me, which led me to suppose that Mr. & Mrs. Dent knew of your recieving them and made no objection. I have too an opportunity of sending it to Jeff. Bks. to be mailed.—Be shure and answer it and all my others soon—and I am sorry Julia that I wrote the letter sent in one of Mrs. Porters.[8] Burn it up wont you? I would feel much freer if the consent desired in that letter was obtained, but as it is not, I will have to wait until I get back there to get it; unless you can satisfy me that there is no parental objection.—What is the reason that John Dent[9] has not written to me? He must have been much engaged electioneering this Summer! Give my love to Ellen and the rest of the family. Again, be shure and write soon and relieve from suspense your most *Devoted* and *Constant* l——

U S G

P. S. I have carefully preserved the lock of hair you gave me. Recollect when you write to seal with the ring I used to wear: I am anxious to see an impression of it once more.

u s g

ALS, DLC-USG, postmarked Jefferson Barracks Mo., Aug. 20, 1844.

1. 2nd Lt. Thaddeus Higgins from Pa., USMA 1840, was assigned to the 4th Inf. In 1842–44 he was in garrison at Jefferson Barracks. For his death, see letter of Sept. 14, 1845, below.

2. Bvt. 2nd Lt. Frederick Tracy Dent, roommate of USG at USMA, was his future brother-in-law.

3. Bvt. 2nd Lt. Norman Elting, USMA 1843, was with the 6th Inf. Both Elting and Dent were stationed at Fort Towson, Indian Territory, six miles north of the Red River.

4. Fanny Morrison, the daughter of Capt. Pitcairn Morrison, was married to 2nd Lt. Thaddeus Higgins, mentioned above, in 1845.

5. Lt. Col. John Garland of Va., Capt. Gouverneur Morris of N.Y., and Capt. Pitcairn Morrison of N.Y., were officers of the 4th Inf. Bvt. Capt. Philip Nordbourne Barbour of Ky., USMA 1834, was with the 3rd Inf.

6. Julia Dent and her sister Ellen.

7. Bvt. 2nd Lt. Charles Edward Jarvis of Me., USMA 1843.

8. The wife of 2nd Lt. Theodoric Henry Porter of the 4th Inf.

9. Julia Dent's brother.

To Julia Dent

———

> Camp Necessity La.
> Grand Ecore & Texas Road
> Aug. 31st 1844

MY DEAR JULIA

Your two letters of July and August have just been recieved and read you can scarsely immagine with how much pleasure. I have waited so long for an answer to my three letters (I have written you three times Julia one of them you probably had not time to get when you wrote yours) that I began to dispare of ever recieving a line from you; but it come at last and how agreeable the surprise! Take example in punctuality by me Julia, I have rec'd your letters only to day and now I am answering them. But I can forgive you since the tone of your last letter, the one in pencil, is so conclusive of constancy. I am sorry to hear that Mrs. Dent thinks there is nothing serious in our engagement with me nothing is more serious or half as pleasant to think of—Since the arrival of your letters I have read them over and over again and will continue to do so until another comes. I have not been into Camp Salubrity yet to deliver to Mr. Hazlitt verbally the messages you sent him, but I wrote him a note this morning containing them. Mr. Hazlitt has been quite unwell for a few days past—You probably have heard from Mr Porters letters that for the last three weeks my company have been road making—The day we came out it rained very hard all day—the men had heavy Knap sacks to carry through the mud and rain for a distance of about five miles and no shelter to go under at the end of their journey—My fare was just the same only I had nothing but myself to carry—The first night we had to lay our wet beds on the still damper ground and make out the best we could—Musketoes and Wood ticks by the hundreds pestered us —On the whole I spent a few miserable nights and not much better days at the begining of my first experience at campaigning, but now I find it much better—We will probably be through and return to Camp Salubrity in ten days more—I have just rec'd a letter from Fred, he is about my most punctual correspondent, he speaks of Louise Stribling. I think [s]he certainly is not married nor wont be unless she gets Fred—Fred is very well but hartily tired of Fort Towson—He proposes that [him] and [me] should each get a leave of absence next Spring and go to Missouri   I would accept his proposal but I intend going sooner— I shall try very hard to go in the Fall—The happiness of seeing you again can hardly be realized, and then like you I have so much that I would like to say and dont want to write.—Julia do tell me the secrets that Georgia M¹ disclosed to you—I think I can guess them from what follows in your letter—Georgia M is a very nice modest and inexperienced girl and can very easily be made to believe anything her oldest sister tells her—I know very well that Fanny has told her that I was in love with her and she foundes her reasons for thinking so upon what ~~followed~~ took place at you house—You remember the occurrence of the apple seeds? Fany has tried to find out from Mr. Hazlitt which I loved best Georgia or Julia—Mr. Hazlitt would not tell her which he thought because to please her he would have to tell what he believed to be a story, and to have said you (as he believed though of course he new nothing about certain) he thought would give an unnecessary offense. Hazlitt told me of the conversation he had and it displeased me so much with Miss F. that I said things of her which I would not commit to paper—Believe me my dear Julia what ever Miss Georgia may have told you she no doubt believed herself, but in believing she has allowed herself to be the dupe of one older than she is, but whose experience *in love affairs*, ought to be worth a great deel more than it is.—Tell me what she said in your next letter—Dont let Mrs. Dent see this part of my letter for of all things I dont like to have to speak ill of a third person, and if I do have to speak so I would like as few as possible to know it.—I am very far from having forgotten our promise to think of each other at sun seting—At that time I am most always on parade and no doubt I sometimes appear very absent minded—You say you were at a loss to ascribe a meaning to t[he] blank lines in my first letter! Nothing is easyer, they were onl[y] intended to express an attachment which words would fail to express   Julia do not keep anything a secret from me with persons standing in the relation that we do to each other there should be no backwardness about making any request—You commenced to make a request of me and checked yourself—Do not be affraid that any thing you may request will not be granted, and just think too the good you might do by giving good advice—No one is so capable of giving good advice as a lady, for they always practice just what they would preach—No doubt you have laid down to Fred. just the course he ought to take, and if he follows the advice he must do well—How fortunate he must feel himself to have a sister to correspond with   I know I should have been proud to have had such a one to write to me all the years of my absence. My oldest sister[2] is old enoug[h] to write now and I intend to direct all my home letters to her—She loves you and Ellen already without ever having seen you just from what she has heard me say—You say Julia that you often dream of me! do tell me some of your good ones; dont tell me any more of the bad ones; but it is an old saying that dreams go by contraries so I shall hope you will never find me in the condition you drempt I was in—And to think too that while I am writing this the ring I used to wear is on your hand—Parting with that ring Julia was the strongest evidence I could have given you (that is—in the way of a present) of the depth and sincerity of my love for you—Write to me soon, much than the last time and if Mrs. Porter is not there, or not writing at the time take a little ride and put ~~it~~ your letter in the Post Office—On the road think of some of the conversations we used to have when we rode out together

Most Truly and Devotedly Your Lover
ULYSSES

To Julia

P S I think in the course of a few days Julia I will write to Col. Dent to obtain his consent to our correspondence; I will ask nothing more at present but when I get back to St. Louis I will lay the whole subject before him Julia do not let any disclosed secrets such as Miss Georgia told you, make you doubt for a moment the sincerity depth & constancy of my feeling, for you and you alone out of the whole acquaintance. Find some name beginning with "S" for me Julia You know I have an 'S in my name and dont know what it stand for.

U.S.G.

P.P.S. Tell Ellen that I have not been into Camp yet to see the playthings she sent Mr. Hazlitt but I will go tomorrow morning if I have to walk. I think there is no danger of us quarreling since we have agreed so long together; but if we do get into a scrape I will let her know it. Remember me to Miss Ellen, Mrs. Porter Mrs. Mary Dent and your Fathers family all.[3]

USG

ALS, DLC-USG. Camp Necessity was located about five miles northwest of Natchitoches. Grand Ecore is about three miles north of Natchitoches.

  1. Georgia and Fanny Morrison were daughters of Capt. Pitcairn Morrison.
  2. Clara Rachel Grant was born in Georgetown, Ohio, Dec. 11, 1828. Other children in the Grant family were Samuel Simpson Grant, born Sept. 23, 1825; Virginia Paine Grant, born Feb. 20, 1832; Orvil Lynch Grant, born May 15, 1835; and Mary Frances Grant, born July 28, 1839.

3. Mrs. Mary Dent was Mrs. George Wrenshall Dent, formerly Mary Isabella Shurlds, who married George Dent on Oct. 14, 1841.

To Julia Dent

Camp Salubrity La
Near Nachitoches
Sept. 7th 1844

MY DEAR JULIA

I have just written the letter you desired I should, and which I have long thought it a duty to write. You can scarsely concieve the embarrassment I felt in writing such a letter, even in commencing the first line. You must not laugh at it Julia for you have the chance   I send it unsealed that you may read it before delivering it. I wrote it at our little camp in the woods on the road to Texas while alone by my self, at night. I immagined all the time that I saw your Pa & Ma. reading it and when they were done, raising all kinds of objections. ~~Age~~ Youth and length of acquaintance I feared might be brought against us but asshure them my dear Julia that the longest acquaintance, or a few years more experience in the world could not create a feeling deeper or more durable. While I have been writing this there has been three or four officers in the tent bothering and talking to me all the time but they have just gone out thank fortune. They do not suspect that I am writing to you. It has only been a few days since I recieved your letters. I answered them immediately, wont you be as punctual in answering mine in the future? You dont know Julia with how much anxiety and suspense I await there arrival. But here I am asking you to write soon and in the same letter asking permission to have you write, and without knowing that the favor will be granted. If the proper consent is obtained I know you will follow the example of punctuality I have set.

I wrote to Fred a day or two ago: I told him I would accept his invitation to go to Mo. next Spring if I did not go sooner, but at present the prospect is so fair for the 4th Regiment going to Jefferson Barracks to spend next winter that I am in hopes that shorter leaves will be long enough for me to visit Gravois.[1] You dont know how much I want to get back there once more. Another of our little walks up or down the creek would be so pleasant, and then too you could tell me what you say you want to tell and cant write. In your next wont you tell me all about the secrets Miss Georgia made known to you. I do asshure you Julia that you need not let anything she can tell you, about me, give the least trouble.

Mrs. Capt. Page and Mrs. Alden have each written to their husbands that they saw General Scott lately[2] and he says that he intends sending our Regiment up the Mississippi as soon as possible; and if he does we will get to Jeff. Bks. about November where we will have to stay until the river breaks up above which will be about next May. It is now about Eleven o'clock P. M. and Mr. Porter and me are each sitting writing letters to go to Gravois. All the time I am writing mine I am thinking that probably Julia has on, the ring that I left her, and who knows but just at this time she may be dreaming of me! How much I flatter myself dont I? to think that your thoughts might be upon me during your sleep.

Mr. Porter is through writing his letter and waiting to get this to seal them up. You know he is Post Master? He says that when you write to me again you must put a little cross on the outside that he may know the letter is for me. The last one he opened before he found it out—Mr. Hazlitt I believe I told you has been sick. His health is improving gradually, but he is very tired of this country. He says he does not consider it [livin]g atall; but merely spining out an existance. He d[esir]es to be remembered to you and Ellen and the rest of the family. He has never seen any of the play things yet that Ellen sent him. Possibly they will be here to-morrow for I understand that Mr. Wallen's[3] baggage is just arriving. Mr. Hazlitt says he wishes you would write him just one letter—Remember me to all the people at Gravois little Davy⁴ and all.

ULYSSES

P. S. Julia dont let any one but your Pa. & Ma read the letter I have directed to them will you?

U

ALS, DLC-USG.

    1. The Dent estate of White Haven was located on Gravois Creek.
    2. Capt. John Page of Mass., and Capt. Bradford Ripley Alden, of N.Y., USMA 1831, were assigned to the 4th Inf.; Maj. Gen. Winfield Scott had been commander of the army since July 5, 1841.
    3. 2nd Lt. Henry Davies Wallen of Fla., USMA 1840.
    4. David Porter, son of 2nd Lt. Theodoric Henry Porter.

To Robert Hazlitt

December 1, 1844

There were five days' races at Natchitoches. I was there every day and bet low, generally lost. Jarvis¹ and a number from Jessup were there. Jarvis was pretty high and tried to be smart all the time. He fell over the back of a bench at the racecourse and tumbled over backward in his chair in front of Thompson's Hotel during his most brilliant day. He undertook to play brag at our camp and soon succeeded in ridding himself of twenty dollars all in quarters. The game of brag is kept up as lively as ever. I continued to play some after you left and won considerable, but for some time back I have not played and probably will never play again—no resolution, though.

Henry E. Chambers, *Mississippi Valley Beginnings: An Outline of the Early History of the Earlier West* (New York and London, 1922), p. 358.
    In addition to the text given, Chambers summarized other portions: "Grant refers to the state of excitement under which the men were laboring, for they expected daily to be hurried off to the Texan frontier. He speaks of 'Corpus or San Antonio' as two possible points of destination, reports all property not absolutely necessary to present needs packed up for transportation and stored at

Grand Ecore. He intimates his own personal doubts as to any movement of the regiment in the near future, notwithstanding these preparations. He tells of the muttered curses heaped upon the heads of the regimental officers who put the men at work building two long lines of blockhouses as winter quarters more comfortable than tents, when the men believed such labor unnecessary in view of the expected early departure."

1. Bvt. 2nd Lt. Charles Edward Jarvis of Me., USMA 1843.

To Julia Dent

Camp Salubrity
Near Nachitoches La.
January 12th 184~4~5

MY DEAR JULIA

It has now been nearly two months since I heard from you and about four since I wrote the letter to your parents to which I hoped so speedy an answer. Of course I cannot argue any thing very strong in favor of my request being granted from their not answering it, but at the same time they do not say that I shall not write to you, at least as a friend, and therfore I write you this Julia, and direct it to Sappington P. O.[1] expecting your Pa & Ma to know that you get it. The fact is I thought I must hear from you again—The more than ordinary attachment that I formed for *yourself* and family during my stay at Jeff. Bks. cannot be changed to forgetfulness by a few months absence. But why should I use to you here the language of flattery Julia, when we have spoken so much more plainly of our feeling for each other? Indeed I have not changed since and shall hope that you have not, nor will not, at least untill I have seen all of you once more. I intend to apply for a leave in the spring again and will go to St. Louis. For three months now I have been the only officer with my company and of course cannot leave even for one week.[2] Julia can we hope that you pa will be induced to change his opinion of an army life? I think he is mistaken about the army life being such an unpleasant one. It is true the movements of the

troops from Jeff. Bks. so suddenly and to so outlandish a place
would rather create that opinion, but then such a thing hardly
occurs once a lifetime.

Mr. Hazlitt returned about one month ago looking as lazy
and healthy as ever. I was away from camp when he returned and
did not get home until about midnight. I woke him up and him
and me had a long talk from that until morning. He told me all
about what a pleasant visit he had at Jeff. Bks. or rather on the
Gravois. Was he plagued much about Miss Clara while there?
You dont know how much I wished to be along with him! He
regrets very much that he didnot return by St Louis.—I must
tell you something about Mr. Hazlitt since he returned. He has
got him a little pony about the size of the one I had at Jeff. Bks.
it is a little "Jim a long Josy"³ of a thing and if you were to see
it you would think it was going to drawl out *"y-e-s im* hisn" just
as you know Mr. Hazlitt does himself; he rode his pony to a
Ball four or five mile from camp a few days ago and as he was
joging along the road, neither pony nor man thinking of anything I suppose, the little thing stumbled and away went Hazlitt
over its head rolling in the dust and dirt. When he got up he
found the pony laying with its head in the other direction so it
must have turned a complete summer-set. I was not at the Ball
myself, and therefore didnot see Hazlitts exhibition and it was
several days before he told me of it. He could'nt keep it a secret.
You ought to be here a short time to see how we all live in our
winter houses. They are built by puting posts in the ground as if
for a fence and nailing up the outside with shingles. I have plank
for my house but there is but one or two other officers that have.
The chimneys are of mud and sticks and generally are completed
by puting a barrel or two on top to make them high enough.
Mr. Porter, Wallen, & Ridgley⁴ have built themselves fine
houses expecting their families here. Mr. Por[ter] went three
or four weeks ago to visit his wife [. . . . .] the mouth of Red
river. If they were here they might live very pleasantly for the
weather is so warm that we need but little or no fires. Mr. Hazlitt
and me keep bachilors hall on a small scale and get along very

pleasantly. We have an old woman about fifty years old to cook for us and a boy to take care of our horses so that we live as well as though we were out of the woods—Mr. Hazlitt wishes to be remembered to all of you. He says that you must write to him right off.—I hear from Fred. very often. He was well the last time he wrote. Julia you must answer this quick wont you? I know you can. Give my love to all the family

Fare well
ULYSSES

ALS, DLC-USG.

1. Sappington Post Office in Carondelet Township was the mail station closest to the Dent estate of White Haven.
2. By Regt. Order 70, July 18, 1844, USG was transferred from Co. I to Co. A, 4th Inf. In the absence of Capt. Charles H. Larnard of R.I., USMA 1831, USG commanded Co. A from Oct. 24, 1844, to Jan. 25, 1845. See *Calendar*, Oct. 31, 1844.
3. "Jim Along Josey," a minstrel song by Edward Harper, was published in 1840. Words and music are in John Lair, *Songs Lincoln Loved* (New York and Boston, 1954), p. 43.
4. Either 2nd Lt. Henderson Ridgely of Mo., or 1st Lt. Randolph Ridgely of Md., USMA 1837.

To Bvt. Brig. Gen. Roger Jones

Camp Salubrity La.
March 11th 1845

SIR

I have rec'd my commission as a Bvt. 2d Lieut. in the army of the U. States and hasten to acknowledge my acceptance of the rank it confers.

I am Sir
Your Obt Svt.
U S Grant

To Gen. R. Jones Adj. Gen.   Bvt. 2d Lt. 4th Inf

ALS, DNA, RG 94, ACP 4754/1885, envelope marked "On Pub. Serv." and postmarked Natchitoches, March 18, 1845. USG had been a bvt. 2nd lt. since his graduation from USMA.

To Julia Dent

——————

Camp Salubrity
Near Nachitoches La.
Tuesday, May 6th 1845

MY DEAR JULIA

I have just arrived[1] at Camp Salubrity after a tolerably pleasant trip of only one week from St. Louis, with one days detention at the mouth of Red River. I am here just in time; one day later I would have probably ~~had~~ an excuse to write. Whilst at the mouth of Red river I met with Lt. Baker who is strait from Fort Towson.[2] He left there only about one week ago. Fred. is very well, and would have been in Missouri with me but his commanding officer refused him a leave. It was right mean in him was'nt it?—Evry thing at Camp Salubrity Looks as usual only much greener from the contrast between the advancement of the season here and in the North. Though we are so far South and vegetation so far advanced a fire this evening is very comfortable. The officers are all collected in little parties discussing affairs of the nation. Annexation of Texas, war with Mexico, occupation of Orregon and difficulties with England are the general topics. Some of them expect and seem to contemplate with a great deal of pleasure some difficulty where they may be able to gain laurels and *advance a little in rank.* Any moove would be pleasant to me since I am so near promotion that a change of post would not affect me long. I have advanced three in rank very lately, leaving only five between me and promotion.—Mr. Hazlitt has gone to Fort Jesup and wont be back for a week; he left this morning before I got here.—It seems very strange for me to be siting here at Camp Salubrity writing to you when only a little more than one short week ago I was spending my time so

pleasantly on the Gravois.—Mrs. Porter started a few days ago
for Washita[3] and of course took little Dave. along so that I
could not give him the kiss you sent him. Mr. Porter was very
particular in his enquiries about all of you, and if he knew that I
was writing would send his love. When I got to Nachitoches I
found Mr. Higgins and Beaman[4] there just ready to start on a
leave of absence. I am sorry that Miss Fanny dont know that he
is on the way. I wanted him to tell me if he intended to bring her
to Salubrity with him but he would not say yes nor no. Tell me
what the probabilities are.—Have you heard yet from Col. Dent?
I supose Brand must have written you a very amusing ~~lett~~ account of his adventures in the East.—I supose Capt. Cotton[5]
has taken Lizzy to Green Bay before this. Does John pretend to
be as much as ever in love?—The first thing I did after geting
here was to get my letters from the Post Office. I found one from
Miss J. B. D. that afforded me a great deel of pleasure, and one
from home that had come by the way of St. Louis.—Is Miss
Jem~~mi~~ma Sappington[6] married yet?—Tell John not to take it so
hard as he appeared inclined to when he first heard of it.—I wrote
to Fred. on my way down the Mississippi and told him of the
pleasant visit I had, and how disappointed you all were that he
was not along. I shall always look back to my short visit to Mo.
as the most pleasant part of my life. In fact it seems more like a
pleasant dream than reality. I can scarsely co[nvince] myself of
the fact that I was there so short a ti[me] ago. My mind must be
on this subject something like what Hercules Hardy's was whilst
he was a prisoner among the Piannakataws in Guiana. I send
you the story[7] that you may read it.—Remember me very kindly
to Mrs. Dent and Ellen and Emmy and your brothers and to your
Aunt Fielding and your Cousins.[8] Dont neglect to write as soon
as you get this.

                                              I am most devotedly your
Julia   Ulysses S. Grant

P. S. I promised to write to Lewis Dent as soon as I got here but
I am so busily engaged building myself a new house that I will

not have much time for a while. Mrs. Wallen is here safe and looks very delicate.—I am going to follow your advice Julia and have me a good and comfortable house.

U.

The letter you wrote me before I went to Mo. was very different from what I expected to find it. It was not near so cold and formal as you led me to believe. I should not have written this last Post script should I?

u

ALS, DLC-USG.

1. USG had a leave of absence from April 1 to May 5, 1845, by special order of March 29, 1845 (Muster Roll, Co. A, 4th Inf., April, 1845, DNA, RG 94). During his leave he asked the Dents in St. Louis for permission to marry Julia. *Memoirs,* I, 51.

2. 2nd Lt. Charles Tainter Baker of Conn., USMA 1842, was in the 6th Inf. For Fort Towson see letter of July 28, 1844.

3. Fort Washita, Indian Territory, was located on the Washita River about thirty miles above its confluence with the Red River.

4. 2nd Lt. Jenks Beaman of Vt., USMA 1842, of the 4th Inf.

5. Capt. John Winslow Cotton of Mass., USMA 1823, 3rd Inf.

6. Jemima Sappington, later Mrs. Jemima Sternhauer, was the daughter of John Sappington of Carondelet Township, elected to three terms in the Mo. legislature as a Whig.

7. The story has not been found. A paperbound edition of *Adventures of Hercules Hardy,* published by Garrett & Co., New York, is listed in *Bibliotheca Americana, 1852–1855.*

8. John Fielding, uncle of Julia Dent, came from Augusta, Ky., to become the first president of St. Charles College in Mo. Unpublished memoirs of Julia Dent Grant.

To Julia Dent

Camp Salubrity La.
Near Nachitoches
June 1845

My Dear Julia

It is now seven weeks since I wrote to you and about three weeks since I began anxiously to expect an answer, but as none has come yet I conclude that either you have never recieved my letter or els you have rec'd and answered it and the answer has been miscarried. Is it not so Julia, for I know you intended to be punctual in writing to me. If you knew how much I prized a letter from you you certainly would be. I do not expect to recieve many more letters from you while at this place, judging from present appearances. All due preparations are now going on for our removal. The Texan Congress has already met and it is thought will soon accede to our terms of Annexation and then in we go without delay, that is, some of the troops from these parts will. The 4th is hardly considered as one bound for Texas unless in case of difficulty with Mexico, but if we do not go there we will go some place else, and I know that I shall be glad enough to get any place away from here. If any difficulty with the Mexicans takes us across the Western frontier the 6th will be as likely to go as the 4th and then I may have the pleasure of meeting Fred. on the *Rio Grand*. We will be excellent friends you may depend upon it when we get so far away. That will be the time for Fred. to prove himself a second Napoleon as you always said he would. I got a letter from Fred. a few days ago. He is in good health, he says he scarsely ever gets a letter from home. The last one he says was from Ellen, and that now you, John, Lewis, Wrenshall and your pa are all indebted to him a letter. So Julia I am not the only one you are negligent in writing to! But I dont believe you deserve so severe a charge as negligence. Are you all well on the Gravois? At Camp Salubrity it is very healthy although it is warm enough to through a Regiment into a fever. You dont know how tired I am geting of this place! I believe it is because I never hear from you. Your Pa has returned before this time I suppose. Did he have a pleasant trip? Brand no doubt has a great many amusing adventures to relate. Write to me Julia as soon as you recieve this whether you have written to me before or not. Col. Dent told me that he would write to me as soon as he returned from the East; if he has not done it yet, ~~you~~ wont you remind him of his promise. Remember me to you Aunt Fieldings family. I will wind up this time Julia with a short letter with the very good intention of writing you a very long one in answer to the first one I get from you. Mr. Porter has not heard from Mrs. Porter since she arrived at her mothers infact has not heard that she did arrive. She has been gone now nearly two months. Mrs. Wallen is very well; she enquires when I heard from you last when ever she sees me but unfortunately I have to tell her that I never hear. Miss Fanny Morrison is married I presume. The Captain is building a very comfortable house for her and Higgins. He says he expects Miss Clara along. Mr. Hazlitt wishes to be reminded to all at White Haven.[1]

Yours as ever
ULYSSES

To Julia

ALS, DLC–USG, postmarked Natchitoches, June 25, 1845.

    1. White Haven was the name of the Dent house.

To Julia Dent

––––––––

N. Orleans Barracks La.
July 6th 1845

MY DEAR JULIA

I recieved your letter a day or two before leaving Camp Salubrity but after we knew that we were to go.[1] You dont know how glad I was to get it at that time. A weeks longer delay in writing to me and I probably would not have heard from you for months, for there is no telling where we are going or how letters will have to be directed so as to reach us. Our orders are for the Western borders of Texas but how far up the Rio Grand is hard to tell. My prediction that I would recieve but few letters more at Camp Salubrity has proven very true. I hope you have sent me a letter by Mr. Higgins. How unfortune Miss Fanny has been. The Brevets that are going to Texas are probably better off than those of higher rank. I am perfectly rejoiced at the idea of going there myself for the reason that in the course of five or six months I expect to be promoted and there are seven chances out of eight that I will not be promoted in the 4th so that at the end of that time I shall hope to be back to the U. States, unless of course there should be active service there to detain me and to take many others there.—I was very much in hopes Julia that I would recieve a letter from your pa before leaving Camp Salubrity giving his full consent to our engagement. Now —that I am going so far away and dont know how long it may be before I can hear from you I shall be in a greatdeal of suspense on the subject. Soldiering is a very pleasant occupation generally and is so even on this occation except so far as it may be an obsticle in the way of our gaining the f unconditional consent of your parents to what *we*, or at least I, believe is for our happiness. —Mrs. Wallen will soon go to Jefferson Barracks to remain until her husband has quarters comfortably arranged for her where the troops may be posted. She will be writing to Mr. Wallen, wont you ask her how she directs her letters and write to me? If you knew how happy I am to get a letter from you you would write often. Mrs. Wallen asked me if I would not have a letter for her to carry when she went to St. Louis and I told her that I would so if you will call on her when she arrives which will probably be about the 1st of August you may find another letter from me.—From what I have seen N. Orleans Barracks is the most pleasant place I have ever been stationed at. It is about four miles below the city, but it is so thickly settled all the way along that we appear to be in town from the start. The place is much more handsomely fixed than Jeff. Bks.—In a few days the 3d Infantry will join us here, and not long after two companies are expected from Fort Scott.[2] I dont know what the probabil- ities are for Fred. going to Texas, I know he is anxious to go and I should be happy to meet him there.—You ask if Fred. has done any thing out of the way that his commanding officer [w]ould not give him a leave! Certa[inly] he [has] [n]ot; the comd.g off. probably thin[ks] that he has not been long enough

in s[e]rv[ice] to have a leave, or els there is too many officer[s] ,
absent already, or something of the kind. There are but few
Commanding officers as indulgent about giving young officers
leaves of absence as the one I am serving under. (Col. Vose).[3]
I recieved a letter from Fred. but a few weeks ago and he said
nothing to me about being ordered farther into the wilderness.
probably some of the Indians in those parts have been pestering
the frontier setlers. Dont be frightened but about his geting
home again and I shall hope too to be with him. Next time I ask
for a leave of absence it will be for six months, *to take a trip North*.

Give my love to all your family, and your Aunt Fieldings
also. Mr. Hazlitt wishes to be remembered. He says that he was
not two months in answering your letter.

Write without failing and I will trust to providence for
geting the letter. for ever yours most devotedly

u s GRANT

Julia

P. S. Remind your pa.about writing to me and you plead for us
wont you Julia? I will keep an account of all the Mexicans and
Comanches that we take in battle and give you a full account.
I have a black boy to th take along as my servant that has been
in Mexico. He speaks English Spanish and French I think he
may be very useful where we are going. fare well my Dear
Julia for a scout among the Mexicans

U

ALS, DLC-USG, postmarked New Orleans, July 9, 1845.

1. The 4th Inf. left Grand Ecore on July 3, 1845, and arrived at New Orleans
on July 5, 1845.
2. Fort Scott, Kan., four miles from the Mo. border, protected the military
road from Fort Leavenworth to Fort Gibson in Indian Territory.
3. Col. Josiah H. Vose of Mass., commanded the 4th Inf.

To Julia Dent

———

N. Orleans Barracks La.
July 11th 1845

MY DEAR JULIA

I wrote you a letter a few days ago in which I promised to write again by Mrs. Wallen. It was my intention then to write you a very long one but she starts much sooner than I expected so that I will only trouble you with a short note, and it too will probably reach you before the letter sent by Mail. There is now no doubt Julia but we will all be in Texas in a very short time. The 3d Infantry have arrived on their way and in a week or so we will all be afloat on the Gulf of Mexico. When I get so far away you will still think of and write to me I know and for my part I will avail my self of evry opportunity to send you a letter. It cannot well be many months that I will be detained in that country unless I be promoted to one of the Regiments stationed there and the chances are much against that. I have never mentioned any thing about *love* in any of the letters I have ever written you Julia, and indeed it is not necessary that I should, for you know as well as I can tell you that you alone have a place in my *my*—What an out I make at expressing any thing like love or sentiment: You know what I mean at all events, and you know too how acquerdly I made known to you for the first time my love. It is a scene that I often think of, and with how much pleasure did I hear that my offer was not entirely unacceptable? In going away now I feel as if I had some one els than myself to live and strive to do well for. You can have but little idea of the influance you have over me Julia, even while so far away. If I feel tempted to do any thing that I think is not right I am shure to think, "Well now if Julia saw me would I do so" and thus it is absent or present I am more or less governed by what I think is your will.

Julia you know I have never written anything like this befor and wont you keep any one from seeing it. It may not be exactly

right to keep it from your parents, but then you will get a letter
from me by Mail about the same time which they will probably
see. Am I giving you bad advice? if you think so act just as you
think you ought.—Mrs. Wallen will give you all the news afloat
here. Dont forget to ask ~~Mrs~~ her how she intends to direct her
letters to Mr. Wallen and send mine to the same address, and
now I must close with sending the most devotional love of

U S G

To Julia

ALS, DLC–USG, envelope marked "Politeness of Mrs. Wallen."

To Julia Dent

———

[*July 17, 1845*]
N. Orleans Barracks La.

My Dear Julia

I wrote to you several days ago expecting that Mrs. Wallen
would start the next day for St. Louis and would be the bearer
of my letter, but at the time that she expected to get off she was
taken sick and has not been able to start until now, so my Dear
Julia I write you a second sheet hoping that any addition to one
of my letters will be as agreeable to you as a Post Script to one
of your letters is to me. Since I wrote you the first sheet several
things of importance, or at least new, have taken place. One
company of ~~the~~ Artillery is now between this and the mouth of
the Mississippi river to join us for Texian service. Mr. and Mrs.
Higgins have arrived and appear to be as happy as you please.
Mrs. Higgins for some time persisted in accompanying her
husband into the field but she has at length given it up.—Something melancholy has taken place too. On the evening of the
15th Inst. Col Vose, for the first time since I have been in the
Army, undertook to drill his Regiment. He was ~~possibly~~ probably some what embarrassed and gave his commands in a loud
tone of voise; before the drill was over I discovered that he put

his hand to his breast when ever he commenced to give any command, and before he was through with the parade he was compelled to leave the field and start for his qarters, which were hardly fifty paces off, and just upon ~~arriving~~ arriving there he fell dead upon the poarch. He was buried to-day (July the 15th)[1] with millitary honors.

That evening late I was sent to town ~~late~~ to have the Obituary notice published; the next evening I was sent again to have the order and time of the funeral put in the papers and was returning between 1 and 2 o'clock at night when I discovered a man and woman that I thought I knew, footing it to the city carrying a large bundle of clothes. I galloped down to the Barracks to asc[er]tain if the persons that I suspected were absent or not and found that they were. I was ordered immediately back to apprehend them, which by the assistance of some of the City Watchmen I was able to do. I had the man put in the watch house and brought the *lady* back behind me on my horse to her husband, who she had left asleep and ignorent of her absence. Quite an adventury was'nt it?

Mrs. Higgins and husband have arrived just in time to find us *en route* for Texas. I believe she will return to Jeff. Bks. in a day or two. She brings news Julia which if I did not believe she was mistaken in would give me some trouble of thoughts. She says that I have a dangerous rival in Missouri, and that you do not intend to write to me any more &c. &c. Of course Julia I did not believe this, yet the fact of any one saying it was so gave me some uneasiness. I knew, or at least thought I knew, that even if any thing of the kind was so that you would let me know it and not tell it to a disinterested person. I am right in this am I not? You must not think Julia that I have been questioning and pumping to get the above information; it was voluntarily given and not to me but to another who come and told me. You will write to me soon wont you and contridict the above statement. Mrs. Higgins told me to-day that she would carry any letters or packages that I might have to send you. I will send these by Mrs. Wallen and when the other asks me for my letters I will tell her that I understand that you do not intend writing to me any more and of course cant expect me to be writing ~~to be writing~~ to you. If you direct your letters to me at N. Orleans La. or Corpus Christi Texas they will be forwarded to where I am. This makes five letters I have written you since I was in Mo. wont you in turn write me one immediately and another in two or three weeks after? Give my love to all your fathers and your Aunt Fieldings families.

Yours affectionately

Julia   U S GRANT

P. S. We will start for Texas in the course of three or four days. While you are reading this I will be thinking of you at Corpus Christi, that is if so fortunate as to get there safely. In a few months I shall hope to be back promoted. I now have but three now between me and promotion; a few months ago I had nine or ten, dream of me Julia and rest assured that what I have heard has not weight enough to chang my love for you in the slightest.

U S G to Julia

ALS, DLC-USG, envelope marked "Politeness of Mrs. Wallen."

1. Col. Josiah H. Vose died on July 15; the funeral was July 17, 1845.

To Julia Dent

———

Corpus Christi Texas
Sept. 14th 1845

MY DEAR JULIA

I have just recieved your letter of the 21st ultimo in which you reproach me so heavily for not writing to you oftener. You know my Dear Julia that I never let two days pass over after recieving a letter from you without answering it; But we are so far separated now that we should not be contented with writing

a letter and waiting an answer before we write again. Hereafter
I will write evry two or three weeks at farthest, and wont you
do the same Julia? I recieved your letter before the last only
about three weeks ago and answered it immediately. Your letters
always afford me a greatdeal of happiness because they assure
me again that you love me still; I never doubted your love Julia
for one instant but it is so pleasant to hear it repeated, for my
own part I ~~feel as though~~ would sacrifice evrything Earthly
[. . .] to make my Dear Julia my own forever. All that I would ask
would be that my Regiment should be at a healthy post and you
be with me, then I would be content though I might be out of the
world. There are two things that you are mistaken in Julia, you
say you know that I am in an unhealthy climate and in hourly
expectation of War: The climate is delightful and very healthy,
as much so as any climate in the world and as for war we dont
believe a word of it. We are so numerous here now that we are
in no fear of an attack upon our present ground. There are some
such heavy storms here on the coast the later part of Sept. and
October however that we will probably be moved up the Nuices
river to San Patricio,[1] an old deserted town, that the Indians
have compelled the inhabitants to leave.—Since the troops have
been at Corpus Christi there has not been a single death from
sickness, but there has been two or three terrible visitations of
providence. There has been one man drownd in the breakers; a
few weeks ago a storm passed over camp and a flash of lightning
struck a tent occupied by two black boys killing one and stuning
the other, and day before yesterday the most terrible accidents of
all occured. For the last few weeks there has been an old worn
out Steam Boat, chartered by government, runing across the
bay here, and day before yesterday there happened to be a several
officers and a number of soldiers aboard crossing the bay; the
boat had scarsely got out of sight when the boilers bursted tear-
ing the boat into atoms and througing almost evry one aboard
from twenty to fifty yards from the wreck into the Briny Deep.
Some were struck with iron bars and splinters and killed immediately others swam and got hold of pieces of the wreck and

were saved. Among the killed was Lt. Higgins and Lt. Berry[2] both of the 4th Infantry. It will drive Fanny almost mad I fear. Capt. Morrison takes Mr. Higgins' death very hard. When he was killed he was standing talking with several officers; the others were uninjured. The number killed and wounded I have not heard accurately state[d], but I believe there was 9 killed and about 17 wounded one or two probably mortally.

Do you hear much about War with Mexico? From the accounts we get here one would supposed that you all thought the Mexicans were devouring us. The vacancies that have lately occured brings me about first for promotion and if by chance I should go back to the States I may have the pleasure of seeing my Dear Julia again before the end of the year; what happiness it would be to see you again so soon! I feel as though my good fortune would take me back. If I should be promoted to a Regt. in Texas I will have to remain untill na[. . . .] affairs look a little more settled and we become permanent in this country, which is a delightful one so far a[s] climate and soil is concerned, but where no one lives scarsely except the troops, and then I will go back and either remain there, or—May I flatter myself that one who I love so much would return with me to this country, when all the families that are now absent join there husbands?— If so Julia you know what I would say.

The mail is just going to close so I must stop writing. I intended to have written another sheet but I will have to put off my long letter until next time. Give my very best love to all your family and also Mrs. Fieldings. Dont neglect writing to me very soon Julia for you dont know anxious I always am to get a letter from my *Dear Dear* Julia and how disappointed I always feel when I am a long time without one from her. I very often look at the name in the ring I wear and think how much I would like to see again the one who gave it to me. I must close, so good by my Dear Julia

U S Grant

ALS, DLC-USG, postmarked New Orleans, Sept. 20, 1845.

1. San Patricio was about twenty-five miles inland from Corpus Christi on the Nueces River.

2. 2nd Lt. Benjamin A. Berry of S.C., USMA 1841.

To Julia Dent

———

Corpus Christi Texas
Oct. 10th 1845

MY DEAR JULIA

Yesterday evening we had a mail which was the first for several weeks and ~~and~~ as it was a very large one I was in hopes that I would hear from you, but how disappointed I was! not a single letter out of several hundred to the officers at this place was directed to me. I wrote you my third letter since I have been in Texas a few days ago but finding an opportunity of sending a letter all the way *by politeness* I write to you again Mr. Reeves[1] will deliver this in person and no doubt will have a great deal to tell you about us all here. What we are to do is hard to surmise, but as I have told you in several previous letters it is supposed that we will remain until spring and then a large proportion return to the States. Those that remain will probably commence puting up quarters for a permanent post, and really I dont know but it would be desirable to remain in Texas. It is just the kind of country Julia that *we* have often spoken of in our most romantic conversations. It is the place where we could gallop over the prairies and start up Deer and prairie birds and occationally see droves of wild horses or an Indian wigwam. The climate is delightful and healthy and the soil fertile, and when protected by troops no doubt will be settled up very rapidly.—The more we see of the Mexicans the more improbable it seems that we can ever get into war with her. Yucatan, one of ~~her~~ Mexico's most powerful states has told Mexico to do their own fighting for they wont assist, besides this they are on the eve of a revolution ~~in~~ with their own subjects, and so far as we have seen, the poorer and less ambitious and much the most numerous class of Mexicans are much better pleased with our form of government than their own; infact they would be willing to see us push our claims beyond the Rio Grande if we would promise not to molest them in their homes and possessions.—The weather is geting quite cold here and no doubt we will suffer conciderably this winter, but it is all for glory you know so we should never complain.— When I wrote to you last I mentioned that I had been promoted, and I believe I said, to the 4th Inf.y, but I was mistaken in my calculation. I am promoted but the news has not yet had time to come from Washington, but I believe I go to the 8th Inf.y so I will of course remain in Texas this winter. Next Summer though I shall go back to the States either with my Regiment or on leave.

Have you seen Mrs. Higgins since the death of her husband? She must have taken it very hard, Capt. Morrison could not have taken it harder if Mr. Higgins had been a son instead of a son-in-law.

Have you heard from Fred. lately? I have not heard from him since I have been in Texas. Tell John[2] that if he wants to come into the army, this Winter will probably be his chance. It is strongly rumored at Washington that there will be two Regiments of Infantry and one of Dragoons raised this comeing session of Congress and if so there will be a great many citizens appointed. Tell him to apply to Mr. Benton[3] to use his influence right off. Are you all well on the Gravois? remember me to evry one I know there. Write to me soon Julia and be assured that I am ever yours devotedly

U S Grant

Julia

ALS, DLC-USG, envelope marked "politeness of Mr. Reeves" and postmarked St. Louis, Nov. 7, 1845.

1. Probably 1st Lt. Isaac Stockton Keith Reeves, of S.C., USMA 1838, of the 1st Art.
2. John Dent, brother of Julia Dent.
3. Senator Thomas Hart Benton of Mo.

To Julia Dent

———

[*Oct., 1845*]
Corpus Christi Texas

MY DEAR JULIA

In my last letter I promised to write to you evry two or three weeks and it is now about that time since I wrote and you see how punctual I am. I fear Julia that there was a long time between the receipt of my letters from N. Orleans and my first from Texas but you must reflect that I had writen you three without having recieved an answer and before writing again I wanted to hear from my *Dear Dear* Julia. I always do and always will answer your letters immediately and if you knew how delighted I always am to hear from yourself you would write often too.

The late casualty in the 4th Infantry promotes[1] me so that I am now permanently at home in this Regiment. I should have prefered being promoted to a Regiment that is now in the States, because then I would get to see again, *soon*, one who is much dearer to me than my commission, and because too, there is hardly a probability of active service in this remote quarter of our country, and there is nothing els, excepting a fine climate and soil, to make one wish to stay here.—There is now over half of the Army of the U. States at Corpus Christi, and there must of course be a breaking up and scatterment of this large force as soon as it is found that their services will not be required in this part of the country. It is the general opinion that on account of the length of time the 4th has already been encamped, here and at Camp Salubrity, and the general unsettled position that it has been in since the begining of the Florida war, that we will be the first out of Texas. Once in quarters again no doubt we will remain for a good long time.

The most of the talk of war now comes from the papers of the old portion of the U. States. There are constantly bands of Mexican Smugglers coming to this place to trade, and they seem to feel themselvs as secure from harm here as though they were citizens of Texas, and we on the other hand, although we are occupying disputed Territory, even acknowedging our right to Texas, feel as secure from attack as you do off in Missouri. There was a time since we have been here when we were in about half expectation of a fight and with a fare prospect of being whipped too; that was when there was but few of us here and we learned that General Arista[2] and other officers of rank were on the Rio Grande ready to march down upon us. I be We began to make preparations to make as stout a defence as possible. Evry working man was turned out and an intrenchment began and continued for about a week and then abandoned.

Now my Dear Julia that a prospect is ahead for some perminancy in my situation dont you think it time for us to begin to settle upon some plan for consumating what we believe is for our mutual happiness? After an engagement of sixteen or seventeen months ought we not to think of bringing that engagement to an end, in the way that all true and constant lovers should? I have always expressed myself willing you know my Dear Julia to resign my appointment in the army for the sake of overcomeing the objections of your parents, and I would still do so; at the same time I think they mistake an army life very much. No set of ladies that I ever saw are better contented or more unwilling to change their condition than those of the Army; and you Julia would be contented knowing how much and how dearly devoted I am to you—I cannot help writing thus affectionat[ely] since you told me that no one but yourself reads my letters.

Your Pa asks what I could do out of the Army? I can tell you: I have at this time the offer of a professorship of mathematics in a tolerably well endowed College in Hillsboro, Ohio, a large and flourishing town, where my salery would probably equal or exceed my present pay. The Principle of the Institution got my father to write to me on the subject; he says I can have until next spring to think of this matter. The last letter I wrote was to make all the enquiries I could about the situation and if the answer proves favorable I shall give this matter serious concideration.

I am now reading the Wandering Jew, the copy that belonged
to Mr. Higgins and the very same numbers read by yourself.
How often I think of you whilst reading it. I think well Julia has
read the very same words that I am now reading and not long
before me. Yesterday in reading the 9th No I saw a sentence
marked around with a pencil and the word *good* written after it.
I thought it had been marked by you and before I knew it I had
read it over three or four times. The sentence was a sentiment
expressed by the Indian Prince Djalmo on the subject of the
marriage of two loving hearts, making a compareison you may
recollect.[3] Was it you that marked the place. I have written so
long a letter that I must close. Remember me to evry body on
the Gravois. Mr. Hazlitt also wishes to be remembered.

Give my love to Ellen. How is Ellen's soft eyed lover
comeing on that she wanted me to quiz somebody down here
about? She did not say so but I know she wanted some of her
friends here to hear of him just to see how jealous she could make
them[.]

Good bye my Dear Julia and dont forget to write soon.

Yours most affectionately

Julia   ULYSSES

ALS, DLC-USG, postmarked New Orleans, Oct. 13, 1845.

1. USG's commission as full 2nd lt. dated from Sept. 30, 1845, when the
4th Inf. was fully assembled in Texas.

2. General Mariano Arista was superseded in command before hostilities
began, but he was restored to command on April 24, 1846.

3. *Le Juif Errant* by Eugene Sue appeared in ten volumes in 1844–45. A
lush melodrama describing an involved Jesuit plot, it also contained social criti-
cism and an exposition of Fourierist theory. Harper published an American
edition in 1846 in which the speech of Prince Djalmo reads: "—for two drops of
dew blending in the cup of a flower are as hearts that mingle in a pure and virgin
love; and two rays of light united in one inextinguishable flame, are as the burning
and eternal joys of lovers joined in wedlock." II, 127.

To Julia Dent

———

Corpus Christi Texas
Nov. 11th 1845

MY DEAR JULIA

I was gratified this morning with recieving a letter from you which was the first for two months. You dont know how dis-appointed I have always felt for the last month when I go to the Post Office and find no letter from my *Dear Dear Julia.* I do not recollect what the report was that you say I spoke of in one of my last letters, but it was nothing concerning either of us and certainly nothing like what you suspected.—Next Spring at farthest I think the 4th Infantry will be going back to the United States and no doubt will be permanent for many years unless some other difficulty should spring up to make it necessary to make us miserable again for another year or two. I always feel as though any place would be pleasant if I could only often see my Dearest Julia, and without that I will always be more or less discontented. How can your Pa continue to disapprove of a Match which so much affects the happiness of both? I say both because I judge you by myself. Dont you think he will finally yeald? How can I say finally though when we have been waiting already so long? I think my *Dear Julia* that the question of our marriage should be fully and irrevocably settled soon in justice to you. You know my Dear Julia that evry one who knows either of us believes that we are engaged and if it should turn out after all (I can scarsely bear to think such a thing possible though) that the engagement should be broken off by the objections of your parents, wont people say that I have done very rong and acted very unjustly to you not to have had a decission of the qustion much sooner. You know my views my Dear Julia on the subject of the interferance of parents in matters of such vast importance. You know that I think that evry thing possible should be done to reconcile parents to a marriage, at the same time, before an engagement is allowed to run on for years the party should make up their mind as to how they should act in case of a final refusal. I have always thought that you were of the same opinion as myself on this subject; am I not right Julia? I am fully satisfied that we could be happy and at the same time independent of the world. Any one so much loved as you are Julia must be contented. Wont you write to me soon and tell me if you think as I do. I would not propose any thing that I did not think would be for your own happiness for believe me I am not altogether selfish, I think of Julia as much as I do of myself.—I believe I told you some time ago that I am promoted such is the case anyhow but I was not fortunate enough to get in a Regiment in the U. S. I go to the 7th Infantry which is encamped here but I have made application to transfer[1] with Lt. Gardner of the 4th Inf.y and no doubt will be able to get back. No doubt Mr. Rieves[2] has answered the questions you ask me about the particulars of the death of Mr. Higgins. I intend writing to Fred. to day. He owes me a letter but I shant be particular about that. He is very much like his sister Julia about writing he likes to have about two letters for one. No reproach reproach upon you though Julia, if I thought you would write me one letter for evry two I would write about twice a week—The portion of the Army at Corpus Christi (amounting to between four and five thousand) would no doubt spend a very unpleasant winter here if we didnot have such a fine climate. We have no quarters but our linen tents and of course cannot have fires, but we are so far South the cold is but little felt. I dont see that there is much difference between the winters and the summers in fact, except that there is more rain in the winter. Give my love to Ellen and the rest of the family at White Haven and if you can do write to me soon. The letter you speak of Julia as having read over so often could have been nothing but the most affectionate for I have not felt any other way. I do not recollect a word of what I wrote. I have written this in a great hurry and in consequence have told you but little news but I will write soon again and write much longer.

I shall look for a letter from you very soon now in answer to the one Mr. Rieves delivered to you

ULYSSES

To Julia

P. S. You have no doubt heard that Mexico has consented to appoint commissioners to settle the question of the boundary between this country and their own without any fighting. No doubt the whole affair will be settled by spring and the troops here distributed. Some two or three Regiments no doubt will have to remain to build and Garrison posts on the frontier of this country.

Julia at home they are very anxious to have me resign evry letter I get is on the subject of my resignation. I have the offer of a professorship in a college in Ohio[3] which they would prefer my taking to remaining in the Army but I have not concluded to accept the offer. I will come to some conclution on the subject between this and Spring. What do you think about it Julia? No one now can have more influance than just yourself. Tell me plainly what you think about my resigning for a place of the kind. If you can muster courage mention the matter to your Pa.

Adieu

Julia   U S G

ALS, DLC-USG.

1. For USG letter to AGO requesting transfer, see *Calendar*, 1845, Oct. 24. On Oct. 23, 1845, 2nd Lt. Franklin Gardner of Iowa, USMA 1843, wrote to Bvt. Brig. Gen. Roger Jones, "I have the honor to request that I may be allowed to change Regiments with Lieut. Grant from the 4th. to the 7th. Regiment of Infantry." Gardner's letter was favorably endorsed by both Col. William Whistler of the 4th Inf. and Bvt. Brig. Gen. Zachary Taylor. DNA, RG 94, Letters Received. USG was promoted to 2nd Lt. Sept. 30, 1845; Gardner on Sept. 12, 1845. Bvt. Brig. Gen. Roger Jones to Secretary of War William L. Marcy, Dec. 12, 1845, *ibid.*, ACP Branch, Letters Sent, Nominations. USG was transferred from the 4th to 7th Regt. by General Orders No. 50, AGO, Nov. 5, 1845. He was transferred to Co. C, 7th Inf., on Nov. 23, 1845, but returned to Co. C, 4th Inf., on Dec. 14, 1845, after receipt of General Orders No. 52, AGO, Nov. 15, 1845.

2. Reeves.

3. See letter of [*Oct., 1845*].

To Bvt. Capt. W. W. S. Bliss

Camp Near Corpus Christi Texas
Nov. 20th 1845

SIR

Having just recieved notice of my promotion to the 7th Infy and having made application some twenty days ago for a transfer to the 4th Infy I respectfully apply for leave of absence until action of the War Department has been had on my application, with permission to accompany an escort which is about leaving this Camp with the Pay Master.

Very Respectfully
Your Obt. Svt.

To W. W. S. Bliss   U S GRANT
Ast. Adj. Gen   2d Lt. 7th Infy

ALS, Abraham Lincoln Book Shop, Chicago, Ill. Bvt. Capt. William Wallace Smith Bliss of N.H., USMA 1833, 4th Inf., was on the staff of Bvt. Brig. Gen. Zachary Taylor. On Nov. 28, 1845, by Special Orders 55, USG was granted 30 days leave "for the purpose of visiting the interior." DNA, RG 94, Orders of Gen. Zachary Taylor. For an account of the trip, see letter of Jan. 2, 1846. On Nov. 20, 1845, Taylor wrote the AGO to acknowledge receipt of a letter of promotion for USG. Copy, DNA, RG 94, Mexican War, Army of Occupation, Letters Sent.

To Julia Dent

[*Nov.–Dec., 1845*]

MY DEAR JULIA

There is one subject that is ever upermost with me and I have alluded to it several times before but I could not resist this fine opportunity, when I know you will get my letter, to mention it again. I take an extra sheet for it not that I have said so much on the first but :—I cant tell why—

I was so much in hopes that I would have a letter from you

that I could scarsely bear to leave the office without one, I wanted to write such a long one to you and wanted it to be an answer; but I know very well My Dear Julia that letters are a long time traveling as far as we are separated, and then too ladies think themselvs punctual if they answer a letter in a month after it is recieved. This is no reproach upon you Julia for I have had two —and beautiful ones too—since the 4th has been in Texas; but you will write oftener even than this ~no~ in the future wont you. You have often heard me say how delighted I always am to get a letter and now that you are so far away I believe I feel still more anxiety about hearing from you. It is not true that absence and distance conquer love.

The subject spoken of as being ever upermost, is my love for *my Dear Julia,* and the consequence (matrimony) of a love so pure. It is now about a year and a half Julia since I first confessed my love for you, and since that time we have been engaged, and yet but little has been said as to when we should be united We have always lived in hopes that your Pa would remove the only obstacle in our way and I took his answer to me as almost a complete removal. He told me that before giving ~his final consent~ a positive answer he would have to speak to you. I thought that he ~with you wish~ would decide as you wished, and I thought I well knew how that was. I cant believe yet my *Dear Dear Julia* but that he will give his consent. I would do anything to gain his permission to our engagement but if he should still refuse: have you ever decided how we then should or ought to act? I shall always recollect ~how~ Miss C. O'F's[1] views upon this subject; it was you told me them, and I perfectly agree with her. I think we should try to gain the consent of all interested parties as long as there was hopes but only allow the best of reasons to change our intention. Do you think with me on this subject? The Army seems to be the only objection and really I think there can be no happyer place to live. As I told you in my last letter I am at this time thinking strongly of resigning but I do not think I will ever half so well contented out of the Army as in it.

I shall not believe my Dear Julia that the difficulties alluded to above will ever be met with. I will continue to think that when my Regiment is permanant at some post where the officers have their families that you will consent to go there too, and there will be no serious objections made. We have loved each other now so long and without any abatement, so far as I am able to answer, that it seems to me they ~~must~~ (I mean your Father & Mother) must agree that even admiting that we might possibly be unhappy after marriage we would be still more so were they to break off the engagement. I say we because I measure your love by my own Julia. It may be vanity but I do not think so.

It is now 8 o'clock A. M. and I have to march on Guard this morning so that I can have but a few minuets more to write.

I have been reading the Wandering Jew but I have only got 15 Numbers of it.[2] If you have the numbers after fifteen will you send them to me ~~Julia~~. I have no way of geting them except by writing to my friends to send them and what one more properly than Julia?

Give my love to Ellen. Ask her how Mr. some one in the country is coming on. Write soon and very often and I will do the same—Adieu

                                        Your most affectionate
Julia   Ulysses

ALS, DLC-USG.

1. Caroline O'Fallon, daughter of Col. John O'Fallon of St. Louis, was a close friend of Julia Dent.
2. See letter of [*Oct., 1845*].

To Julia Dent

———

                                        Corpus Christi Texas
                                        Jan. 2d 1846

My Dear Julia

I have just returned from a tour of one month through Texas, and on my return I find but one single letter from my Dear Julia and that one but a few lines in length. You dont know how disappointed I felt, for in my two or three last letters, which remain unanswered yet, I said something that I was somewhat impatient to recieve an answer too.

On the 2d of Dec. myself and some fifteen other officers started for San Antonio which is about one hundred and fifty miles from here and laying beyond a district of country which heretofore has been rendered uninhabitable by some bands of Indians—The Comanches and others—who have always been at the enemies of the white man. Of course we had to camp out during the journey and we had very disagreeable weather to do it in too. Some of the old Texans say they have scarsely ever seen as disagreeable a winter as this one has been. From San Antonio I went across to Austin, the seat of Government. The whole of the country is the most beautiful that I ever have seen, and no doubt will be filled up very rapidly now that the people feel a confidance in being protected. San Antonio has the appearance of being a very old town. The houses are all built of stone and are begining to crumble. The whole place has been built for defence, which by the way was a wise precaution, for untill within three or four years it has been the scene of more blood shed than almost any place of the as little importance in the world. The town is compact, the houses all one story high only, the walls very thick, the roofs flat and covered with dirt to the depth of two or more feet and they have but few doors and windows and them very small so the town cant be burned down, and a few persons in side of a house can resist quite a number. Austin in importance or at least in appearance is about equal to Carondolett.[1] The inhabitants of San Antonio are usually mostly Mexicans. They seem to have no occupation whatever.

I have but little doubt Julia but that my Regt. the 4th Inf.y (I was promoted to the 7th but I have transfered to the 4th) will go up the Miss. river in the course of a few months now, but so far as I am concerned myself I dont know but I would prefer remaining in Texas. On you account Julia I would prefer going back but even here I think you would be contented.

Here it is now 1846 Julia, nearly two years since we were first engaged and still a time when or about when our marriage is to be consumated has never been talked of. Dont you think it is now time we should press your father further for his concent? If you would speak to him on the subject I think he would give his concent; you know he told me that you never spoke to him of our engagement and infact would hardly give him a chance to speak to you of it. If you think it best I will write again to him.

You know Julia what I think we would be justifiable in doing if his concent is still witheld and I hope you think nearly with me. Wont you give the matter a serious concideration and tell me soon, very soon if we agree. You alone Julia have it in your power to decide whether in spite of evrything we carry our engagement into effect. You have only to decide for me to act. If you will set a tim[e] when I must be in Missouri I will be there no matter if my Reg.t is still in Texas. The matter is one of importance enough to procure a leave of absence, and besides for the love I bear my dear Julia I would not value my commission to highly to resign it. I ought not to commit this to paper where there is danger that it may be seen before you get it, but I cannot help it, it is ~~for~~ what I feel and have expressed before. My happiness would be complete if a return mail should bring me a letter seting the time—not far distant—when I might "clasp that little hand and call it mine."

Your Devoted Lover
U<small>LYSSES</small>

Julia

ALS, DLC-USG, postmarked New Orleans, Jan. 12, 1846.

1. Carondelet, a small town south of St. Louis, was later absorbed by the city.

To Julia Dent

————

Corpus Christi Texas
Jan. 12th 1846

MY DEAR JULIA

I have just been deligted by ~~the~~ recieving a long and interesting letter from the one I love so much and from the tone of her
letter I am left with the hope that for the remainder of the time
that we two are not one, she will be punctual in answering my
letters. You do not know the pleasure it gives me to recieve
letters from you my Dear Julia or you would write oftener. I
write to you very often besides answering all your letters. You
beg of me not to resign : it shall be as you say Julia for to confess
the truth it was on your account that I thought of doing so,
although all the letters I get from my father are filled with
persuasion for me to resign. For my own part I am contented
with an army life, all that I now want, to be happy is for Julia to
become mine, and how much I would sacrifize if her parents
would give now their willing concent. By Spring at farthest I
hope to see the 4th Inf.y (You know that I have transfered from
the 7th to the 4th) settled and that too on the Mississippi river,
unless something should take place to give us active employment. Has Mr. Reeves ever delivered you the letters sent by
him. It is astonishing Julia what a place Corpus Christi has
become. Already there are two Theaters and a printing office
evry night there is a ~~performance~~ play at one or the other. It
seems strange to hear you talking of sleigh riding, for here we
have although it is January weather warm enough for light clothing. Such a thing as a sprinkle of snow is rarely seen at Corpus
Christi.

From my last letter you will see that I have been on a long
trip through Texas and that I think the country beautiful and
promising. If it should turn out after all that my Regiment
should be retained here (it is not the opinion of any one that it
will be kept) I could have but little to complain of. Your letter,

and indeed all your letters, show your willingness to accompany me to any permanant Military post. It is very pleasant to hear such confessions from the one we love and in return I have to say that I would make any sacrifice for my Julias happiness. But what an uninteresting letter I am writing you it seems to me that the more I write the worse I get.—I have not heard from Fred. since I have been in Texas. I have written to him once and I think twice since he wrote to me last. Tel him he must write soon. Fred is now about 3d for promotion. There has been two resignations at Corpus Christi that he has not heard of.—Mr. Ridgely and Mr. Sykes[1] have gone to St. Louis on a sick leave; if I had known sooner that they were going I would have sent a letter by them.

I have written you several letters that remain [u]nanswered so I shall look for an[other] letter [in] evry Mail. Give my love to all at White Haven. Soon I hope to see you again my dear dear Julia and let us hope that it will be to never separate again for so long a time or by so great a distance.

Your Devoted
ULYSSES

Julia

ALS, DLC-USG, postmarked New Orleans, Jan. 23, 1846.

1. 2nd Lt. George Sykes of Md., USMA 1842, 3rd Inf.

To Julia Dent

———

Corpus Christi Texas
Feb 5th 1846

MY DEAR JULIA

Two or three Mails have arrived at Corpus Christi in the last few days and by each I confidently expected a letter from you, but each time I was disappointed. As a consolation then I come to my tent and got out all the letters yo[u have] ever written me—How many do you think they amounted to? only 11 Julia, and it is now twenty months that we have been engaged. I read all of them over but two and now write to you again Julia in hopes that hereafter I will get a letter from you evry two or three weeks. You dont know with what pleasure I read your letters or you would write much oftener.

At present the prospect of the 4th Infantry, or any other Regiment, geting back to civilization is by no means flattering. Our march is still onwards to the West. Orders have been recieved here for the removal of the troops to the Rio Grand (to Francis Isabel)[1] and before you get this no doubt we will be on our way.—Continue to direct your letters as before, ~~to~~ the care of Col. Hunt[2] N. Orleans and they will reach me. In all probability this movement to the Rio Grande will hasten the settlement of the boundary question, either by treaty or ~~a~~ the sword, and in eather case we may hope for early peace and a more settled life in the army, and then may *we—you and I Julia—* hope for as speedy a consent on the part of[3] your parents to our union? You say they certainly will not refuse it. I shall continue to hope and believe that it will be as you say.

I wrote to you a short time ago that I thought our engagement should be carried into effect as early as possible ~~Julia~~. I still think so and would be very happy to have you set the time at no very distant day, with the condition if the troops are not actively emploid. Of course Julia I never even dremed of such a thing as asking you to come to a Camp or ~~an~~ temporary ~~unsettled~~ and distant post with me. I would not wish to take you from a home where you are surrounded by evry comfort and where you are among friends that you know and love. That is not what I proposed. If you should consent that I might "clasp that little hand and call it mine" while the troops are still in their present unsettled state I would either resign as my father is anxious to have me do, or return by myself leaving my Dear Julia at a comfortable home while I was fighting the battles of our Country.—Has John made application for an appointment in one of the new Regiments that are to be raised I hope he has not let the oportunity slip. With Mr. Bentons[4] influance he could probably get a Captaincy.—I got a letter from Fred. a few days ago. He is well and is now looking out for promotion. He is anxious to get to the 4th I[nf.y] and says that if he is not promoted to it h[e] intends to make a transfer to get to it if he can.—Dont neglect to write to me often Julia. If you have but a little to write say that, it gives me so much pleasure even to see your name in your own hand writing. About the time you get this I will be on the march (on foot of course) between this and San Isabel or Francis Isabel. In the evenings just think that one who loves you above all on this Earth is then resting on the ground (thinking of Julia) after a hard days march.—Give my love to Ellen Emmy and the rest at White Haven.

Your most affectionately
U S GRANT

Julia

ALS, DLC-USG.

    1. Francis Isabel or Point Isabel was a coastal town a few miles above the Rio Grande.
    2. Lt. Col. Thomas F. Hunt of N.C., deputy q. m. gen.
    3. Two words crossed out.
    4. Senator Thomas Hart Benton of Mo.

To Julia Dent

Corpus Christi Texas
Feb. 7th 1846

DEAREST JULIA

    I have just been delighted by a long and interesting letter from my Dear Julia and although I wrote to you but two or three days ago I answer this with my usual punctuality. You say you write me letter for letter well I am satisfied that my love is returned and you know how anxious one is to hear often from the one they love and it may appear to me that you do not write as often as you really do. Your letter was one of the sweetest you have ever written me and your answer to the question I have so often asked was so much like yourself, it was just what I wanted to hear you say; boldness indeed: no my Dear Julia that is a charge that can never be laid to you.—There is a part of your letter that is entirely incomprehensible to me. I dont know whether you are jesting or if you are serious.[1] I first loved Julia I have loved no one els.—The chance of any of the troops geting out of Texas this spring is worse than ever, before long we will be on our way farther West but no doubt it will be but a few months until the boundary question will be settled and then we may look for a general dispersion of troops and I for one at least will see Missouri again.—Does your pa ever speak of me or of our engagement? I am so glad to hear you say that you think his consent will be given when asked for. I shall never let an opor-tuntiy to do so pass.—As to resigning it would not be right in the present state of affairs and I shall not think of it again for the present.—So John is again a Bachilor without a string to his bow. no doubt he will remain single all his life The extract from some newspaper you send me is a gross exageration of the morals and health of Corpus Christi. I do not believe that there is a more healthy spot in the world. So much exposure in the winter season is of course attended with a goodeal of sickness but not of a serious nature. The letter was written I believe by a soldier of the 3d Inf.y. As to the poisning and robberies I believe they are entirely false. There has been several soldiers murdered since we have been here, but two of the number were shot by soldiers and there is no knowing that the others were not. Soldiers are a class of people who will drink and gamble let them be where they may, and they can always find houses to visit for these purposes. Upon the whole Corpus Chri[sti] is just the same as any other plase would be where there were so many troops. I think the man who wrote the letter you have been reading deservs to be put in the Guard house and kept there until we leave the country. There he would not see so much to write about.—Do you get the paper I send you evry week?—I know Julia if you could see me now you would not know me, I have allowed my beard to grow two or three inches long. Ellen would not have to be told now that I ~~was~~ am trying to raise whiskers. Give my love to all at White Haven.

> Your Devoted lover
> ULYSSES

Julia

ALS, DLC-USG, postmarked New Orleans, Feb. 18, 1846.

1. Eleven lines crossed out.

To Julia Dent

————

> Corpus Christi Texas
> March 3d 1846

MY DEAR JULIA

I have not recieved a letter from you since my last, but as I may not have an opportunity of writing to you again [for] several weeks I must avail my self of this chance of writing to my dear Julia. This morning before I got awake I dreamed that I was some place away from Corpus Christi walking with you leaning upon my arm, your hand was in mine and I felt very happy. How disappointed when I awoke and found that it was but a dream. However I shall continue to hope that it will not be a great while befor such enjoyment will be real and no dream. —The troops have not yet left this place but the movement is to commence now in a few days. The 4th Inf.y is the last to leave. We are to go into camp on this side of the Rio Grande just opposite to Matamoras,[1] a town of considerable importance in Mexico, and as we are informed, occupied by several thousand troops who it is believed by many will make us fight for our ground before we will be allowed to occupy it. But fight or no

fight evry one rejoises at the idea of leaving Corpus Christi. It
is to be hoped that our troops being so close on the borders of
Mexico will bring about a speedy settlement of the boundary
question; at all events it is some consolation to know that we
have now got as far as we can go in this direction by any order
from Government and therefore the next move will be for the
better. We may be taken prisoners it is true and taken to the
City of Mexico and then when we will be able to get away is
entirely uncertain. From the accounts recieved here I think the
chances of a fight on our first arrival on the Rio Grand are about
equal to the chances for peace, and if we are attacked in the
present reduced state of the troops here the consequences may
be much against us.—Fred is now about 2d or 3d for promotion
and I have no doubt but this moove will make him a 2d Lieut.—
But I have said enough on this subject for the present. A few
weeks more and we will know exactly what is to take place and
then the first thing, I will write to one who in all difficulties is
not out of my mind. My Dear Julia as long as I must be separated from your dear self evry moove that takes place I hail
with joy. I am always rejoised when an order comes for any
change of position hoping that soon a change will take place that
will bring the 4th Inf.y to a post where there are comfortable
quarters, and where my Dear Julia will be willing to accompany
me. In my previous letters I have spoken a great deal of resigning
but of course I could not think of such a thing now just at a time
when it is probable that the services of evry officer will be called
into requisition; but I do not think that I will stand another year
of idleness in camp.—You must write to me often Julia and
direct your letters as heretofore. I will write to you very often
and look forward with a great deal of anxiety—to the time when
I may see you again and claim a kiss for my long absence.—Do
you wear the ring with ~~my in~~ the letters U. S. G. in it Julia.
I often take yours off to look at the name engraved in it.—While
writing this I am on guard ~~fo~~ of course for the last time [at] this
place.—Give my love to all at White Haven.

Mr. Hazlitt is well and also Capt Morrison. Tell John not

to let his chance of geting into one of the new Reg.t that will probably be raised, slip by unimproved.

> Your Most Devoted
> ULYSSES

Julia

ALS, DLC-USG, postmarked New Orleans, March 16, 1846.

1. Matamoros was commonly spelled "Matamoras" by American troops.

To *Julia Dent*

———

> Camp Near Matamoras
> March 29th 1846

MY DEAR JULIA

A long and laborious march, and one that was threatened with opposition from the enemy too, has just been completed, and the Army now in this country are ~~now~~ laying in camp just opposite to the town of Matamoras. The city from this side of the river bears a very imposing appearance and no doubt contains from four to five thousand inhabitants. Apparently there are a large force of Mexican troops preparing to attack us. Last night during the night they threw up a small Breast work of Sand Bags and this morning they have a piece of Artillery mounted on it and directed toward our camp. Whether they really intend anything or not is doubtful. Already they have boasted and threatened so much and executed so little that it is generally believed that all they are doing is mere bombast and show, intended to intimidate our troops. When our troops arrived at the Little Colorado, (a river of about 100 yards in width and near five feet deep where we forded it) they were met by a Mexican force, which was represented by there commander to be large and ready for an attack. A parly took place between

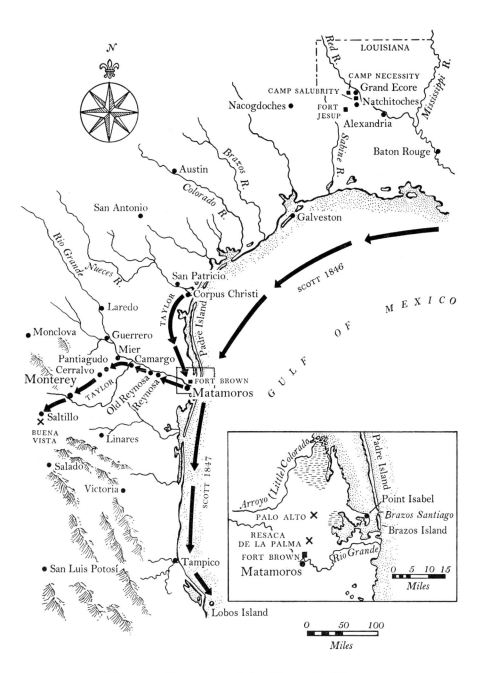

Northern Campaign of the War with Mexico

Gen. Taylor[1] and their commanding officer, whose name I have forgotten, the result of which was, that if we attempted to cross they would fire upon us. The Mexican officer said that however much he might be prepossessed in our favor himself he would have to obey the orders of his own Government, which were peremptory and left him but one course, and that was to defend the Colorado against our passing, and he pledged his honor that the moment we put foot into the water to cross he would fire upon us and war would commence. Gen. Taylor replied that he was going over and that if he would allow them fifteen minuets to withdraw their troop and if one of them should show their his heads after he had started over, that he would fire upon them; whereupon they left and were seen no more until until we were safely landed on this side. I think after making such threats and speaking so positivl[y] of what they would do and then let so fine an opportunity to execute what they had threatened pass unimproved, shows anything but a decided disposition to drive us from the soil. When the troops were in the water up to their necks a small force on shore might have given them a greatdeel of trouble.—During our whole march we have been favored with fine weather, and alltogether the march has been a pleasant one. There are about forty miles between the Nuices and the Colorado rivers that is one continuous sandy desert waste, almost without wood, or water with the exception of Salt Lakes. Passing this the troops of course suffered considerably.—Here the soil is rich and the country beautiful for cultivation. When peace is established the most pleasant Military posts in our country I believe will be on the Banks of the Rio Grande. No doubt you suppose the Rio Grande, from its name and appearance on the map to be a large and magnificent stream, but instead of that it is a small muddy stream of probably from 150 to 200 yards in width and navigabl[e] for only small sized steamers. I forgot to mention [that] we recieved before we arrived here, the proclamation[2] of Col. Majia the Commander-in-Chief I believe, of the Mexican forces. It was a long wordy and threatning document. He said that the citizens of Mexico were ready to expose their bare breasts to the Rifles of the Hunters of the Mississippi, that the Invaders of the North would have to reap their Laurels at the points of their sharpened swords; if we continued our march the deep waters of the Rio Grande would be our Sepulcher the people of our Government should be driven East of the Sabine and Texas re-conquered &c. &c. all of which is thought to mean but very little.

The most beliggerent move that has taken place yet occured yesterday. When we had arrived near this place a party of Mexican soldiers siezed upon two of our Dragoons and the horse of a Bugler boy who had been sent in advance to keep an eye in the direction of the enemy and to communicate if they saw any movement towards our column. The prisoners are now confined in the city. It is quite possible that Gen. Taylor will demand the prisoners and if they are not given up march over and take the city or attempt it.

I am still in hopes notwithstand all warlike appearances that in a few months all difficulties will be settled and I will be permitted to see again My Dear Dear Julia. The time will ~~will~~ appear long to me until this event but hope that has so long borne me out, the hope that one day we will meet to part no more for so long a time, will sustain me again. Give my love to all at White Haven and be sure to write soon and often. I have not heard from Fred. very lately. Vacancies have occured here which make him I think 2d from promotion and another will probably take place soon in the case of an officer who is to be tried for being drunk on duty.—I will write again in a few days, but dont put of answering this until you get my next.

ULYSSES

Julia

ALS, DLC-USG, postmarked New Orleans, April 14, 1846.

1. Bvt. Brig. Gen. Taylor reported that he had spoken to an officer "who was represented as the adjutant general of the Mexican troops." Taylor to AG, March 21, 1846, *HED*, 30–1–60, p. 124.

2. The proclamation of Gen. Francisco Mejia, Matamoros, March 18, 1846, is *ibid.*, pp. 125–29.

To Bvt. Brig. Gen. Roger Jones

                                        Camp Near Matamoras
                                        March 29th 1846

SIR

I have the honor of acknowledging the receipt of my commission as a 2d Lieutenant in the 4th U. S. Infantry.

                                        Respectfully
Gen. R. Jones   Your Obt. Svt
Adj Gen   U S GRANT
U.S.A.   2d Lt. 4th Infy

ALS, DNA, RG 94, ACP 4754/1885. Rec'd April 17, 1846. The commission dated from Sept. 30, 1845, when the 4th Inf. was first fully assembled in Texas.

To Julia Dent

                                        Camp Near Matamoras Tex.
                                        April 20th 1846

MY DEAREST JULIA

I have just rec'd your letter of the 19th of last month. You may Judge ~~of my~~ with how much gratification when I tell you that it is the first letter I have got from you for about ten or twelve weeks with the exception of a few lines about seven weeks ago which come along with the copy of the Wandering Jew you sent me.[1] Evry thing is very quiet here. We are only seperated by a narrow stream from one of the largest Cities of Mexico yet not a soul dare cross. Evry thing looks beliggerent to a spectator but I believe there will be no fight. The Mexicans are busily engaged in throwing up fortifications on their side and we are engaged the same way on ours. Occationally they make a threa[t] but as yet their threats have all ended in bombast. I believe I told you of their threats when we cross the Colorado?

We have been threatened of just as certain violance since that. About ten days ago Gen. Ampudia[2] arrived at Matamoras with additional forces, reported at three thousand; he gave Gen. Taylor notice that he must retire from this ground to go East of the Nuices within twenty four hours from that time or War would be the inevitabl[e] consequences. The Mex. Gen. went on to say that in case of War he would do all in his power to have the rules and usages of the most civilized warfare observed and hoped that Gen. Taylor would co-opporate with him in so humane an object.—Gen. Ampudia is known to be one of the most inhuman of the Mex. Genls. He has gone so far as to boil the heads of one or two of his prisoners in oil so as to preserve them.—Gen. Taylor made a courtious but decided reply, to the amount that we would not leave but by force. After all this how could we expect anything els but war? yet evry thing has passed off as before. It is now the opinion of many that our difficulty with Mex. will be settled by negociation and if so I hope my dear Julia to hear the 4th Inf.y ordered to the upper Mississippi before the end of warm weather yet. At all events I shall try to get a leave of absence as soon as there ceases to be a probability of difficulties, and then my Dear Julia may I hope to claim you as my partner for life. The Regiments that remain in this country will have beautiful stations but it is not likely that the 4th will be one of them.—I got a letter from Fred. a few days ago. He says he is third for promotion then, but since he wrote there has been vacancies enough to promote him and all the rest of our class and one or two over. He either goes to the 2d Inf.y which is stationed in Michigan or to the 5th which is here, so either you or I will see him soon. Mr. Hazlitt has not got here yet from Corpus Christi When we left, a number of Officers were left behind to c[ome] around by water, H. among them.—Do wri[t]e to [me] often Julia while we are separated so far and let us hope, as I [sin]cerely do, that before many months it will not [be nec]essary for us to write inorder to convey our thoug[hts] [to e]ach other. Fred. says in his letter that he hopes [that ne]xt time he sees me to take me by the hand as a *Brevet brother*. Give my love to evry one at White Haven. Has John tried to get into one of the new Regiments that are likely to be raised? I have heard that Sarah Walker is engaed, is she married yet? I used to think that Mr. Cloud was waiting for her.—Write as soon as you get this.

Your Devoted U<small>LYSSES</small>

Will Miss Julia accept the compliments of her friend Lt Wallen I hope the time is not far distant, when I shall welcome her to the 4th Infantry. Laura has left N. Orleans for St Louis I hope that you will meet her., when you do Kiss her for me.

yours truly H. D. W

P. S. My Dear Julia   Mr. Wallen asked me to allow him to put a few lines in my letter and I see he has hoped to see something which one much more concerned in than himself most sincerely hopes that he may not be disappointed and that one is

your Devoted U<small>LYSSES</small>

P. P. S. I have just rec'd another letter from you my Dear Julia of about two weeks later date than the one I got this morning. You dont know how hapy I was at geting two letters in such quick succession from one so dear to me, and such sweet letters as they were too! I know my Dear Julia that you are going to write to me very often, and you know how punctual I am in answering. I shall write to you again in one week.

Your devoted U<small>LYSSES</small>

ALS, DLC-USG, postmarked New Orleans, April 29, 1846.

    1. See letter of [*Oct., 1845*].
    2. Gen. Pedro de Ampudia arrived in Matamoros on April 11, 1846. His message to Bvt. Brig. Gen. Taylor is printed in *HED*, 30–1–60, p. 140.

To Julia Dent

———

Point Isabel Texas
May 3d 1846

MY DEAR JULIA

I wrote you a long letter in answer to your last sweet letter a few days ago and intended to bring it with me to this place but when we started I left in such a hurry that I forgot it. I gave you a long account of our difficulties in it and as I now have but a few minuets to write I will send you the other letter as soon as I get back. At present I can only give you what has happened without any of the circumstances. Col. Cross[1] has been killed by the Mexicans. Cap.t Thornton[2] with three other officers and about fifty Dragoons fell in with a camp of some two thousand Mexicans and of course were taken. One officer and six or seven men were killed and four wounded all the others were taken prisoners. Lt. Porter[3] with twelve men were attacked by a large number of Mexicans and Mr. Porter and one man was killed the rest escaped.—Gen. Taylor left Matamoras with about two thousand troops for this place on the 1st of May intending to give the ~~me~~ Mexicans a fight if we fall in with them. We marched nearly all night the first night and you may depend My Dear Julia that we were all very much fatigued. We start again at 1 o'clock to-day and will probably have an engagement. We understand that there is several thousand encamped not far from this place. There was about six hundred troops left in our Fort opposite Matamoras and the presumption is they have been attacked, for we have heard the sound of ~~Cannon~~ Artillery from that direction ever since day light this morning. As soon as this is over I will write to you again, that is if I am one of the fortunate individuals who escape. Dont fear for me My Dear Julia for this is only the active part of our business. It is just what we come here for and the sooner it begins the sooner it will end and probably be the means of my seeing my dear Dear Julia soon. You dont know how anxious I am to see you again Julia. Another year certainly cannot roll round before that happy event. ~~My~~ I must now bring my letter to a close. I wish I had time to write a much longer one. Give my love to all at White Haven. Write to me soon Julia.

> Your Most devoted
> U. S. GRANT
> 4th Inf.y

ALS, DLC-USG, postmarked New Orleans, May 13, 1846.

1. Col. Trueman Cross of Md., was killed April 21, 1846.
2. Capt. William Anderson Thornton of N.Y., USMA 1825, 4th Art.
3. 2nd Lt. Theodoric Henry Porter of Pa., 4th Inf., was killed April 19, 1846.

To Julia Dent

————

> Head Quarters Mexican Army
> May 11th 1846

MY DEAR JULIA

After two hard fought battles[1] against a force far superior to our own in numbers, Gen. Taylor has got possesion of the Enemy's camp and now I am writing on the head of one of the ~~Drums~~ captured drums. I wrote to you from Point Isabel and told you of the march we had and of the suspected attack upon the little force left near Matamoras. About two days after I wrote we left Point Isabel with about 300 waggons loaded with Army supplies. For the first 18 miles our course was uninterupted but at the end of that distance we found the Mexican Army, under the command of General Arista[2] drawn up in line of battle waiting our approach. Our waggons were immediately parked and Gen. Taylor marched us up towards them. When we got in range of their Artillery they let us have it right and left. They had I believe 12 pieces. Our guns were then rounded at them and so the battle commenced. Our Artillery amounted to 8 guns of ~~eight~~ six pound calibre and 2 Eighteen pounders. Evry moment we could see the charges from our pieces cut a way through their ranks making a perfect road, but they would close up the interval without showing signs of retreat. Their officers made an attempt to charge upon us but the havoc had been so great that their soldiers could not be made to advance. Some of the prisoners that we have taken say that their officers cut and slashed among them with their Sabres at a dreadful rate to make them advance but it was no use, they would not come. This firing commenced at ½ past 2 o'clock and was nearly constant from that until Sun down.

Although the balls were whizing thick and fast about me I did not feel a sensation of fear until nearly the close of the firing a ball struck close by me killing one man instantly, it nocked Capt. Page's³ under Jaw entirely off and broke in the roof of his mouth, and nocked Lt. Wallen and one Sergeant down besides, but they were not much hurt. Capt. Page is still alive. When it become to dark to see the enemy we encamped upon the field of battle and expected to conclude the fight the next morning. Morning come and we found that the enemy had retreated under cover of the night. So ended the battle of the 8th of May. The enemy numbered three to our one besides we had a large waggon train to guard. It was a terrible sight to go over the ground the next day and see the amont of life that had been destroyed. The ground was litterally strewed with the bodies of dead men and horses. The loss of the enemy is variously estimated from about 300 to 500. Our loss was comparitively small. But two officers were badly wounded, two or three slightly. About 12 or 15 of our men were killed and probably 50 wounded. When I can learn the exact amount of loss I will write and correct the statements I have made if they are not right. On the 9th of May about noon we left the field of battle and started on our way to Matamoras. When we advanced to about six miles we found that the enemy had taken up a new position in the midst of a dense wood, and as we have since learned they had recieved a reinforcement equal to our whole nu numbers. Grape shot and musket balls were let fly from both sides making dreadful havoc. Our men [con]tinued to advance and did advance in sp[ite] of [their] shots, to the very mouths of the cannon an[d] killed and took prisoner the Mexicans with them, and drove off with their own teams, taking cannon ammunition and all, to our side. In this way nine of their big guns were taken and their own ammunition turned against them.[4] The Mexicans fought very hard for an hour and a half but seeing their means of war fall from their hands in spite of all their efforts they finally commenced to retreat helter skelter. A great many retreated to the banks of the Rio Grande and without looking for means of crossing plunged into this water and no doubt many of them were dround. Among the prisoners we have taken there are 14 officers and I have no idea how many privates. I understand that General Lavega,[5] who is a prisoners in our camp has said that he has fought against several different nations but ours are the first that he ever saw who would charge up to the very mouths of cannon.

In this last affray we had we had three officers killed and some 8 or ten wounded. ~~wh~~ how many of our men suffered has not yet been learned. The Mexicans were so certain of sucsess that when we took their camp we found thir dinners on the fire cooking. After the battle the woods was strued with the dead. Waggons have been engaged drawing the bodies to bury. How many waggon loads have already come in and how many are still left would be hard to guess. I saw 3 large waggon loads at one time myself. We captured, besides the prisoners, 9 cannon, with a small amount of ammunition for them, probably 1000 or 15000 stand of fire arms sabres swords &c. Two hundred and fifty thousand rounds of ammunition for them over 400 four hundred mules and pack saddles or harness. Drums, musical instruments camp equipage &c, &c. innumerable. The victory for us has been a very great one. No doubt you will see accounts enough of it in the papers. There is no great sport in having bullets flying about one in evry direction but I find they have less horror when among them than when in anticipation. Now that the war has commenced with such vengence I am in hopes my Dear Julia that we will soon be able to end it. In the thickest of it I thought of Julia. How much I should love to see you now to tell you all that happened. Mr. Hazlitt come out alive and whole. When we have another engagement, if we do have another atall, I will write again; that is if I am not one of the victims. Give my love to all at White Haven and do write soon my Dear Julia. I think you will find that history will count the victory just achieved one of the greatest on record. But I do not want to say to much about it until I see the accounts given ŧ by others. Dont forget to write soon to your most Devoted

ULYSSES

P. S. I forgot to tell you that the Fortifications left in charge of Maj. Brown[6] in command of the 7th Inf.y was attacked while we were at Point Isabel and for five days the Mexicans continued to throw in shells. There was but 2 killed, Maj. Brown & one soldier, and 2 wounded.

ALS, DLC-USG.

1. The battles of Palo Alto (May 8) and Resaca de la Palma (May 9), 1846.
2. Gen. Mariano Arista had taken command of Mexican forces at Matamoros on April 24, 1846.
3. Capt. John Page of Mass., 4th Inf., died July 12, 1846, of wounds received at Palo Alto.
4. Brig. Gen. Zachary Taylor reported the capture of seven pieces of artillery. Taylor to AGO, May 9, 1846, *HED*, 30–1–60, p. 296. USG's factual statements about the battles are in general agreement with official reports.
5. Gen. R. Diaz de La Vega.
6. Maj. Jacob Brown of Mass., died May 9, 1846, of wounds received May 6, 1846. The fort he had defended, now at Brownsville, Tex., had originally been named Fort Taylor, but was renamed Fort Brown on May 17, 1846.

To Julia Dent

Matamoras Mexico
May 24th 1846

MY DEAR JULIA

I recieved your letter of the 5th Ins. about one week ago and would have answered it (as I do all your sweet letters) immediately but I had written to you but a few days before and I

wanted to see what moove we would make next before I wrote
again. Since the battles of the 8th & 9th ins. which resulted so
disastrously to the Mexicans we have had but little trouble with
them. It is pretty well ascertained now that the loss of the
Mexi[cans] in the two days fight amounted to near three
thousand from killed wounded and desertion, whilst our force
only amounted to two thousand. We followed up our success by
crossing the Rio Grande and driving the remaining four thousand
Mex. troops from the city and taking possession our selvs. You
would be surprised at the difference between an American town
and a Mexican one and indeed there is just as much difference
between the people. The inhabitants are generally more like
Idians in looks and habits than white men.[1] and I think too after
so sound a thrashing as our small force gave their large one, we
will be able with the assistance of the great number of volunteers
that have come to our aid, to bring Mexico to speedy terms.
Where the 4th Infy will be when you get this letter is hard to
surmise. No doubt Gen. Taylor will take possession of all the
towns on or near the river within the next few weeks and I may
be at one of them far up the river. Whereever I am I shall continue to write to my Dear Julia very often and hope that the day
is not far distant when I shall hold that little hand again in mine.
Do not feel alarmed about me my Dear Julia for there is not half
the horrors in war that you immagine,[2] One thing though, if we
ever get whiped by them we will no doubt meet with cruel treatment. Some of their officers are perfect gentlemen, but it would
be impossible for them to ~~con~~ restrain the soldiers.

My Dearest Julia does you Pa or Ma ever speak of our engagement, or do they think that time and distance can make us
forget each other? I would love to hear you say that you believed
they would never make further objections. Dont they know
whenever you get a letter from me? I feel as if I shall never be
contented until I can see you again my Dear Julia, and I hope it
will be never to leave you again for so long a time. I get all your
letters, some times though they are a long time on the way.
I expect before long to see Fred. down here for I am almost

certain he is promoted to one of the Texas (or rather Mexico) Regiments. No doubt he will be very much pleased to come here. If he does come I will get him to ask for a leave of absence at the same time I do. Does Fred. ever say any thing about Miss L. S.³ in his letters now? I dont believe they correspond. I think it very likely you will see Capt. Morrison in Missouri in a month and then you can hear an account of the battles fought on the borders of Mexico. He does not say that he will leave but evry one thinks that his family afflictions⁴ of late have been so great as to justify him in taking a leave of [ab]sence. Has John made application for the Rifle Regiment? I [fi]nd that the member of Congress⁵ who got me my appointm[ent] as a Cadet is applying to get me into the new Regt. if it is [. . . .]. It is very warm at Matamoras, enough so to have vegitab[les] nearly all winter. I think if I ever get to a good cold [c]lim[ate] ~~again~~ once more I will not want to come South again.

Give my love to all at White Haven Julia and write very soon to one who loves you most devotedly

ULYSSES

P. S. The two Flowers you sent me come safe but when I opened your letter the wind blew them away and I could not find them. Before I seal this I will pick a wild flower off of the Bank of the Rio Grande and send you. My Dear Julia do you ever see me anymore in your dreams? how much I wish you could see me in reality! I am certain that you would not know me. I am as badly Sun burnt as it is possible to be, and I have allowed my beard to grow three inches long. Adieu My Dear Dear Julia

ULYSSES

ALS, DLC-USG, postmarked New Orleans, May 30, 1846.

1. Two lines omitted.
2. Half a line omitted.
3. Probably Louise Stribling.
4. See letter of Sept. 14, 1845. Capt. Morrison was the father-in-law of 2nd Lt. Thaddeus Higgins.
5. Thomas L. Hamer of Ohio.

To Julia Dent

––––––––

Camp At Matamoras Mexico
June 5th 1846

I recieved a few days ago My Dearest Julia your sweet letter of the 12th of May. How often I have wished the same thing you there express, namely that we had been united when I was last in Mo. You dont know how proud and how happy it made me feel to hear you say that willingly you would share my tent, or my prison if I should be taken prisoner. As ~~you~~ yet my Dearest I am unhurt and free, and our troops are occupying a conquered city. After two hard fought battles against a force three or four times as numerous as our own we have chased the enemy from their homes and I have not the least apprehention that they will ever return here to reconquer the place. But no doubt we will follow them up. I believe the General's plan is to march to Monteray, a beautiful little city just at the foot of the mountains, and about three hundred miles from this place. That taken and we will have in possession, or at least in our power the whole of the Mexican territory East of the Mountains and it is to be presumed Mexico will then soon come to terms. I do not feel my Dear Julia the slightest apprehention as to our sucsess in evry large battle that we may have with the enemy no matter how superior they may be to us in numbers. I expect soon to see Fred. here to join us in the invasion of Mexico. I see that his promotion to the 5th Inf.y was confirmed a month ago at Washington. I have no doubt he will be very glad to get away from Towson[.]¹ Possibly too John Dent may be coming here as a Captain in a new Regiment. Before you get this letter Julia you will probably ~~hear~~ see or hear of Cap.t Morrison and Lt. Wallens return to the U. States. They have been sent on the recruiting service and will not probably return until next Fall. From the papers we recieve from the States one would judge that there is great excitement about us there, but believe me my Dear Julia you need not feel any alarm for our wellfare. The greatest danger is from exposure to the rain sun and dew in a very warm climate. But for my part I am never sick, and I think I have become well acclimated to the South.

My Dearest Julia when you write to me again tell me if your Pa ever says any thing about our engagement and if you think he will make any further objections. I think from what he said to me when I was there last Spring he will not; but he has not written to me as he said he would do. But Julia I hope many months more will not pass over before we will be able to talk over this matter without the use of paper. How much I do want to see you again; but I know you would not recognize me. When you see me, as you say you often do in your dreams, you see me as I was not as I am, for climate has made a change. I mean a change in appearance, but in my love for Julia I am the same, and I know too that she has not change[d] in that respect for she writes me such sweet letters when she does write. In six weeks I have had four letters from you Dear Julia which is much more than I ever recieved in the same time before. wont you continue to write to me often for it gives me so much pleasure to read and to answer your letters.

Julia if the 4th Inf.y should be stationed permanantly in the conquered part of Mexico would you be willing to come here or would you want me to resign? I think it probable though that I shall resign as soon as this war is over and make Galena my home. My father is very anxious to have me do so. Speaking of your coming to Mexico dearest I do not intend to hint that it is even probable that the 4th Inf.y will remain [here] for I think it will be one of the first to leave [this] Country.—Give my love to all at White Have and write very soon and very often to

                                        ULYSSES

Julia

ALS, DLC-USG, postmarked New Orleans, June 15, 1846.

    1. Fort Towson near the Red River.

To Julia Dent

———

Camp at Matamoras Mex
June 10th 1846

How much gratified I have been my Dearest Julia in recieving
another sweet letter from you. Indeed of late you have been so
punctual in your answers that it makes up for the long time I was
without a letter atal from you. I know if you were aware of the
happines[s] it gives me to hear from my Dearest Julia you would
continue to write often. You say in your letter I must not grow
tired of hearing you say how much you love me! Indeed dear
Julia nothing that you can say sounds sweeter. I have written
you a great many letters since I have been on the Rio Grande
no doubt you have recd them all? The occational mails that we
get here shows us how great the excitement in the States is for
our wellfare and indeed when I look back at the condition we
were in I do not think our danger was much over[ove]rated.
We were in an enemy's country without a friendly house to
retreat to in case of defeat, and surrounded by a well armed force
out numbering us three to one, besides evry Mexican citizen
would have been ready to have taken our lives as soon as they
saw us well beaten. But at present my Dearest Julia we are very
differently situated. Now our force is three or four times as great
as it was and the enemy is no where to be found. Our troops are
encamped in the suburbs of one of the largest of Mexican towns,
and soon no doubt will start out to continue their conquest.—I
would not be surpprised if the next letter (but one) I write you
dear love should be written on the road from here to Monteray.
We are very anxious to push forward for that is our only hope
of a speedy peace. How much I should love Julia to walk through
Matamoras once with you to let you see the difference between
a Mexican town and and an Mexican population and that of an
American. The Mexican house is low with a flat or thatched roof,
with a dirt or brick floor, with but little furnature and in many

cases the fire in the middle of the house as if it was a wig–wamb. The majority of the inhabitants are Indians[1] I believe that our present force is sufficient to keep off any force that Mexico can bring, provided we are kept in one body.

I see that John is not appointed in the new Regiment that has been raised. Did he apply. I fear Dear Julia that you will not be able to see Fred. this Summer as you have expected, but likely he and I will be able to get a leave of absence at the same time; then dearest wont you become mine for ever. Whenever Fred. writes to me he always asks how our engagement is likely to please your Pa & Ma, or calls me a ~~Bvt~~ Brivet Brother or something of that sort. Fred. has already got three 2d Lieut's below him in his own Regiment and will probably have two if not three or four more in the next few Months. Mr. Sykes has just returned from St. Louis but he did not tell me that he had seen you.[2]

My Dear Julia now that we are so far distant from each other you are my constant thought when ~~I am~~ alone. When I lay down I think of Julia until I fall asleep hoping that before I wake I may see her in my dreams. I know too Dearest from your letters that I am not forgotten. The many pleasant hours spent with you often pass in review before my memory. It certainly cannot be a great while [before] a recurrence of similar happiness. I often take the ring, which bears your name, from my finger and think of the day I first wore it. You recollect we were returning from the City. I dont believe you will be able to read this letter so I will close it and try and write plainer next time. Remember me to Ellen & Emmy and all at White Haven and dont forget Dearest Julia to write soon very soon to you devoted

Ulysses

ALS, DLC-USG, the top left-hand corner of the envelope sheet has "Point Isabelle June 16th," 1846.

1. Three lines omitted.
2. See letter of Jan. 12, 1846.

To John W. Lowe

Matamoras Mexico
June 26th 1846

DEAR LOWE

I have just recieved your letter of the 6th of June, : the first I have had from you since my Reg.t took the field in anticipation of the Annexation of Texas. Since that time the 4th Infantry has experienced but little of that ease and luxury of which the Hon. Mr. Black speaks so much. Besides ha[r]d marching, a great part of the time we have not even been blessed with a good tent as a protection against wind and weather. At Corpus Christi our troops were much exposed last winter which the citizens say was the severest season they have had for many years. From Corpus Christi to this place (a distance of about 180 miles) they had to march through a low sandy desert covered with salt ponds and in one or two instances ponds of drinkable water were separated by a whole days March. The troops suffered much but stood it like men who were able to fight many such battles as those of the 8th & 9th of May, that is without a murmer. On our arrival at the Rio Grande we found Matamoras occupied by a force superior to ours (in numbers) who might have made our march very uncomfortable if they had have had the spirit and courage to attempt it. But they confined their hostilities (except their paper ones) to small detached parties and single individuals as in the cases you mention in your letter, until they had their force augmented to thrible or quadrouple ours and then they made the bold efforts of which the papers are so full. About the last of April we got word of the enemy crossing the river no doubt with the intention of cuting us off from our supplies at Point Isabel. On the 1st of April [*May*] at 3 o'clock General Taylor started with about 2000 men to go after and escort the Waggon train from Point Isabel and with the determination to cut his way, no matter how superior their numbers. Our march on this occation was as severe as could be made. Until 3 o'clock at night we scarsely halted, then we laid down in the grass and took a little sleep and marched the ballance of the way the next morning. Our March was mostly through grass up to the waist with a wet and uneven bottom yet we made 30 miles in much less than a day. I consider my march on that occation equal to a walk of sixty miles in one day on good roads and unencumbered with troops. The next morning after our arrival at Point Isabel we heard the enemies Artillery playing upon the little Field work which we had left Garrisoned by the 7th Inf.y and two Companies of Artillery. This bombardment was kept up for seven days with a loss of but two killed and four or five wounded on our side. The loss of the enemy was much greater though not serious. On the 7th of May General Taylor started from P. I. with his little force encumbered with a train of about 250 waggons loaded with provisions and ammunition. Although we knew the enemy was between us and Matamoras and in large numbers too, yet I did not believe, I was not able to appreciate the possibility of an attack from them. We had heard so much bombast and so many threats from the Mexicans that I began to believe that they were good for paper wars alone, but they stood up to their work manfully. On the 8th when within about 14 miles of Matamoras we found the enemy drawn up in line of battle on the edge of the prairie next a piece of woods Called Palo Alto. (Which is the Spanish for Tall Trees.) Even then I did not believe they were going to give battle. ~~and did not~~ Our troops were halted out of range of Artillery and the waggons parked and the men allowed to fill their canteens with water. All preparations being made we marched forward in line of battle until we recieved a few shots from the enemy and then we were halted and our Artillery commenced. The first shot was fired about 3 o'clock P. M. and ~~the~~ was kept up pretty equally on both sides until sun down or after, we then encamped on our own ground and the enemy on theirs. We supposed that the loss of the enemy had not been much greater than our own and expected of course that the fight would be renewed in the morning. During that night I believe all slept as soundly on the ground at Palo Alto as if they had been in a

palace. For my own part I dont think I even dreamed of battles.
During the days fight I scarsely thought of the probability or
possibility of being touched myself (although 9 lb. shots were
whistling all round,) until near the close of the evening a shot
struck the ranks a little ways in front of me and nocked one man's
head off, nocked the under Jaw of Capt. Page entirely away, and
brought several others to the ground. Although Capt. Page rec'd
so terrible a wound he is recovering from it.[1] The under jaw is
gone to the wind pipe and the tongue hangs down upon the
throat. He will never be able to speak or to eat. The next morning
we found to our surprise that the last rear guard of the enemy
was just leaving their ground, the main body having left during
the night. From Palo Alto to Matamoras there is for a great part
of the way a dense forest of under growth, here called chapparel.
The Mexicans after having marched a few miles through this
were reinforced by a conciderable body of troops. They chose a
place on the opposite side from us of a ~~pond~~ long but narrow
pond (called Resaca de la Palma) which gave them greatly the
advantage of position   Here they made a stand. The fight was a
pel mel affair evry body for himself. The chapparel is so dense
that you may be within five feet of a person and not know it. Our
troops rushed forward with shouts of victory and would kill and
drive away the Mexicans from evry piece of Artillery they could
get their eyes upon. The Mexicans stood this hot work for over
two hours but with a great loss. When they did retreat there
was such a panic among them that they only thought of safty in
flight. They made the best of their way for the river and where
ever they [. . . . .] it they would rush in. Many of them no doubt
were drowned. Our loss in the two days was 182 killed &
wounded. What the loss of the enemy was cannot be certainly
ascertained but I know that acres of ground was strewed with
the bodies of the dead and wounded. I think it would not be an
over estimate to say that their loss from killed wounded, take
prisoners, and missing was over 2,000; and of the remainder
nothing now scarsely remains. So precipitate was their flight
when they found that we were going to cross the river and take

the town, that sickness broke out among them and as we have understood, they have but little effective force left. News has been recieved that Parades[2] is about taking the field with a very large force. Daily, volunteers are arriving to reinforce us and soon we will be able to meet them in what ever force they choose to come. What will be our course has not been announced in orders, but no doubt we will carry the war into the interior. Monteray, distant about 300 miles from here, will no doubt be the first place where difficulties with an enemy await us. You want to know what my feelings were on the field of battle! I do not know that I felt any peculiar sensation. War seems much less horrible to persons engaged in it than to those who read of the battles. I forgot to tell you in the proper place of the amount of property taken. We took on the 9th Eight pieces of Artillery with all their ammunition something like 2,000 stand of arms, muskets, pistols, swords sabres Lances & 500 mules with their packs, camp equipage & provisions and in fact about evry thing they had. When we got into the camp of the enemy evrything showed the great confidence they had of sucsess. They were actually cooking their meal during the fight, and as we have since learned, the women of Matamoras were making preparations for a great festival upon the return of their victorious Army.—The people of Mexico are a very different race of people from ours. The better class are very proud and tyrinize over the lower and much more numerous class as much as a hard master does over his negroes, and they submit to it quite as humbly. The great majority ~~are of the~~ inhabitants are either pure or more than half blooded Indians, and show but little more signs of neatness or comfort in their miserable dwellings than the uncivilized Indian. —Matamoras contains probably about 7,000 inhabitants, a great majority of them of the lower order. It is not a place of as much business importance as our little towns of 1,000. But no doubt I will have an opportunity of knowing more of Mexico and the Mexicans before I leave the country and I will take another occation of telling you more of them.

Dont you think Mr. Polk has done the Officers of the Army

injustice by filling up the new Regt. of Riflemen from citizens?
It is plain to be seen that we have but little to expect from him.—
I have now written you a long letter; as soon as any thing more
is done I will write again. If you have an opportunity I wish you
would let them know at home that I am well. I dont think I have
written in the last few weeks.—I should like very much to see
you here in command of a volunteer company.[3] I think you
would not be affected by the climate. So far our troops have had
their health remarkably well—

Remember me to your own and Judge Fishback's fa[mi]ly.
I suppose Tom[4] has grown so much that he almost thinks of
volu[nteerin]g for the Mexi[can] Wars himself.—I shall be
pleased to hear from you as often as you will make it convenient
to write and will answer all your letters—

Yours Truly
U S GRANT
4th Inf.y

J. W. Lowe Esq.
Batavia O——

ALS, InU. John William Lowe, born in 1809 in New Brunswick, N.J., moved to
Batavia, Ohio, in 1833 and studied law under Thomas L. Hamer. He was friendly
with both USG and his father. Carl M. Becker, "John William Lowe: Failure in
Inner-Direction," *Ohio History*, 73, 2 (Spring, 1964), 75–89. See *Calendar*,
Dec. 8, 1840.

1. See letter of May 11, 1846.
2. See letter of July 25, 1846.
3. Unsuccessful in both law and politics, Lowe joined the 2nd Ohio Inf.
Regt. as capt. and left for Mexico in Sept., 1847. Becker, "Lowe," p. 78.
4. In 1837 Lowe married Manorah Fishback, daughter of Judge Owen T.
Fishback of Batavia, Ohio. Tom was their son.

To Julia Dent

Matamoras Mexico
July 2d 1846

My Dear Julia

117951

I recieved last evening your letter of the 10th of June, in which you speak of this Earthly paradise. If it is a Paradise where it rains about four hours each day why then Matamoras is the place. I have no doubt though I should like the place very much if it was only the home of My Dearest Julia, but I know that I shall never be contented until I am with her once more. I am afraid Julia that Matamoras will be very sickly this Summer. The whole of this country is low and flat and for the last six weeks it has rained almost incessantly so that now the whole country is under water. Our tents are so bad that evry time it rains we get a complete shower-bath. I dont believe that we will leave here for two or three months and then we will either have some hard fighting or bring our difficulties in this quarter to a speedy close. Now that the Oregon boundary is no longer in dispute I think we will soon quiet Mexico and then dearest Julia, if I am not one of the unfortunate who fall, nothing will keep me from seeing you again. I really am very much in hopes that an other Spring will not roll around before I will be able to call Julia my own dear, (shall I say wife,) Just think it is now going on three years ~~since~~ since we were first engaged! You never will tell me Julia if you think your Pa & Ma will say no. I dont think they can but I would like to hear you say ~~so~~ that they will not.— I did not let the flowers in your last letter blow away. When I opened the letter and saw the rose leaves I just thought that only two short weeks ago Julia had them in her own hands and here I am and have not seen her fore more than a year. If I was in Mo. and you were here I know what I would do very soon; I would volunteer to come to Mexico as a private if I could come no other way. But I recollect you did volunteer some time ago, or what showed your willingness to do so, you said that you wished we had been united when I was last in Mo. ~~for~~ and how willing you would be to share even a tent with me. Indeed Julia that letter made me feel very happy. How much I ought to love you when you express a willingness to sacrifice so much just for me.—I believe you have burned some of my letters for you say you only have twenty five of them and it seems to me I have written a great many more; at all events I will write more in the future and you must write often too wont you Julia? So you have read that rediculous falsehood about the cause of Lt. Deas[1] crossing the river. There was not a word of truth in the whole statement except that he swam the river. It was a strange fancy that struck him at a time when he was not duly himself. Fred. has not got here yet. I wonder what can keep him? I shall pick a quarrel with him as soon as he gets here for not writing to me. He is a great deal worse than you are about writing; but I ought not to say a word about your writing now for you are so much more punctual than you used to be. I will write to you again in a few days but you must not wait to get another letter before you answer this. I would like to make a bargai[n] for each of us to write, say, evry Sunday [. .] then just think I would hear from my Dear love fifty two times in a year. Remember me to all at White Haven.

Your Devoted
Ulysses

Julia

P. S. You say that I must not let Fred. read your letters. I know now how to get you to write often. Evry time that two weeks elapse without geting a letter from my Dearest Julia I will just take out one of the old ones and give it to Fred. to read. You had better look out and write often if you dont want him to read them.

U S Grant

P. P. S. Since writing the above I have heard that Fred is in N. Orleans on his way here. I suppose he will be here in two or three days. I'll make him write to you as soon as he comes.

ALS, DLC-USG, "Pt Isabel July 9th," 1846, on top left-hand corner of envelope sheet.

1. 1st Lt. Edward Deas of S.C., 4th Art., swam across the Rio Grande into Mexican territory on the evening of April 13, 1846. He told friends that he was seeking Col. Trueman Cross, whom he believed to be a prisoner in Matamoros. Cross had been killed but his body had not yet been found. A newspaper reported that Deas was actually in search of a Mexican beauty. Bvt. Brig. Gen. Taylor later reported that Deas "was laboring under mental alienation at the time he committed the unfortunate act." He was discovered in Matamoros when the city was occupied, and he rejoined the army. Edward J. Nichols, *Zach Taylor's Little Army* (New York, 1963), p. 60.

To Julia Dent

———

Matamoras Mexico
July 25th 1846

MY DEAREST JULIA

It must be about two weeks since I have written to you, and as I am determined that a longer time shall never pass with my Dearest hearing from me, whilst I am in an enemie's country, I write to you again, notwithstanding I have not heard from you for some time. Do not understand me though to cast any censure upon you, ~~though~~ for you may have written me a dozen letters and me not recieved one of them yet, for I believe it is about two weeks since we have had a Mail, and there is no telling when we will have another. You must not neglect to write often Dearest so that whenever a mail does reach this far-out-of-the-way country I can hear from the one single person who of all others occupies my thoughts. This is my last letter from Matamoras Julia. Already the most of the troops have left for Camargo and a very few days more will see the remainder of us off. Whether we will have much more fighting is a matter of much speculation. At present we are bound for Camargo and from thence to Monteray, where it is reported that there is several thousand Mexican troops engaged in throwing up Fortifications, and there is no doubt either but that Parades[1] has left Mexico at the head of nine thousand more to reinforce them, but the latest news says that he has been obliged to return to the City of Mexico on account of some rupture there. But a few months more will determine what we have to do, and I will be careful to keep my Dear Julia advised of what the army in this quarter is about. Fred. has not arrived here yet but I am looking for him daily. His commission arrived some time ago, and also a letter from St. Louis for him. I have them both in my possession, and wrote to him to hasten on. His Reg.t. (the 5th Infantry) is already in Camargo. A few months more of fatigue and privation, I am much in hopes, will bring our difficulties to such a crisis that I will be able to see you again Julia, and then if my wishes pre-vailed, we would never part again as merely engaged, but as,— you know what I would say.—No doubt a hard march awaits us between Camargo and Monteray. The distance is over two hundred miles, and as I have understood, a great part of it without water. But a person cannot expect to make a Campaign without meeting with some privations.

Fred. and me will probably be near each other during the time and between us I am in hopes that I will hear from my Dear Julia evry week, but write oftener to me than to Fred.—Since we have been in Matamoras a great many murders have been committed, and what is strange there seemes to be but very week means made use of to prevent frequent repetitions. Some of the volunteers and about all the Texans seem to think it perfectly right to impose upon the people of a conquered City to any extent, and even to murder them where the act can be covered by the dark. And how much they seem to enjoy acts of violence too! I would not pretend to guess the number of murders that have been committed upon the persons of poor Mexicans and our soldiers, since we have been here, but the number would startle you.—Is Ellen married yet? I never hear you mention her name any more. John I suppose is on his way for [the] seat [o]f war by this time. If we have to fight [we] may all meet next winter in the City of Mexico.

There is no telling whether it will be as prisoners of war or as a conquering force. From my experience I judge the latter much the most probable.—How pleasant it would be now for me to spend a day with you at White Haven. I envy you all very much, but still hope on that better times are coming. Remember me to all at White Haven and write very soon and very often to

ULYSSES

Julia

ALS, DLC-USG, "Pt Isabel July 30," 1846, on envelope sheet.

1. Gen. Mariano Paredes y Arrillaga had deposed and replaced José Herrera as President of Mexico on Jan. 4, 1846, because of Herrera's willingness to negotiate with the United States. As Mexican arms suffered reverses, threats of revolt increased. It was announced, erroneously, that Paredes was leading an expedition against the American army. Actually, Paredes turned over the management of affairs to Vice President Bravo, also believed to favor negotiations. Before anything could come of the plans of Paredes or Bravo, they were overthrown by a revolution led by Antonio López de Santa Anna.

To Julia Dent

Matamoras Mexico

Aug. 4th 1846

MY DEAREST JULIA

I have just recieved a letter from you, the first for about a month, and you deserve a very short one in answer for not writing sooner. My Regiment is all in Camargo with the exception of two Companies. They went up by water. My comp.y and one other of the 4th Inf.y and two of the 3d Inf.y were retained to ~~exeort~~ escort a battery of Artillery by land through all the mud and water, and you may depend there is no scarsity of it. It will take us about ten days to get there and then I will be so far separated from my Dear Julia that you need not look for a letter for one month after this, but my next will be a long one. It is now after [noon] and I have to go to town yet to [mail] this and for other business so tha[t you] must be satisfied with a very [short] one this time. Fred. has not joined us yet. I have a big bone to pick with you the next time I see you. If I dont get back to Missouri soon I will write to Ellen to give you the scolding I want so much to give myself. Indeed Julia I would give all the glory to be gained in our battles to see you again now. I am very much of the opinion however that there will not be many more battles to fight. No doubt you hope there will be no more, but if you would believe the volunteers, they are anxious to see as hard fighting as they do hard times. You can see from this letter Julia how we live. Dont you see that the paper has been perfectly saturated with water? That is the way with evry thing else, even to ourselvs. Give my love to evry body at White Haven When I get to Camargo I will answer your letter, for I consider this no answer. But I dont want you to take the [s]ame view of the subject and put [off] writing until you get another.

Adieu My Dearest Julia
Ulysses

ALS, DLC-USG.

To Julia Dent

Camargo Mexico
August 14th 1846

My Dearest Julia

After a fatiguing march of over a hundred miles my company has arrived at this place. When we left Matamoras, on the 5th of August, it had been raining a great deal so that the roads were very bad, and as you may well guess, in this low Latitude, the weather was none of the coolest. The troops suffered considerably from heat and thirst. Matamoras is a perfect paridice compared to this place. The recent high waters over-run this place so much as to make the ~~this place~~ most of the houses untenable, and at present a great many families are living, or rather staying, (for I do not consider that the poorer class of Mexicans live atall) under mere sheds, without any other protection. I might attempt a discription of the Mexican people but then you have your Brother Lewis with you who has been so recently among them and can tell you all about them. Fred. has not joined us yet but I am looking for him now daily. Very soon now the troops at this place will start for Monteray, and then I fear, my Dear Julia, that there will be several months that we will not hear from each other very often. Dont neglect to write very frequently so that when a Mail does come I may hear from *my Dearest Julia.*

Whether there will be a fight at Monteray or not is a matter about which there are various opinions. It is well known that there is now at Monteray about Two thousand Mexican troops, busily engaged in throwing up defences, and the Government too is making her best endeavors to get as great a body together as she can. But it is thought doubtful whether she will be able to get any reinforcement before our arrival, and in that case, it is reported, that the Northeren provences intend to refuse to furnish their quota of troops. Upon the whole, taking the expression of opinion here the chances are about equal whether there will be another battle or not. The Volunteers and other troops who have arrived since the battles of the 8th & 9th of May are, of course, very anxious to have another fight, but those who were present those two days are not so particular about it. For my part I believe we are bound to beat the Mexicans whenever and where ever we meet them, no matter how large their numbers. But then wherever there are battles a great many must suffer, and for the sake of the little glory gained I do not care to see it. After the way in which the President has taken to show his feelings for the Army, especially I think we have but little reason to want to see fighting.—Do you recollect that some months ago I told you that now I had got to the far South Western limits of our Territory and the next moove must necessarily take me nearer my Dearest Julia? but at present the prospect is very different. Where this moove is to end there is no telling. All I have to wish,

Dear Julia, is that you may feel as contented and as little alarm as I do. If I could but see and talk to you frequently Julia I would not care to be any place else. How happy we must both be after so long a separation, when we meet again. How often I think of our pleasant walks & rides & talks!—It has been two or three days since I wrote the above. Since that reports continue to reach us which leaves but little doubt that we will have a big fight at Monteray. Fred. is not yet with us but I am expecting him now evry day. How anxious I am to see this affair over that I may go back and be with my Dea[r] Julia again! I will write to you evry opport[unit]y I have of Mailing a letter after we leave this, and I shall expect a letter from you Julia by evry Mail that reaches us. Even then I fear I will not hear from you half as often as formerly. I have not been very well for a few days and have been busy in my new duties. I am Quarter Master to the Regiment.[1] Give my love to all at White Haven Tell Ellen that Mr Dilworth[2] speaks of her very often. Adieu My Dearest Julia—

U S GRANT

Julia

ALS, DLC-USG.

1. USG had commanded Co. C since July 22, 1846, but relinquished command on Aug. 14, 1846 (according to the co. muster), or Aug. 16, 1846 (according to the regt. muster), to become act. asst. q. m. For USG protest against q. m. duties, see following letter.
2. 2nd Lt. Rankin Dilworth of Ohio, USMA 1844.

To Bvt. Col. John Garland

———

[*August, 1846*]

I respectfully protest against being assigned to a duty which removes me from sharing in the dangers and honors of service

with my company at the front, and respectfully ask to be permitted to resume my place in line. Respectfully submitted.

U. S. GRANT
2nd Lt. 4th Inft.

John W. Emerson, "Grant's Life in the West . . .," *The Midland Monthly* VII, 1
(Jan., 1897), 36. This protest was returned with an endorsement by Bvt. Col.
John Garland. "Lt. Grant is respectfully informed that his protest can not be
considered. Lt. Grant was assigned to duty as Quartermaster and Commissary
because of his observed ability, skill and persistency in the line of duty. The
commanding officer is confident that Lt. Grant can best serve his country in
present emergencies under this assignment. Lt. Grant will continue to perform
the assigned duties."

On Aug. 29, 1846, Bvt. Maj. William W. S. Bliss wrote to Garland. "The
Commanding General desires that you will retain Lieut. Grant in his position of
QuarterMaster to the 4th Infantry—his services being represented as very
useful by Major Allen." Copy, DNA, RG 94, Mexican War, Army of Occupation, Letters Sent.

To Bvt. Maj. Gen. Thomas S. Jesup

———

Pontia Gurdie, Mexico
September 6th 1846.

SIR;

I have the honor to transmit, herewith, a monthly report of
Privates of the 4th Infantry employed on extra duty: also a
"Summary Statement" of moneys received, expended, and re-
maining on hand for part of August, 1846.

Very respectfully
Your obt. Servt.
U S GRANT
2d Lt. 4th Inf.y
a. a. q. m.

Maj. Genl. Thomas S. Jesup.
Quartermaster Genl.
U. S. Army.
Washington, D.C.

LS, DNA, RG 92, Letters Received. This is the earliest report known of USG as quartermaster.

Bvt. Maj. Gen. Thomas Sidney Jesup of Ohio, served as quartermaster-general from 1818 to 1860.

To Julia Dent

———

Ponti Agrudo, Mexico.
September 6th 1846.

MY DEAREST JULIA

We have left Camargo on our way for Monteray, where it is possible we will have a grand fight. We are now within Six days march of Monteray but it is probable we will not start from here, or from Ser albo,¹ quite a fine city Twelve miles from Ponti Agrudo, for some ten or twelve days yet. When we do start I will write again if an opportunity occurs to send the letter. I am much in hopes my Dearest Julia after this moove our difficulties will be brought to a close, and I be permitted to visit the North again. If ever I get to the states again it will be but a short time till I will be with you Dearest Julia. If these Mexicans were any kind of people of they would have given us a chance to whip them enough some time ago and now the difficulty would be over; but I belive they think they will out-do us by keeping us runing over the country after them.² I have traveled from Matamoras here, by land, a distance of two hundred miles. In this distance there is at least fifteen thousand persons, almost evry one a farmer and on the whole road there is not, I dont belive, ten thousand acres of land cultivate[d] On our way we passed through Reynoso, Old Reynoso Camargo, & Mier, all of them old deserted looking places, that is if you only look at the houses, but if you look at the people you will find that there is scarsely an old wall standing that some family does not live behind. It is a great mistery to me how they live—Fred. is not with us yet. If he does not make haste he will not have the pleasure of making himself heard of more than heard from, as you told me he said he ~~y~~ would. Have you heard from John since he started with Col. Kearny?[3] No doubt he is hartily tired of soldiering by this time?—I suppose you have heard long ago of the freak Col. Harney took?[4] He is now some place further interior than we are. Whether he and his six hundred men are ever heard of again I think a doubtful matter. So much exposure as the troops have been subjected to has been the cause of a great deel of sickness, especially among the Volunteers. I think about one in five is sick all the time. The regulars stand it some better but there is a great deel of sickness with them too. Gen. Taylor is taking but Six thousand men with him to Monteray. The most of the Volunteers he has left behind.

Julia aint you geting tired of hearing of war, war, war? I am truly tired of it. here it is now five months that we have been at war and as yet but two battles. I do wish this would close. If we have to fight I would like to do it all at once and then make friends.—

It is now above two years that we have been engaged Julia and in all that time I have seen you but once. I know though you have not changed and when I *do* go back I will see[5] the same Julia I did more than two years ago. I know I shall never be willing to leave Gravois again until Julia is mine forever. How much I regret that we were not united when I visited you more th[an] a year ago. But your Pa would not have heard to anything of the kind at that time. I hope he will make no objections now! Write to me very often Julia, you know how happy I am to read your letters. Mr. Hazlitt is very well. Give my love to all at White Haven. Has Ellen & Ben Farrer made up yet? the time is now geting pretty well up ~~I~~ and I am afraid that I may loose my bet.—

ULYSSES

Julia

ALS, DLC-USG.

1. Cerralvo was about twelve miles southwest of Pantiagudo.
2. Two lines crossed out.
3. Brig. Gen. Stephen Watts Kearny of N.Y., had been ordered from Fort Leavenworth to occupy Santa Fe, and then into Calif. Kearny's army of 1700

left in detachments in June and July, 1846, reached Santa Fe on Aug. 18, 1846, and pushed on for Calif., Sept. 25, 1846.

4. Col. William Selby Harney of La., led an unauthorized expedition across the Rio Grande, discussed in *HED*, 30–1–60, pp. 410–11, 425.

5. Two words crossed out.

To Julia Dent

————

Camp Near Monteray Mex.
Sept. 23d 1846

MY DEAR JULIA

It is now after night and an opportunity occurs of sending a letter tomorrow to where it can be mailed, and you know my Dear Julia I told you I would not let a single chance escape of writing to you. If I could but see you I could tell you a volume on the subject of our last three days engagement, but as I write this I am laying on the ground with my paper laying along side in a very uneasy position for any one to give a detailed account of battles so you must be satisfied with it a simple statement of facts, and the assurance that in the midst of grape and musket shots, my Dearest Julia, and my love for her, are ever in my mind. We have indeed suffered greatly but sucsess seems now certain. Our force is but six thousand that of the enemy is probably much greater, but is not known. The siege of Monteray was commenced on the 20th Ins. but we did not fire our first gun until the morning of the 21st. Monteray is a city of from six to ten thousand inhabitants. The houses are all low and built of stone. In the town and on all the commanding points the Mexicans have erected fortifications and seem determined to fight until the last one is taken by shere force. Already all those on the high points of ground have been taken and many Mexican lives with them. We are now playing upon them with pieces of Artillery and ammunition that we have captured but they still hold their citadel and Artillery enough to man it. Our loss has been very great, particularly in the 3d & 4th Inf.y. The killed and wounded officers runs as follows (leaving out a number of Volunteers who I do not know the names of.)

1st Inf.y Capt. Lamotte an arm off, Lt. Terrett badly wounded and in the hands of the Mexicans, Lt. Dillworth lost a leg.[1] 3d Inf.y Capt. Morris, Capt. Field Maj. Barbour, Lt. Irwin & Lt. Hazlitt killed Maj. Lier severely wounded, the ball passing in at the nose and out at the ear.[2] His recovery doubtful. 4th Inf.y Lt. Hoskins & Lt. Woods killed and Lt. Graham severely wounded.[3] 5th Inf.y I[n] the other Regt. there was more or less killed or wounded but the loss not so severe. I passed through some severe fireing but as yet have escaped unhurt

Of course My Dear Julia if I get through (and I think the severest part is now over) I will not let an opportunity of writing to you escape me. I have not had a letter from you since we left Matamoras which was on the 5th of August but I know there must be one or two on the way some place I am geting very tired of this war, and particularly impatient of being separated from one I love so much, but I think before I see another birth day I shall see Julia, and if she says so, be able to call her my own [. . .] Dear for ever. It is about time for [me] to close writing until Monteray is entirely ours, so give my love to all at White Haven and write very soon to

ULYSSES

Julia

ALS, DLC-USG.

1. Capt. Joseph Hatch La Motte of N.C., USMA 1827, survived; 1st Lt. John Chapman Terrett of Va., was killed at Monterey; 2nd Lt. Rankin Dilworth of Ohio, USMA 1844, died Sept. 27, 1846, of wounds received at Monterey.

2. Capt. Gouverneur Morris of N.Y., survived the battle; Capt. George P. Field of N.Y., USMA 1834, killed at Monterey; Bvt. Maj. Philip Nordbourne Barbour of Ky., USMA 1834, was killed at Monterey; 1st Lt. Douglass Simms Irwin, of Wash. D.C., USMA 1840, was killed at Monterey; 2nd Lt. Robert Hazlitt of Ohio, USMA 1843, was killed at Monterey; Maj. William W. Lear of Md., died Oct. 31, 1846, of wounds received at Monterey.

3. 1st Lt. Charles Hoskins of N.C., USMA 1836, was killed at Monterey; Bvt. 1st Lt. James Sterrett Woods of Pa., USMA 1844, was killed at Monterey; 1st Lt. Richard Hill Graham of Ky., USMA 1838, died Oct. 12, 1846, of wounds received at Monterey.

To Julia Dent

————

Camp Near Monteray Mex.
Oct. 3d 1846

MY DEAREST JULIA

I wrote to you while we were still storming the city of Monteray and told you then that the town was not yet taken but that I thought the worst part was then over. I was right for the next day the Mexicans capitulated and we have been ever since the uninterupted holders of the beautiful city of Monteray. Monteray is a beautiful city enclosed on three sides by the mountains with a pass through them to the right and to the left. There are points around the city which command it and these the Mexicans fortified and armed. The city is built almost entirely of stone and with very thick walls. We found all their streets baricaded and the whole place well defended with artillery, and taking together the strength of the place and the means the Mexicans had of defending it it is almost incredible ~~to say~~ that the American army now are in possession here. But our victory was not gained without loss. 500,[1] or near abouts, brave officers and men fell in the attack. Many of them were only wounded and will recover, but many is the leg or arm that will be buryed in this country while the owners will live to relate over and over again the scenes they witnessed during the siege of Monteray. I told you in my last letter the officers that you were acquainted with that suffered, but for fear the letter may not reach you I will inumerate them again. Capt. Morris of the 3d Inf.y Maj. Barbour Capt. Field Lt. Irwin Lt. Hazlitt Lt. Hoskins and Lt. Terrett & Dilworth since dead. Lt. Graham & Maj. Lier dangerously wounded.[2] It is to be hoped that we are done fighting with Mexico ~~now~~ for we have shown them now that we can whip them under evry disadvantage. I dont believe that we will ever advance beyond this place, for it is generally believed that Mexico has rec'd our Minister and a few months more will restore us to amity. I hope it may be so for fighting is no longer a pleasure. Fred. has not joined us yet and I think it a great pity too, for his Regiment was engaged at a point where they done the enemy as much harm probably as any other Reg.t but lost but very few men and no officer. Monteray is so full of Orange Lime and Pomgranite trees that the houses can scarsly be seen until you get into the town. If it was an American city ᵻᵼ I have no doubt it would be concidered the handsomest one in the Union. The climate is excellent and evry thing might be produced that any one could want³ I have written two pages and have not told you that I got a letter a few days ago from my Dear Dear Julia. It has been a long long time since I got one before but I do not say that you have not written often for I can very well conceive of letters loosing their way following us up. What made you ask me the question Dearest Julia "if I thought absence could conquer love"? You ought to be just as good a judge as me! I can only answer for myself alone, that Julia is as *dear* to me to-day as she was the day we visited St. Louis together, more than two years ago, when I first told her of my love. From that day to this I have loved you constantly and the same and with the hope too that long befofore this time I would have been able to call you *Wife*. Dearest Julia if you have been just as constant in your love it *shall not* [. . . .] long until I will be entitled to call you by the [. . . .] affectionate title. You have not told me for a long time Julia that you still loved me, but I never thought to doubt it. Write soon to me and continue to write often. Now that we are going to stay here some time I am in hopes that I will get a number of letters from you. I forgot to tell you that by the terms of the capitulation the Mexicans were to retire beyond Linariz⁴ within seven days and were not to fight again for eight weeks and we were not to advance for the same time. Fred. certainly will join soon and then I will make him write often. Give my love to all at White Haven

ULYSSES

Julia

P. S. I am going to write to you evry two weeks if I have an opportunity to write so you may know if you dont get letters that often that some of them are lost

U.

ALS, DLC-USG, envelope marked "Pt Isabel Oct 24," 1846.

    1. The AGO reported later that 205 regulars and 282 volunteers were killed and wounded at Monterey. *HED*, 31–1, 24, pp. 10, 28.
    2. See letter of Sept. 23, 1846.
    3. Two lines crossed out.
    4. Linares.

To Julia Dent

———

Camp Near Monteray Mex.
Oct. 20th 1846

My Dear Julia

    How very very lonesome it is here with us now. I have just been walking through camp and how many faces that were dear to the most of us are missing now. Just one month ago this night the 4th Inf.y left this camp not to return again until it had lost three of its finest officers. (Lt. Graham has since died)[1] I came back to my tent and to drive away, what you call the Blues, I took up some of your old letters, written a year or so ago and looked them over, I next took up a Journal that I kept whilst at Jefferson Barrack and read as far as to where I had mentioned "that of late I could read but very little for I was so busy riding about and occationally visiting my friends in the country—who by the way are becoming very interesting."[2] That part Julia must have been written about the time I first found that I loved you so much. It brought the whole matter to mind and made me think how pleasantly my time passed then. It seems very hard that I should not be able now to spend a few days in the year as I did then evry week. How long this state of things is to continue is yet a problem but it is to be hoped not long. When you walk down the branch to Aunt Fieldings do you ever think of our walks on that road? How very often they come to my mind. This is my third letter since the battles to you Julia so that if you dont hear from me often it is not my fault.[3]—

We occationally get reports here that negociations are going or that proposals of the kind have been made by this ~~country~~ Government. I hope sincerely that such is the case for I am very anxious to get out of the country. This is the most beautiful spot that it has been my fortune to see in this world, but without you *dearest* a Paradice would become lonesom.—Fred. is not with us yet and I am now giving up the hope of seeing him here. I have had his commission for a long time and the other day I concluded to send it to him. One or two of the Mails comeing this way from Camargo have been robed lately and the letters sent to Gen. Ampudia and by him to Gen. Santa Ana. ~~H~~ Ampudia was polite enough to inform Gen. Taylor of the fact.—Before you get this no doubt there will be great excitement in the states in concequence of the battle of Monteray, and no doubt you will hear many exaggerated accounts of the valorous deeds per-formed by individuals. I begin to see that luck is a fortune. It is but necessary to get a start in the papers and there will soon be deeds enough of ~~your~~ ones performances related. Look at the case of Capt. Walker![4] The papers have made him a hero of a thousand battles.—Give my love to all at White Haven and write to me very soon. I would like to know Julia if your Father ever says or hints a word on the subject of our engagement?

Farewell my Dearest until my next letter which will be in a week or two

Your Devoted
ULYSSES

Julia

P. S. The Mail has not left here since writing the above. All are well except many slight cases of Fever & Ague. Capt. Ridgely[5] of the Artillery, hose name no doubt you have often seen in print, met with a severe accident yesterday, the 26th

He was riding through Monteray and his horse fell with him and fractured his scull. His life is dispaired of.

U

ALS, DLC-USG.

1. See letter of Sept. 23, 1846.
2. In his *Memoirs* I, 52, USG mistakenly says that his journal was lost when his belongings were packed at Jefferson Barracks for the move to Camp Salubrity. He adds: "Often since a fear has crossed my mind lest that book might turn up yet, and fall into the hands of some malicious person who would publish it." It has not turned up yet.
3. Seven lines crossed out.
4. Capt. Samuel Hamilton Walker of Tex., who led the Texas Mounted Rifles, was killed Oct. 9, 1847, in the battle of Huamantla.
5. Bvt. Capt. Randolph Ridgely died Oct. 27, 1846. See Maj. Gen. Zachary Taylor to AG, Oct. 28, 1846, *HED*, 30–1, 60, pp. 433–34.

To Julia Dent

———

Camp Near Monteray Mexico
November 7th 1846

My Dear Julia

I got one of the sweetest letters from you a few days ago that I have had for a long time and the least I can do in return is to write you at least three pages in, return; even if I have nothing more to write than that I love you, and how very much. I have written very often to you since the battle of Monteray and intend to continue to do so, but still I hope that I may have but few more letters to write you. How happy I should be if I knew that but a very few more letters were to pass between my Dearest Julia and myself,—*as mere lovers,*—that is to say, how happy I should be if soon Julia was to become mine forever. You say in your letter that you wish it was our country that was being invaded instead of Mexico, that you would ask for quarters but doubted if Mr. Grant would *grant* them. Indeed dearest I am one of the most humane individuals you are acquainted with, and not only would I give quarters to any one who implores them; but if Julia says she will surrender herself my prisoner I will take the first opportunity of making an excursion to Mo. But you must not expect your parole like other prisoners of war for I expect to be the Sentinel that guards you myself. Indeed dearest Julia it cannot be a great while longer that we are to be separated by so many miles space! Very soon now the troops at this place will be on their way for either Tampico or San Louis Potosi at either of which places there will be likely to be a big fight. Some troops will remain here to Garrison the city but who will remain is not known. Before we leave of course I will write again. So many battles must of course result in a final peace and I hope matters will be rushed so as to bring about a speedy settlement of all our difficulties.

November 10th As the Mail only leaves this place once a week I have put off finishing this letter until to-day—Mail day—, Since writing the above orders have been published for the 5th & 8th Infantry and Artillery Battalion, the whole commanded by Gen. Worth,[1] to march upon Saltillo on the 12th Instant. The 7th Inf.y and one comp.y of artillery Garrison Monteray, so it is presumed that before two weeks we will take the field again. I get but few letters from home now and write but very short ones in answer. Some time ago my Father had one of my letters published[2] so hereafter I intend to be careful not to give them any news worth publishing. I have not had a letter from Clara or Virginia[3] for some time. When I write again I will tell Clara that if she will write to you she will get an answer. Clara is very anxious to have me come home and wants me to take Julia with me. Will I have that pleasure *dearest*? This will be my last Winter in Mexico until I return to the U. States even if I have to resign. I have never yet seen a place where I would as leave be stationed as at Monteray if the population was an American one—and if Julia was here.

The climate ~~here~~ is excellent, the soil rich, and the scenery beautiful;[4] Did you understand what I meant in the firs[t] of this letter where I hope but few letters m[ore] would pass between

us as mere lovers? Of course though you know that I meant I
hoped that it would not be long until I would be with you and
then it would not be necessary to write. But in the mean time
write very often as I do. I do not know that you get all my letters,
but I write very often. Does Sarah Walker take the death of Mr.
Terrett very hard?[5] You say she used to get very long letters
from him! Are all well at White Have? Give them my love and
write to me soon. Dream of me and tell me your dreams. When
you wrote *kiss* on your letter I kissed before I knew whether you
had kissed it or not, and frequently after Tell Ellen I will pay
her off for trying to play a trick off on me. you say it was her
wrote the word on the corner of the sheet of paper. I wrote to
Fred. a short time a go and sent him his commission and a letter
that I have had for him a long time. Farewell Dearest Julia, I
shall write to you again in about one week and my next ~~wil~~ after
that will as likely be from Tampico as any place els

ULYSSES

Julia

ALS, DLC-USG.

<ol>
<li>Bvt. Maj. Gen. William Jenkins Worth of N.Y.</li>
<li>This letter has not been located.</li>
<li>Sisters of USG.</li>
<li>Four lines crossed out.</li>
<li>See letter of Sept. 23, 1846.</li>
</ol>

To Julia Dent

———

Monteray Mexico

December 27th 1846

MY DEAREST JULIA

Again I write you from Monteray. You know I told you that
my next letter would probably be written from some place far
away. The troops moved as I expected but the 4th Inf.y and one
company of Artillery was left to Garrison this city and will

probably be here for the ballance of the war. Gen. Worth Gen. Wool & Gen. Butler[1] are all at or near Saltillo with from four to five thousand troops, Gen. Taylor is on his march for Victoria with the greater part of the Army, and I would not wonder if he continued on to Vera Cruze. After Gen. Taylor had been out about three days from this place an Express reached here from Gen. Worth announcing that Santa Anna's army was advancing upon them The Express was forwarded to Gen. Taylor and he returned but finding that the danger ahead was not so great as was threatened he has again taken up his line of march for Victoria. There is but little doubt but that Santa Anna is at San Luis Potosi with an army of from 20 to 30 thousand but I do not believe that he intends advancing but will wait for us to go to him. The citizens of this place have become very much allarmed at the threats of the Mexican General and have nearly all left the town, but I think in a few weeks they will find that Santa Anna is not coming as fast as he says, and the inhabitants will return. A report reached here a day or two since that the Mexican congress has passed a resolution to admit a Minister from the U. States to treat. I hope it may be true.

You say Julia that your Pa said as soon as he heard that I was QuarterMaster that he pronounced me safe for Qr. Mrs. did not have to go into battle; that is very true but on the 21st of September I voluntarily went along with the Regiment and when Mr. Hoskins was killed I was appointed acting adjutant to take his place and in that capacity continued through the fight.[2]

I have written you two pages my Dearest Julia without telling you that I had recieved your sweet letter of the 7th of November. I feel very happy when I can get such long letters from you Dearest and then this one has some such good news in it! You say your Pa often asks about me and then he named me when you were counting apple seeds? When I read this I felt as though I was just geting his concent to our long long engagement. How long it does seem since I saw you last! You ask when my next birth day will be On the 27th of April I will be 25 years old. Just think when we were first engaged I was but twenty two and I thought then that long before one year passed Julia would have been mine forever. I regret very much that such was not the case. I see from your letter that Ellen is as full of mischief as ever, she takes evry opportunity to tease you as she did about your dreaming of seeing me with whiskers! I expect when I see her she wont be satisfied with teasing me about them but will pull them and to show you that they are long enough to be pulled I will send you a lock of them.

Julia [w]hy did you not tell me some of your drea[ms] you say you frequently do dream of me now? I [think] a great deel about my dear Julia but of late I but seldom dream. You must write very often to me Julia and tell me if you got a letter containg a check for Mrs. Porter. In your last letter you did not say whether Mrs. P. is still at the Barracks or not? Give my love to all at White Haven and kiss Emmy for me. Do ask your Pa to write to me some time and say that he will give me Julia. Fred has not written to me for a long time. I bid you good by Dear Julia hoping that before a great while I will be able to see you.

U<small>LYSSES</small>

Julia

P. S. I have got Emmy's kiss and the hundred you send. Recollect I am going to collect them all when I see you next, besides paying you the hundred I send you in return

U.

ALS, DLC-USG, marked "Pt. Isabel Jan. 9, 1847."

1. Bvt. Maj. Gen. William Jenkins Worth, Brig. Gen. John Ellis Wool, of N.Y. and Maj. Gen. of Vols. William Orlando Butler, of Ky.
2. USG discusses his services at Monterey in *Memoirs*, I, 110–17.

To (Mrs. Thomas L. Hamer)

———

[*Dec., 1846*]

When Major Hamer wrote, three days before his death, no one expected a fatal ending. But neither the skill of our surgeons, nor the loving attention of friends, availed to save him. He died as a soldier dies, without fear and without a murmur. His regret was that, if death must come, it should not come to him on the field of battle.

He was mindful the last of all of those at home who would most suffer.

He died within the sound of battle, and that was a pleasure to him as a brave soldier. He was buried with the "honors of war," and with the flag of his beloved country around him.

All things will be forwarded in due course of regulations.

Personally, his death is a loss to me which no words can express.

> Respectfully, your obedient servant,
> U. S. GRANT,
> Second Lieutenant and Quartermaster.

John W. Emerson, "Grant's Life in the West," *The Midland Monthly*, VII, 1 (Jan., 1897), 35. Brig. Gen. Thomas L. Hamer died Dec. 2, 1846. Hamer as Congressman had appointed USG to USMA. Emerson also prints (34) a letter from Hamer to a friend written shortly before his death. "I have found in Lieutenant Grant a most remarkable and valuable young soldier. I anticipate for him a brilliant future, if he should have an opportunity to display his powers when they mature. Young as he is, he has been of great value and service to me. To-day, after being freed from the duty of wrestling with the problem of reducing a train of refractory mules and their drivers to submissive order, we rode into the country several miles, and taking our position upon an elevated mound, he explained to me many army evolutions; and, supposing ourselves to be generals commanding opposing armies, and a battle to be in progress, he explained suppositious maneuvers of the opposing forces in a most instructive way; and when I thought his imaginary force had my army routed, he suddenly suggested a stragetic move for my forces which crowned them with triumphant victory, and himself with defeat, and he ended by gracefully offering to surrender his sword! Of course, Lieutenant Grant is too young for command, but his capacity for future military usefulness is undoubted."

Unknown Addressee

————

[*Dec., 1846*]

Here we are, playing war a thousand miles from home, making show and parades, but not doing enough fighting to much amuse either the enemy or ourselves, consuming rations enough to have carried us to the capital of Mexico. If our mission is to occupy the enemy's country, it is a success, for we are inertly here; but if to conquer, it seems to some of us who have no control that we might as well be performing the job with greater energy. While the authorities at Washington are at sea as to who shall lead the army, the enterprise ought and could be accomplished.

John W. Emerson, "Grant's Life in the West and his Mississippi Valley Campaigns," *The Midland Monthly*, VII, 2 (Feb., 1897), 139–40.

To Bvt. Maj. Gen. Thomas S. Jesup

————

Camp Palo Alto Texas
Jan. 31st 1847.

GENERAL

Here with I enclose you my Monthly Summary Statement for the month of Jan. 1847 and Muster Rolls.

On the night of the 6th of Jan. 1847 I had stolen from my Quarters in monteray a chest containing all my Quarter Master funds besides several hundred dollars more. This money I am not able at present to replace and as it was not through negligence of mine that it was stolen it would be but justice that Government should loose the amount and not me.

Very Respectfully
Your Obt. Svt.

Gen. T. S. Jesup	U S GRANT
Qr. Mr. Gen	2d Lt. 4th If.y
Washington D. C.	A. A. Q. M.

ALS, USG 3. There is no further correspondence concerning these stolen funds although a similar theft in June, 1848, became the subject of a claim presented to Congress. See document of June 27, 1848.

To Julia Dent

———

Camp Palo Alto Texas
Feb. 1st 1846 [1847]

MY DEAREST JULIA

From the heading of my letter you will see that since my last the 4th Inf.y has materially changed its Position. Two days before we left Monteray we thought we were stationary for some time to come but as soon as Gen. Scott took command evrything was changed and now here we are prepairing to embark, I believe, for a small Island[1] laying between Tampico and Vera Cruze no doubt soon to make a decent upon the City of Vera Cruze. As soon as we are stationary I will write again. I am affraid Julia that you do not get all my letters for I see that at home they get none of them. Evry few weeks I get a letter from there beging me to write. They say they have not had a letter from me since the troops went to Monteray. Of course I have written a number. At Vera Cruze we will probably have a desperate fight but our little Army goes so much better prepaired than it has ever done before that there is no doubt as to the result. I fear though that there is so much pride in the Mexican character that they will not give up even if we should take evry town in the Republic. Since we left Monteray I have been very far from well and now I could remain behind if I would but I think by the time our sea voyage is completed I will be well and while I am in the country I want to see as much of it as possible. Evry letter I get from home begs of me to leave Mexico and I think if Mr. Polk does the Army another such insult as he did in officering the Rifle Reg.t I ~~think~~ I will leave.—My Dear Julia you cannot know the anxiety I feel to see you I would almost be willing to be sick enough to leave the country just to get back to Gravois once more. This is a very pretty country to look at but I am geting so thoroughly tired of it that I begin to think like one of our Captains who said that if he was the Government he would whip Mexico until they would concent to take the Sabine for their boundary and he would make them take the Texans with it.[2]—When we leave here I think I shall give up Quarter Mastering and go back to my Company. Fred. never writes to me any more. Is he still at Baton Rouge? His Reg.t is encamped here with us and will sail with us—I heard from some one that Fanny Higgins is engaged to be married.[3] Is it so? What do the people in the States think about peace? do they think there ever will be peace again between the U. States and Mexico? Tell Fred. when you write to him not to think of applying to be relieved from where he is, for he would soon find that he did not know when he was well off. How was John & Lewis the last time you heard from them?

I have nothing left to write dearest Julia except how much I love you and how very anxious I am to see you again and all that you know for I I have told it to you with the utmost candor a thousand times. Give my love to the whole family and a kiss to Misses Ellen & Emmy and a Thousand for Miss Julia. How often I take the ring from my finger just to see the sweet name engraved in it! Write very often to me Julia and I will promise more than an equal number.

                                                    ULYSSES

Julia

P. S. Dearest Julia since writing the above I rec'd a letter from Mrs. Porter. It was sealed with black wax and the direction did not seem to be in your hand This allarmed me a little but you cannot immagine my allarm when I saw your brother's name was signed to the last page. But the sweet note from your dear self restored me to confidence of my dearest Julias health. You must not neglect to write as your pa advises you for all your letters reach me. Two or three months ago I sent Mrs. Porter a check on Col. Cumming[4] enclosed in a letter to you. Did you ever get the letter? If you did not Mrs. Porter will not loose the money for no one els could draw it but it will take some time for me to find out if you got it and to send another. write Dearest Julia

U

ALS, DLC–USG, envelope postmarked New Orleans, Feb. 13, 1847.

1. The Island of Lobos. Maj. Gen. Winfield Scott, appointed by President James K. Polk to command the Vera Cruz expedition on Nov. 19, 1846, reached Camargo, Mexico, on Jan. 3, 1847, and issued orders for the transfer of troops from Taylor's army.

2. "Captain [Charles H.] Larnard said to Grant one day: 'People think this is a very cruel war. For my part I would carry on this war against Mexico until she agreed to take these Texans and keep them and make the Rio Colorado the boundary between the United States and Mexico.' " Henry Carey Baird," Recollections of General Grant at the 'Carey Vespers,' June 25, 1865 . . ." *USGA Newsletter*, III, 3 (April, 1966), 20.

3. See letter of Sept. 14, 1845.

4. Perhaps Lt. Col. David H. Cummings of 2nd Tenn. Inf.

To Julia Dent

———

Ship North Carolina
Island of Lobos Mexico
Feb.y 25th 1847

MY DEAREST JULIA

There is now laying at this Island over thirty transports ready to fall down to Anton Lizardo as soon as the remainder of

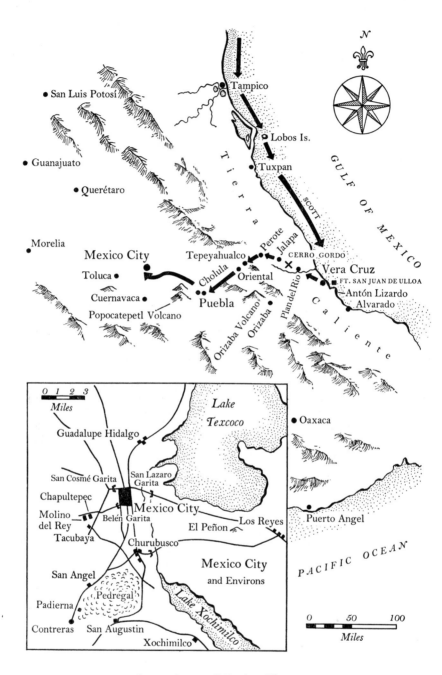

Campaign to Mexico City, 1847

the Army joins us which will probably be in the course of six or
seven days. Lobos is a small Island about one mile in circum-
ference and ten miles from the main land. It is covered with the
India rubber tree (You must recollect we are now in the Torrid
zone) which like some others of the Tropical trees has a number
of different trunks. The limbs bend over until they touch the
ground and there take root and grow as large as the parent tree.
On the ship North Carolina we have over four hundred troops.
A great part of the time we have had a very heavy sea and often
you would think the ship would capsize. It rocks so much now
that I am affraid I will not sucseed in writing so that you can
read it. I have not been troubled with sea sickness but have
almost recovered from my former illness. There has been several
cases of small Pox here among the volunteers and one Reg.t, the
Mississippi Reg.t has lost in the last few weeks about one hundred men. Their sickness has resulted principally from being
crouded and not keeping up a strict Police. We have lost no one
aboard our vessel. The general opinion now is that we will have
a fight when we attempt to disembark and a big one at Vera
Cruz. It is to be hoped that it will be the last! There is a report
here that Gen Taylor has had a fight with Santa Anna some
place beyond Monteray and repulsed him but it is not generally
believed.[1] We will all have to get out of this part of Mexico
soon or we will be caught by the yellow fever which I am ten to
one more affraid of than of the Mexicans. Gen. Scott will have
with him about twelve thousand land troops and a large Naval
force. Fred's Reg.t is here. I should like to see him here but if I
was in his place I never would make application to come to
Mexico. I have long since been tired enough of this country[2] but
I suppose I will have to see the war out. In my next no doubt I
will have news of a great battle to relate. If we are likely to be
stationary for several months after the battle I will apply for a
leave of absence for a few months. If I should sucseed in geting
a leave I will make my way for St. Louis as fast as possible. My
anxiety to see you my Dearest Julia increases with the space
which separates us. Vera Cruz is 20° degrees south of Jeff. Bks.

I have dreamed of you twice since my last letter. All my dreams agree in one particular, that is in our marriage, either that the day is set or the seremony is being performed.

Feb. 27th Having no opportunity of Mailing this I left one page blank to fill up when an opportunity did occur. To-morrow a mail leaves here and I can not fail to improve it. My Dearest Julia time can not suffice to make my absence from you more bearable. I begin to believe like some author has said,—that there are just two places in this world—One is where a person's intended is, and the other is where she is not. At one of these places I was always very happy and hope ere long to return, at the other I feel much discontent. Dont you think Julia a soldiers life[3] is insupportable? Just think in all this time there has been but three battles fought towards conquering a peace. If we have to fight I would like to see it all done at once[4] Julia you must write to me often and when I get off [the] rocking ocean I will write a long letter; that will probably be from Vera Cruz.— Give my love to all at White Haven and dream of me yourself dearest. At least I have the pleasure of dreaming of you some times but not half so often as I would like. My love a thousand times over to you dearest Julia and twice as many kisses. Adieu

ULYSSES

To Julia

ALS, DLC-USG, postmarked New Orleans, March 15, 1847.

    1. Maj. Gen. Taylor had won the battle at Buena Vista, Feb. 22–23, 1847.
    2. One word crossed out.
    3. Four words crossed out.
    4. Five words crossed out.

To Julia Dent

———

Camp at Vera Cruz Mex.
April 3d 1847

MY DEAREST JULIA

It has been longer since I wrote you last than I have ever before gone without writing, but I wanted to wait until the Seige of Vera Cruz was completed and the fighting over. You will no doubt read flaming accounts of the taking of this City and the Castle San Juan de Ulloa. Yesterday I visited the Castle and find that its strength has never been exagirated. The City is a solid compact place the houses generally built of stone and two or three stories high, the churches like most Catholic churches are very much ornamented. The whole place is enclosed by a stone wall of about fifteen feet in hight and four or five feet thick. Taking into account all the out works of the place it seems as if it would be impossible for any enemy in the world to come and drive us away. Fred is here and well. I see him evry day. I will leave the discription of the battle here to him. I am doing the duties of Commissary and Quarter Master[1] so that during the siege I had but little to do except to see to having the Pork and Beans rolled about. It is not known when the troops will leave here but they will move some place soon, ~~bfore~~ before the sickly season. How much my Dearest Julia I would be pleased to hear that Mexico has agreed to treat. I think they must do so soon for Gen. Taylor at his end of the line of opporations has routed Santa Anna and totally disorganized his army.[2] Here Gen Scott has taken the key to their whole country and the force that Garrisoned this place are all prisoners of war on their Parole not to fight during the war.—Do you recollect Dearest about six months ago I told you that another Birth day certainly would not roll round before I would be with you. Well here it is near the time and I have not started yet. I have always been so much in hopes that the war would soon end that I have not followed the desire of my Father to resign. He insists that evry officer of the Regular army ought to resign after the appointments that have been made. I believe he is right and if there is no prospect soon of the War closing I will go any how. I rec'd one of the sweetest letters from you about ten days ago! You speak of Captain Gardenier[3] in it, is there not a report that he and Mrs. Porter are to be married I have heard so. Remember me to Mrs. P. and dont forget to send me the poetry you promised. We have a very pretty encamping ground here and though the Sun is very hot yet the sea brease makes it quite comfortable.[4] It is a great pity that[5] people[6] compose the Mexican soldiery should be made the tools for some proud and ambitious General to work out his advancement with. Julia aint it a hard case that this Mexican war should keep me two long years as it has done from seeing one that I love so much. But tim[e] only strengthens and proves the reality of their [being] such a thing as love—If I could but see you and have a long talk I could then serve out this war with some degree of contentment, but as it is I am very impatient. Fred was in here a while ago and no doubt would have had some message if he knew who I was writing to. Fred. knows of our engagement and has spoken of you to me once or twice.—I often take the ring you put on my finger off and look at the sweet name in it. Give my love to your Pa Ma Ellen Emmy &c. Write very often my Dearest Julia to

ULYSSES

ALS, DLC-USG, postmarked New Orleans, April 17, 1847.

1. Bvt. Col. John Garland wrote to Bvt. Brig. Gen. Roger Jones, April 1, 1847. "I have *this day* appointed 2nd Lieutenant U. S. Grant, 4th Infantry, Regimental Quarter Master, subject to approval of General Head Quarters." The appointment was approved by Jones and Secretary of War William L. Marcy on July 6, 1847. LS, DNA, RG 94, Letters Received.
2. At Buena Vista.
3. Capt. John Randolph Barent Gardenier of N.Y., USMA 1828, 1st Inf.
4. Two lines crossed out.
5. Four words crossed out.
6. One word crossed out.

To Julia Dent

Castle of Perote Mexico
April 24th 1847

MY DEAR JULIA

You see from the above that the great and long talked of Castle of Perote is at last in the hands of the Americans. On the 13th of this month the rear Division of Gen. Scott's army left Vera Cruz to drive Santa Anna and his army from the strong mountain passes which they had fortified, with the determination of driving back the Barbarians of the North, at all hazards. On the morning of the 17th our army met them at a pass called Cierra Gorda[1] a mountain pass which to look at one would suppose impregnable. The road passes between mountains of rock the tops of which were all fortified and well armed with artillery. The road was Barricaded ~~and~~ by a strong work with five pieces of artillery. Behind this was a peak of the mountains much higher than all the others and commanded them so that the Enemy calculated that even if the Americans should succeed in taking all the other hights, from this one they could fire upon us and be out of reach themselvs. But they were disappointed. Gen. Twiggs'[2] Division worked its way around with a great deel of laibor and made the attack in the rear. With some loss on our side and great loss on the part of the Enemy this ~~fort~~ highest point was taken and soon the White flag of the enemy was seen to float. Of Generals and other officers and soldiers some Six thousand[3] surrendered as prisoners of war Their Artillery ammunition supplies and most of their small arms were captured. As soon as Santa Anna saw that the day was lost he made his escape with a portion of his army but he was pursued so closely that his carriage, a splendid affair, was taken and in it was his cork leg and some Thirty thousand dollars in gold. The pursuit was so close that the Mexicans could not establish themselvs in another strong pass which they had already fortified, and when they got to the strong Castle of Perote they passed on leaving it too with all of its artillery to fall into our hands. After so many victories on our part and so much defeat on the part of the Mexicans they certainly will agree to treat. For my part I do not believe there will be another fight unless we should pursue with a very small force.—From Vera Cruz to this place it is an almost constant rize Perote being about Eight thousand feet above the ocean. Around us are mountains covered with eternal snow and greatly the influance is felt too. Although we are in the Torrid zone it is never so warm as to be uncomfortable nor so cold as to make a fire necessary. From Vera Cruz to this place the road is one of the best and one that cost more laibor probably than any other in the world. It was made a great many years ago when Mexico was a province of Spain. On the road there a great many specimens of beautiful table land and a decided improvement in the appearance of the people and the stile of building over any thing I had seen before in Mexico. Jalapa is decidedly the most beautiful place I ever saw in my life. From its low Latitude and great elevation it is never hot nor never cold. The climate is said to be the best in the world and from what I saw I would be willing to make Jalapa my home for life with only one condition and that would be that I should be permitted to go and bring my Dearest Julia. —The 5th Inf.y, Fred's Reg.t was was not present at the fight of Cierra Gorda. A few days before we left Vera Cruz the 5th Inf.y was ordered down the coast to Alvarado to procure horses and mules for the use of the army, and ~~and~~ when we left they had not returned. My Dearest Julia how very long it seems since we were together and still our march is onward. In a few days no doubt we will start for Puebla and then we will be within from Eighty to a Hundred miles of the City of Mexico; there the march must end. Three years now the 4th Inf.y has been [on] the tented field and I think it is high time t[hat] I should have a leave of absence. Just think Julia it is now three long years that we have been engaged. Do you think I could endure another years separation loving you as I do now and believing my love returned? At least commission and all will go in less time or I will be permitted to see the one I have loved so much for three long years. My Dearest dont you think a soldiers life a hard one! But after a storm there must be a calm. This war must end some time and the army scattered to occupy different places and I will be satisfied with any place wher I can have you with me. Would you be willing to go with me to some out-of-the-way post Dearest? But I know you would for you have said so so often.— Your next letter will probably reach me in Puebla the 3d city in size in the Republic of Mexico. Write to me often Julia I always get your letters. I will write again as soon as the army makes another halt Has your pa ever said anything more about our engagement? You know in one of your sweet letters you told me something he had said which argued that his consent would be given. Remember me affectionately to you father and mother Miss Ellen & Emmy.

ULYSSES

Julia

P. S. Among the wounded on our side was Lt. Dana[4] very dangerously. In the Rifle Reg.t one officer, Lt. Ewell, was killed Mr. Maury lost his hand Mason and Davis a leg each.[5] A great many Volunteer officers were killed and wounded. I have not had a letter from you since the one I answered from Vera Cruz but there have been but few mails arrived since. I hope to get one soon.

U

ALS, DLC-USG.

1. Cerro Gordo.

2. Bvt. Maj. Gen. David Emanuel Twiggs of Ga.

3. Maj. Gen. Scott reported 3000 prisoners in a letter to Maj. Gen. Zachary Taylor, April 24, 1847, *HED*, 30–1, 60, p. 948.

4. 1st Lt. Napoleon Jackson Tecumseh Dana of Me., USMA 1842, 7th Inf., survived.

5. 1st Lt. Thomas Ewell of Tenn., was killed at Cerro Gordo; Capt. Stevens T. Mason of Va., died May 15, 1847, of wounds received at Cerro Gordo; and 2nd Lt. Thomas Davis of Ill., died April 20, 1847, of wounds received at Cerro Gordo. Bvt. 2nd Lt. Dabney H. Maury of Va., USMA 1846, had his left arm shattered. He was told by a surgeon on the field that amputation was necessary, but at the hospital five miles in the rear was told that the arm could be saved. Al-

though the arm was saved, Maury was crippled for life. Dabney Herndon Maury, *Recollections of a Virginian in the Mexican, Indian, and Civil Wars* (New York, 1894), pp. 36–37.

Addressee Unknown

———

April 24, 1847

It was war pyrotechnics of the most serious and brilliant character. While it was a most inspiring sight, it was a painful one to me. I stood there watching the brigade slowly climbing those ragged heights, each minute nearer and nearer the works of the enemy with our missiles flying over their heads, while white puffs of smoke spitefully flashed out in rapid succession along the enemy's line and I knew that every discharge sent death into our ranks. As our men finally swept over and into the works, my heart was sad at the fate that held me from sharing in that brave and brilliant assault. But our batteries did their duty, and no doubt helped in achieving the glorious result.

Jalapa is the most beautiful part of Mexico we have seen. I suppose we move on toward the Capital at once.

John W. Emerson, "Grant's Life in the West . . .," *The Midland Monthly*, VII, 3 (March, 1897), 226.

Resignation Endorsement

———

[*April, 1847*]

I should be permitted to resign the position of Quartermaster and Commissary. Why should I be required to resign my position in the Army in order to escape this duty: I *must* and *will* accompany my regiment in battle, and I am amenable to court-martial should any loss occur to the public property in my charge by reason of my absence while in action.

John W. Emerson, "Grant's Life in the West . . .," *The Midland Monthly*, VII, 3 (March, 1897), 219. This was an endorsement upon a USG letter resigning his quartermaster post which had been returned to him by Bvt. Col. John Garland with the following endorsement.

> I. The resignation of Lieutenant Grant is not accepted, and Lieutenant Grant is informed that the duty of Quartermaster and Commissary is an *assigned* duty, and not an *office* that can be resigned. As this duty was imposed by a military order from a superior officer, the duty cannot be evaded except by a like order relieving Lieutenant Grant from the duty.
>
> II. The good of the service requires that Lieutenant Grant continue to perform the duties of Quartermaster and Commissary in the Fourth Infantry. However valuable his services might be, and certainly would be, in *line*, his services in his present assigned duties cannot be dispensed with, and Lieutenant Grant will continue in their discharge.

The letter with both endorsements was forwarded to brigade, division, and general headquarters, and eventually to the war department, with Col. Garland's course approved at each stop.

To John W. Lowe

Tepey Ahualco Mexico
May 3d 1847

DEAR LOWE

Just as the troops were leaving Vera Cruz I recieved a letter from my young friend Tom[1] and yourself. Now that we will probably be stationary for four or five days I avail my self of the opportunity of answering. I see that you have written me several letters which you have not recieved answers to. I always make it a point to answer all your letters and am only sorry that I dont get more of them. You say you would like to hear more about the war. If you had seen as much of it as I have you would be tired of the subject. Of our success at Vera Cruz you have read evry thing. The strength of the town its Forts and Castle the

papers are full and they do not exagerate. On the 13th of April
the rear Division of Gen. Scotts army left Vera Cruze to ascend
the mountains and drive Santa Anna from his strong position in
one of the Passes. On the night of the 15th Gen. Worth arrived
at Plana del Rio three miles from the Battle ground. Gen. Twiggs
with his Division had been there several days prepairing for an
attack. By the morning of the 17th the way was completed to go
arround the Pass, Cierra Gordo, and make the attack in the rear
as well as in front. The difficulties to surmount made the undertaking almost equal to Bonapartes Crossing the Alps. Cierra
Gorda is a long narrow Pass the mountains towring far above
the road on either side. Some five of the peaks were fortified
and armed with Artillery and Infantry. At the outlett of the
Mountain Gorge a strong Breast work was thrown up and 5
pieces placed [into] embrasure sweeping the road so that it
would have been impossible for any force in the world to have
advanced. Immediately behind this is a peak of the Mountains
several hundred feet higher than any of the others and commanding them. It was on this hight that Gen. Twiggs made his attack.
As soon as the Mexicans saw this hight taken they knew the day
was up with them. Santa Anna Vamoused with a small part of
his force leaving about 6000 to be taken prisoner with all their
arms supplies &c. Santa Anna's loss could not have been less
than 8000 killed, wounded taken prisoners and misen. The pursuit was so close upon the retreating few that Santa Anna's
carriage and mules were taken and with them his wooden leg
and some 20 or 30 thousand dollars in money. Between the
thrashing the Mexicans have got at Buon Vista, Vera Cruz and
Cierra Gorde they are so completely broken up that if we only
had transportation we could go to the City of Mexico and where
ever els we liked without resistance. Garrisons could be established in all the important towns and the Mexicans prevented
from ever raising another army. Santa Anna is said to be at
Orazaba, at the foot of a mountain always covered with snow
and of the same name. He has but a small force. Orazaba looks
from here as if you could almost throw a stone to it, but it looked

the same from Jalapa some fifty miles back and was even visable from Vera Cruze. Since we left the Sea Coast the improvement in the appearance of the people and the stile of building has been very visable over any thing I had seen in Mexico before. The road is one of the best in the world. The scenery is beautiful and a great deal of magnificent table land spreads out above you and below you. Jalapa is the most beautiful place that I ever saw. It is about 4000 feet abov[e the] sea and being in the Torrid zone, they have th[ere] everlasting spring. Fruit and vegitables the year around. I saw there a great many handsome ladies and more well dressed men than I had ever seen before in the Republic. From Jalapa we marched to Perote and walked quietly into the strong Castle that you no doubt have read about. It is a great work. One Brigade, the one I belong to is now 20 miles in advance of Perote. Soon no doubt we will advance upon Puebla. I am Regtl Quarter Master appointed under the new law allowing one to each Reg.t and giving extra allowances.—Remember me to all your family and Judge Fishbacks.[2] Tel Tom he must write to me again

I will be much pleased to recieve all the letters you will write to me and all that Tom will write too. I will write to Tom from Puebla. I suppose we will be there in a few days. If you see any of the Beth[el] people please remember me to them. Tell them I am hartily tired of the wars. If you were to s[ee] me now you would never recognize me in the world[.] I have a beard more than four inches long and it [is] red.

> Your Friend   U. S. GRANT
> 4th Inf.y

ALS, InU. See letter to Lowe, June 26, 1846.

1. Thomas Lowe, son of John Lowe.
2. Judge Fishback was Lowe's father-in-law.

To Julia Dent

———

No (1)
Puebla Mexico
May 17th 1847

MY DEAREST JULIA

I rec'd your sweet letter marked No (1) at Tepeyahualco
the evening before we left there and would have answered it that
night but I was very sick with the chills & fever. In that letter
you spoke of what a good nurse you are. How much I wished
then I could be with you! We started the next morning for this
place and I was sick all the way but I am well now. At a little
town about ten miles from here our troops had a small fight but
no one on our side was hurt. A few of the Mexicans were killed.
Santa Anna is said to be ten or twelve miles in our advance
fortifying a Bridge but I suppose we will not go there for a few
weeks to molest him. Puebla is much the largest city we have
yet seen in Mexico. It contains from 80 to 90 thousand inhabitants. The houses are large and well built. It surpasses St. Louis
by far both in appearance and size ~~but~~ the mass of the people are
the same[1] beings that we have seen all over the country. At a
certain ring of the church bell or when the senior Priest of the
place passes you might see them on their nees in the streets all
over the city[2] Although we are now within a few days march of
the capitall of the Mexican Republic I do not see that the chances
for peace brighten in the least. The people are proud ~~ignorant~~
and subject to the will of a few and they have no government to
act for them.—The 5th Inf.y is now with us. I see Fred frequently.
Of course we are the best friends in the world and I will do as you
request, keep him out of mischief. How much my Dearest Julia
I regret that I had not taken my Fathers advice and resigned
long ago. Now no doubt I would have been comfortably in business and been always near one of whom I am always thinking and
whom I love better than all the world besides. The night after I
rec'd your last letter I dreamed that I had been ordered on the

recruiting service and was near where you were. In my dream,
I said now I have often dreamed of being near my dear Julia but
this time it is no dream for here are houses that I recollect well
and it is only two days travel to St. Louis; but when I woke up
in the morning and found that it was but a dream after all how
disappointed I was! My Dearest how much I wish I could see
you here for one day to see all the grand churches, the beautiful
public walks &c. &c. they are far superior to anything you
expect. The churches of the city are very numerous and extravigantly furnished. We are now quartered in a Convent. This
place from its elevation is very healthy and much more pleasant
both in summer and winter, so far as climate is concerned, than
Jeff. Bks. You ask if Fred. is in earnest about his attachment for
Miss Cross. I believe he is but you must not tell him that I told
you so. He recieves letters from her. My Dearest Julia if this
war is to continue for years yet as it may possibly do (but I do
not think it will) can I stay here and be separated from you
(whom I love so much) all the time? I have no intention of
anything of the kind. In the course of a few months more I will
see you again if it costs me my commission which by the way I
value very low for I have been a very long time ballancing in my
mind whether I would resign or not. At one time about two years
ago or near that, I was offered a proffessorship in a College in a
very pretty town in Ohio and now I regret that I did not go there.[3]
I often think how pleasantly I would have been settled now had
I gone. No doubt you would have been with me dearest and I
have always been happy when I was near you. My Dearest Julia
before now I would have applied for a leave of absence and in-
sisted upon geting it had your father and mother given their
consent to our engagement. I do not doubt but they will give it,
but when I go to Mo. I would like you to become mine forever
my dearest, and if I am to stay in the army I would come back
myself and see the war out. Mexico is a delightful country[4]
May 23d   My Dearest Julia I have had no opportunity of mailing this since we have been here. I am now perfectly recovered
from the chills and fever of which I had an attack. There is but

little news here. Santa Anna is taking a position between here
and the City of Mexico but the people of the country seem to be
disatisfied with him and there are very many of them who would
be glad to hear of his death either by violance or otherwise.—
Fred is well. You must remember me and him to Mr. Elting.⁵
Give my love to all at White Haven. Ask Ellen if I have won
that bet. I bet that her and Ben Farrer would make friends in
two years.—You must write to me often dearest for I get all
your letters. Number them and I will tell you if I loose any.
I intend writing to you very often so that if any letters should be
lost you will hear still often enough to know how much I love
you and whether I am sick or well.—I have not heard from Mr.
Dana⁶ lately but the last I heard he was improving. He is in
Jalapa. I rec'd the two flowers you kissed and sent me. It is very
pleasant my Dearest to get a kiss from you even on a flower that
has to travel two thousand miles to reach me but how much
more pleasant it would be if I could be with you to steal a real
one! I think I will be entitled to several when I get back to Mo.
—When you write to John and Lewis remember me to them.
Tell them they must whip the Mexicans badly at their end of
Mexico, we have whiped them so often here that we are geting
tired. Write often very often Dearest

to Your affectionate
ULYSSES

ALS, DLC-USG.

1. Three words crossed out.
2. One and a half lines crossed out.
3. See letters of [*Oct.*] and Nov. 11, 1845.
4. One line crossed out.
5. 2nd Lt. Norman Elting of N.Y., had resigned Oct. 29, 1846.
6. See letter of April 24, 1847.

To Julia Dent

———

No 2.

Puebla Mexico

May 26th 1847

MY DEAREST JULIA

I wrote you a long letter a few days ago and marked it No 1 and now I will write you again believing that it is doubtful if the other ever reaches. There are no troops going from here to Vera Cruze and the road is so infested with Mexican armed men that a mail stands but a small chance of reaching there, but coming this way they are well guarded with the new troops that are constantly arriving   I cannot venture to write you as I otherwise would lest some day my letter might be in the hands of the enemy. I am very well and so is Fred. I saw him this morning. As I told you in my other letter, Puebla is a beautiful, large, and well built city, surpassing anything we had seen before in Mexico. The climate is delightful but yet I long very much to be back to my old home and particularly to the first home I had after entering the army. You must write me long letters my Dearest Julia and expect short ones for a short time until the line from here to the sea coast is more safe. Remember me to all at White Haven and wish for my speedy return to the states. I will closeing this hoping that you may recieve my other letter yet fearing that you will not.

My Dearest Julia Adieu

ULYSSES

ALS, DLC-USG.

To Julia Dent

————

Puebla Mexico
August 4th 1847

MY DEAREST JULIA

A few days ago I wrote you a short letter in answer to yours telling me of the report you had heard, hearing at that time that a privat express was going to Vera Cruz, but after writing it I found that the express had left before I had as much as heard that one was to leave.—You must not attribute you geting but few and but short letters from me to any disinclination on my part to writing them. No my dearest I would be willing to write you a whole sheet evry day if you could but get my letters. I have told you before, but I will now repeat it, that but few Mails go from here to Vera Cruz and those are in great danger of being captured as several of them have been. Mails coming in this direction are much safer from the fact that troops are constantly joining the army from that direction.—I recieved another letter from you by some troops that come in last evening and one too that gave me more happiness than any previous one that I have ever recieved. It not only assured me that you were satisfied falsity of the report you mentioned in your previous one (why did you not tell me my Dearest the object the man could have had in perpetrating such a falshood) but it set me at rest on another subject. You know how often I have asked you if your Pa would give his concent to our engagement. I know now that he will and I am happy. My greatest trouble now is how am I to get back and when. I think certainly by Fall. If I thought another year was to pass over first I would be miserable. The same mail that brought your letter brought [me] several from home. My sister Virginia said in her's that of all ~~the~~ persons in the world except myself she wants most to see you and she wants to see us both in Bethel soon. I sincerly hope Dear Julia that her wish may be gratified. This waring in a foreign country does very well for a while but a person who has attachments at home will get tired of it in much less time than I have been at it. I believe I have told you before that of all the countries and all the climates on Earth no other people are so blessed by Nature as the inhabitants of this part of Mexico.[1] The church has all the power, all the wealth[2] I think I would be safe in saying that three fourths of the expence of building Puebla has been in churches and church property.—When we will move towards Mexico is not known unless it is by the Commanding-General. We hear a great many reports of there being a strong peace party in the city of Mexico who are only waiting our approach to come out boldly but I do not know how true it is. I have not seen Fred. for a day or two but I know he is well. Give my love to all at White Haven. I will close this with a P.S. when I find I can mail it

Yours most Devotedly
Ulysses

Julia

August 8th P. S.   I have not yet had an opportunity of mailing this letter and do not know when I will have—To morrow we start for the City of Mexico where no doubt we will have another big fight. Rest assured my Dearest Julia I will not let an opportunity of geting out of Mexico escape me after I have once seen the Capittal.

U

ALS, DLC-USG.

1. Two lines crossed out.
2. One-half line crossed out.

Addressee Unknown

———

[*Aug. 22, 1847*]

I wondered what must be the emotions of General Scott, thus surrounded by the plaudits of his army.[1] The ovation was genuine, and from the hearts of his men. This has been the greatest battle of all, and it looks now as if the city would yield without another. May heaven grant it, for the slaughter of our men is greater than ever before, and worse than death is the awful suffering of the torn and wounded on both sides.

While the cheers were going up for General Scott, General Rincon,[2] one of the captured Mexican prisoners confined in the church, was standing at a window leaning out; he uncovered his head, and his countenance lighted up, and his eyes sparkled with every manifestation of delight. I have no doubt but the old veteran, animated with the chivalrous instincts of the true soldier, when he heard the plaudits which the General received from the brave men he had so recently led to victory, forgot that *he* was defeated and a prisoner, and for the moment entered into the enthusiasm of the occasion.

Too much blood has been shed. Is it ended, or will hostilities be resumed? We are prepared for either event. I have tried to study the plan of campaign which the army has pursued since we entered the Valley of Mexico, and in view of the great strength of the positions we have encountered and carried by storm, I am wondering whether there is not some other route by which the city could be captured, without meeting such formidable obstructions, and at such great losses. If I should criticise, it would be contrary to military ethics, therefore I do not. There is no force in Mexico that can resist this army. To fight is to conquer. The Mexicans fight well for a while, but they do not hold out. They fight and simply quit. Poor fellows; if they were well drilled, well fed and well paid, no doubt they would fight and persist in it; but, as it is, they are put to the slaughter without avail.

John W. Emerson, "Grant's Life in the West . . .," *The Midland Monthly*, VII, 4 (April, 1897), 323–24. The final paragraph, printed on a separate page of Emerson's article, is assumed to be part of this letter.

1. The description is of Maj. Gen. Winfield Scott's reception by his army after the victory at Churubusco, Aug. 20, 1847.
2. Gen. Manuel Rincón had defended the convent at Churubusco.

Addressee Unknown

———

[*Sept. 12, 1847*]

You will thus see the difficult and brilliant work our army has been doing. If Santa Anna does not surrender the city, or peace be negotiated, much more hard fighting may be expected, as I foresee, before the city is captured. My observations convince me that we have other strong works to reduce before we can enter the city. Our position is such that we cannot avoid these. From my map and all the information I acquired while the army was halted at Puebla, I was then, and am now more than ever, convinced that the army could have approached the city by passing around north of it, and reached the northwest side, and avoided all the fortified positions, until we reached the gates of the city at their weakest and most indefensible, as well as most approachable points. The roads and defenses I had carefully noted on my map, and I had communicated the knowledge I had acquired from Mexican scouts in our camp, and others I met at Puebla who were familiar with the ground, to such of my superiors as it seemed proper, but I know not whether General Scott was put in possession of the information. It is to be presumed however, that the commanding General had possessed himself of all the facts.

It seems to me the northwest side of the city could have been approached without attacking a single fort or redoubt, we would have been on solid ground instead of floundering through morass and ditches, and fighting our way over elevated roads, flanked by water where it is generally impossible to deploy forces.

What I say is entirely confidential, and I am willing to believe that the opinion of a lieutenant, where it differs from that of his commanding General, *must* be founded on *ignorance* of the situation, and you will consider my criticisms accordingly.

John W. Emerson, "Grant's Life in the West . . .," *The Midland Monthly*, VII, 5 (May, 1897), 433.

To Julia Dent

————

City of Mexico
September 1847

MY DEAREST JULIA

Because you have not heard from me for so long a time you must not think that I have neglected to write or in the least forgotten one who is so ever dear to me. For several months no mail has gone to Vera Cruz except such as Editors of papers send by some Mexican they hire and these generally fall into the hands of the enemy who infest the wole line from here to the sea coast. Since my last letter to you four of the hardest fougt battles that the world ever witnessed have taken place, and the most astonishing victories have crowned the American arms. But dearly have they paid for it! The loss of officers and men killed and wounded is frightful. Among the wounded you will find Fred's name but he is now walking about and in the course of two weeks more will be entirely well. I saw Fred. a moment after he received his wounded[1] but escaped myself untouched. It is to be hoped that such fights it will not be our misfortune to witnessed again during the war, and how can be? The whole Mexican army is destroyed or disbursed, they have lost nearly all their artillery and other munitions of war; we are occupying the rich and populace valley from which the great part of their revenues are collected and all their sea ports are cut off from them. Evry thing looks as if peace should be established soon; but perhaps my anxiety to get back to see again my Dearest Julia makes me argue thus. The idea of staying longer in this country is to me insupportable. Just think of the three long years that have passed since we met. My health has always been good, but exposure to weather and a Tropicle Sun had added ten years to my apparent age. At this rate I will soon be old.—Out of all the officers that left Jefferson Barracks with the 4th Infantry but three besides myself now remains with us, besides this four or five who joined since, are gone. Poor Sidney Smith[2] was the last one killed. He was shot from one of the houses after we entered the city.

Mexico is one of the most beautiful cities in the world and being the capital no wonder that the Mexicans should have fought desperately to save it. But they deserve no credit. They fought us with evry advantage on their side. They doubled us in numbers, doubled us and more in artillery, they behind strong Breast-works had evry advantage and then they were fighting for their homes.[3] It[4] truly a great country. No country was ever so blessed ~~with~~ by nature. There is no fruit nor no grain that cant be raised here nor no temperature that cant be found at any season. You have only to choose the degree of elevation to find perpetual snow or the hotest summer. But with all these advantages how anxious I am to get out of Mexico. You can redily solve the problem of my discontent Julia. If you were but here and me in the United States my anxiety would be just as great to come to Mexico as it now is to get out.

Oct. 25th   At last a mail is to leave here for the U States I am glad at finally having an opportunity of leting you hear from me. A train is going to Vera Cruz and with it many of the wounded officers and men. Fred. is geting too well to be one of them. I am almost sorry that I was not one of the unfortunates so that now I could be going back. It is to be hoped that in future mails will be much more frequent though in fact it is generally believed that as soon as congress meets the whole army will be ordered from this valey of Mexico. There is no use of my teling you any more that I will take the first opportunity of geting back to Mo. for I have told you that so often, and yet no chance has occured. At present Gen. Scott will let no officer leave who is able for duty not even if he tenders his resignation. So you see it is not so easy to get out of the wars as it is to get into them. — Write to me often dearest Julia so if I cant have the pleasure of sending letters often to you let me at least enjoy the receipt of one from you by evry Mail coming this way. —No doubt before this the papers are teaming with accounts of the different battles and the courage and science shown by individuals. Even here one hears of individual exploits (which were never performed) sufficient to account for the taking of Mexico throwing out about four fifths of the army to do nothing. One bit of credit need not be given to accounts that are given except those taken from the reports of the different commanders.

Remember me my Dearest Julia to you father & mother and the rest of the family and pray that the time may not be far distant when we may take our walks again up and down the banks of the Gravois. Truly it will be a happy time for me when I see that stram again.

Farewell My Dearest Julia
U S GRANT

ALS, DLC-USG.

    1. 1st Lt. Frederick Dent received a thigh wound at the battle at Molino del Rey. USG discovered him and placed him on a wall to attract medical attention.
    2. 1st Lt. Sidney Smith of Va., died on Sept. 16, 1847, of wounds received two days earlier during the capture of Mexico City.
    3. Three lines crossed out.
    4. Two words crossed out.

To Julia Dent

———

Tacabaya Mexico
January 9th 1848

MY DEAR JULIA

Since I wrote to you last one Brigade has moved to this place which is about four miles from the City of Mexico and from being so much higher than the City is much more healthy. One Brigade has gone to Toluca and it is rumored that before a great while we will move to some distant part, either Queretero, Zacetecus, San Louis Potosi or Guernivaca[1] unless there is a strong probability of peace. It is now however strongly believed that peace will be established before many months. I hope it may be so for it is scarsely suportible for me to be separated from you

so long my dearest Julia. A few weeks ago I went to the commanding officer[2] of my Regiment and represented to him that
when the 4th Inf.y left Jefferson Barracks, three years ago last
May, I was engaged, and that I thought it high time that I should
have a leave of absence to go back. He told me that he would
approve it but I found that it would be impossible to get the
Comd.g Gen. to give the leave so I never made the application.
I have strong hopes though of going back in a few months. If
peace is not made it is at all events about my turn to go on
recruiting service. As to geting a sick leave that is out of the
question for I am never sick a day. Mexico is a very pleasant
place to live because it is never hot nor never cold, but I believe
evry one is hartily tired of the war. There is no amusements
except the Theatre and as the actors & actresses are Spanish but
few of the officers can understand them. The better class of
Mexicans dare not visit the Theatre or associate with the
Americans lest they should be assassinated by their own people
or banished by their Government as soon as we leave. A few
weeks ago a Benefit was given to a favorite actress and the
Govorner of Queretero hearing of it sent secret spies to take the
names of such Mexicans as might be caught in indulging in
amusements with the Americans for the purpose of banishing
them as soon as the *Magnanimous Mexican Republic* should drive
away the Barbarians of the North. I pity poor Mexico. ~~In~~ With
a soil and climate scarsely equaled in the world she has more poor
and starving subjects who are willing and able to work than any
country in the world. The rich keep down the poor with a
hardness of heart that is incredible. Walk through the streets of
Mexico for one day and you will see hundreds of begars, but
you never see them ask alms of their own people, it is always of
the Americans that they expect to recieve. I wish you could be
here for one short day then I should be doubly gratified. Gratified
at seeing you my dearest Julia, and gratified that you might see
too the manners and customs of these people. You would see
what you never dreamed of nor can you form a correct ~~I~~ idea
from reading.[3] All gamble Priests & civilians, male & female

and particularly so on Sundays.—But I will tell you all that I know about Mexico and the Mexicans when I see you which I do hope will not be a great while now. Fred. is in the same Brigade with me. I see him evry day. He like myself is in excellent health and has no prospect of geting out of the country on the plea of sickness.—I have one chance of geting out of Mexico soon besides going on recruiting service. Gen. Scott will grant leaves of absence to officers where there is over two to a Company. Inf my Reg.t there [are three] or four vacancies which will be fi[lled] soon [. . . .] h and will give an oportunity for [one] or two now here to go out. Give my love to all at White Haven and do not fail to write often dearest Julia. I write but seldom myself but it is because a mail but seldom goes from here to the sea coast. Coming this way it is different for the Volunteers are constantly arriving.

When you write next tell me if Mrs. Porter and Mrs. Higgins are married or likely to be.

Adieu My Dearest Julia

ULYSSES

ALS, DLC-USG, postmarked New Orleans, Feb. 15, 1848.

    1. Querétaro, San Luis Potosí, and Cuernavaca, are shown on the map. Zacatecas is about 400 miles northwest of Mexico City.
    2. Bvt. Col. Francis Lee of Pa., USMA 1822.
    3. Ten words crossed out.

To Julia Dent

———

Tacabaya Mexico
Feb.y 4th 1848

MY DEAREST JULIA

I recieved a few days ago your long sweet letter enclosing one from my father. By the same Mail I got another from home directed to Gen. Worth en[quiring] of the Gen.l my fate if I

was dead, or if al[ive] my whereabout; by the same Mail I also
got o[ne] from my sister Clara anouncing that they had at last,
after waiting six months, recieved a letter from me. She says
that they had recived a letter from Wren.[1] a few days before and
that you had desired to be remembered, and she begs me to come
home soon and take Julia along. How happy I should be to do so
and I hope it will not be long before I may claim that privilege.
There are several vacancies in the 4th Inf.y for 2d Lieutenants
and as soon as they are filled some two officers will be sent on
the recruiting service and I am certain that the commanding
officer will send me for one.—We are now stationed in the little
Village of Tacabaya about four miles from the City of Mexico
and you dont know how lonesom it is. But I ride into town all-
most evry day to pass away an hour or two. I do hope that if the
Mexicans dont make peace soon that our Government will decide
upon occupying this whole country then the married officers
would bring their families here and with the society we would
then have I would not want a better station, except I would never
be satisfied unless you were here too, my Dearest Julia. Would
you come to Mexico? I look forward to the the time for my going
back to Missouri with a great anxiety and dont you think it too
bad that I have never got leave to go! Fred. is here in Tacabaya
and is very well.—I asked him why he had not written to you
and he says he has written by evry mail. There was a time when
no mail went from here to the U. States for about five months
and it was in consequence of this that they never heard from me
from at home. I never let an opportunity of sending a letter pass
without writing.

    Feb.y 13th   A train starts for Vera Cruz in a day or two
and I will now close this letter. Peace news is stronger than ever.
Commissioners have agreed upon terms of peace and if Congress
confirms their conditions it is thought that we will all be on our
way in sixty days from this time. If I was certain that in this time
we were going how long the time would appear—How strange
it will be for you to see the 4th Inf.y again and how sad too.
When we left Jefferson Barracks I was a Brevet 2d Lieutenant

and the youngest officer in the Regiment now there are some fifteen Lieutenants below me all new faces in the Reg.t. One after another has fallen until but few of the old ones are left. Dont you recollect Cap.t Alvord & Lt. Gore?[2] they are both here and the proudest men now that they are married. They both speak frequently of you. I saw Cap.t Gardinier in town af a few days ago.[3] The first thing he asked me was about you. He told me that I need not blush for he knew all about our engagement, that [you] used to make rather a confident of him. I used to think so from the way you spoke of him sometimes in your letters.—I should like to see Fanny Higgins very much to see the alteration it makes in her having her eyes straitened.[4]—I have not yet delivered the message that Ellen sent to Jarvis but I will and he will take it in the greatest earnest too. Tell Miss Ellen that I cannot give up that I have lost that bet that we made some years ago but on the contrary she is the loser. Give my love to your Pa & Ma and the res[t of] the family and write dearest Julia very often. If [a] Mail does not start for a few days I will try and write to Wrenshall. You say that I must send back the letter you sent me from my home but I do not know what I have done with it. The letters I get from you I keep with me generally about a week so that I can read them over and over again when ever I am by my self—then I put them [in] my chest.

Julia wont you send me your Daguerotype? How very much I would like to have it to look at since I must be deprived of seeing the original.

Write my Dear Julia as often as you can to one who loves you so much

 ULYSSES

ALS, DLC-USG.

1. Refers to Julia's brother, George Wrenshall Dent.
2. Bvt. Maj. Benjamin Alvord of Vt., USMA 1833, and Bvt. Maj. John H. Gore of Md.
3. See letter of April 3, 1847.
4. USG's interest may have been based on Julia's strabismus. See Ishbel Ross, *The General's Wife* (New York, 1959), pp. 220–22.

To Julia Dent

Tacabaya Mexico
March 22d 1848

MY DEAREST JULIA

I recieved a day or two ago your sweet letter, sweeter because it had been so long since I had recieved one before. Two Mails come to the City of Mexico without bringing a letter from you. I never let a Mail go from here without writing to you still you accuse me of neglect and say that you had determined to not write again until you had recieved an answer to some of your last letters. You must not make any such resolutions as this dear Julia for as I have told you a thousand times before I am never so happy as when I hear from you and I could not neglect you. You say in your sweet letter that you would be happy to come to me! How happy I should be if such a thing was possible. If you were here I should never wish to leave Mexico. but as it is I am nearly crazy to get away. I applied for leave of absence a few weeks ago but Gen. Butlter[1] refused to give it. The only chance at present is for peace to be made which we are very sanguine will be made, but you know more on this subject than we do here. I see that you and my sister have commenced a correspondence. I hope it may prove interesting but unless Clara takes more pains in writing to you than she does writing to me I fear that her letters will fail to interest you. I have not seen Fred. for more than a week but as a mail starts from here to-day I suppose he will write to you.—Tacubaya is a very healthy place but it is so dull here. It is about four miles to the City and as I have several horses at my disposal I generally gallop into town evry day and spend an hour or two. I wish you could be here to take one of these rides with me and see the beautiful Valley of Mexico. The whole Valley is spread out to the view covered with numerous lakes, green fields, and little Villages and to all appearance it would be a short ride to go around the whole valley in a day, but you would find that it would take a week. It is always spring here the winter months being the most pleasant.—Herr Alexander, the great Jugler, has been amusing the people of Mexico for the last ten days. A great many respectable Mexicans male & female attend which argues well that these people at least believe that we will have pease. Before the armistice and treaty were entered into the Mexican people could not visit a place of amusement which was attended by the Americans. Their own people would not allow them.

I have no news to tell you Dearest Julia. Those officers who, you know are generally well. I have not seen Cap.t Gardinier, who says he is your confidant, for some time, but he is in town and I know wants to be remembered to you.—I dont intend to make any more bets with Miss Ellen for I see that she would claim the wager, win or loose. I will forgive the debt this time. Give my love to all of the family and to my acq[uain]tances. From your letter I suppose Georgia[2] [M.] is married before this? Remember me to Misses Geo[rgia] and Fanny.—Write often dearest Julia to one who always thinks but one who unhappily cannot dream of you often. If I could only always see you and talk with you in my dreams whenever I closed my eyes to sleep, I should be much better satisfied. Adieu my dearest Julia

Ulysses

ALS, DLC-USG.

1. Maj. Gen. of Vols. William Orlando Butler succeeded to command of U.S. forces in Mexico on Feb. 18, 1848, when Maj. Gen. Winfield Scott was relieved. W. L. Marcy to Scott, Jan. 13, 1848, *HED*, 30–1, 60, p. 1044.

2. Georgia Morrison, sister of Fanny Morrison Higgins. Both were daughters of Maj. Pitcairn Morrison.

To Julia Dent

———

Tacubaya Mexico
May 7th 1848

DEAREST JULIA

I have not recieved a letter from you for two months or more until two days ago, but when one did come it was most welcom. It has been a good while since I wrote to you but I can easily explain the reason. On the 3d of April I started with a party to go to the top of Popocatapetl the highest mountain in North America. From the mountain a portion of us went across into the Valley of Cuernavaca to visit the great mammoth cave of Mexico. On this trip I was absent from Mexico sixteen days and in the mean time a mail went off. The day after my return another mail started but I did not hear of it until I saw it leaving, so you see my dearest Julia you cannot attach any criminality to my apparent neglect. What must I think of you. just think two long months without hearing from one that I love so much.[1] Well I do not blame you[2] so long as you dont forget me and love me as you say you do.

There is a great deal of talk of peace here now. The knowing ones say that the Mexican Congress will ratify the terms proposed and that the advance of the American Army will be on its way for Vera Cruz in three weeks.[3] I atleast hope dear Julia that it will not be long before I can see you again. It is too bad aint it? just think we have been engaged almost four years and have met but once in that time, that was three years ago.

I see Fred almost evry day. I told him what you desired me to. Fred read me a little of Miss Ellen's letter[4]

The trip to the snow mountain and to the cave was very pleasant and would have been more so had we succeeded in geting to the top, but the weather was so unfavorable that all failed. The day that we arrived at the foot of the mountain we ascended about one half of the way to the top and there encamped for the night. We had been there but a short time when it began to blow

rain, hale & snow most terrificaly and of course we were in bad
plight next morning for ascending a mountain which is difficult
at best   Next morning however we started through a snow
storm which had continued from the night before and the wind
blowing hard enough almost to carry a person away. The snow
on the mountain drifted so rapidly that it was impossible to see
over thirty or forty yards in any direction so we lost the view
that we would have had of the surrounding valleys. We ploded
on for several hours through all these difficulties when all found
that it was perfect madness to attempt to go farther, so we turned
back when about 1000 feet below the Crater. That night about
the time we were going to lay down, first one person would
complain of his eyes hurting him then another and by 9 o'clock
evry one was suffering the most excrusiating pain in the eyes.
There was but little sleeping done by the party that night. Next
morning nine of the officers were blind so that they were obliged
to have their horses led   One day however restored evry one so
far that it was determined not to give up the expediti[on]   We
then divided, a portion waiting for a favorable [day] succeeded
in reaching the top of the Mountain, the rest of us passing over
a low ridge commenced descending and after twenty miles of
gradual descent arrive in tierra Calliente, or hot county, Here
much to our surprise on approaching quite a large ~~large~~ town
we were halted by some Mexican officers who forbid our entring
the place. The commander said that the place was occupied by
Mexican troops and by the terms of the Armistice we were
obliged to content our selvs out side of town that night. We
met troops at three other places before we reached the cave.
They showed no hostile feeling but were very punctillious in
their observance of the armistice. The fact is they wanted to
annoy us by making 'us go around without seeing their towns.
Traveling through tierra Calliente is a beautiful and strange
sight to a Northerner. All seasons of the year you will find
vegetation in full bloom. We passed some of the most beautiful
sugar Plantations in the world and finest buildings in the world.
They beat any in Louisiana. Evry one has on it fine coffe fields

and orchards of Tropical fruits such as oranges Bananas and twenty kinds of fruit that I never heard of until I came to Mexico. I have written so long that I must close with telling you that after six days travel from the snow Mountain through this beautiful valley we arrive at the great cave of Mexico and explored it to a considerable distance. The cave is exceedingly large and like the Mammoth cave of Kentucky its extent has never been found out. Some of the formations are very singular. One would think that they were works of art. We had with us torches and rocketts and the effect of them in that place of total darkness was beautiful.[5]

Give my love to all at home. Dont forget to write often. Two months is too long to wait for a letter from one that I love so much.

Adieu My Dear Dear Julia
ULYSSES

P. S. I would take another sheet and give you a more minute discription of my trip but there is an officer waiting, very impatiently for me to get through and go to town where I am obliged to. Dont neglect to write very soon and very often Dearest Julia

ALS, DLC-USG, postmarked Vera Cruz, May 11, 1848.

    1. Two lines crossed out.
    2. Two words crossed out.
    3. The Mexican Congress ratified the Treaty of Guadalupe Hidalgo on May 25, 1848, and the two governments exchanged formal notifications five days later. The evacuation of U.S. troops from Mexico City began that same day (May 30) and was completed on June 12, 1848.
    4. Five lines crossed out.
    5. An account of the expedition is in *Memoirs*, I, 180–90.

To Bvt. Brig. Gen. Roger Jones

———

Head Quarters, 4th Infantry
Tacubaya, Mexico
May 19th 1848.

SIR

I have the honor to inform you, that their has been no Recruits enlisted in the Regiment, during this Quarter, consequently my Recruiting Account remains the same as per last Return

Sir
I am very Respectfully
To   Your Obed. Servt.
Genl. R. Jones   U S GRANT
Adjt. Genl. U S A   1st Lt. 4th Inf.y
Washington, D C   Recruiting Officer

LS, DNA, RG 94, Letters Received.

To Julia Dent

———

Tacubaya Mexico
May 22d 1848

MY DEAREST JULIA

I have just recieved your sweet letter of the 17th of April and hasten to answer it. I have no doubt but this will be my last letter from Mexico. Peace is certain and already evry preparation is being made to move the troops to Vera Cruz. I think by the 1st of June there will not be an American soldier in the City of Mexico and by the last of June probably not on Mexican soil. What will be our destination it is hard to guess but we will have some perminant station and I am determined to have a leave of absence. So my dear Julia I think by July at farthest I shall be able to claim some of the kisses that you have sent me in your letters. No doubt many troops will be sent on the Rio Grande and others to Calafornia but wherever they go officers who have families will take them along. If the 4th go to Calafornia will you go with me? But I know you will. You have often told me that you were willing to go with me any place. I am happy at the idea of geting away from Mexico at last because I will be able to see my dear dear Julia again and I hope not to separate. But for this I would be contented to remain in Mexico for ever.

Our Commissioners left the City this morning for Caratro and no doubt will give us full news of the confirmation[1] of the Treaty being co by the Mexican Government in the course of a week. Byt that time all will be ready to start and away we will go for our homes, many of us with lighter hearts than we started here with.

Even on the extreme borders of our Territory, with the society that a Garrison will necessarily make, and with you there too, I shall be very happy.

Fred has recieved his sword. I see him evry day is quite well. I told him that you were going to write to him the next week. I send you this letter by Cap.t Morris[2] who is going out of the country on a sick. leave.

I suppose you have read of the attempt to rob a large house in the City of Mexico and in which several officers were concerned? The officers are Lt. Tilden 2d Inf.y & Lts. Dutton & Hare Pa. Volunteers.[3] They have been tried and their guilt established and on Thirsday next are to be hung. Tilden was a Cadet one year with Fred and me. I will write you but a short letter this time but with the firm belief that I shall be the bearer of the next one myself.

Give my love to your family. I will make Fred write before we leave the City of Mexico.

Yours devotedly
ULYSSES

Julia

ALS, DLC-USG, marked on envelope "Politeness of Cap.t Morris 4th Inf.y."

    1. The Mexican Congress met at Queretaro. For the confirmation, see letter of May 7, 1848.
    2. Bvt. Maj. Gouverneur Morris.
    3. 1st Lt. Bryant Parrot Tilden of Mass., USMA 1840, resigned June 6, 1848; 1st Lt. Benjamin F. Dutton and 1st Lt. Isaac Hare of the 2nd Pa. Vols.

To Julia Dent

———

Tacubaya Mexico
June 4th 1848

MY DEAREST JULIA

    I wrote you a letter about two weeks ago saying that I should not probably ever write to you again from this part of Mexico. But as there is a Mail going in a few days, and it will probably go faster than the troops will march, I will write to you again and for the last time, from here. Peace is at last concluded and the most of the troops are on their way to Vera Cruz. On Thursday next the last of the troops in the Valley of Mexico will leave and I think by the 25th or 30th of July I may count on being in St. Louis. The thought of seeing you so soon is a happy one dearest Julia but I am so impatient that I have the *Blues* all the time. A great many of the business people, in fact nearly all of them, want to see us remain in the country. Already a revolution is looked for as soon as our backs are turned. People who have associated with the Americans are threatened with having their ears & noses cut off as soon as their protectors leave. Gen. Terrace[1] of the Mexican army lives here in Tacubaya with his family. He has five daughters young ladies who are very sociable with officers of the U. S. Army. A few weeks ago an Aid-de-Camp of Gen. Velasco[2] threatened to mark their faces as soon as we left. The threat reached the ears of one of the officers who was in the habit of visiting the young ladies and he gave the valient A. D. C. who was going to make war against innocent females, a good thrashing in a public place, and much to the amusement of the by-standers. Already some barbarities have been committed such as shaving the heads of females, and I believe in one or two cases they cut their ears off.[3] Yesterday an officer had his horse saddle and bridle stolen in broad day light and from the very dencest part of the city. Such thefts are very common. I most hartily rejoice at the prospect of geting out of Mexico though I prefer the country and climate to any I have ever yet seen.

I am going to write you but a short letter dearest Julia because I expect to start at the same time this does. Our march to Vera Cruz I fear will be attended with much fatigue and sickness. Already the rainy season is begining to set in and at Vera Cruz there has been several cases of Yellow fever. Evry precaution will be taken to keep the troops from geting sick however.

We are all to halt and encamp before we get to the coast and as fast as transportation is ready the troops will be marched aboard at night and push off immediately.

Give my love to all. Fred. is well. Write to me again as soon as you recieve this and direct as usual. Wherever a Mail meets us it will be stoped and we will get our letters.

Adieu but for a short time
Ulysses

Julia

ALS, DLC-USG.

1. Gen. Terrace is apparently Gen. Terrés.
2. Gen. Velasco may be Velázquez.
3. Four lines crossed out.

Sworn Statement

———

Camp Jalapa Mexico
June 27th 1848.

Statement

About the 6th of June, at Tacubaya Mexico, I took to Capt Gore's room the sum of $1000.00 Qr. Mr. funds, to be locked up in his trunk for safe keeping, my own chest having previously had the lock broken. I also deemed it safer to have Public money in the room of some Officer who did not disburse public funds, because they would be less likely to be suspected of having any conciderable amount about them. On the night of the 16th of June 1848 as Shown by the accompanying affidavits, the trunk containing these funds was Stolen from the tent of Capt. Gore whilst he and Lieut De Russy 4th Infantry were both sleeping in the tent

U. S. GRANT
1st Lt. 4th Inf.y
Reg.l Q M

sworn to before me, this 27th day of June 1848, at Camp near Jalapa Mexico.

H. D. WALLEN
1 Lt. 4th Infantry
Judge advocate
Genl Court Mar.l

DS, Mr. and Mrs. Philip D. Sang, River Forest, Ill. This document was discussed by Mary A. Benjamin, "Grant and the Lost $1000," *The Collector*, LXIX, 2, 3 (Feb.–March, 1956), 17–20. Also described was the report of a board of inquiry, called by Gen. Worth at USG's request, composed of Bvt. Col. Francis Lee of Pa., 1st Lt. De Lancey Floyd-Jones of N.Y., USMA 1846, and Bvt. Capt. Maurice Maloney, which concluded "that no blame can attach to Lt. U. S. Grant, that he took every means to secure the Money—that the place he deposited it was the most secure in camp, and they exonerate him from all censure." Also described were three affidavits, each written by USG and attested by 1st Lt. Henry Davies

Wallen. Bvt. Maj. John H. Gore, June 26, 1848, swore to the facts USG had presented. 1st Lt. Floyd-Jones swore "that I assisted Lieut. U. S. Grant . . . in counting a bag of Money that he brought into his quarters sometime early in the month of June. The amount was exactly one thousand Dollars, which we (Lieut. Grant and myself) put in a bag and the said Lieut. Grant took the money and said he would place it in Captain Alvords trunk—We understood afterwards that the money was placed in the trunk of Captain Gore. . . ." 2nd Lt. John De Russy of N.Y., USMA 1847, swore "On or about the night of the 16th of June, whilst encamped in the vicinity of Puebla the trunk containing said funds was stolen from the tent of Capt. Gore, this whilst Capt. Gore and myself were both sleeping in the tent."

Exoneration by board of inquiry did not relieve USG of the necessity of reimbursing the government. On Jan. 30, 1849, David Fisher of Wilmington, Ohio, presented the House of Representatives with "The Memorial of U. S. Grant, of the United States Army, praying to be released from further payment to the government, of public moneys which were stolen from him near Jalapa, in Mexico; which was referred to the Committee on Military Affairs." *House Journal*, 30–2, p. 345. The same petition was reintroduced in the next congress by Jonathan Morris of Batavia, Ohio, the son of Jesse Grant's friend, Senator Thomas Morris. *Ibid.*, 31–1, p. 1073. Again no action resulted. See letter of June 20, 1852.

To Julia Dent

Bethel Ohio
August 7th 1848

Monday evening
MY DEAREST JULIA

I have just arrived at home and find all my family in good health. They had not recieved my letter written from the mouth of the Ohio so I took them all by surprise. About seven miles from home a young lady took passage in the same stage with [*me*] and hearing that my name was Grant enquired if I was not a brother of Virginia Grant's. She said that she had been at the same boarding-school with my sister and would call and see her while the stages were changing. From this we got into conversation and rode quietly up to my fathers house where I was quite attentive in assisting the young lady out and looking after her baggage. They all thought as much as could be that it was Julia that I had brought home, and infact upon making some calls an hour or two afterwards I was told that she had understood that I had brought Mrs. Grant home with me. See how easy it is in a country vilage to give a report circulation!

I felt as unhappy Dear Julia after leaving you as I did happy upon seeing you first. The whole way, I done nothing but think of you, and of how happy I should be at our next meeting. But then you know how very much I love you and how could we part without ~~without~~ my grieving. I will leave here on Thursday and reach St. Louis Sunday night or Monday morning. One of my Sisters would accompany me only they say they cannot get ready by the time I want to start.

After my arrival Dear Julia I hope we shall never be so long separated again. My feelings since I left you the last time convinc

AL, DLC-USG. The letter ends in mid-word, mid-page, and apparently never was completed. The bulk of the 4th Inf. left camp near Jalapa, Mexico, on July 11, 1848, and arrived at Camp Jefferson Davis, East Pascagoula, Miss., on July 23, 1848. "Annual Return of the Alterations and Casualties . . . Fourth Regiment of Infantry . . . 1848," DNA, RG 94. That same day USG was replaced as regt. q.m. by 1st Lt. Henry D. Wallen, and USG began a sixty day leave by special orders no. 124 of Maj. Gen. Zachary Taylor which included permission to apply for a two month extension. Copy, DNA, RG 98, Western Division, Special Orders. USG returned to St. Louis from Bethel and married Julia Dent on Aug. 22, 1848.

To Bvt. Maj. Gen. Roger Jones

Bethel Ohio
Sep.t 1st 1848

G EN.

I have the honor, herewith, to transmit the enlistments of Charles, & William Saunders,[1] together with the written concent of their mother, their only surviving parent.

I am Sir
Your Obt. Svt.
U. S. G RANT

To Gen. R. Jones
Adj.t Gen.

1st Lt. 4th Inf.y
Recruiting Officer

My Recruiting Return, & Account Current with Lt. Maloney's[2] receipt for the Recruiting funds in my possession are made out for transmittal, but the present Reg.l Commander refuses to sign them on account of his not having been in Command during the time for which they were made out. I cannot therefore forward them until they are signed by the former commander, Maj. Lee 4th Infy who is now absent.

Respectfully
Your Obt. Svt.
U. S. G RANT

Gen. R. Jones
Adj. Gen U.S.A.

1st Lt. 4th Inf.y
Recruiting Officer

ALS, DNA, RG 94, Letters Received.

1. Charles and William Sanders enlisted in the 4th Inf. for five years at Palo Alto, Tex., Feb. 1, 1847. On April 21, 1847, John M. McCalla, Second Auditor, wrote to USG. "I herewith respectfully return for correction the enlistments of William and Charles Sanders—they being minors, the written consent of the mother must be obtained. See par. 22 of the Revised Recruiting Regulations." Copy, DNA, RG 217, Second Auditor Letters Sent. See letter of Feb. 12, 1850. William and Charles Sanders were thirteen and twelve years old when they enlisted.

2. Bvt. Capt. Maurice Maloney, born in Ireland, joined the 4th Inf. as a private on Nov. 5, 1836, and was then serving as regt. adjt. The regt. was commanded by Col. William Whistler of Md., who had succeeded Col. Josiah Vose on July 15, 1845, but had not served in Mexico.

To Maj. Gen. Zachary Taylor

———

Bethel Ohio
Sep.t 1st 1848.

G<small>EN</small>

I have the honor, very respectfuly to request an extension of two months to my present leave of absence

I am Sir
Very Respectfully
Your Obt. Svt.
U. S. G<small>RANT</small>
1st Lt. 4th Inf.y

ALS, PHi. A notation in DNA, RG 94, AGO Index 1848 Supplement indicates that this letter was returned to USG on Sept. 7, 1848. See following letter.

To Colonel

———

Bethel Ohio
Sep.t 12th 1848

C<small>OL</small>.

My application for an extension of two months to my leave of absence, recieved from Gen. Taylor, has been returned, together with Gen. Orders No 49 which says that leaves are granted by Comdrs. of Divisions. I have the honor therefore very respectfully to request an extension of two months to the leave of absence, for sixty days, given to me by Gen. Taylor on the 25th of July, with permission to apply for such extension.

Please direct to St. Louis Mo.

Very Respectfully
Your Obt. Svt.
U. S. G<small>RANT</small>
1st Lt. 4th Inf.y

ALS, de Coppet Collection, NjP. See following letter.

To Captain

————

Bethel Ohio
Sept 12th 1848

CAP.T

I have just had returned to me an application for an extension of leave of absence together with Orders No 49 which state that leaves of absence are granted by Div. Commanders. I have the honor therefore very respectfully to request an extension of two months to the leave already granted by Gen. Taylor.

I would at the same time submit this application as my report required by Gen. Orders No 49 of the 31st of August.

Please direct to me at St. Louis Mo.

Very Respectfully
Your Obt. Svt.
U. S. GRANT
1st Lt. 4th Inf.y

ALS, IHi. This letter may have been addressed to Bvt. Maj. George Deas of Pa., asst. adjt. gen. for Maj. Gen. Winfield Scott. On Sept. 20, 1848, by Special Orders no. 6, Scott extended USG's leave for two months. Copy, DNA, RG 98, Eastern Division, Special Orders. USG's leave was also extended for two months by Special Orders no. 22 of Oct. 13, 1848. *Ibid.* The duplication of orders was probably caused by USG's two letters of application, and both covered the same two months.

To Bvt. Maj. Gen. Thomas S. Jesup

————

St. Louis Mo.
Oct. 16th 1848

GEN.

I have not forwarded my accounts as Reg.l Qr. Mr. in consequence of Maj. Lee having left the Reg.t before they were completed, and those which required his signature Col. Whistler, who succeeded him in the command of the Reg.t, will not sign. I shall start for my Reg.t in about three weeks and immediately upon my joining will forward all my accounts.

Respectfully
Your Obt. Svt.

Gen. T. S. Jesup   U. S. GRANT
Q. M. Gen.   1st Lt. 4th Infy
Washington   Reg.l Q.m.

ALS, DLC–James K. Polk.

To Bvt. Maj. Gen. Roger Jones

————

Mad. Bcks.
Sackets Harbor N. Y.
Dec. 17th 1848

GEN

I have the honor of acknowledging the receipt, this day, of my commission as a 1st Lt. in the 4th Reg.t U. S. Infantry

I am Sir
Very Respectfully
Your Obt. Svt.

To R. Jones   U. S. GRANT
Adj. Gen U. S. A.   1st Lt. 4th Infy

ALS, DNA, RG 94, ACP 4754/1885. Promotion to 1st lt. was dated to Sept. 16, 1847. The commission, dated Feb. 7, 1848, is reproduced in facsimile in William H. Allen, *The American Civil War Book and Grant Album* (Boston and New York, 1894).
 USG reported on Nov. 17, 1848, to regimental headquarters in Detroit, Mich., and then was reassigned to Madison Barracks, Sackets Harbor (near Watertown), N.Y. On Nov. 30, 1848, Bvt. Col. Francis Lee, commanding at Madison Barracks, wrote to 1st Lt. Patrick Calhoun, act. asst. adjt. gen. for Bvt. Maj. Gen. Edmund Pendleton Gaines. "Lieut Grant of 'I' Company—you will perceive is reported 'on leave,' ordered to join his Company.' I report him so by direction of the Adj of my regiment. I have had no report from Lieut Grant—and I know not his whereabouts: his services are wanted here to organize his Com-

pany, acquire the necessary arms clothing &c. &c. I respectfully request he be ordered to his post." On Dec. 11, 1848, Bvt. Lt. Col. William Grigsby Freeman of the AGO endorsed the letter. "Lt. Grant's leave has expired or will soon expire, & it is probable he has joined his company before this time." DNA, RG 94, Letters Received. On Dec. 2, 1848, Lee had written from Madison Barracks to Bvt. Maj. Gen. Thomas S. Jesup that "Lieut. U. S. Grant, regimental quarter master of the 4th Infantry, arrived here to day, and has reported to me for duty; he will relieve Br. Major [Joseph Rowe] Smith in the duties of quarter master as a matter of course." ALS, DNA, RG 92, Consolidated Correspondence 598, "Madison Barracks." USG also commanded Co. I.

To Bvt. Maj. Gen. Thomas S. Jesup

————

Madison Barracks
Sackets Harbor N. Y.
Jan. 15th 1849

GEN.

I would respectfully request to know whether the purchase of Bed sacks for the troops at this Post would be allowed as a proper disbursment out of Qr. Mr. Funds, under the following circumstances

On the 9th of Dec./48 when the troops arrived at this Post there was not clothing of any kind at the place, and the season, and the inclemency of the weather made it absolutely necessary for the health and comfort of the troops that Bed sacks should be immediately procured. The distance of Government clothing from this post, and the time that must have necessarily elapsed befor it could have been forwarded, would have subjected the soldiers to great exposure.—I made the purchas[e] at the time and respectfully submit the matter for your decission

I am Sir
Very Respectfully
Your Obt. Svt.
U. S. GRANT

Gen. T. S. Jesup   1st Lt. 4th Infy
Q. M. Gen U. S. A.   Regl Qr Mr.

ALS, DNA, RG 92, Letters Received, Clothing. On Jan. 23, 1849, Bvt. Maj. Gen. Thomas S. Jesup replied, "I have to acknowledge your letter of the 15th inst. I cannot decide 'whether or not the purchase of Bed Sacks for the Troops at your post be a proper Disbursement' until it is satisfactorily explained to me why those Troops were not supplied with their Clothing and Equipage on their passage through New York. The Clothing Depot being at Philadelphia every article required by the Troops could have been supplied to them during the time they were in N.Y. Harbour" Copy, *ibid.*, Letters Sent, Clothing. See letter of Jan. 30, 1849.

To Bvt. Maj. Gen. Thomas S. Jesup

——————

Madison Barracks
Sackets Harbor N. Y.
January 19th 1849

Gᴇɴ.

I would respectfully represent to you that the fences in rear of the officers quarters at this post are in a very dilapidated condition, the most of them having fallen down or are sustained by props. I understand that they were built in 1819 since which time but little repairs have been put upon them.

There is 1158 feet of fencing, 8 feet high which would require 9264 feet of plank, 927 posts, and 2316 feet of Scantling.—I would respectfully ask if the Qr. Master General will authorize the purchase of lumber to make the above repairs.

The Eave troughs and leaders on the quarters of officers and soldiers are leaky and in many places broken causing, in wet weather, damage to the Public buildings.

I am Gen.
Your very Obt. Svt.
U. S. Gʀᴀɴᴛ
1st Lt. 4th Inf.y
Reg.l Q. M.

To Gen. T. S. Jesup
Qr. Mr. Gen. U. S. A.

ALS, DNA, RG 92, Consolidated Correspondence 598. For the reply, see next letter.

To Bvt. Maj. Gen. Thomas S. Jesup

————

Madison Barracks
Sackets Harbor N. Y.
January 19th 1849

GEN.

I would respectfully report to you that the two dwelling houses and store house (Property of the U. States) in the town of Sackets Harbor are in such a state of decay that they will scarsely stand, and they are a nuisance to the citizens of the place, both from their combustible nature and the character of the people who occupy them.

I am Gen.
Very Respectfully
Your Obt. Svt.
U. S. GRANT
1st Lt. 4th Inf.y
Reg.l Q. M.

To Gen. T. S. Jesup
Qr.Mr. Gen. U. S. A.

ALS, DNA, RG 92, Consolidated Correspondence 956. Bvt. Maj. Gen. Jesup replied, Jan. 25, 1849. "In regard to the houses in the town, you will call upon the commanding officer for a Board, to examine and report upon their condition. Should their report be adverse to retaining them, you will either sell them, on condition that are removed, or you will use the materials at the Post as may be most advantageous. The repairs reported as necessary to the fences &c. you will have made." *Ibid.*, Q.M. Letter Books.

To Bvt. Maj. Gen. Thomas S. Jesup

————

Madison Barracks
Sackets Harbor N. Y.
January 27th 1849

GEN

I respectfully report to you the necessity of a horse and cart being allowed at this post in addition to the two horses and wagon now on hand and for authority to make the necessary purchase. I am told that three horses have always been allowed here and at present we find it almost impossible to do without them.

I am Gen.
Very Respectfully
Your Obt. Svt.
U S GRANT
1st Lt. 4th Inf y
Reg l Q. M.

To Gen. T. S. Jesup
Q. M. Gen. U. S. A.

ALS, DNA, RG 92, Consolidated Correspondence 598. Bvt. Maj. Gen. Jesup authorized this purchase on Feb. 9, 1849. *Ibid.*, Q.M. Letter Books.

To Bvt. Maj. Gen. Thomas S. Jesup

———

Madison Barracks
Sackets Harbor N. Y.
January 30th 1849

GEN.

I have the honor to acknowledge the receipt of your letter of the 23d inst enquiring why the Troops at this Post were not supplied with their Equipage on their passage through N. Y. In answer I have to state that the 4th Infantry arrived in N. Y. Harbor about 10 O'clock at night, reshipe[d] and left the next day for their several destinations. The Troops being badly supplied with clothing, at Post in a high Latitude and in an inclement season of the year it was absolutely necessary for their health and comfort that Bedsacks should be immediately suplied which I accordingly did and would now respectfully ask for the approval of the Qr. Master General to the disbursment.

I am Gen.

Very Respectfully

Your Obt. Svt.

U. S. GRANT

To Gen. T. S. Jesup   1st Lt. 4th Inf.y

Q. M. Gen. U. S. A.   Reg.l Q. M.

ALS, DNA, RG 92, Letters Received, Clothing. See letter of Jan. 15, 1849. On Feb. 8, 1849, Bvt. Maj. Gen. Thomas S. Jesup replied to USG, "I have to acknowledge your letter of the 30th Ultimo, in answer to mine of the 23d January. Forward the account to this Office for examination." Copy, *ibid.*, Letters Sent, Clothing. On Feb. 12, 1849, Jesup wrote to USG, "The Voucher for the purchase of Bed Sacks, accompanying your Quarterly Account Current, for 4th Qur 1848, has been received and examined and the disbursement is approved." *Ibid.* See *Calendar*, April 24, 1849.

To Bvt. Maj. Oscar Fingal Winship

———

Madison Barracks

Sackets Harbor N. Y.

February 10th 1849

MAJ.

I very respectfully represent to the commander of the 1st & 3d military Deparments, to be refered to the commander of the Eastern Division, the injustice which I immagine has been done me by ordering me from Detroit to this Post. I am Regimental Quarter Master, and have been, since the first creation of that appointment.

Owing to the scarsity of officers at this Post it might not appear as such manifest injustice were it not taken into account that another officer (Lt. H. D. Wallen) whos proper Company was at Madison Bck's at the time, was retained at Detroit to fill the proper duties of my office.

I would, most respectfully, as a desission upon the question, whether or not Head Quarters of a Regiment is the proper place for the Reg.l Q. Master, and if it is, that I may recieved order to to proceed to Detroit.

> I am Maj.
> Very Respectfully
> Your Obt. Svt.
> U. S. GRANT
> 1st Lt. 4th Infy
> Reg.l Q. M.

To Maj. O. F. Winship
Asst. Adj.t. Gen. U. S. A.

ALS, DNA, RG 98, 1st and 3rd Military Departments, Letters Received. Bvt. Maj. Oscar Fingal Winship of N.Y., USMA 1840, was adjt. gen. for Bvt. Maj. Gen. John E. Wool. On Feb. 20, 1849, Winship replied. "Your letter of the 10th instant, in reference to your being ordered on duty at Madison Barracks, has been received and laid before the General Commanding, the 1st and 3. Military Departments, who instructs me to say that the circumstances of the case are not made sufficiently explicit for him to form an opinion, as to the justness of your complaints. He desires you will state whether your appointment as Regimental Quartermaster, has been regularly withdrawn, and if not whether you are still in the performance of that duty, or are merely doing Company duty at Madison Barracks, togeather with all the circumstances, under which you were ordered to that Post." Copy, *ibid.*, Letters Sent. See letter of Feb. 23, 1849.

To Bvt. Maj. Gen. George Gibson

———

> Madison Barracks
> Sackets Harbor N. Y.
> February 16th 1849

GEN.

I send you voucher No 14, Abstract of Contingencies, for 2d quarter 1848 to replace the one already forwarded which was informal for want of signature. Voucher No 13, same Abstract, I have been obliged to forward to Detroit for signature. As soon as signed it will be sent to the Office of the Com. Gen.

I am Gen.

Very Respectfully

Your Obt. Svt.

U. S. GRANT

To Gen. Geo. Gibson   1st Lt. 4th Infy

Comy Gen. U. S. A.   A. A. C. S.

ALS, DNA, RG 217, Third Auditor's Account number 8905. On Oct. 25, 1848, Bvt. Maj. Gen. George Gibson, Commissary General of Subsistence, had written USG that "Vouchers Nos 13 & 14. Abs. of Contingencies 2d qr. are informal for want of signature to the receipts." Copy, DNA, RG 192, Letters Sent. USG's letter was forwarded to the Third Auditor's office, where it was noted that he was allowed $10.80 in the settlement of March 15, 1850.

To Bvt. Maj. Oscar Fingal Winship

Madison Barracks

Sackets Harbor N. Y

February 23rd 1849

MAJ.

I have the honor to acknowledge the receipt of your letter of the 20th inst, requiring me to set forth more fully, than I did in my protest, the particulars of the injustice of which I complain. In answer I respectfully submit the following.

When the law was passed, early in 1847, authorizing the appointment of Regimental Quarter-Master, I received that appointment in the 4th Inf.y, and have held it ever since. I am now performing the duties of the appointment and receive the extra emoluments attached to it. In no way either by resignation or removal, have I vacated the office of Reg.tl Quarter-Master, neither has the Co.l Commanding ever considered that I had.

In the latter part of July last, I obtained a leave of absence, and Lieut. H D Wallen was assigned to my duties. Shortly after this the Regiment was ordered to its present station, and Lieut

Wallen was retained at Pascagoula, Mississippi, in some capacity, I beleive Depot Commissary, and only rejoined the Regiment about two weeks before my leave expired. Immediately upon his arrival at Detroit, Head Quarters of the Reg.t, he was placed on duty as acting assistant Quarter Master and acting Commissary and orders were forwarded to me to report for duty at this post. Before this order reached me I was on my way to Detroit with my family, not doubting but that Head Quarters was my proper station, and that I would be allowed to remain there. What then was my surprise immediately upon my arrival at Detroit, to receive[d] orders to make a long and comfortless trip, at an inclement season of the year, a family with me, and another officer allowed to take my place, when his company was at the very post which I was required to join? It was not for me to decide, but I could not see, by what authority a Reg.tl Commander, could detain an officer from his company, particularly where his services were so necessary as at this post. It could not well be to avoid a trip from Detroit to Madison Barracks, for if Lieut Wallen, had ~~have~~ proceeded to this place immediately upon his arrival at Detroit, he could have been here before the close of Lake navigation, and I would have been spared a long trip by land.

Lieut Wallen belonged to one of the companies at this post, and at that time there was but one officer present for duty with the two companies. This fact was known at Head Quarters of the Reg.t, and was assigned as a reason why it was necessary to send an officer here, and it had necessarily to be either Lieut. Wallen or myself.

The injustice of which I complain is, that being Reg.tl Quarter Master, Head Quarters of the Reg.t, seems to be my proper station. I was ordered from there and another officer, whose proper place was with his company, retained to perform my duties notwithstanding I was there, on the spot, ready to resume them. I was compelled therefore to make a long and expensive trip, at an inclement season of the year, (navigation having already closed on Lake Ontario.) for the ostensible reason that it would be inconvenient for Lt. Wallen to move there with his wife and child. I was at Detroit with my family, and had to undergo this very inconvenience, and at an expense amounting to double the allowance made by Government for transportation. It was also assumed that the appointment of Reg.tl Quarter Master, expired with the war. Finding that this supposition was incorrect, Lt. Wallen effected a transfer with Lt. Maloney, then Adjutant of the Reg.t, and whose company was at Detroit, which transfer was annulled by the commander of the Eastern Division of the Army, on the ground that it was taking an effective officer from his Comp.y and giving it an ineffective one.

After this I was in daily expectation, of receiving orders to return to Detroit, and would have received such orders no doubt, had not Lieut Wallen succeeded in getting permission, to retain his position until the opening of Lake navigation.

Since that time the Adjutant of the Reg.t has resigned his office of Adj.t and Lieut. Wallen appointed in his place.

The above statement makes known the facts of which I complain, as consisely as I can express them, and I respectfully submit this to the Commander of the 1st and 3d Military Departments for his decision

I am Maj
Very Respectfully
Your Ob.dt Serv.t
U. S. GRANT

To Major O F Winship   1st Lieut 4th Inf.y
Asst. Adj.t Gen.l U S A   Reg.tl Q.r M.r

LS, DNA, RG 98, Eastern Division, Letters Received. See letter of Feb. 10, 1849. On Feb. 24, 1849, Bvt. Col. Francis Lee wrote to Bvt. Maj. Oscar Fingal Winship. "I have the honor to transmit, herewith, a statement made by Lieut Grant Regtl Q.M., for the decision and action of Majr Genl. Wool. In my judgment of this matter Lieut Grant has, unquestionably, been hardly & wrongfully dealt by. He was sent from his proper station undoubtedly, for the mere accommodation and gratification of another officer, not that the good of the service required it. Both Lieutenants Wallen and Grant were at Detroit, the Hd Qrs of the Regt, Lieut Wallen's company was here—so was Lieut Grant's—this was Lieut Wallen's legitimate station, Detroit was Lieut Grant's, nevertheless, Lieut Grant was sent here to preform company duty—for I had only one officer with two companies—

and Lieut Wallen detained, at Detroit, to perform the very duties the law ap creating regimental Quarter Masters contemplated Lieut Grant should do. Lieut Wallen's transfer with Lieut Maloney the then Adjt. of the regiment, whose company was at Detroit, was disapproved by Majr Genl Scott. I protested against it, through Majr Genl Gaines, on the ground that it was entailing on this Post an unavailable officer for an available one. Lieut Wallen was ordered here on the earliest opening of navigation, the order has been defeated by Lieut Maloney resigning his adjutantcy, and Lieut Wallen being appointed in his place. I have only two officers here, Lieut Grant is one of them, commands a company, and is Quarter Master and commissary. If the service would permit, I would be glad to get another officer or two, the Captains of both the[se] companies are permanently absent, as is one first Lieutenant. Lt Wallen,—I don't know what has become of Lieut Forsythe, 2d Lieut of I Company: he has never reported, I have heard nothing of him since he was promoted to the Reg.t, the 8th of last October." Both letters were forwarded to Bvt. Maj. Gen. Edmund Pendleton Gaines by Bvt. Maj. Gen. John E. Wool with the endorsement, "It would appear that injustice has been done Lieut Grant Regt. Quarter Master. As the Colonel of the Regiment, who is beyond my control, may have other reasons for the course he has pursued towards Lieut Grant than appears in his letter, the subject is submitted for consideration to the General Commanding of Division." *Ibid.*, Eastern Division, Letters Received.

On Feb. 25, 1849, Lee again wrote to Winship. "I have the honor to just have received Dept Order No. 10, detailing both Lieut Grant and Lieut Hunt on a Gen Court martial to assemble at Oswego on the 1st of March. This leaves me without a company officer, and as muster is on the 28th inst. muster rolls returns &c to be made out, the presence of one officer, at least, with two companies, would but seem indispensable. In the event that the session of the court is likely to be protracted for any considerable time, I would respectfully ask that one of these officers (Lieut Grant) be relieved, and be sent back to his post: Lieut Grant is regimental q. m., and is doing the duties of both commissary & Quarter master." For USG's service on the court see letters of Feb. 27, March 1, 1849. 2nd Lt. Lewis Cass Hunt of Mo., USMA 1847, also served on the court.

To Julia Dent Grant

Adams N. Y.
Feb.y 27th 1849

MY DEAREST JULIA

With a very bad pen, bad ink, and a sheet of Fools Cap paper, furnished by the same Frost that we stoped with when we passed through Adams, I pen you these lines—We are thus far on our journey without difficulty or accident.

How often I thought of you I can not say but it was a number of times. We found no sleighing and to-morrow will have, no doubt, a tedious trip in the stage. As soon as I arrive at Oswego I will write to you, but as we will be on the road until after night you will probably miss a day recieving letters.

We didnot come on the same road that you Clara[1] & I took, and therefore did not see the old house in which we spent such an unpleasant night. When you write to me dont forget to tell me of any news that you may get in letter whilst I am gone.—

I find that I love you just the same in Adams that I did in Sackets Harbor. A thousand kisses and much love to you.

U.

ALS, DLC-USG. USG was ordered to serve on a general court martial at Fort Ontario, Oswego, N.Y., by district orders 10, Feb. 22, 1849. DNA, RG 94, First and Third Military Departments, orders.

1. Clara Grant, oldest sister of USG.

To Julia Dent Grant

Oswego N. Y.
Feb.y 28th 1849

MY DEAREST JULIA

It is 11 O'Clock at night and Mr. Hunt[1] and myself have just arrived and had time to get our suppers. You see how punctual I am in writing to you. I found your note stuck to the top of the valise and read it with the greatest pleasure. Although I may not dream of you I think of you *very very* often and of how much I love you.

All the officers of the Court Martial are here and we think that we will not be detained more than two or three days.

Our ride to-day was very fatiguing. All the seats were taken and Mr. Hunt and myself were obliged to take a passage on top of the stage. Bad roads compelled the stage to travel abo[u]t as slow as a person would walk. I think you may look for me home on Monday. If I am the least bit sick I certainly will tell you.

To-morrow when I am rested I will write you a longer letter.

Adieu My dear dear Julia

U

ALS, DLC-USG.

1. 2nd Lt. Lewis Cass Hunt of Mo., USMA 1847.

To Julia Dent Grant

———

Oswego N. Y.,
March 1st 1849

M<small>Y</small> D<small>EAREST</small> J<small>ULIA</small>

We are through the Court Martial and will start home day-after-tomorrow We meet again to-morrow too read over the proceedings and will be too late for the stage so that Saturday is the day that we will start. Either Saturday night or Sunday night, about 1 O'Clock at night, you may look for me. I can not tell you anything except how *very very* much I love you and how often I think of you. It is possible that we will go by the way of Syracuse if it causes no detention, and I think it will not.

I am affraid that from our late arrival at this place that my letter may not have got in the Mail so that, although I have written daily, you may miss two days in geting letters. To-morrow I shall look for a letter from you. This is the last letter you need look for from me. The first stage that starts after the one that carries this will carry me so there is no object in writing again.

I am very well. A thousand kisses and much love to you my dearest Juje

U

ALS, DLC-USG. Madison Barracks post returns (DNA, RG 94) state that USG returned on March 4, 1849. The court had heard the cases of three privates and one musician who had deserted. In every case the soldier was found guilty, ordered to forfeit all pay and allowances, "to be marked indelibly with the letter D one and a half inches long, on his left hip, and to be drummed out of service." DNA, RG 153.

To Bvt. Maj. Oscar F. Winship

—————

March 9, 1849

Having received orders to join headquarters of the [*4th*] Infantry at Detroit Michigan I would respectfully request permission to remain at this port until the earliest opening of navigation on the lakes. At this time no boats are running, and I would therefore be obliged to make the trip most of the way by stage with my family which at this season of the year is most insupportable for females. The journey would require at this season about seven days of constant land travel, stopping neither day nor night.

The Flying Quill (Goodspeed's), Sept.–Oct. 1954. Bvt. Maj. Oscar Fingal Winship was an asst. adjt. gen. on the staff of Bvt. Maj. Gen. John E. Wool. USG was ordered to join the headquarters of the 4th Inf. at Detroit by Eastern Division Special Order 18, March 2, 1849. Copy, DNA, RG 98, Eastern Division, Special Orders. USG reported at Detroit on April 18, 1849. Madison Barracks and Detroit Barracks Post Returns, DNA, RG 94. On March 15, 1849, Bvt. Lt. Col. William Grigsby Freeman replied to USG. "Your letter of the 9th inst. has been received, and for the reasons therein stated Major General Scott authorizes you to defer a compliance with 'Special Orders,' No. 18, directing you to join the Head Quarters of your regiment at Detroit, until the opening of lake navigation." Copy, *ibid.*, RG 98, 1st and 3rd Military Departments, Letters Received; *ibid.*, Eastern Division, Letters Sent.

To Bvt. Maj. Gen. George Gibson

Madison Barracks
Sackets Harbor N. Y.
March 28th 1849

GEN.

I have just recieved yours of the 23d inst. informing me that I have given Lt. P. Andrews 2d Art.y credit for 100$ on my accounts for 2d quarter 1848. The name should read 1st Lieut. Geo. P. Andrews 3d Artillery.

I am Gen
Very Respectfully
Yr. Obt. Svt.
U. S. GRANT
1st Lt. 4th Inf.y
A. A. C. S.

To Gen Geo. Gibson
Com.y Gen. Sub.

ALS, DNA, RG 217, Third Auditor's Account number 8905. On March 23, 1849, Bvt. Maj. Gen. George Gibson had written to USG. "On the examination of your account 2d. quarter .48 it is observed that you credit Lt. P. Andrews 2d Art: an officer unknown to this Dept. and whose name does not appear on the Official Army Register with $100, you will therefore as early as practicable furnish this office with the correct name of the officer from whom you received the money." Copy, DNA, RG 192, Letters Sent. Bvt. Maj. George P. Andrews of N.C., USMA 1845, was regt. q.m. for the 3rd Art.

To Bvt. Maj. Gen. Roger Jones

Madison Barracks
Sackets Harbor N. Y.
March 30th 1849

GEN.

I have the honor, very respectfully, to return my commission as Bvt. 1st Lt. in the 4th Inf.y U. S. A.

I am Gen
Very Respectfully
Your Obt. Svt.
U. S. GRANT
1st Lt. 4th Inf.y

To Gen R. Jones
Adj.t Gen. U. S. A.

ALS, DNA, RG 94, ACP 4754/1885. Bvt. Maj. Gen. Roger Jones, Jan. 14, 1850, endorsed the letter to Secretary of War G. W. Crawford. "The declining of his *brevet of 1st Lieutenant*, seems to require a statement of the facts of the case, at this time, as the Army Register is about being published.

"While a *2d Lieutenant*, this Officer was nominated by the late President and confirmed by the Senate, 'to be *captain* by brevet for gallant and meritorious conduct in the battle of *Chapultepec*, to rank from *September 13, 1847*.' The brevet of Captain, being an advance of *two* grades, was afterwards found to be a mistake, and accordingly, by direction of the Secretary of War, the promotion was not announced in orders. The Secretary of War further directed, that at the next meeting of the Senate, that the error should be corrected.

"It appears that at the next session of the Senate, Lieut. Grant was again nominated ~~by~~ and *confirmed*, as a *brevet 1st Lieutenant*, 'for gallant and meritorious conduct' in a previous battle—that of '*Molino del Rey*,' to rank from *September 8, 1847.*—and this is the brevet which this officer declines, as seen by his letter; but it was without any knowledge of the previous brevet of Captain having been conferred, & with-held—

"The brevet of 1st Lieutenant, dated September 8, 1847, being a proper basis for the brevet of Captain, places this officer in a proper position to receive the one of higher grade, prematurely conferred, and on that account, it may be supposed witheld by the Department.—I therefore respectfully recommend, that the *commission* of Captain by brevet be now issued to this meritorious officer, (now a 1st Lt. in his Regt.) believing it to be just and proper and in conformity with the intentions of your predecessor." Crawford replied the following day. "The President directs that action be suspended on this case." Jones returned to the matter on March 1, 1851. "Laid before the Sec. of War this morning, who agrees to the propriety of issuing now, the *Brevt* of *Captain*, as previously nominated, & confirmed by the Senate.—" The Senate reconfirmed both brevets on March 10 and the commission of bvt. 1st lt. was returned to USG on May 29, 1851. See *Calendar*, Aug. 24, 1848, Dec. 11, 1848.

To Julia Dent Grant

Detroit Michigan
April 27th 1849

M Y D E A R E S T J U L I A

I recieved your Telagraphic dispach yesterday morning from which I see that you are on your way to St. Louis. I hope you may find all at home well, and get this soon after your arrival. This you know is my Birth day and I doubt if you will think of it once.—I have a room and am staying at present with Mr. Wallen.[1] Wallen and family are as well as can be expected under present circumstances.

I have rented a neat little house in the same neighborhood with Wallen and Gore[2] In the lower part of the house there is a neat double parlour, a dining room, one small bedroom and kitchen. There is a nice upstares and a garden filled with the best kind of fruit. There is a long arbour grown over with vines that will bear fine grapes in abundance for us and to give away. There are currents and plum & peach trees and infact evrything that the place could want to make it comfortable.[3]

I will have a soldier at work in the garden next week so that bv the time you get here evrything will be in the nicest order. I find Detroit very dull as yet but I hope that it will appear better when I get better acquainted and you know dearest without *you* no place, or home, can be very pleasant to me. Now that we are fixed to go to hous keeping I will be after you sooner than we expected when you left. I think about the 1st of June you may look for me. Very likely Ellen will come along and spend the Summer with us.—I hope dearest that you had a very pleasant trip. I know that you have thought of me very often.[4] I have dreamed of you several times since we parted.

I have nothing atal to do here. I have no company and consequently do not go on Guard or to Drills. Mr. Gore and myself are to commence fishing in a day or two and if sucsessful we will spend a great many pleasant hours in that way.

When I commence housekeeping I will probably get a soldier to cook for me, but in the mean time if any good girl offers I will engage her to come when you return.

Dearest I nothing more to write except to tell you how very very dear you are to me and how much I think of you. Give my love to all at home and write to me very soon and often. Yours devotedly

ULYS

P. S. I recieved two letters here for you which I opened and read; the one from Annie Walker I forwarded to you at Bethel. One from Elen I did not send inasmuch as you would be at home so soon. Give my love to Sallie & Annie.

U

ALS, DLC-USG. The letter, postmarked Detroit, April 28, 1849, was sent to JDG "Care of Mr. F. Dent," her father.

1. 1st Lt. Henry Davies Wallen had recently become regt. adjt.
2. Bvt. Maj. John H. Gore.
3. The house, at 253 E. Fort Street, was later moved to the Michigan State Fair Grounds as an exhibit by the Michigan Mutual Liability Company, Detroit. See *Michigan History Magazine*, XXI (Spring, 1937), 208–10.
4. Five words crossed out.

To Mr. Earl

Detroit Michigan
May 3d 1849

MR. EARL

DEAR SIR

Please send me one Military frock coat (Infantry) made to the measure of Capt. J. H. Gore 4th Inf.y but about ½ an inch shorter in the waist than his. Also one dark vest.—I should like to recieve the above articles before the end of this month, if possible, inasmuch as I expect to make a visit to St. Louis for a few days in the Month of June, leaving here on the 1st proxim[o]

Capt. Gore & Lieut Collins,¹ both of the 4th Inf.y, have requested me to say that they would like to have the clothing ordered by them, forwarded as soon as possible.

Please send me, in addition to the above articles, a Cap bugle with the figure four

I am Sir
Your Obt. Svt
U. S. GRANT
1st Lt. 4th Inf.y

ALS, CSmH. Presumably the addressee is J. Earl, Jr., with whom USG corresponded about clothing Sept. 16 and Nov. 4, 1851.

1. Joseph Benson Collins of Washington, D.C., enlisted as a private in 1846 and was commissioned a 2nd lt. in the 4th Inf. on March 29, 1848.

To Julia Dent Grant

Detroit Michigan
May 20th 1849

MY DEAREST JULIA

I recieved your long sweet letter by yesterdays Mail and you know with what pleasure I read it. It is the second recieved since your arrival. Dr. & Mrs. deCamp¹ brought the latest news from St. Louis. They say that you were very well and half inclined to come with them but that your Mother vetoed it.

But in ten days from now dearest I will start after you. If Ellen is comeing with you you might telagraph me and let me know exactly they day you would start and I could meet you at Chicago. But it will probably be better if I should go all the way to St. Louis. I want to see them all there.

I recieved a long lecture from Clara yesterday. Virginia is sick so that the Dr. has to attend her twice each day. The rest are

all well and I am glad to hear that Father is trying to sell his
Bethel property or exchange it for City property.² They have
not heard from you since you left Louisville.—Clara had just
written Mrs. Lee³ a long letter.

I have moved into our house and will get it in the best order
I can before I start for you. The owner of the house furnishes the
materials for the repairs that are wanted and the soldiers do the
work. I will have the house thoroughly whitewashed and painted.
Gregorio⁴ is living with me and a soldier is cooking for me at
present, but I will not keep him after I start to get you.

I have no horse yet but if I can get a good one in St. Louis
without paying too much I will bring one along from there.

We heard of the dreadful fire in St. Louis the same afternoon that it was raging so. Is it possible that it was as distructive
as it is represented to have been? The fire may drive off the
Cholera⁵ but it will be at a fearful expense to many citizens. I will
send this letter by Col. Bainbridge who is going immediately to
St. Louis and will deliver it at least five days sooner than it
would go by Mail. One letter next Sunday will be the last I shall
write. Any after that would not get to you as soon as I will myself.
I will not stay in St. Louis more than a day or two if the Cholera
is raging, if it is not I will stay eight or ten days.

Dont be allarmed about my fishing—I will take good care
of myself and not get my feet wet as you fear.

I have not become acquainted with may of the people of
Detroit yet and have not visited any of the young ladies. You
know I told you that I would be quite a gallant while you [are]
absent, but as I see no one that I like half as well as my own
dear Julia I have given up the notion

There has not been a single case of the Cholera here yet and
the city authorities are doing all they can, in the way of having
the streets and yards cleaned and limed, to keep it off.

Why dont Ellen write to me some time[.] I have written to
her! But I know how [it] is, She is too lazy even to keep up ~~even~~
the correspondence with her dear little Mc. What has become
of Elting?⁶ Write to me as soon as you get this and then you

need not write again. Give my love to all at home and a thousand kisses for yourself.

Your devoted

ULIS

ALS, DLC-USG. The letter was carried to St. Louis by Bvt. Lt. Col. Henry Bainbridge of Mass., USMA 1821, 7th Inf. It was addressed to Julia Grant at the Dent St. Louis town house at the corner of "Fourth & Cerra" [Cerre].

1. Dr. Samuel G. I. De Camp of N.J., was an army surgeon with the rank of maj.

2. Jesse Grant later moved to Covington, Ky.

3. Probably Mrs. Francis Lee, wife of Bvt. Col. Francis Lee of the 4th Inf. Clara Grant had visited USG at Sackets Harbor when the Lees were stationed there.

4. Gregorio was the servant brought from Mexico by USG.

5. The great fire in St. Louis, May 17, 1849, came in the midst of a great cholera epidemic which killed 4547 people in the first seven months of 1849. "Cholera Epidemics in St. Louis," *Missouri Historical Society, Glimpses of the Past,* III, 3 (March, 1936), pp. 56–72; J. Thomas Scharf, *History of Saint Louis City and County* (Philadelphia, 1883), I, 819–21; II, 1574–9.

6. 2nd Lt. Norman Elting had resigned his commission on Oct. 29, 1846. He taught school in St. Louis County, Mo., 1847–49.

To Julia Grant and Ellen Dent

Detroit Michigan

May 26th 1849

MY DEAR DEAR JULIA

I write to you dearest for the last time until it happens that we are again separated, which I sincerely hope will never take place. I know now how dearly I love you, and will never give my consent to your making another long visit without me, unless it should be absolutely necessary.

By another year I can get a leave of absence for four months and I do not know but that I could it at this time if I wanted it. I watch the papers regularly to see how the Cholera is at St. Louis and it distresses me, not a little, to see such unfavorable accounts. Dearest I do wish that you was away from there. Both of us would be uneasy about dear friends I know, who would still be in the midst of the disease, but I hope that by this time it is quiting the City.—If I am not unfortunate I will be in St. Louis on the 4th or 5th of June at the outside and if the Cholera is bad I think we will start back in a day or two after.[1] Should there be no danger I will remain a week or ten days at home.

I am geting along very well with our house. A soldier has been at work for several days white washing and painting. The place looks very different now from what it did when I wrote to you before. Mrs. Wallen, Mrs. Gore and all the rest here are very well. They seem anxious to see you. Our quiet town is very healthy and there seems to be but little apprehension about the Cholera. I am going to write you but a short letter because you will not recieve more than a day or two before I see you myself dearest Julia and I doubt if I do not beat it to St. Louis.

Give my love to all at home and tell Wrenny[2] that he will now be relieved of his trouble as Carrier. You know he says in your letter "Devil take the P. Office I'm Carrier." Ten kisses to all except yourself dearest, those due you I will pay in kind very soon.

Yours affectionately
ULIS

P. S. I will write in the next page a few lines in reply to the note Ellen wrote in your last letter

U.

Kiss

DEAR SISTER, OR MISS VANITY I SHOULD SAY.

Dont you know that you are as vain as you can be and all just because some silly fellows, not knowing any other way to keep up conversation, have flattered you. But you did'nt understand them and as I think a goodeal of you myself,[3] I will forgive it all.

Now I can tell you that if I did get the "old maid of the family," as you say, I got the very one I wanted, and the only one I wanted, and very much too to the disappointment of her Sister (Nellie I mean) and another lady spoken of in your note.

Besides you [had] better look out or this same Sister Nellie [will] be a much "Older Maid" before she finds one with all the qualifications, (*that she can get.*) However be ready to come here with us to Detroit and we may be able to find you a beaux inasmuch as you are a stranger and people may not have time to find you out. But you must not look your "Uglyest" for if you should you would loose so by the contrast with "Sis" that evrybody would be at dagers ponts with me for showing such good taste in my selection (you know how disappointed[4] when you found that it was not you I was going to see) that none of the beaux would look at you. Give my love to evrybody. I sent you ten kisses in the other part of my letter but as I expect to be in St. Louis so soon and dont know but that you might claim them *all* I will take nine of them back and have them distributed among the little girls across the way

Your affectionate brother
ULIS.

ALS, DLC-USG, postmarked Detroit, May 28, 1849.

    1. USG was on leave June 1–June 20, 1849. DNA, RG 94, 4th Inf. Return.
    2. Julia Grant's brother.
    3. One and a half lines crossed out.
    4. Two words crossed out.

To P. Clayton

———

Detroit Mich.
July 30th 1849

MR. CLAYTON
SIR.

I have recieved your letter of the 17th of July, showing a deficiency of vouchers for property turned over to different officers, by me, as Act. Adjutant and as A. A. Q. M. of the 4th Inf.y

Upon examination of my old papers I find vouchers (which I herewith respectfully enclose) for all except the following articles; viz:

> *6* Six Canteens & Straps.
> *50* Fifty prs boots. (Issued to Lt. H. M. Judah)[1]
>> *1* One Wall Tent.
>> *1* One Sgts Wool Jacket.
>> *3* Three Flannel Shirts.
>> *1* One Blanket.

The receipts for the fifty prs. of boots issued to Lt. H. M. Judah, 4th Inf.y I can not find. But upon examination of the Company books of (E) Co. 4th Inf.y, which he Lt. Judah commanded at that time, I find they are duly noted and the men receiving them charged. I have written to Lt. Judah to obtain a renewal of the receipts, and as soon as received I will forward them.

The Wall Tent, Fly and poles is now on hands, as shown by my Quarterly return. At the end of the present quarter I will forward the receipt of the Asst. Q. M. at this place, for the tent, and strike it from my returns.

The Woolen Jacket Sgts. with which I am charged should be (upon examination of my Return for part of 3d quarter /48) one pair of Sgts. Wool Ovealls.

The Pay Master is now absent from this place but upon his return I will forward his receipts for the following articles; viz:

> *6* Six Canteens & Straps. $1.92
> *1* One Sgts Wool O'Alls.   2.21
> *3* Three Flannel Shirts.   2.32½
> *1* One Blanket.   2.25

which, with Lt. H. M. Judahs Receipts, and the vouchers herewith inclosed, I believe settles the deficiencies innumerated.

> I am Sir
> Very Respectfully
> Your Obt. Svt.
> U. S. GRANT
> 1st Lt. 4th Inf.y
> Reg.l Q. M.

ALS, Harry N. Burgess, Arlington, Va. The addressee, Philip Clayton, was Second Auditor of the Treasury Department.

1. Bvt. Capt. Henry Moses Judah of N.Y., USMA 1843, was then stationed at Fort Ontario, N.Y.

To P. Clayton

———

Detroit Mich.
February 12th 1850

SIR

I have just received your letter informing me that on examination of my recruiting accounts for May, 1848, a balance has been found due the United States, in the sum of Six Dollars, being the amount paid to Wm Saunders, (by way of Bounty) who puts his mark to the voucher forwarded, also that the enlistment has never been received at your Office

I can only state that the enlistment was duly made out and forwarded, together with the written consent of the mother, who was the only guardian of Wm Saunders. Herewith I enclose you the descriptive list of the above named recruit as taken from the Descriptive Book of the Regiment

The duplicate of the voucher sent with the enlistment has been lost and Wm Saunders being now absent from this place it is impossible to get it renewed immediately but as soon as possible I will secure another properly witnessed

The duplicate of the enlistment will be found on file in the Adjutant Generals Office

I am Sir
Very Respectfully
To P. Clayton Esq   Your Obt. Servant
2d Auditor Treasy   U. S. GRANT
Washington D. C.   1st Lt. 4th Inf.y

LS, DNA, RG 217, Second Auditor's Account 11615. See letter of Sept. 1, 1848. On Jan. 28, 1850, Philip Clayton, Second Auditor of the Treasury, wrote to USG. "Your recruiting account for May 1848, has been examined and adjusted, and a balance found due the United States of $6.00, differing in that sum from your statement, being the enclosed Vouchers of *Wm Saunders*, who signed by mark, and has no attesting witness, and whose enlistment also, has not been received by this office." Copy, *ibid.*, Second Auditor, Letters Sent. On March 12, 1851, Clayton again wrote to USG. "A settlement has been made in this office, which has this day been confirmed by the 2d. Comptroller, shewing your a/c balanced on account of Expenses of Recruiting." *Ibid.*

To Bvt. Brig. Gen. Thomas Lawson

Detroit Mich
March 25th 1850

SIR

Herewith I enclose a statement of purchases made by me as Act Asst Comy. of Subs. of the 4th Infy. for the Hospital of the same Regt. The purchases were made on the certificate of the attending surgeon of the Regt.; and are disallowed at the 2d Auditors office, with these remarks. viz "These items have been excluded from Lieut Grants Subs. account and should be referred by him, to the Med. Dept. whence they will be referred to the 2d Auditor for adjustment" I respectfully request that the Surgeon General will approve of the purchases, so that the accounts will pass at the auditors office to my credit.

I am Sir
Very Respectfully
Your Obt Servant
U. S. GRANT
1st Lt. 4th Inf.y
A. A. C. S.

To Genl T. Lawson
Surgeon Genl U. S. A.

LS, DNA, RG 217, Second Auditor's Account 10127. Accompanying papers show that the expenditure of $43.25 was allowed. Bvt. Brig. Gen. Thomas Lawson of Va., served as surgeon-general 1836–61. See *Calendar*, March 16, 1850.

To Bvt. Maj. Oscar F. Winship

Detroit Michigan
June 14th 1850

Maj.

I have the honor to apply for a leave of absence for four months for the purpose of visiting my friends in Missouri and the state of Ohio.

I am induced to make this application at this time for the reason that my services can probably be better dispensed with at present than at any future time, there being at this Post, with one comp.y, a Commanding officer, Adjutant and three Company officers besides myself. Urgent family reasons also induce me to respectfully submit this application.

I am Maj.
Very Respectfully
Your Obt. Svt.

To Maj. O. F. Winship   U. S. Grant
A. A. Gen. East.n Div.   1st Lt. 4th Inf.y

ALS, DNA, RG 108, Letters Received. The letter was favorably endorsed by Col. William Whistler, Bvt. Maj. Gen. Hugh Brady, and Bvt. Maj. Gen. John E. Wool, and forwarded to Bvt. Lt. Gen. Winfield Scott. Four months' leave was granted by Scott's Special Orders No. 59, June 21, 1850. Copy, *ibid.*, RG 94, Headquarters of the Army, Special Orders.

The "urgent family reasons" mentioned by USG probably involve the birth of USG's son Frederick Dent Grant on May 30, 1850, in St. Louis. Julia Dent Grant had been advised by Maj. Charles Stuart Tripler, surgeon at Detroit, to return to her parents for the birth of her first child. Unpublished memoirs of Julia Dent Grant.

Deposition

State of Michigan,
City of Detroit,
ss.

Ulysses S. Grant being duly sworn, deposeth and saith, that on or about the 10th day of January a. d. 1851 & for 25 days previous thereto, within the City of Detroit, Antoine Beaubien did neglect to keep his Side walk free and clear from Snow and Ice on Jefferson Avenue in front of house owned and occupied by him and did then and there commit many other acts contrary to the ordinances of said city; further deponent saith not.

U. S. Grant

Sworn to and subscribed before me this 10th day Jan. a, d. 1851.

J. Van Rensselaer   City Clerk

DS, Detroit Historical Museum, Detroit, Mich. A printed form with space provided for offense and date, only the signature is by USG. A virtually identical document printed by *Richardson* (134) gives the same date, same avenue, but names "Zachary" Chandler as the offender. Zachariah Chandler, born and educated in N.H., came to Detroit in 1833 as a merchant. In 1851 he was mayor of Detroit. Chandler later served as U.S. Senator from Mich., 1857–75, and as Secretary of the Interior under USG. According to Richardson, Chandler conducted his own defense against USG's charges before a jury, asserting that "If you soldiers would keep sober, perhaps you would not fall on people's pavements and hurt your legs." The jury found for USG, assessing court costs to Chandler and a fine of six cents.

To Bvt. Maj. Gen. Thomas S. Jesup

Detroit Michigan
Apl. 7th 1851

Gen.

Your instructions of the 31st Ult. are just recieved, and agreeable to them the public team will be disposed of and the teamster discharged.

I would respectfully report that the transportation of fuel to the public offices, and other transportation of a public nature, requires the service of a team a portion of evry day in the week.

I will be pleased to recieve instructions as to how this transportation is to be procured.

> I am Gen.
> Very Respectfully
> Your Obt. Svt.
> U. S. GRANT

To Bvt. Maj. Gen. T. S. Jesup   1st Lt. & Bvt. Capt. 4th Inf y
Qr. Mr. Gen. U. S. A.   A. A. Q. M.

ALS, DNA, RG 92, Consolidated Correspondence 254. Bvt. Maj. Gen. Thomas S. Jesup replied on April 12, 1851. "What transportation other than that for fuel, which should be delivered monthly, is required at your post? and how many public offices have you to supply? The estimates for the Quarter Master's Department having been reduced by Congress one half, notwithstanding their reduction upon close calculation in this office, renders it necessary for us to furnish nothing not absolutely required for the public service and not positively within the letter of the regulations." Copy, DNA, RG 92, Q. M. Letter Books.

To Bvt. Capt. Irvin McDowell

———

Detroit Michigan
April 8th 1851

CAPT.

Your note of the 7th has been recieved, and in reply, I respectfully submit the following report of quarters at Detroit Barrack, assignable for officers.

In reply to your first question I have to state that there are no *public* quarters assignable for officers.

There is one old frame building, within the enclosure of the garrison, which is rented for officers quarters. It is in a dilapidated state, so much so that the officers occupying it about one year ago, applied for a Board of Survey to condemn it as unfit for assignment.

Herewith I submit a plan of the building with the dimensions of each apartment.

I am very Respectfully sir
Your Most Obt. Svt.
U. S. GRANT
1st Lt. & Bvt. Capt. 4th Inf y
A. A. Q. M.

Capt. I. McDowell
Asst. Adj. Gen.

Plan and discription of hired quarters, for officers, at Detroit Barracks Michigan.

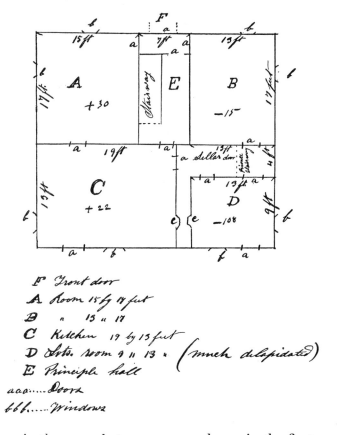

F Front door
A Room 15 by 17 feet
B "   13 " 17
C Kitchen 19 by 13 feet
D Stv. room 9 " 13 " (much delapidated)
E Principle hall
aaa......Doors
bbb......Windows

Rooms in the second story same as shown in the first excep the room over C is but 17 feet long and is the only assignable room in the house which has a fire place. All the other rooms are

warmed by stoves, the pipes leading to the chimney going up
from the kitchen.

U. S. GRANT
1st Lt. & Bvt. Capt. 4th Inf.y
A. A. Q. M.

ALS, Burton Historical Collection, MiD. Bvt. Capt. Irvin McDowell of Ohio,
USMA 1838, who later commanded at Bull Run, was then asst. adjt. gen. at
army headquarters, 2nd Department.

To Bvt. Maj. Gen. Thomas S. Jesup

———

Detroit Michigan
April 14th 1851

GEN.

Your instructions of the 31st of March, requiring the sale
of the public team, and discharge of the teamster &c. at this post,
have been complied with.

I would most respectfully represent the necessity, and ask
the favor, that the first part of your instructions, that requiring
the discharge of the clerk, may be suspended.

In addition to my duties at the garrison I am now doing the
duties of Asst. Qr. Mr. for the 2d Mil. Dept. which duties, alone,
have been performed heretofore by an Asst. Quarter Master who
has always been allowed the assistance of a clerk.

If the good of the service will permit this favor I feel assured
that the Quarter Master General will allow it.

I am Gen.
Very Respectfully
Your Obt. Svt.

To Bvt. Maj. Gen. T. S. Jesup   U. S. GRANT
Qr. Mr. Gen. U. S. A.   1st Lt. & Bvt. Capt 4th Infy
Washington D. C.   A. A. Q. M.

ALS, DNA, RG 92, Consolidated Correspondence 254. Bvt. Maj. Ebenezer
Sprote Sibley of Mich., USMA 1827, reported to Bvt. Maj. Gen. Thomas S.

Jesup on April 1, 1851, that USG had that day assumed his q.m. duties. DNA, RG 92, Consolidated Correspondence 254.

Jesup replied to USG on April 22, 1851, "You can retain your Clerk until the 30th of June." Copy, DNA, RG 92, Q.M. Letter Books.

To Bvt. Maj. Gen. Thomas S. Jesup

Detroit Michigan
April 17th 1851

GEN.

Your note of the 12th Inst. enquiring for the number of public offices to supply with fuel and the amount of other transportation necessary has just been recieved.

There are four public offices supplied by the Act. Asst. Qr. Mr. with fuel. In addition to this the bread has to be taken daily from the Bakehouse to the garrison, a distance of one mile, and a load of slops and matter collected by the police party taken, also daily, from the Barrack. The rations for issue are taken monthly from the store house in the city to the Barracks.

I am Gen.
Very Respectfully
Your Obt. Svt.
U. S. GRANT

To Bvt. Maj. Gen. T. S. Jesup   1st Lt. & Bvt. Capt. 4th Infy
Qr. Mr. Gen. U. S. A.   Act. Asst. Qr. Mr.

ALS, DNA, RG 92, Consolidated Correspondence 254. On April 28, 1851, Bvt. Maj. Gen. Thomas S. Jesup replied to USG. "I have received your letter of the 17th instant in answer to mine of the 12th reporting the number of public offices at Detroit to be supplied with fuel; and the transportion required. The fuel should be delivered at the offices monthly, and its delivery thus, be made one of the conditions of the contract. The carrying of the bread from the bake house to the garrison is an expense that cannot, under any circumstances, be borne by the United States, who furnish the flour, but do not receive any of the profits. Those who receive the profits should bear all the expenses incident to them. The officers' servants and the police party must dispose of the slops and other matter collected by them. The issue of provisions to the troops is usually made at the commissary's store house, but if the distance from it to the barracks is so great as to render it absolutely necessary, a dray or truck may be hired for their delivery at the barracks. The insufficient appropriations made for the army render it necessary to retrench every expenditure not within the letter of the Regulations, and to curtail those conveniencies which ample appropriations permitted to the service without additional cost, or detriment to the public interests. Inconsiderable as may be the saving at each post by the reductions made at it, still in the aggregate, they make a sum applicable to our frontier defences, of great importance to us with our present limited means." Copy, DNA, RG 92, Q.M. Letter Books.

To Bvt. Maj. Gen. Roger Jones

————

Detroit Michigan
May 19th 1851

Gen.

When the last list of Brevets was published my name appeared in it as having recieved the Brevet rank of Captain in the 4th U. S. Inf. y.

The other officers at this post, who were promoted at the same time, recieved their commissions some five weeks since, and I have not yet recieved mine, I would respectfully notify you of the fact.

I am Gen.
Very Respectfully
Your Obt. Svt.
U. S. Grant
1st Lt. & Bvt. Capt. 4th Infy

To Gen. R. Jones
Adjt. Gen. U. S. A.
Washington D. C.

ALS, DNA, RG 94, ACP 4754/1885. For the confusion concerning USG's bvt. rank, see letter of March 30, 1849.

To Julia Dent Grant

————

Detroit Michigan
May 21st Wednesday [*1851*]

Dearest Julia

As I promised you I write on this day, and for the last time to Bethel.[1] Since you have been gone I have been a little lonesome but have got along very well. I generally visit Mrs. Gore and Mrs. Grayson evry day and occationally take a ride.[2]

Mrs. Grayson's horse run off with their buggy a day or two after you left and tore it to pieces. The very next day she run off with Maj. Gore's and scarsely left enough of it to get mended.

Mrs. Gore has not been sick yet but from the Maj. staying so close to his room I would not be surprised to hear of her being taken at any time.—I like the place I am boarding at, very well. Col. Grayson and Clarke are going there too so we will just four at our table.

I have no news to write you dearest Julia except I would like to see you and Brink.[3] very much. You must write me a greatdeel about the little dog. Is he walking yet?

Your scarf got here last Sunday. I will send it to you at St. Louis so as to be there by the time you arrive.

Last Sunday night, at Church, I lost the ring you gave me so long ago off of my finger and could not find it.[4] I am in hopes the sexton will find it and give it to me by next Sunday. It distresses me very much to think it is gone and at first I had a notion not to tell you of it but to get one just like it, with your name in it, and wear that.

Mr. Hunt[5] has been spending several days here. He is looking very bad and is almost as bald as Dr. Tripler.[6] He says Harritt Camp is to be married this Summer shure enough. All our acquaintances at Sackets Harbor are well.

Mrs. Gore sends a greatdeel of love to you. She says she has no idea that she would miss you so much. Capt. Brent[7] will be here in a day or two and relieve me. I will then make a visit to Grosse Isle and likely to Fort Gratioit.[8]

Give my love to all at home and to our friends around. Write to me often and long letters dearest Julia. I am looking for a letter from you this evening.—Mr. Kercheval and Miss Allice were at the Broadway house at the same time you was but they did not find [it] out that you were there until after you had started.

Good buy dearest.
Ulyss

ALS, DLC-USG.

1. Bethel, Ohio, was the home of Jesse Grant, USG's father.
2. Wives of Bvt. Maj. John H. Gore and Bvt. Lt. Col. John B. Grayson, of Ky., USMA 1826.
3. Brink is apparently Frederick Dent Grant, born May 30, 1850.
4. See letter of July 27, 1851.
5. Probably 2nd Lt. Lewis Cass Hunt of Mo., USMA 1847.
6. Dr. Charles Stuart Tripler of N.Y., maj. and surgeon.
7. Capt. Thomas Lee Brent of Va., USMA 1835.
8. Fort Gratiot, Mich., was located on the St. Clair River near Port Huron.

To Julia Dent Grant

———

Detroit Michigan
Wednesday 28th May 1851

DEAREST JULIA

You will no doubt be astonished to learn that we have all been ordered away from Detroit. Maj. Gore goes with his company to Fort Gratioit. Col. Whistler is ordered to move his Head quarters to Fort Niagara; but as there are not sufficient quarters there he has represented the matter to Washington and no doubt our destination will be changed to Sacket's Harbor.[1] Wont this be pleasant. I will write to you again before we leave here and tell you all about it. Dr. Tripler goes with us and Capt. McDowell goes to Jefferson Barracks. I will send your scarf by him.

Mrs. Gore is thoroughly disgusted at the idea of going to Gratiot. She seems really distressed at the idea of being separated from you. She starts to-day so as to be there before her troubles come on.

I think now I will send for you sooner than you expected to return when you left. When you come I will meet you at Detroit and we will spend a week here and at Fort Gratioit. If Ellen is not to be married this Fall get her to come with you and spend this Winter.

There is no possible news in Detroit. Evry thing is about as when you left. People all pretend to regret our depature very much and I presume some of them are sincere. For my part I am glad to go to Sackets Harbor. I anticipate pleasant housekeeping for the next year or two. I shall provide nothing in the way of furnature until you arrive except a carpet for one room.

I hope dearest Julia you have not been as unfortunate about geting letters this time as you was the last time you left me. I have had but one from you yet but I am expecting another now evry day.

You have none idea dearest how much I miss little Fred. I think I can see the little dog todeling along by himself and looking up and laughing as though it was something smart. Aint he walking? I know they will all dislike to see him leave Bethel.

Write to me very soon dearest and tell me all about what kind of a trip you had from Cincinnati, how you found all in St. Louis &c. &c.

Give my love to all of them and kiss them for me. Kiss Freddy and learn him to say papa before he comes back. Dont let him learn to say any b[ad] words.—Mrs. Gore says Jim is learning to talk but I guess he talks about as he did when you left.

Good buy dearest Julia and dont forget to write very often. I will write punctually evry week as I promised.

ULYSSES

P. S. I am about selling my horse and if I do I will send you $50.00 by my next letter.

U

ALS, DLC-USG, postmarked Detroit, May 28, 1851, and addressed "Care of Mr. F. Dent, St. Louis, Mo."

1. Col. William Whistler was reassigned to Sackets Harbor.

To Julia Dent Grant

————

Detroit Michigan
June 4th 1851

DEAREST JULIA.

I wrote you in my last that we had all been ordered away from here and that it was uncertain whether we would go to Sacket's Harbor or to Fort Niagara. We are still in suspense but I suppose this evenings mail will decide. Maj. Gore's Comp.y left for Gratiot last Friday. The Maj. and Mrs. Gore are still here. Mrs. Gore has a very fine daughter.[1]

Day after to-morrow is the time set for our departure but I presume I shall not leave for several days after.

The Biddle house opened this morning and I commenced with them. Your letter from Bethel got here in due time and in answer to your fears relative to boarders let me tell you that there was no boarders but Col. Grayson Clarke a clerk and myself. I have the room I took over Mr. Rood's Book store yet and find it quite as pleasant as it would be at the hotel.

Capt. McDowell leaves to-day or to-morrow for Jeff. Bcks. I gave the Capt. your scarf. Mrs. McDowell will give you all the news from Detroit. Dont neglect to call upon her soon after her arrival.

Mrs. Whistler & Louisa[2] came strait for Detroit as soon as they heard that we were to be moved. I am very glad they were away when the order arrived. McConnell[3] got the Col. to apply to have our destination changed to Sackets Harbor and the old lady dislikes it very much. You know then as a matter of course that if she had been here the Col. would never have dared apply for the change.

There is no news of importance in Detroit. Col. Chapman[4] of the 5th Inf.y is here on his way to join his Regt. I sent some word to Fred. by him.

Dearest Julia I miss you very much and little Fred. too. You dont tell me whether he walks yet or not. Why dont you write more about him. I think I can see the little dog making faces and trying to talk. Was he not a great favorite at our house? I know they hated to see him leave very much.

I have not written home since the order for our change. When you write tell them.

I have been very busy for a few days turning over quarter Master property to Capt. Brent, geting the Comp.y baggage moved to Gratiot and recieving provisions for the next year. I do not visit any except at Mrs. Gore's, and not there now, so the only amusement I have is to take a long ride on horse back evry day. We have had the most terrible weather since you left. The whole country is flooded and it is quite cold enough for overcoats. It seems as if summer never would come.

I will close this letter my dearest Julia and write you another in a few days. You need not answer this until you hear from me again. As soon as I know here we are going I will let you know where to direct.

Kiss all of them at home for me and tell Freddy that he is comeing to see his pa before a great while. I told you I believe dearest that I should buy no furnature except carpeting for one room. When you come we will get evry thing nice and nothing but just what we want. The few things we have I will pack up carefully and have them shiped.

Good buy dearest and kiss all of them for me again.

Your affectionate husband
Ulys

Kiss and let Fred. kiss

ALS, DLC-USG.

1. Eight words crossed out.
2. Louisa Whistler was the daughter of Col. William Whistler.
3. Bvt. Capt. Thomas Rush McConnell of Ga., USMA 1846, then regt. adjt. of the 4th Inf.
4. Bvt. Lt. Col. William Chapman of Md., USMA 1831.

To Bvt. Maj. Gen. Roger Jones

————

Detroit Michigan
June 7th 1851

GEN.

I have the honor of acknowledging the receipt of my Commissions as Brevet 1st Lieut. & Brevet Captain in the 4th U. S. Infantry.

I am Gen.
Very Respectfully
To Bvt. Maj. Gen. R. Jones   Your Obt. Svt.
Adjt. Gen. U. S. Army   U. S. GRANT
Washington D. C.   1st Lt. & Bvt. Capt. 4th Infy

ALS, DNA, RG 94, ACP 4754/1885. See letter of May 19, 1851. The commissions as bvt. 1st lt., March 3, 1849, and as bvt. capt., May 27, 1851, are reproduced in facsimile in William H. Allen, *The American Civil War Book and Grant Album* (Boston and New York, 1894).

To Julia Dent Grant

————

Detroit Michigan
June 7th 1851

DEAREST WIFE.

We have just recieved the order changing our destination to Sackets Harbor and I hasten to write to you so that you can write to me soon. I know you will write as soon as you get this wont you dearest?

Maj. Gore is ordered to Saut St. Marie.[1] Col. Whistler has gone to Kentucky so McConnell and myself will have the old lady, with all her traps, on our hands for the journey.

I know you will be delighted, as I am with the prospect of geting back to Sacket's. My hope is that they will let us remain there long enough to enjoy it.

Mrs. Gore is doing very well and so is her little girl. She has not yet given her a name. Mrs. Grayson wants her named after her and I can see plainly that she is quite peaqued that Mrs. Gore will not do it. She talks of calling her Bell.

There is no news of importance in Detroit. I have sold my horse for $110.00 since I wrote to you last, so now I am deprived of those long rides I have been taking evry evening. We leave here however next Teusday (this is Saturday) so that I shall not want him much more.

I hope dearest Julia you had a pleasant trip from Bethel to St. Louis and that dear little Freddy has been well all the time. You dont know how anxious I am to see him. I never dreamed that I should miss the little rascle so much. I know they were all delighted to see him in St. Louis. You must write me a greatdeel about him as soon as you get this. I have not had a letter from you since you second one. I suppose you wrote again from Bethel. The Arrow is not yet in but when she comes I shall expect to find a letter from you.

I have not heard from home since you wrote to me nor have I written to let them know that we have been ordered to Sackets Harbor. I will write in a day or two.

Give my love to all our friends and kiss them all at home for me. Let Fred. kiss his Grandma and Aunts for me. Dont they think the world and all of the littl[e] dog? If he is as good as he used to be I know they must. Be sure and write me long and frequent letters and I will continue as punctual as I have been in writing to you.

I send you with this letter a check for $50.00 made payable to you father. I think likely this will be the last money I will send you for I expect that you will come back sooner than you expected when you started. I told you that I would meet you here when you returned. This is in case you do not travel in company with some one going all the way[.]

Adieu dear dear Julia. A thousand kisses to you and Fred.

ULYSSES

ALS, DLC-USG.

1. Bvt. Maj. John H. Gore was assigned to command Fort Brady at Sault Ste Marie.

To Julia Dent Grant

Niagara Falls
New York
June 11th 1851

Dearest Julia

    I am at the above place on my way to Sacket's Harbor and as I have a half hour to spare it cannot be better employed than in writing to you dearest. I wrote to you as soon as we learned where we were going and inclosed you a check for $50.00. I hope you got it all safe. Mrs. Whistler and Louisa are along but they stop just below here. We have had the most terrible weather since you left. There has been scarsely a dry day and it is cold enough for overcoats and big fires.—All the Detroit people seemed to regret our leaving them very much and I think they intend to get up some representation to get us back.—I believe I told you Maj. Gore was going to Saut St. Marie!

    I think dearest Julia if you know any one traveling this way next month you had better come back. I want to see you and Fred. very much and as we are going to where there are good quarters there is no difficulty in the way of our keeping house comfortably[.]

    I have not had a letter from you since the one in which you told me you would leave Bethel on the next Wednesday. You must write to me more punctually wont you dearest? Did you get home without any trouble? and was dear little Fred. well all the way. I feel so anxious all the time lest he should have another attack like the two he had before you left.

    There was nothing new in Detroit when I left. Mrs. Gore was doing very well but I have not seen her since she was confined. I believe she is satisfied with going to the Saut. Mrs. Grayson has been very kind to her through all her sickness.

    I boarded at the new hotel from the time it was opened until I left and so enough to show me that we would not be comfortable nor satisfied. Col. Dibble is evidently too close to get along with boarders, or with the public, after the other hotel is completed.

I have no more time to write dearest so good buy dearest. Give my love to all at home and kiss little Freddy for me. Remember me to all our friends. Adieu again.

Ulysses

P. S. Tell you pa to have the direction of my paper changed when he is in town some time, (I presume you are in the country) and finds it convenient. Dont forget to tell me if you got the money I sent you all safe.

Ulys.

ALS, DLC-USG.

To Julia Dent Grant

———

Sacket's Harbor
June 16th 1851

Dearest Julia

You will see from the above that we are already at Sacket's Harbor[.]¹ I wrote to you from Niagara Falls last Wednesday to let you know that we were on the way. Sacket's Harbor is just the same place it was when we were here before. There are no new faces to be seen and but few of the old inhabitants have left. The garrison however will be more pleasant than when we were here before. Besides the Col's family and ourselvs there are in the garrison three other families. Dr. Christie of the Navy Lieut. Stevens' Navy and Dr. Bailey of the Army.² I have been to see some of our old acquaintances and they all seem anxious to see you back again. I was at Mrs. Kirby a few days ago. Mrs. Kirby and her second daughter are absent, and have been, all winter. I shall make no preparation for housekeeping until you come on. A bed-room carpet will be the extent of my purchases. I think you will be here dearest Julia in July or August at the out side. I am geting quite uneasy about you and

Fred. I have not had the scratch of a pen from you since about a week after you left. Wont you write often?

Miss Harriett Camp is to be married soon. She admitted the fact to me her self. Mr Sternes and Mr. Barbour have both been married since we saw them. Sacket's Harbor is as dull a place as can be immagined. There is no building and no improvements going on of any sort. The place must look up now however. They have their rail road completed to within seventeen miles of here and the ballance is nearly graded and will be completed by October. Sackets Harbor is now within about fourteen hours travel of N. York City.

A few of the ladies of Watertown have adopted the new Turkish dress. I saw a lady here in the street with it on a day or two ago. The dress is really beautiful[.] It is a very great improvement on the old stile, but at the same time I should regret exceedingly to see or hear of any friend of mine wearing it until the dress has been fully adopted and has seased to attract attention. I suppose you see it occationally at St. Louis!

Dearest you have no idea how uneasy I feel not hearing from you. Had it not been that Fred. was so sick just before leaving Detroit I should feel no alarm. As it is I am in constant dred lest I may hear bad new from the dear little dog. I am very anxious to see him and his ma. K[iss] him for me. I suppose he is runing ab[out] now. I tell evry body who inquires about him that he is. —Since you left I have been as well as it is possible for a person to be all the time. I hope dearest that I will soon hear that you and Fred. have been just as well.

Give my love to all at your house and kiss them for me. Tell me if Ellen is to be married in the Fall. Remember me to all our friends and write soon. Dont neglect to call on Mrs. McDowell soon. Adieu dearest Julia.

U<small>LYSSES</small>

(Kiss)

ALS, DLC-USG.

1. Post returns of Madison Barracks (DNA, RG 94) place USG's arrival on June 12, 1851. He assumed command on June 17, 1851, the date of departure of

Lt. Col. Benjamin L. E. Bonneville, and held command until June 27, 1851, when Col. William Whistler arrived. 4th Inf. Return, *ibid*.

2. Surgeon Peter Christie had served in the navy since 1812. Lt. Thomas H. Stevens entered the navy as a midshipman in 1836. Dr. Joseph Howard Bailey of N.Y., had served as asst. surgeon since 1834.

To Julia Dent Grant

Sackets Harbor N. Y.
June 22d 1851

DEAREST JULIA

Here it is the 22d of June and yet I have not heard a word from you. I am really geting quite uneasy lest something is the matter. I have written you some six weeks since I have heard a word and in one of the letters inclosed you a check. I do not hear if you got it, if you are at home or anything from you. Dearest why dont you write? You know how you scold when I neglect writing more than a week. I am begining to be like you was when you said you did not care a cent for any of them at home for you had no friends. Your not writing keeps me in constant suspense lest poor little Freddy may be sick again. Write to me as soon as you get this and dont neglect in future to write at least once evry week. I have not gone an entire week without writing to you but once since you left me.

All our things arrived from Detroit, and I moved into Garrison, yesterday. The Col. has not arrived yet but we look for him this week.

I have selected for my quarters the rooms Col. Smith formerly occupied, on the opposite side of the sally port from where we lived before. Evrything looks much better about the Barracks than they did when we were here before. The fences have been put up and the place repaired.

Since I have been here I have visited Watertown and Brownville each twice and taken an occational ride into the country. Things look just as they did evry where except in Watertown.

That you know was burned down about two years ago. It has been built up however better than it was before and evry thing looks flourishing. In a few weeks they will have their Rail road completed. New York City and Watertown then will be within about twelve hours travel of eachother.

The people in Sacket's Harbor are making great preparations for celebrating the 4th of July. Having the 4th Infantry Band here is such a treat to them that they expect extra doings this year from formerly.

I have got no news to write you and, as it has been so long since I heard from you, no questions to answer. I think I must hear this week and then no doubt will find enough to fill a sheet just in replying to what you have to say.

If Ellen is not to be married this Fall bring her on here to spend the Winter with us. I know she will be delighted to come. I have said in some of my former letters that you had better return soon if you find a good opportunity of coming. Write to me about the time you expect to start and I will meet you on the road. If you find some one of your acquaintances visiting N. York you can come with them as far as Syracuse and I will meet you there. Let me know if the girl you have got is comeing with you so that if she is not I may look out and engage one before you get here.

Do write soon and often dearest Julia. Kiss all of them at home and kiss dear little Fred. evry night for his pa. Has he improved much since he left? If the little dog had not been so sick before he left Detroit I would not feel the least uneasiness, but as it is I feel a constant dread lest I shall hear bad news. I know I shall be afraid to open the first letter I get from you. Tell me if you have got all my letters, that is to say about two letters per week, or at least ~~three~~ three letters evry two weeks. Adieu dearest Julia. A thousand kisses for you. Dream of me.

                                                        ULYS.

ALS, DLC-USG.

Advertisement For Wood

———

Notice

Sealed Proposals will be received at the Office of the Regimental Quarter Master 4th U S Infy, Madison Barracks N. Y. until the 15th day of July 1851, at 2 o'clock P. M, for supplying the Troops at Madison Barracks N.Y. with wood for the year ending June 30th 1852.

The wood to be of straight and sound body, split, (or round if not over six inches in diameter) 4 feet from tip to scarf, free from all limbs, rot, gnarled or dead wood. One fifth to be hickory, and the balance about an equal proportion of Rock Maple, Upland Beach and Iron Wood, to be neatly and compactly piled, 4, 6 or 8 feet high in the yard at Madison Barracks at such times and in such quantities as the Regimental Quarter Master or his successor shall designate[.] Bonds will be required for the faithful performance of the contract, and each bid should give the names of the two bondsmen

U S Grant

Regtl Qtr Master's Office   Bvt Capt. & R. Q. M. 4th Infy
Madison Barracks
June 24th 1851

D, DNA, RG 92, Consolidated Correspondence 956. S. T. Hooker, on July 10, 1851, agreed to deliver wood as described for $2.70 per cord. *Ibid.* On July 21, 1851, the formal contract was signed. DS, *ibid.*, RG 217, Army Contracts. On Aug. 29, 1851, however, Lt. Col. Charles Thomas, deputy q.m. gen., told USG "Your letters dated the 24th instant, one enclosing an agreement made by you with Samuel J. Hooker for wood for the troops at Madison Barracks and the other a report on the stores on hand and required, is received. Your attention is called to paragraph 980, General Regulations of the Army: You will report the difference of price between hickory wood, and maple or beach, both of which are equal, if not superior to the standard; and should the former be more costly, by what authority it was contracted for. Stoves not being provided for by Regulations, the question of supplying them will be submitted to the Quarter Master General on his return to this office." Copy, *ibid.*, RG 92. Q.M. Letter Books. See letter of Sept. 4, 1851.

To Julia Dent Grant

———

Sackets Harbor N. Y.
June 29th 1851

DEAREST JULIA

After a lapse of more than one month I at length recieved a
letter from you yesterday. I do not see that you had any excuse
whatever for not writing before. It seems that you had stayed
in the city some days and then moved to the country and remained there some time before writing.[1] My dearest dont you
know that I must have been very uneasy all that time? I knew
that you had left Bethel, alone, and that dear little Fred. had
been sick and was so liable to be so again. Do not neglect to write
for so long a time again. I have written to you very often and I
suppose you think all is well so long as you hear from me. But
I shant scold any more until you neglect me again.

I am highly delighted with Sacket's Harbor and only hope
that we may remain here for a long time to come. The people
are very clever and there are several very pleasant families in
the garrison. We all amuse ourselvs by riding over the country
fishing, sailing &c. Evry few days the ladies get up a picknick
and take a sail. At Sacket's Harbor we are within half a day of
Niagar Falls the same time from N. York City and within a day
of Montreall or Boston. Next week I am going down to
Montreall and Quebeck Canada to spend a few days. My next
letter will probably be from Quebec. If I see anything interesting
to write about I will give you a full account If Ellen was here
now she would have a fine opportunity of seeing the finest cities
in Canada.

Col. Whistler and family are here. They are all well and the
same as ever. The old woman knows the price of eggs and
chickens here as well as the oldest inhabitants though she has
not commenced keeping house. Mr. Hunt is not very well.
McConnell made up his mind to be disgusted with Sacket's
Harbor so he is not now willing to see anything good in the place.

I think you had better not start for Sacket' Harbor during the month of July nor August if it is sickly on the river, but if it is not sickly come in August by all means. I will meet you in Detroit when you do come if you have not got company further. If you find company going to N. York City you can travel with them as far as Rome N. Y. and I can meet you there. In fact so far as economy goes you might go to N. York City better than for me to go all the way to Detroit, and then you would get to see that great city.

Dearest you must take good care of l[ittle] Fred. and learn him to say pa before he gets [here.] Do you think he recollects me? Has he any more teeth? You dont tell me anything about him. Have you seen Mrs. McDowell and Maj. Morrisons family. Remember me to all of them. I suppose that by the end of this week I will get some letters from you in answer to my skolding ones. I know you wont make it necessary for me to schold any more.

Give my love and kiss all at home for me. A thousand kisses for you and Freddy. Tell me if Bridget[2] will come with you to Sacket's Harbor. Adieu dearest Julia.

ULYSSES

Have you paid Grimsley?

ALS, DLC-USG.

1. Presumably Julia Grant had been at the Dent town house in St. Louis, then at White Haven.
2. The servant referred to in USG letter of June 22, 1851.

To Julia Dent Grant

———

Sacket's Harbor N. Y.
July 3d 1851

MY DEAREST JULIA

To-day I start for Montreal and Quebec. It is but a little over half a days travel to the former place and a little over a day to the latter. I will keep a memorandum of all that I see and if there is any thing worth relating I will tell you in my next. When I got a letter from you I expected to recieve another very soon but none has come yet, I think however when I come back there will be two or three for me. Dont you feel the least uneasiness about me dearest. I will take just as good care of myself as if you were along. I regret though that you are not along. The scenery on the St. Lawrence is said to be magnificent, and Quebec is said to be entirely foreign in appearance, customs and evry thing els. But we will see and tell you more about it in a day or two.

Mrs. Whistler, Louisa and myself went to Watertown a few days ago and Mrs. W. and I got a carpeat each, both off of the same piece. I think it a very nice one and I have no doubt you will think so too. We have a soldier here who is an eligant cabinet maker and I have got him at work making us a fine center table, two handsome parlor chairs and lounges.

The weather here is delightful. Summer is the time to enjoy Sackets Harbor to advantage so you must come before it entirely passes away. I am delighted that you are not in the city for I see that the cholera is raging there to a considerable extent. I have nothing particular to write you dearest Julia except to take good care of our dear little boy. Dont let him forget his pa and when you write write a greatdeel about him. I want to see him so badly that I can hardly wait. I expect if he should stay there long his Aunt Ell. would learn him more badness than he would unlearn in five years. Kiss him evry day for me dearest Julia.

In your letter you did not say anything about how many letters you had recieved from me. As you did not complain I presume you had recieved all that I had written. You did not tell me if Ellen was to be married in the Fall. I told you in one of mine to ask her to come here and spend the winter if she was not to be married, or at least come and make us a visit.

Give my love to all at home and kiss them all for me. A thousand kisses for your self dearest Julia. Do not fail to write very of [ten] to your affectionate husband.

U<small>LYSS</small>

P. S. Dearest I will be as good while [on] this little exkursion as you can desire   Dont fail to write to me the time you will leave St. Louis, who you are going to travel with and where I must meet you.

Adieu dear Julia, Dream of me often. I dreamed of you a few nights ago—

U.

ALS, DLC–USG.

To Bvt. Maj. Oscar Fingal Winship

—————

Montral Canad East
July 5th 1851

Maj. O. F. Winship
Asst. Adjt. Gen. U. S. Army
Albany N. Y.

Herewith I inclose you an application for an extension of ten days to the leave of absence I already have for seven days.

Please direct to me in the City of N. York. When I left Sacket's Harbor it was my intention to have gone from this place directly to Albany and carry my applycation to you in person. As it is I shall not go by the way of Albany.

I am Maj.
Very Respectfully
Your Obt. Svt.
U. S. GRANT
Bvt. Capt. 4th Inf.y

ALS, DNA, RG 98, Eastern Division, Letters Received. On July 3, 1851, by orders no. 56, Col. William Whistler granted USG leave for seven days "with permission to apply at Division Head Quarters for an extension of ten days." *Ibid.* On July 9, 1851, by special orders no. 29, USG's leave was extended for ten days by command of Bvt. Maj. Gen. John E. Wool. DNA, RG 98, Eastern Division, Special Orders. See following letter.

To Bvt. Maj. Oscar Fingal Winship

―――――

New York N. Y.
July 11th 1851

MAJ.

I left my station, Sacket's Harbor N. Y. with a leave of absence from the commanding officer of the Post, for seven days, with permission to apply for an extension of ten days. That leave, with the application for the extension, I mailed to you on the 5th inst. but having recieved no reply I would respectfully request that my leave, which commenced on the 4th of July, may be extended until the 21st inst.

I am Maj.
Very Respectfully
Your Obt. Svt.
U. S. GRANT
1st Lt. & Bvt. Capt. 4th Infy

To Maj. O. F. Winship
Asst. Adj. Gen. U. S. Army
Troy N. Y.

ALS, DNA, RG 98, Eastern Division, Letters Received. On the same day USG sent a similar letter addressed to Bvt. Maj. Oscar F. Winship at Albany. "I left Sackets Harbor N.Y. with a leave of absence for seven days, from the 4th inst. with permission to apply to Div. Hd quarters for an extension of ten days. That leave, with an application for the extension, I mailed to you with the request that the reply might be sent to this city. I would state that I have recieved no reply to my application and respectfully request ten days extension to my present leave of absence." *Ibid.* At the time these letters were written the extension of leave had already been granted. See preceding letter.

To Julia Dent Grant

Camp Brady
West Point N. Y.
July 13th 1851

My Dearest Julia

I wrote to you last from Quebec on last Sunday.[1] In that letter I gave you a little discription of the place and my travels. From there I returned to Montreal and thence up lake Champlagne. My trip has been a very pleasant one and I really felt very glad to get back to the old place where I spent, what then seemed to me, an interminable four years. Evry thing looks as natural as can be, and although I only got here yesterday evry thing seems like home. I should really like very much to be stationed here. Most of the officers are persons who were cadets with me In passing up lake Champlagne the boat stoped for a few minuets at Plattsburg, but I did not see Capt. Wallen[2] or any of the officers stationed there.

I shall leave here to-morrow, probably not to visit the place again—for years. When I get back to Sacket's Harbor I shall remain there until I am ordered away or go to meet you. I suppose I will find at letter at the Harbor from you in which you will say something about when you expect to return. I want to see you and Freddy very much, now particularly, since we are where we can keep house. I will get evrything as comfortable as I can as soon as I go back so that when you come back there will not be much but some little furnature, crockery &c. to get to commence

I occationally see accounts from St. Louis stating that there has been so many deaths, from Cholera, in S the city for the last week. These accounts distress me a goodeal. But knowing that you are in the country is a great relief. I hope you and Freddy are quite well. Does the little dog run about yet? I know he must, and try to talk too. I expect he wont know me when he sees me again. His grandma and pa will be sorry to see the little fellow leave them I know, but they wont miss him like I do. By next Summer he will be big enough for me to take him out riding and walking. Who does he like best at his grandpas? I know it is not his aunt Ell. Give my love to all at home dearest Julia and write to me very often. I have but little to write about at present but I will write you a long letter in about one week. I am just as well as it is possible to be. [. . . .] The President that is to be, (I mean Gen. Scott)[3] is here at present. He is looking very well. His wife and daughter are stoping here at the hotel on the Point. The General stops at the hotel about two miles below here. There are a great many visiters here now attending the Cadets parties which take place evry other evening   I should like to attend one of them again but I do not k[now] that I can. Next summer if we are st[ill] at Sacket's Harbor I will get a leave for a week and bring you here. It is one of the most beautiful places to spend a few days you ever saw. Adieu dear dear Julia, kiss Fred. and all of them at home for me. Come back to me as soon as you think it safe to travel with Fred.

Your affectionate husband
ULYS.

ALS, DLC-USG.

1. This letter has not been found.
2. Capt. Henry Davies Wallen.
3. Bvt. Lt. Gen. Winfield Scott was the Whig nominee for President in 1852, losing to Franklin Pierce.

To Julia Dent Grant

———

Sacket's Harbor N. Y.
July 27th 1851

DEAREST JULIA

I got a sweet letter from you yesterday, but like all your others you had but a few moments to write, nor did you acknowledge the receipt of any letter. I wrote to you from Quebec and from West Point but I cannot tell if you ever recieved either of the letters. In fact I have seen nothing from you that shows whether you know that I have ever taken a trip since comeing to Sacket's Harbor. Mrs. Whistler says that you care nothing about me, that you have got off among the beaux now and are playing the young lady again. I do not believe that though. It seems that you have been dreaming about me which is an evidence that you have not forgotten me entirely. I wish you were here; the Summers are so pleasant and there are several pleasant families in garrison[.] I have a horse and buggy and all to-gether you would enjoy yourself very much   When you write to me I dont believe you ever think of my letters. I have asked you so many questions which you never answer. I wanted to know if Ellen was to be married this Fall and if she was not if she would'nt come here with you and spend the Winter. I want to know if Bridget will come with you and a great many other questions I have asked.

Yesterday afternoon Mrs. Whistler, Louisa and myself went to Watertown and Brownville. I called at Col. Bradleys. They enquired very particularly after you, as in fact all your old acquaintances have done. You speak of comeing on here in September if I recommend it it. I would recommend your come-ing as soon as you have an opportunity if you think it safe for Fred. How many teeth has the little dog got? and does he have any more attacks of sickness? I want to see the little rascal so bad I can hardly wait until September. Elijah Camp[1] talks of going near St. Louis next month and if he does I think you had better come with him. If he goes I will write to you in time for you to get ready and meet him.

If you have an opportunity of traveling with anyone with whom you are acquainted who is visiting New York you had better come with them as far as Syracuse and let me know so that I may meet you there. I should think you would find families traveling in that direction all the time. Will they miss Fred. much from your house? I know they will. Does he try to talk yet?—I found your ring[2] the other day. I suppose in taking my handkerchief out of my pocket the ring sliped off and it has laid there ever since, and although I have worn the coat a great deel, and had my hand in the pocket a hundred times, since, I never found the ring until a f[ew] days ago.

Give my love to you pa, ma, sisters and all of them at home and dont dearest Julia neglect to write to me often and let me know what letters you get from me. Kiss little Fred. and all of them for me. There is nothing new to write about from here. I am enjoying excellent health as I ~~all~~ always do. Good buy dearest Julia and dont forget the scolding I have given you in this, and try not deserve it again.

Your affectionate husband
ULYS

ALS, DLC-USG, postmarked Sackets Harbor, July 28, 1851.

1. Elijah Camp was a special contractor for Madison Barracks. See *Calendar*, Feb. 26, March 9, 20, 1849.
2. See letter of May 21, 1851.

To *Julia Dent Grant*

———

Sacket's Harbor N. Y.
August 3d 1851

DEAREST JULIA

I got another, and a long sweet letter from you the last week. If you would write to me as regularly as the two or three last letters I would be perfectly satisfied and see how easy it would be. I do not think you had better wait until September to come here but you should start the first good opportunity, unless by waiting a few weeks you can be present at Nelly's wedding.[1] When you come give me notice so that I may meet you on the road some place. The best place would be Rome N. York if you should be with company going to N. York City. I am very well and enjoy myself as well as could be expected when away from you and

Fred. Does the little dog understand all that is said to him? I expect him and his pa will be taking a ride evry evening when he comes here, and often he will let his ma go along. There are several nice families living in Garrison and plenty of children for Fred. to play with.

Sackets Harbor is as dull a little hole as you ever saw but the people are very clever as you know very well and all together we could not have a more pleasant station. I presume however it will not be our luck to remain here long. We will be much more comfortably fixed than we have ever been before and it usually happens in such cases with the Army that they are moved as soon as they are comfortable.

You have never told me whether you have recieved your crape shawl! I sent it by Capt. McDowell whose lady you should have called upon. You have before this I know.—Does Fred. continue well? Tell his Grandpa & ma that when he gets big enough to travel by himself he may go and stay with them for six months. Does he give much trouble? I expect now that he is runing about it takes one person all the time looking after him to keep him out of mischief.

I got a letter from Maj. Gore a few days ago   He writes that they are all well and as contented as people could expect to be at the Saut.² Mrs. Gore & Jim send love to you and Fred.

The only amusement we have here is fishing, sailing and riding about the country. I have an eligant horse and a buggy to take you and Fred. out with evry day. I hope dearest Julia that you and Fred. enjoy good health annd are having a pleasant visit. I wish very much that I could be with you but I have been on leave of absence so much in the last three years that I cannot think of asking again for several years to come. Tell Fred. that he must be a good boy and not let grandpa & grandma say that he is naughty and that they are tired of him. I see dearest t[hat] you have been suffering again with the neu[ral]gia. Dont you think you might muster courage enough to have the tooth pulled that causes all that pain? I think you might. The pain of extracting it is but for a moment while the pain it gives you is for years.

Give my love to all at home and kiss Fred. for me. Remember me to Maj. Morrison's family and to Capt. McDowell's. Write soon to me dearest Julia and very often.

Your affectionate husband

ULYS

ALS, DLC-USG.

    1. Ellen Dent married Dr. Alexander Sharp.
    2. Sault Ste Marie.

To Julia Dent Grant

Sacket's Harbor N. Y.

August 10th 1851

MY DEAREST JULIA

My regular day for writing has come again but this time I have no letter of yours to answer. I am looking for a long letter now evry day. I am so sorry that you are not here now. Sacket's Harbor is one of the most pleasant places in the country to spend a summer. It is always cool and healthy. There are several pleasant families in garrison and the parade ground would be such a nice place for Fred. to run. I want to see the little dog very much. You will start now very soon will you not? Evry letter I get now I shall expect to hear that you are geting ready to start. I have not got a particle of news to write you only that I am well and want to see Fred. and you very much.

I have had some very nice furnature made in garrison and otherwise our quarters look very nice. All that we want now to go to housekeeping is the table furnature. That I will not buy until you come on lest I should not please you. The furnature made in garrison is nicer than I could buy in Watertown and more substantial. It consists of lounges, chairs and a center table.

I know dearest Julia you will dislike very much to leave

home, and I know that they will miss you and Fred. very much; but you know that you must come after while and you might just as well leave soon as late. Write to Virginia and see if she will not come with you if you come that way. I have told you to ask Nelly two or three times but you never say anything about whether she can come or whether she is to be married this fall or anything about it. I suppose however from your always sending your letters by McKeever to the post office that she is to be married to him soon.—What news do the boys send from California? Are they doing as well as formerly? I suppose they say nothing more about comeing home now.

Col. Whistler confidantly expects to be ordered away from here in the spring. What leads him to think we will go I dont know. I hope his prediction may not prove true.

Tell Fred. to be a good boy and not annoy his grandpa & ma. Is he geting big enough to whip when he is a bad boy? I expect his aunt Ell. annoys him so as to make him act bad evry day. When he comes here I will get him his dog and little wagon so that he can ride about the garrison all day. You dont tell me, though I have asked so often, how many teeth he has.

I have not heard from home now for a long time, and to tell the truth I have not written since I was at Quebec.

I hope all are well at your house. Give my love to them all and write soon.

Dont forget to avail yourself of the first good opportunity to come on here.

Adieu dearest Julia. A thousand kisses to you and Fred.

ULYS.

ALS, DLC-USG, postmarked Sackets Harbor, Aug. 11, 1851.

To Bvt. Maj. Gen. Thomas S. Jesup

———

Sacket's Harbor N. Y.

August 11th 1851

Gen.

Herewith I enclose you the proceedings of a Board of Survey upon forty five stove, property of the United States.

I would respectfully request permission to dispose of them and to appropriate the proceeds to the purchase of new ones.

I am Gen.

Very Respectfully

Your Obt. Svt.

To Bvt. Maj. Gen. T. S. Jesup	U. S. Grant
Qr. Mr. Gen. U. S. Army	1st Lt. & Bvt. Capt. 4th Inf.y
Washington D. C.	Reg.l Qr. Mr.

ALS, DNA, RG 92, Consolidated Correspondence 956. Col. William Whistler assembled a board of survey consisting of 1st Lt. Edmund Russell and 2nd Lt. Lewis Cass Hunt which reported forty-five stoves "unfit for further service." Lt. Col. Charles Thomas, deputy q.m. gen., replied to USG on Aug. 19, 1851. "You will report the number of good stoves on hand—the whole number required for use at the station and for whom and for what purpose required." *Ibid.*, Q.M. Letter Books. See letter of Aug. 24, 1851.

To Julia Dent Grant

———

Sackets Harbor N. Y.

August 17th 1851

My Dearest Julia.

I got a letter from you a day or so since and if it was not that you are comeing here so soon I would give you a good skolding. Notwithstanding all that I have said to you about neglecting to answer my letters here comes another without one word in reference to any thing that I had written

But as you are comeing so soon I shall say no more about it.

I got a letter from Clara[1] yesterday. She complains of your not writing more frequently. They are very anxious to have you go by Bethel.

I have got all the furnature and evrything nice for house-keeping except the table ware and that you know can be got in a few hours. I shall look for you early next month and infact I dont see why you should not start immediately. You can come to Detroit and there stay until the Steamer Ocean, Capt. Willoughby commanding, comes out and Capt. W. will see you safe[ly] aboard the Lake Ontario Steamer which will land you safely at Sackets Harbor. Recollect to come by no other boat but Capt. Willoughby's. I will write to Capt. W. to see you safely along. This will obviate the necessity of my going to Buffalo perhaps to wait four or five days and then come back without you. The time is so short now until you start that I shall not write again so look for no more letters, nor no more skoldings, from me. Tell Fred. that he must promise to write often to his grandpa & ma. Write as soon as you get this and tell me as near as you can what day you will start, whether Bridget will come with you &c. &c. so that I may know how to provide. There is no difficulty about geting girls here, but if Bridget suits you it will be much better to bring her than to run the risk of get a poor one.

Col. & Mrs. Whistler wish to be remembered to you and say for you to hurry home. I have nothing special to write about so I will close this, my last letter, by sending my love to all at home. Remember me to Capt. & Mrs. McDowell and to Maj. Morrison and family. Adieu dearest Julia, dont forget to write immediately upon the receipt of this.

Your affectionate husband
ULYS.

ALS, DLC-USG.

1. Clara Grant, sister of USG, lived with her parents in Bethel, Ohio.

To Bvt. Maj. Gen. Thomas S. Jesup

———

Sackets Harbor N. Y.
August 24th 1851

GEN.

Yours of the 19th instant requiring a report of the number of good stoves on hand at this post, the whole number required, and for whom required, has been recieved.

The number of stoves that will remain on my return is twelve. The Company will require four, the Band two, the Adjutant's office, Com.y store house, Quarter Master's office and Guard house each one, the Hospital two, the Col. commanding four, Asst. Surgeon two, Adjutant, R. Q. M. and two comp.y officers each one, making in all twenty two stoves.

I would respectfully state that the stoves condemned have been repaired as long as they will possibly bear it and now are worth nothing except for old iron.

In estimating the number of stoves required I have not included cooking stoves, which the Messes must necessarily have, but would enquire whether cooking stoves can be allowed to officers from the Quarter Master Department.

I am Gen.
Very Respectfully
To Gen. T. S. Jesup   Your Obt. Svt.
Qr. Mr. Gen. U. S. Army   U. S. GRANT
Washington D. C.   Bvt. Capt. & R. Q. M. 4th Infy

ALS, DNA, RG 92, Consolidated Correspondence 956. See letters of June 24, Aug. 11, Oct. 17, 1851.

To Lt. Col. Charles Thomas

———

Madison Barracks
Sackets Harbor N. Y.
Sept. 4th 1851

Maj.

Your letter dated the 29th of August 1851 calling my attention to paragraph 980 General Regulations of the Army, and requiring me to report the difference of price between Hickory wood, & Maple or Birch, and enquiring by what authority Hickory was contracted for, if it was the most costly, is recieved. In answer I have to say that in giving out the bid for furnishing wood I have refered to the advertisements for years back, at this post, all of which required a portion of Hickory. The price of Hickory does not vary materially, if at all, from other classes of hard wood, and is cheaper than the standard, oak.

I am Maj.
Very Respectfully
Your Obt. Svt.

To Maj. C. Thomas U. S. Grant
Dept.y Qr. Mr. Gen. U. S. A. Bvt. Capt. & R. Q. M. 4th Infy

ALS, DNA, RG 92, Consolidated Correspondence 956. See June 24, 1851.

To J. Earl Jr.

———

Sackets Harbor N. Y.
Sept. 16th 1851

Mr. J. Earl Jr. Esq.

Please send me in addition to the articles already ordered, a sword belt of the new pattern.

As I am in no particular hurry for my clothing you need not send it until the over coat is made.

> Yours &c.
> U. S. GRANT
> Bvt. Capt. & R. Q. M. 4th Inf.y

ALS, IHi. See letter of May 3, 1849.

To Bvt. Maj. Gen. Thomas S. Jesup

———

> Madison Barracks
> Sackets Harbor N. Y.
> October 17th 1851

GEN.

Herewith I have the honor to enclose to you my Account Current, and other papers, for the 3d quarter 1851.

I would respectfully report that the roof of the Qr. Mr. & Com.y store house is in a very leaky condition. I have made enquiry and find that the expense of a double coat of paint and sand, over the whole roof, would amount to one hundred & six dollars.

Some time since I forwarded to the Qr. Mr. Gen. the proceedings of a Board of Survey condemning forty five stoves on hand at this post, and requested permission to dispose of them and purchase new ones with the proceeds. I would respectfully renew the request.

> I am Gen.
> Very Respectfully
> Your Obt. Svt.

To Gen. Thos. J. Jesup   U. S. GRANT
Qr. Mr. Gen. U. S. Army   Bvt. Capt. & R. Q. M. 4th Inf.y

ALS, DNA, RG 92, Consolidated Correspondence 956. Bvt. Maj. Gen. Thomas S. Jesup replied on Oct. 20, 1851. "In reply to your letter dated the 17th instant

I have to inform you that stoves not being permanent fixtures in public quarters are considered as furniture, and furniture for officers is not authorized or allowed by the Regulations. At the time the stoves reported by you were purchased this Department was in funds, and they were purchased by special authority. At present there is no money on hand from which they can be purchased, even by such authority. You are authorized however to dispose of the stoves which have been condemned and apply the *proceeds* of the sale and nothing more, to the purchase of new ones for the Hospital, public store Houses & offices. The officers must supply their quarters should they consider them necessary for their convenience as they do other articles of furniture.'' Copy, *ibid.*, Q. M. Letter Books.

To J. Earl Jr.

————

Sackets Harbor N. Y.
November 4th 1851

MESSRS J. EARL JR. & CO.
SIRS:

As I have an opportunity of geting the sword belt & pompoon (articles which I wrote to you for some time since) from New York free of the Express charges, I would beg that you do not send me those articles.

Yours &c
U. S. GRANT
Bvt. Capt. 4th Inf.y

ALS, ICHi. See letter of Sept. 16, 1851.

To Bvt. Lt. Col. J. B. Grayson

————

Sackets Harbor N. Y.
November 12th 1851

COL.

I take the liberty of addressing you this note to enquire if the stock holders in the Detroit & Saline, and in the Plymouth roads have been assessed since I left Detroit, and if so, how much ? I would like also to know what dividends these roads will likely pay on the 1st of January. I have sold my stock to Callender,[1] the sale to take effect after the January assessments have been paid and the dividends called in.

I see from my Detroit paper that sporting is on the ascendent in your place and that some of the *nags* make good time. I should like very much to change back again to Detroit.

We are all quite well at this post but frozen up. Give my regards to Mrs. Grayson and John and to all my friends in your City.

Yours Truly
U. S. GRANT

To Col. J. B. Grayson U. S. A.
Detroit Michigan

ALS, Burton Historical Collection, MiD.

1. Bvt. Capt. Franklin Dyer Callender of N.Y., USMA 1839, apparently gave USG a note in payment which is mentioned in letter of June 28, 1852.

To Bvt. Maj. Gen. Thomas S. Jesup

————

Sackets Harbor N. Y.
May 26th 1852

GEN.

The 4th Infantry having recieved orders to repair to Fort Columbus N. Y. preparitory to a move for the Pacific Division, I would respectfully request instructions as to what I shall do with the public property, pertaining to the Quarter Master's Department, at this place.

I would respectfully recommend that the horses, and forage, on hand be sold.

	I am Gen.
	Very Respectfully
To Gen. T. S. Jesup	Your Obt. Svt.
Qr. Mr. Gen. U S A	U. S. GRANT
Washington D. C.	Bvt. Capt. & R. Q. M. 4th Infy

ALS, DNA, RG 92, Consolidated Correspondence 956, Bvt. Maj. Gen. Thomas S. Jesup replied on May 29, 1852. "Your letter of the 26th instant is received. You are directed to sell, to the best advantage, all the means of transportation in your possession. You will also call on the commanding officer of your Post for a 'Board of Survey,' and sell all such property as may be reported as not worth the transportation. You will apply the money thus received to the public use so far as it will go, and, should no officer of the Department arrive at your post to make arrangements for the transportation of the troops before it is necessary for them to move, you will make the necessary contracts, payable only after Congress shall have supplied the Department with funds." Copy, *ibid.*, Q. M. Letter Books.

To Bvt. Maj. Gen. Thomas S. Jesup

—————

Sackets Harbor N. Y.
May 31st 1852

GEN.

Having been directed to provide transportation, to Governer's Island, for the three companies of the 4th Infantry, stationed at Forts Niagara & Ontario and this place, I would respectfully report; that I have not got the means of paying for such transportation, and doubt the propriety of entering into any contract that will depend upon the action of Congress, (the passage of the deficiency bill) to comply with.

I would respectfully request instructions.

	I am Gen.
	Very Respectfully
To Maj. Gen. T. S. Jesup	Your Obt. Svt.
Qr. Mr. Gen. U. S. A.	U. S. GRANT
Washington D. C.	Bvt. Capt. & R. Q. M. 4th Inf.y

ALS, DNA, RG 92, Letters Received. See letter of June 2, 1852.

To Bvt. Maj. Gen. Thomas S. Jesup

———

Sackets Harbor N. Y.

June 2d 1852

GEN.

I have the honor of acknowledging the receipt of your instructions of the 29th May, relative to the manner of entering
into contract for the transportation of troops &c.

I have entered into agreement, conditionally, for the transportation of the three companies of the 4th Infantry, at Fort
Niagara, Fort Ontario, and this place, to Governer's Island,
having been directed by Col. Whistler to do so.

I am Gen.

Very Respectfully

To Gen. T. S. Jesup   Your Obt. Svt.

Qr. Mr. Gen. U. S. A.   U. S. GRANT

Washington, D. C.   Bvt. Capt. & R. Q. M. 4th Inf

ALS, DNA, RG 92, Letters Received. See letter of May 26, 1852. On June 2,
1852, USG signed a contract with Samuel T. Hooker for the transportation of
eight officers and 178 others from Madison Barracks, Forts Ontario, and Niagara,
N.Y., to Fort Columbus, Governors Island, N.Y., at a cost of $10 for each officer
and $8.50 for each of the others. DS, *ibid.*, RG 217, Army Contracts.

To Bvt. Maj. Gen. Roger Jones

———

Madison Barracks, Sacket's Harbor, N.Y.

June 15th, 1852.

GENERAL:

I have the honor to report to you that the Regimental and
non-commissioned Staff, and Company "D" 4th Infantry—com-
prising in all three officers and seventy-one non-commissioned

officers and privates, leave here this morning, for Governor's Island.

> I am, Sir,
> Very respectfully
> Your Obt. Svt.

Bvt. Major Genl. R. Jones   U. S. Grant
Adjt. Genl. U. S. A.   Bvt. Capt. & Act. Adj. 4th Inf.y
Washington, D. C.   Comd.g Post

LS, DNA, RG 94, Letters Received.

To Julia Dent Grant

———

> Governer's Island N. Y.
> June 20th 1852

Dear Julia.

We are all now pretty well settled in camp[1] with the usual comforts; that is, a chest and trunk for seats and a bunk to sleep in. The ladies have come over from the city and are living in a few vacant rooms that are not required by the company of Artillery stationed on the island.

The weather has been exceeding warm for the last few days and very unpleasant for the camp. The great difficulty in living in camp is that persons are so much exposed to the weather. A warm day is much more felt, in a tent, than in the sun; and a tent is but little protection against the cold.

I have been doing nothing but to busy myself making arrangements for the comfort of the camp. I have all to do in making preparation for our departure and I now begin to fear that I shall be so busy as to prevent my going to Washington. I spoke to Col. Bonneville[2] on the subject this morning and he seems to think that it will be out of the question for me to go. If I cannot go I want father to write to our member of congress and have one set of my papers, on the subject of the stolen money,[3] saved. It is very important that they should not be lost.

Governer's Island is situated in the Harbor of N. York City and about one & a half miles from Castle Garden landing. We can go to the city at almost all hours of the day in small boats belonging to Government, and which ply regularly for the convenience of us all. But while it keeps so warm there is but little pleasure in visiting the city. Most of the day we get the benefit of the sea breeze here while in the city we would get but little of it.

How did you and Fred. get along? I am begining to grow impatient to hear now as the time approach[es] when I should hear. Were they all delighted to see Fred.? And how has he behaved? Did Clara get my letter in time to go to the city[4] to meet you? Write soon and answer all these questions.

the ladies that are here are Mrs. Gore, Mrs. Haller, Mrs. Wallen, Mrs. Maloney and Mrs. Collins.[5] Mrs Forsythe[6] was married to a young lady living somewhere about Rochester, but whose name I did not learn, on last Thursday. He has arrived in the city with his bride and will probably be here with her to-morrow. Mr. Jones[7] too will be married this week. He sent invitations for us all to attend his weding to-morrow evening I believe. He is to marry Miss Whitney of Rochester. I never thought she would have him.

Two Companies of our Regiment go round the Cape, Cape Horn, in a sail vessel, and Mr. Hunt goes with them. The Compa[nies] selected to go are Maj. Larnard's and [Maj.] Haller's.[8] They will take their lad[ies with] them.

It is impossible to tell anything abou[t] when we will start.

Give my love to all at home and be sure and write soon and often. I will write again about Wednesday. Kiss Fred. for me. Does he talk about his pa.

Your affectionate husband.

ULYS.

ALS, DLC-USG, postmarked New York, June 21, 1852, and addressed to Julia Grant "care of J. R. Grant Esq. Bethel, Clermont County, Ohio."

1. The 4th Inf. arrived at Governors Island on June 17, 1852.
2. Lt. Col. Benjamin L. E. Bonneville.
3. For previous correspondence on this subject, see June 27, 1848, and for further mention see June 28, 1852.
4. The city of Cincinnati.
5. All wives of officers of the 4th Inf.
6. 2nd Lt. Benjamin D. Forsythe of Ill., USMA 1848.
7. 1st Lt. DeLancey Floyd-Jones of N.Y., USMA 1846, graduated under the name of Jones and added a hyphen later.
8. Bvt. Maj. Granville Owen Haller of Pa.

To Julia Dent Grant

Fort Columbus, Governer's Island N. Y.
June 24th 1852

MY DEAREST JULIA.

It is time now to write my second letter for this week but I must confess that there is but little to write about. I generally go to the city evry day but as I have business with the Quarter Master there I do not get to see much of the city. The other evening I went to see the trained animals you heard me reading about before you left Sackets Harbor. Their performances are truly wonderfull. The monkeys are dressed like men & women, set up and take tea like other persons, with monkeys to wait on the table; they go riding on horseback and in a coach, with dogs for horses, a monkey driving and another acting as footman. During their drive a wheel comes off the carriage and they have an upset. The driver immediately rushes for the dog's heads,— who act as if they were making desperate efforts to run away— and seizes each by the bit and holds them while the footman gets the wheel that come off and brings it to the carriage to be put on again. All this and many other tricks sufficient to fill up an evening they do apparently understanding all the time what they are about. I forgot to say in the begining that I recieved youre note from Cincinnati punctually when due. I was very glad to hear that you had got through without accident to yourself or Fred.

and without loss of baggage. Did Clara meet you at the Broadway house ?[1] I expect she did not get my letter until you got there. There has been no letter come here for you since you left. I have been expecting a letter from St. Louis, and indeed I am anxious to hear from them before we leave. I shall write to them in the course of a few days. What do they say of your arrangement of spending the summer in Ohio? Dont you think you have taken the wisest course?

It seems now more than probable that we will leave here about the 10th of next month, or as soon after that as transportation can be provided. Maj. Larnard's and Maj. Haller's Companies sail by the way of Cape Horn. It will probably take them from five to six months to go round. I should like the trip by the Horn very much for the sake of seeing all the South American ports that the vessel will necessarily put in too for water &c. Mr. Hunt goes with them for the benefit of his health.—Now as the time approaches for going I am anxious to be off. The later in the season we put off going the worse it will be crossing the Isthmus.

Did you get a letter from Mrs. Gore? She wrote one to you and I want you to be sure and answer it soon. Her brother accompanies her to Calafornia. I think on the whole it is a dangerous experiment for the ladies to go to Calafornia. There is one thing certain they make make up their minds before they start to get along with their work without assistance. Some of the ladies of the 2d Infantry who went with their husbands in 1848 have returned and do not intend going back again I believe.

How does little Fred. behave? He has got acquainted well enough I suppose to behave as cuning as he did before he left Sackets Harbor? Does he ever talk about his pa? You must write a greatdeel about the littl[e] dog. I want to see him very much. I do n[ot] feel as if I can be a great while without seeing you and Fred. I did not know but I would get a leave of absence for a short time and go home but I do not believe it possible. All preparation for starting devolvs on me so that out of all the Regiment I am the only one that cannot get a leave of absence. I am going to

Washington² next week however, and if I may find out something there about the time we will start and if there is time I will
go on to Ohio and see you. Adieu my dearest Julia. Give my love
to all at home. Kiss Fred. for me. Write soon.

> Your affectionate husband
> ULYSS.
>
> over

I forgot to say that I found yours and Freds l[e]tter enclosing a
lock of each of your hair. I put them away and will take good care
of them. I am looking for a letter from you now evry day. Have
you rec'd one from St. Louis yet?

> U.

ALS, DLC-USG.

1. In Cincinnati.
2. See preceding letter for the purpose of the trip to Washington.

To Julia Dent Grant

> Fort Columbus, Governer's Island, N. Y.
> June 28th 1852

MY DEAREST JULIA;

I was highly delighted at recieving a letter from you, so soon,
written in Bethel. It relieved me from all apprehension for your
safety. You have had so much experience traveling alone that
you can get along as well as any lady by yourself, but having
Fred. to take care of I felt uneasy until I heard that you had arrived safely. The little dog no doubt is taken care of without
giving you any trouble. I miss him very much.

We still have no idea when we are to sail. The Regiment has
to get two hundred more recruits before they can go; but that

number they will have by the 10th of next month. What is to
detain us more than ten days after that time I dont know.

You want to know what I am doing? It is hard to tell. We
are on the Island about one or one & a half miles from the main
shore where all the officers except myself have to attend two or
three drills per day, and attend four or five roll calls in addition.
Between times we get together and talk over matters relating
to our move &c. Evry body is highly delighted with going and
wants to be off.

Since I have been here I have met a great many persons that
I new before, some from Detroit and some from evry place that
I had ever been. Among them was Capt. Johnston from Georgetown. I thought this an eligant opportunity of sending you something nice and accordingly you may look out for a very pretty
present within three days after you get this letter. The present
~~sent~~ I send to Fred. I thought very appropriate; the one I send
to you is the best I could think of. I intended to send something
to Clara, Gennie and Mary[1] at the same time, but I could not
think what to get so I thought it better to let you buy them a
present.

I send you Capt. Calender's[2] note by this letter. He has paid
my tailors bill so that I have not got a debt against me in the
United States, that I know of, except my public debt, and that I
shall go to Washington on Wednesday to try and have settled.
I met Marshall,[3] member of Congress from Calafornia who I
knew very well in Mexico, and he promises me to take the matter
up as soon as he goes back to Washington. When ever Capt.
Calender makes any payment get some one to credit him with
the amount on the back of his note and send him a receipt for the
amount. He will not pay you anything before next March, but as
the note bears interest that makes no matter. I will send you
$100.00 by my next letter. I would send it by this but having
Capt. Calender's note in it the letter will be so bungling that it
might attract suspicion that would lead to its being opened.
What money you have and what I will send you will answer you
until I can send again from Calafornia.

There seems to be no doubt but we will get the two dollars per day additional pay that has been allowed heretofore to persons serving on the Pacific. If we do get it I will try and save the whole of my pay.

Does Fred. talk and gesticulate as much as he did? Does he go much with his grandpa? I know they are all very much pleased with him and delighted at having him at home. When you have your other little one be sure and have some one to write to me immediately dearest. I hope we will not sail until I hear you are all well over your troubles and I do not think we can sail before that. Mrs. Gore is very well and sends love to you. It is by no means a certain matter that she will go to Calafornia. I think it very foolish in the Major going. His health is such that he can get a sick leave by asking in a minuet. Give my love to all at home. Kiss Fred. for me. Write to me when you get your presents and tell me how you like them. Remember me to Aunt Polly and family, Aunt Ann & family and Uncle Samuel and family.

Has your box from Sackets Harbor reached you yet? It is time now that you had got it. All here that you know are quite well. Capt. Mc⁴ goes in a day or two to see his sister.

Adieu dearest Julia; Dont forget to write soon and often tell me all about yourself and Fred. Tell me what new words Fred. learns to say. I presume in a month or so he will be talking quite plainly.

Adieu again
Your affectionate husband
ULYS.

ALS, DLC-USG.

1. USG's three sisters.
2. See letter of Nov. 12, 1851.
3. Edward Chauncey Marshall was born in Ky., graduated from Transylvania University, and became a lawyer. He moved to San Francisco, later to Sonora, Calif., served in the Mexican War, and was elected to the Thirty-Second Congress (1851–53). For USG's debt, see June 27, 1848.
4. Probably Bvt. Capt. Thomas R. McConnell, whose sister is mentioned in the letter of Jan. 4, 1853.

To Julia Dent Grant

———

Pay Master's Office, New York N. Y.
June 28th 1852

DEAREST JULIA;

Immediately after completing my letter to you this morning
I come to the city on business and while here I thought best to
get the check of one hundred dollars to send you. Dont neglect to
acknowledge the reciept of it as soon as possible.

Your affectionate husband
U. S.

Kiss Fred. for me again. A thousand kisses to yourself.
U.

I have got this check made payable to father so that you can
get him to draw the money for you the first time he goes to the
city.
U.

ALS, DLC-USG.

To Julia Dent Grant

———

Willards Hotel, Washington D. C.
July 1st 1852

MY DEAREST JULIA;

You will see from the above that I have at last got to Washington to attend to my pecuniary matters. The run from New
York here is but a matter of a few hours. I left N. York last
evening and arrived here at six o'clock this morning. I have not
yet seen Mr. Barrere,[1] or any one els on the subject for which I

am visiting here. To-day all places of business are closed and the buildings dressed in mourning for Mr. Clay,[2] whos funeral took place but a few hours since. This evening I shall visit Mr. Barrere and to[-]morrow, if possible, go before the Military Committee and make affidavit of my losses and try to get them to report favorably upon the matter. As soon as this is done I will go back to New York. My leave is only for three days.

The weather is so warm here compared to what I have been accustomed to that I feel as if I would melt away.

I know some ten or twelve members of the two houses of Congress, and officers of the Army who will introduce me to any one els that it may be necessary for me to know, so that on the score of acquaintances to attend to my business I cannot fail. In the morning I will call upon Mr. Cass and Mr. Shields[3] and present my business to them and urge action on the ground that I am now about leaving the vicinity of Washington and might not be able to attend to it hereafter.

I was very much disappointed in the appearance of things about Washington. The place seems small and scattering and the character of the buildings poor. The public buildings are ornimental and the grounds about them highly improved. I have only taken a short stroll around the city so I am not prepared to say much about it.

I believe I never tell you dearest Julia that I am well. But you know I am but seldom otherwise, and if I was I would tell you. I have been as well as could be ever since you left me.

Nothing has transpired, relative to our move, since I last wrote to you. It is ~~not~~ now thought that the Regiment will be filled up in two weeks from this time, and then the Colonel will report his readiness to move. It will probably be some two weeks more after that before vessels can be chartered and us get off. Have you ever got the box shipped to you from Sackets Harbor? I want you to keep me advised on this subject so that I may write to Mr. Hooker[4] if you do not get it in time.

I was looking for a letter from you when I left Governer's Island but it was most to soon to expect one. When I get back

I suppose I will find one and no doubt I will hear of many of Fred's tricks that he has been playing off of late. Has he got so that he makes himself at home yet? How much I want to see the little dog. Dont forget to write me a greatdeel about him dearest! —Have you got your presents yet? and the money I sent you? I suppose so without doubt.

Give my love to all at home and kiss Fred. for me. Remember me to all our friends. A thousand kisses for yourself dearest Julia.

Your affectionate husband
ULYS.

Do you hear often from home and what do they say about your being in Ohio? Write soon.

U.

ALS, DLC-USG.

1. Nelson Barrere, a lawyer of Hillsboro, Ohio, served as a Whig in the House of Representatives of the Thirty-Second Congress (1851–53). On Jan. 12, 1852, he had presented to the House the petition of USG accompanied by the proceedings of the board of inquiry. The matter was then tabled and no further action resulted. *CG*, 32–1, p. 258; *House Journal*, 32–1, p. 191. On Feb. 12, 1852, John S. Gallaher, Third Auditor of the Treasury, wrote to Secretary of the Treasury Thomas Corwin. "A communication from the Hon. A. S. Seymore of the 10th inst. covering sundry papers bearing on an alleged loss of $1000. by Lieut U. S. Grant, in the year 1848 was, yesterday, referred, by you, to this office, for a report. In reply I have to say, that I caused an examination to be made of the a/c.s & correspondence of Lieut Grant, on file in this office, and no mention has been made, by him, of having lost any money whatever—he has charge none to the U. S. and, consequently, no action could be had thereon.— The rule, however, in all such cases, is to *disallow* them, having no discretion to do *otherwise* in the premises—This fact is so generally known, that, it is presumed, Lieut Grant must have been aware of it, and, therefore, appealed *direct* to the only body competent to relieve. The statement of his *money returns*, however, may serve to throw some light on the subject; they commence with the 3rd qr. 1847. & terminate with the 2nd qr. 1851. inclusive, In the 4th qr of 1847. he admits a balance, due the U. S. of $200.28. in the 1st qr. 1848. he claims a balance of $117.14. in the 2nd qr. 1848. he admits $1473.38½ due the U. S. and in this qr. he rec.d $1000. from Maj. Fitzgerald, the same, perhaps now alleged to have been stolen, and which makes up the above balance. This latter balance is continued, to the present time, with slight variations—In his last a/c. *current* 2nd qr. 1851, he admits a balance due U. S. of $1.270.03½." Copy, DNA, RG 217, Third Auditor, Congressional Letters Sent. On Feb. 16, 1852, Corwin wrote to Representative Origen Storrs Seymour, a Conn. Democrat serving on the committee on claims. "I have the honor to return herewith the papers enclosed with

your letter of the 10th inst. asking information in regard to the claim of Lieut Grant. with the report of the 3d Auditor of the 12 inst. stating the facts so far as they are within the the knowledge of any officer of this Dept. You ask for a statement of the rule of the Dept. in such cases. Where public money is alleged to have been lost by a Disbursing Officer, no credit can be given on account of such alleged loss, unless expressly authorized by Act of Congress. I am not aware of any case where this Dept. has undertaken to decide the complicated questions of vigilance, fidelity, and possibility of fraud, & connivance which arise in most of such cases. The accounting officers only settle such accounts upon the proper voucher's. If these are not produced, it has always been held that relief could only be granted by act of Congress." Copy, *ibid.*, RG 56, Letters Sent to Committees of Congress.

2. Senator Henry Clay of Ky. died June 29, 1852.

3. Lewis Cass of Mich. had resigned from the Senate to become the unsuccessful Democratic candidate for President in 1848, and had been reelected to the Senate after the election. James Shields, also a Democrat, was then serving as Senator from Illinois. USG may have known him in Mexico where he served as brig. gen. of vols.

4. Possibly Samuel T. Hooker; see June 24, 1851.

To Julia Dent Grant

———

Girard House, Philadelphia Pa.
Sunday, July 4th 1852

DEAREST JULIA;

I am this far on my way back to New York and having a half an hour I will devote it to writing you a short letter.—I found that Mr. Barriere,[1] who I most wanted to see, had left Washington and would not be back for some ten days. So my mission proved partially a failure. I saw several other member however who promised to give the matter their support when ever it was brought up. Among others General Tailor,[2] from the Zainsville District, told me that if I would write to him he would do all for me in his power. The first day in Washington I could do nothing nor see any one. It was the day of Mr. Clay's funeral and consequently evry house in the city was closed and evry body at the funeral. Judging from appearances, and from the voice of the press, Mr. Clay's death produced a feeling of regret that could hardly be felt for any other man.

Among other things my object in going to Washington was to go before the Military Committee and state all the particulars in my case. But I found that that Committee held no meeting before next Teusday evening, and I could not wait until that time.

I got in here this morning and it being Sunday I had to remain until 5 O'Clock P. M. before there was a train starting for New York; so I took a stroll around and found three old maids, cousins of mother's, who I staid and took dinner with. Their names are Hare. They were delighted to see me and say that I look just as I did nine years ago when they last saw me.[3] They had a great many enquiries to make after all our friends in Ohio, and also after you dearest and little Fred. of whom they have frequently heard. There was a cunning little racal, about Fred's age, seting a few seats in front of me comeing from Baltimore last night, who was all the time busy, lifting the window and puting it down again. I thought I could see you and Fred. as you were going along in the cars.

I have but a moment more til I must close. I expect to find at least one letter awaiting me dearest when I get home.—I presume before this you have got the little presents I sent you and Fred. ? How were you pleased with my selection?

Give my love to all at home and write soon and often. Dont get mad because this is not four pages, for I have no more time. A thousand kisses for yourself and Fred. Adieu dearest Julia.

Your affectionate husband
U<small>LYSSES</small>

ALS, DLC-USG.

1. See preceding letter.
2. John Lampkin Taylor of Chillicothe, Ohio, served as a Whig in the House of Representatives, 1847–55.
3. The last visit to Philadelphia took place on USG's trip west after graduation from USMA.

To Julia Dent Grant

DEAR DEAR JULIA   *[July 5, 1852]*

We sail directly for the Isthmus. I never knew how much it was to part from you and Fred. until it come to the time for leaving[.] Several of the ladies will be left behind by this sudden move. Mrs. Montgomery is probably on her way here, Mrs. Rains is left, and Mrs. Judah[1] will probably be confined this week.

You must be a dear good girl and learn Fred. to be a good boy. I think there will be an opportunity for you to join me in the course of next Winter in company with the other ladies of the Regiment left behind.—I will write to you from evry place we put in shore. You must write to me soon and direct as I have told father.

It distresses me dearest to think that this news has to be broken to you just at this time. But bear it with fortitude. Our seperation will not be a long one anyway. At least lets hope so. Good buy dear dear Julia. Kiss Fred. a thousand times. A thousand kisses for you dearest Julia

AL, DLC-USG.

1. Wives of 1st Lt. Thomas Jefferson Montgomery of Me., USMA 1845; Maj. Gabriel James Rains of N.C., USMA 1827; and Bvt. Capt. Henry Moses Judah of N.Y., USMA 1843.

To Julia Dent Grant

Steamer Ohio
July 15th 1852

MY DEAREST JULIA;

What would I not give to know that you are well at this time? This is about the date when you expected to be sick and my being so far away I am afraid may affect you. I am very well, only sea-sick, and so are all the passengers, notwithstanding we are in latitude 10° North.[1] We have been blessed with remarkably fine weather from the begining; a very fortunate thing for a vessel coming to this latitude in July, with 1100 persons on board.

You see dearest Julia how bad it would have been had you accompanied me to New York. The Regiment had but two days notice before sailing and I had but a few hours. You know I wrote to you Sunday afternoon from Philadelphia when I knew nothing, nor suspected nothing, of the move. The orders to sail were sent by Telegraph and obeyed before there was time to correspond.

There is no insident of the voyage to relate that would interest you much, and then dearest I do not know how this letter will find you. I hope for the best of course, but cannot help fearing the worst. When I get on land and hear that you are all over your troubles I will write you some long letters. I cannot say when you may look for another letter from me. This goes to New York by the vessel we come out upon. To-morrow we commence crossing the Isthmus and I write you this ~~beca~~ to-day because then I may not have an opportunity. I write this on deck, standing up, because in the cabin it is so insufferably hot that no one can stay there.

The vessel on the Pacific puts in at Acapulco, Mexico, and I may find an opportunity of mailing a letter from there. If I do you will hear from me again in about three weeks or less.

Before recieving this dearest I [*hope*] the little one will be born. If it is a girl name it what you like, but if a boy name it after me.[2] I know you will do this Julia of your own choise but then I want you to know it will please me too.

Dear little Fred. how is he now? I want to see him very much. I imagine that he is begining to talk quite well. Is he not? I know he is a great favorite with his Grandpa & ma and his Aunts. Does he like them all? Kiss the little rascal for me.

My dearest Julia if I could onl[y] hear from you daily for the next [. . .] days I would have nothing to regret in this move. I expect by it to do something for myself.

The only ladies with us are Mrs. Gore, Mrs. Wallen, Mrs. Slaughter, Mrs. Collins & Mrs. Underwood.[3] They poor things I fear will regret it before twenty four hours. It is now in the midst of the rainy season and we have to cross the mountains on mules, through passes which are too narrow for two abreast, and the ascent and descent to precipitate for any other animal. Give my love to all at home dearest Julia. I hope you recieved the check for one hundred that I sent you. I have one hundred & fifty dollars in the hands of Col. Swords,[4] Qr. Master in New York which I will direct him to send you.

Adieu Dearest, A thousand kisses for yourself, Fred. and our other little one. I will let no opportunity of mailing a letter pass unimproved. Write often dearest to your affectionate husband

Ulyss

ALS, DLC-USG, postmarked "Steamship."

    1. This latitude extends just above the northernmost coast of Panama.
    2. Ulysses S. Grant, Jr., was born July 22, 1852.
    3. The wives of Bvt. Maj. John H. Gore, Capt. Henry Davies Wallen, 2nd Lt. William Alloway Slaughter, of Ind., USMA 1848, 2nd Lt. Joseph Benson Collins, and 2nd Lt. Edmund Underwood, of Pa., all of the 4th Inf.
    4. Bvt. Lt. Col. Thomas Swords of N.Y., USMA 1829.

Contract

Memorandum of Contract made this day, the twenty first day of July, One thousand Eight hundred and fifty two, between José Ma. Saravia of the first part and U. S. Grant, Bvt. Capt. & R. Q. M. 4th Infantry of the second part:

I, José Ma. Saravia, the first part agree to deliver (as soon) as soon as possible in Panama all the remainder of the 4th Regi-

ment of the U. S. Infantry, including the baggage of the whole
Regiment detained here for want of transportation. The means
of transportation to consist of riding mules, packing mules and
litters for the sick.

I, U. S. Grant Bvt. Capt. & R. Q. M. 4th Infantry the second
part agree to pay twenty dollars for hundred pounds of the
baggage and twenty four dollars American gold for each riding
mule and eighty Dollars for each litter, and also agree that the
part of the first part shall retain said part of 4th Regiment untill
full payment shall be made on delivery of the freight and arrival
of the saddle mules and Litters, and shall it be understood that the
freight is to be paid for each part of the baggage at the time it
will be delivered, and in case of default on the part of the second
part to pay all damages, losses &c there attaining to, to the first
party.

In witness whereof we have hereunto affixed our hands and
seals, the day and date above written.

Witness   U. S. GRANT
Sam Smith   Bvt. Capt. & R. Q. M. 4th Inf.y
Wilson H. Woeff   JOSÉ MA. SARAVIA

DS (facsimile), NN. On official paper of the Republica De La Nueva Granada. The
contract was probably prepared at Cruces, a point some twenty-five miles from
Panama on the Pacific Coast, reached by travellers in 1852 after using the
completed portion of the Panama railroad and the Chagres River. Although
Isthmian transportation had been contracted before USG arrived at Cruces, he
found the contractor unable to supply mules. An outbreak of cholera caused some
travellers to pay as much as forty dollars for a mule to ride twenty-five miles. All
healthy soldiers without families with them were sent ahead; USG remained for
a week in Cruces with the sick and the dependents before transportation could be
arranged, and about a third of the people with him died at Cruces or on the trip to
Panama. The contract with Saravia called for payment of more than double the
normal price and undoubtedly saved many lives. *Memoirs*, I, 194–98. Lt. Col.
Benjamin L. E. Bonneville reported to Bvt. Maj. Edward D. Townsend, Aug. 25,
1852, that "The baggage of the troops (which was ten tons less than the quantity
allowed by the contract) was not taken through to Panama with them, but was
delayed so long at *Cruces*, that the Regimental Quartermaster was obliged to
enter into a contract with the Alcalde of the place, to convey it through." LS,
DNA, RG 98, Pacific Division, Letters Received.

Statement

I Certify that my services were required at Panama where I received orders on the 28th of July to buy Two hundred and forty nine blankets; that they had to be Sent from Panama to the Steamer "Golden Gate", a distance of Several miles; and that it was impracticable for me to be present to see them issued; further that two-hundred and forty-nine were purchased by me and Sent to the Steamer for issue; that when I got aboard there could not be obtained receipts for all the blankets by eleven that had been purchased.

U. S. GRANT
1st Lt. & R. Q. M. 4th Inf.y
Bvt. Capt. U. S. A.

Steamship "Golden Gate"
Panama Bay
Augst 1st 1852

DS, IHi.

To Julia Dent Grant

Steamer Golden Gate
Near Acapulco, Mexico, Aug. 9th 1852

MY DEAREST JULIA;

I wish I could only know that you, and our dear little ones were as well as I am. Although we have had terrible sickness among the troops, and have lost one hundred persons, counting men, women & children, yet I have enjoyed good health. It has been the province of my place as Quarter Master to be exposed to the weather and climate on the Isthmus, while most of the others were quietly aboard ship, but to that very activity probably may be ascribed my good health. It no doubt will be a relief to you to know that we have been out from Panama over four days and no sickness has broken out aboard. All are healthy and evry minuet brings us towards a better climate.

Among the deaths was that of poor Maj. Gore. The Maj. was taken before daylight in the morning and in the afternoon was dead.[1] Mrs. Gore took his death very hard and then to think too of the trip she had to undergo crossing the Isthmus again! My dearest you never could have crossed the Isthmus at this season, for the first time, let alone the second. The horrors of the road, in the rainy season, are beyond description.—Mrs. Gore will be at home, if she is so fortunate as to stand the trip, before you get this. I hope father and Gennie will will go and see her soon. Lieut. Me Macfeely,[2] 2d Lt. of Maj. Gore's Comp.y, accompanied Mrs. Gore and may go to our house to see you. He promised me that he would. I gave him an order on the Qr. Mr. in New York for $150 00 Mr. Hooker owes me which he gets he will send you.

Mrs. Wallen and the other ladies along are tollerably well, but a goodeal reduced. Mrs. Wallens weight when she got across the Isthmus was 84 lbs. Her children, Harry Nanny & Eddy look quite differently from what they did when they left New York. But thank fortune we are fas approaching a better climate. The Golden Gate takes us nearly 300 miles per day.

We have seen from a Calafornia paper our destination. All but one company goes to Oregon. Head Quarters (and of course me with it) goes to Columbia Barracks, Fort Van Couver, Oregon. In consequence of one company of the Reg.t, and all the sick being left at the Island Flamingo, near Panama, to follow on an other steamer, we will remain at Benecia Cal. for probably a month. Benecia is within a days travels of where John[3] is and of course I shall see him. ·

You must not give yourself any uneasine[ss] about me now dearest for the time has passed for danger. I know you have borrowed a goodeal of trouble and from the exagerated accounts which the papers will give you could not help it. From Mrs. Gore however you can get the facts which are terrible enough.

I have not given you any discription of any part of our journey, and as I told you in all my letters dearest, I will not until I hear of your being well. I will say however that there is a great accountability some where for the loss which we have sustained.—Out of the troops at Sackets Harbor some twelve or fifteen are dead, none that you would recollect however except O'Maley, and Sgt. Knox, the one you thought looked so much like Maloney.

Elijah Camp[4] is with us. He goes as sutler, probably with Head Quarters.

Give my love to all at home dearest and kiss our dear little ones for me. Fred, the little dog I know talks quite well by this time. Is he not a great pet? You must not let them spoil him dearest. A thousand kisses for yourself dear Julia. Dont forget to write often and Direct, Hd Qrs. 4th Inf.y Columbia Barracks Fort Van Couver, Oregon.

> Adieu dear wife,
> Your affectionate husband
> ULYS.

P. S. You may be anxious to hear from Maggy.[5] She looks wors than ever. She has been sea-sick ever since she started. She regrets very much that she had not staid with you.

Mrs. Wallen was going to write to you from Panama but Maj. Gore's taking sick prevented.

> Again adieu dear dear wife.
> U.

ALS, DLC-USG.

1. Bvt. Maj. John H. Gore died Aug. 1, 1852.
2. 2nd Lt. Robert Macfeely of Pa., USMA 1850. Julia Grant was then staying with her father-in-law, Jesse Grant, in Bethel, Ohio.
3. John Dent, brother-in-law of USG, was then operating a ferry at Knights Ferry, Calif.
4. See letter of July 27, 1851.
5. Margaret Getz, wife of an enlisted soldier of the 4th Inf., was employed by USG as a servant for two years. See letter of July 19, 1853.

To Julia Dent Grant

———

Steamer Golden Gate
Between San Diego & Sanfransico Ca[l]
August 16th 1852

MY DEAREST JULIA;

There is a bare chance that we may meet a steemer to-day
from San fransisco and if we do the Captain intends to send the
passenger's letter's aboard. If we do meet the steamer you will
get this letter by the same mail as the one I wrote from near
Acapulco, and therefore I can only add that health still prevails
on board, and that I am perfectly well. My greatest anxiety to
write is to let you know that a rumor which you will probably
see in the papers is without foundation; namely that the Golden
Gate, with all her passengers, was lost off Monteray Calafornia.
While in at San Diego this morning we recieved Ꮐ Sanfran-
sisco papers up to the latest dates and saw a rumor to the above
effect, and although the paper did not credit the report I knew
it would distress you until you heard a possitive contradiction.

We will get into San Francisco to-morrow night and in the
course of a few weeks proceed to Oregon. In the mean time I
shall visit John.[1] As soon as I can get my papers off after our arrival at Benecia (which is within two or three hours of San
Franciso) I will apply for a seven days leave and go to Knights
Ferry. The distance is only one days travel.

You dont know dearest Julia how fortunate it is that you are
not along at present. How we will be situated is as yet all in the
dark. It may be that we will have to tramp over the country
looking after Indians for months, or it may be that we will be
quiet, but in tents, without a single comfort. As soon as we are
atal perminent it is our intention to have one of the officers who
have left their wives behind go, at the mutual expense of all, and
bring out all the ladies. It may be Maj. Alvord or it may be me
who will go, or it may be that Col. Buchanan[2] will be comeing

with his wife at that time and arrangements can be made for all
to come with him.

Our voyage on the Golden Gate has been a very pleasant one,
only a little sea sickness. We are not atal crouded, yet there are
enough to make it pleasant.

How I long to hear from you dearest Julia! yet I cannot hope
to hear for a month yet. If I had told you to direct your letters to
Benecia instead of San Diego I might hope to hear sooner. Now
you had better direct as I told you in my letter from Panama: that
is to Columbia Barracks, Fort Van Couver, Oregon. I presume
your letters from San Diego will be forwarded, but the Mail from
there is only semi-monthly. I think the Mails from Fort Van-
Couver are semi-monthly also, and if they are you will hear from
me evry two weeks.

In my last I told you of two or three from Sackets Harbor,
who you would probably remember, that died on the road. Besides those I told you of, there was the Band Master and O'Maley
and the Drummer, Herman.

My dearest what is there that I would not give, or undergo,
to see you and our two dear little ones now! If I could only know
that you three are well I would be perfectly satisfied with my
position. We are going to a fine country, and a new one, with a
prospect of years of quiet, when one settled. Chances must arrise,
merely from the location of land if in no other way, to make
something which if it should not benefit us soon will at least be
something for our children.

I write to you dearest Julia as if I knew that you were perfectly well and able to enter into all these calculations. I would
that I did know so. I cant think otherwise but what a satisfaction
it would be to know, possitively know, that you were.

I wrote to Ellen from Acapulco and told her that she must
send you my letter as soon as she read it. Although you would
get no later news by it I wanted you to get as many letters as
possible.

Give my love to all at home and all our friends. Tell me all
about Fred. and our other little one. Who it looks like! its name

&c. Fred. must talk very well! Often I set upon the deck of the vessel and wish I could see the little dog runing about. Does he ever say anything about his Pa? Dont let him forget me dearest Julia. Kiss him and the babe for me a thousand times dearest.

> Adieu dear der Julia
> Your affectionate husband
> ULYS.

ALS, DLC-USG.

    1. See preceding letter.
    2. Bvt. Maj. Benjamin Alvord of Vt., USMA 1833; Bvt. Lt. Col. Robert Christie Buchanan of Md., USMA 1830.

To Julia Dent Grant

———

> Benecia Calafornia
> August 20th 1852

MY DEAR WIFE.

    We have arrived, all safely, at this place where we will remain, probably, for some three weeks. When we leave here it will be for Fort Van Couver as I have told you in all my previous letters from Panama up to this place.—Benecia[1] is a nice healthy place where our troops will pick up what they lost on the Isthmus in a very short time. I can assure you it was no little that all lost in the way of flesh. Capt. McConnell[2] and myself when we got across were in prime order for riding a race or doing anything where a light weight was required. I have not been sick but the degree of prostration that I felt could not be produced in any other latitude except that of the tropics, and near the equator at that.

    I should not write you now because there is no Mail going for several days but I am going up to the Stanislands, to-morrow, to see John and before I get back the Mail may leave, and I can assure you dearest Julia that I shall never allow a Mail to leave here without carrying a letter to you.

I am staying with Fred. Steel,[3] a class-mate of mine, ~~and~~ who was at our wedding, and when I told him we had a little boy named Fred. he was very much elated. McConnell, Russell and Underwood[4] all joined in telling what a nice boy Fred. is. I really believe Fred. was much more of a favorite with the officers than we thought.

I spent an hour or two with Mrs. Stevens[5] in San Francisco, and she would have come up with us only Stevens was sick. They will be here in a day or two and make this their home. Mrs. Stevens seemed very much disappointed at not seeing you and Mrs. Gore. She sayd that she had heard you say so much about Mrs. Gore that she felt almost like she was an old acquaintance.

I have seen enough of Calafornia to know that it is a different country from any thing that a person in the states could imagine in their wildes dreams. There is no reason why an active energeti[c] person should not make a fortune evry year. For my part I feel that I could quit the Army to-day and in one year go home with enough to make us comfortable, on Gravois,[6] all our life. Of course I do not contemplate doing any thing of the sort, because what I have is a certainty, and what I might expect to do, might prove a dream.

Jim. de Camp come aboard at San Francisco to see Mrs. Wallen and he told her that John was making one hundred dollars per day. This is Friday night and on Sunday night I expect to be with John[7] and then I will write to you, and make him write also, and it is more than probable that you will get the letters at the same time as you get this.

I wish dearest Julia that I could hear from you.—I cannot hope to hear from, after your confinement, for at least a month yet. It distresses me very much. If I could only know that you and our little ones were well I would be perfectly satisfied. Kiss them both for me d[e]arest and dont let Fred. forget his pa. No person can know the attachment that exists between parent and child until they have been seperated for some time. I am almost crazy sometimes to see Fred. I cannot be seperated from him and his Ma for a long time.

Dearest I hope you have been well taken care of and contented at our house. I know they would do evrything to make you comfortable. I have often feared that you would fret and give yourself trouble because I was not there.

Give my love to all at home dear and kiss our little ones for their pa. Write me all about both of them.

Adieu dear dear Julia,

> Your affectionate husband
> ULYSS.

ALS, DLC-USG.

1. Benicia Barracks, at the western end of Suisun Bay, was a few miles from San Francisco.
2. Bvt. Capt. Thomas Rush McConnell of Ga., USMA 1846.
3. Bvt. Capt. Frederick Steele of N.Y., USMA 1843, of the 2nd Inf.
4. Officers of the 4th Inf.
5. The wife of Capt. T. H. Stevens.
6. USG refers to White Haven, located on Gravois Creek.
7. See letter of Aug. 9, 1852.

To *Julia Dent Grant*

————

> Benicia, California
> August 30th 1852

I have just returned from the Stanislaus, bringing John with me.[1] I find that there is a mail just being made up for the states and as I told you in my last letter, (which you will recieve at the same time as this) I now hasten to give you the account of my visit.—I started from here in the evening, by steamboat, for Stocton where I arrived before morning. At Stockton I got a mule and rode over to your brothers, d[is]tant about forty miles. I was very much surprised to find houses almost evry mile, and the road much more crouded with teams than almost any in the Atlantic States. These teams mostly cross your brother's ferry and are carrying provisions, goods &c. for Miners in the Diggings. I was much pleased with the prospect at Knight's Ferry. There are three stages per day, each way, crossing at the ferry, and generally come loaded with from eight to twelve passengers each. All these stop at the hotel, which is kept in connection with their other business, and dine. Lewis can tell you all about their business of course but you will be glad to know what they are doing from me. Their ferry, which is managed by two persons, is drawn across a little river about one hundred & fifty feet wide, by ropes attached to both shores. It takes about one minuet from the time they leave one shore until they reach the other. For this they now charge two dollars which is much less than they formerly got. In connection with this is their tavern, or as it is called, "The Knigt Ferry house" where the passengers by stage, and many teamsters stop and get a dinner at one dollar. They have stables which the stage companies pay them about two hundred dollars per month rent for, and board all their men [w]ith them at ten dollars per week. They have a traiding house where they get pretty much all the dust the Indians, and some other Miners, dig. They have a Ranch where they have several hundred cattle and numerous horses, all worth about thribble what they would be in the Atlantic States. So much for their business, that is the nature of it, as to the profits they are clearing from fifty to one hundred dollars daily.

I found dearest immediately upon my arrival a letter from you encl[os]ing one from Wrenny, and one from Ellen. But they were both written before you had heard of our being orderd from Governer's Island. It was with great pleasure I recieved them but it did not afford me the relief it would to have got one of a later date. Just think dearst I have not had one word from you since you got the news of our departure from Governer's Island.

Our Regiment is now in Camp at this place where we will remain probably two or three weeks when we proceed, by sail vessel, for Columbia Barrack[s] Fort Van Couver. It is detestable going in this way because it will take so long. The way the winds are now prevailing we may be three weeks going about six hundred miles. But there is no danger for it is the dry season and there are no storms.—On account of the Mail closing so soon and wanting to answer Ellen's letter too I can not write you all the particilars that I will hereafter. I feel somewhat tired too for I started, on horse back, yesterday from John's and rode to Stockton, 40 miles, before 3 o'clock leaving John's a little befor [8] o'clock. I had then to come immediately aboard the steamer and was told that we would arrive at Benicia at 12 o'clock and as the boat only merly touches here for less than two minuets of course I could not sleep. Well it was nearly morning before we arrived hence the loss of one nights sleep after a hard days ride. The night befor was almost like it. John had no idea at night of comeing down with me, so we set up until we almost fell asleep talking. We then went to bed, togethe[r], and got probably little more than an hours sleep when I got awake finding myself covered with a meriad of Aunts. We had of course to change our quarters and I could sleep but little more.

Kiss our dear little ones for me dearest Julia. You do not know how anxious I am to see them. Dear little Fred I know, talks quite well! Dont he dear? Is he not a great favorite with all at home? He could not be otherwise. John is very anxious to see him and likes to hear the officers who know him speak of him. Adieu dear dear Julia. Give my love to all at home and be sure to write often. Your affectionate husband

U<small>LYS</small>.

P. S. I forgot to say that I am as well as can be and so is John. Mrs. Stevens is here with us and is well and so are all the children. Mrs. Stevens says she has written to you three times but always directed to Sackets Harbor.

U.

ALS, DLC-USG.

1. See letter of Aug. 9, 1852.

To Board of Survey

Camp near Benecia Calif'o
September 3d 1852

To The Board of Survey Convened
by Orders No 67.

Gentlemen:

I respectfully submit the following statement relative to the loss of Public property whilst crossing the Isthmus of Panama.

The Regiment sailed from New York on the 5th of July under a contract which was to cover all expenses of transportation on land and water. Upon arriving at Navy Bay it was decided, by the contracting parties, or their agents to send the troops by the Gorgona route, and the baggage by the Cruses route.

Upon arriving at Cruses I found that the agent of the contracting party, had entered into a contract with a Mr Duckworth for the transportation of baggage &c from there to Panama.

After waiting three days for Mr Duckworth to furnish transportation I found that, at the terms he had agreed upon he was entirely unable to comply with his engagements. I was obliged therefore to enter into a contract myself for the transportation of our baggage. This detained me two days more in Cruses waiting to see the Regimental baggage packed or safely stored.

During this detention the Cholera broke out among the few troops left with me, as a guard, so virulently that I was obliged, on the recommendation of Surgeon Tripler,[1] to put them under cover. The baggage being protected only by tents was of course liable to the depridations of the inhabitants untill it could be got under cover.

Buildings were procured immediately, upon the Guard being relieved, to put the property in. All the natives that could be induced to work (about ten in number) were employed to pack this property and store it. But there being a large amount, in bulk and weight, it could not be removed in one day, neither could the natives be kept employed at night.—Hence a portion of the property was left one night unprotected.

Had transportation been furnished promptly at Cruses, as it should have been under the contract, it is my opinion that but little or no loss would have been sustained.

> I am
> Gentlemen
> Yours very Respectfully
>
> (Signed)   U. S. GRANT
> Bt Cap.t & Reg.l Qr. Mr. 4th Infy

Copy, DNA, RG 92, Consolidated Correspondence 350. For details on the Panama crossing, see July 21, 1852. Proceedings of the board of survey and the original of USG's report were sent by Lt. Col. B. L. E. Bonneville to Bvt. Maj. Gen. Thomas S. Jesup on Sept. 13, 1852. The documents were copied in the Q. M. office and the originals forwarded to Secretary of War Charles M. Conrad. *Ibid.* The original apparently served as the basis for the text printed in *Richardson*, pp. 141–42. The board of survey consisted of USG, 1st Lt. Thomas Jefferson Montgomery, and 1st Lt. William H. Scott, was ordered on Sept. 4, 1852 "to investigate, and Report upon the losses, and damages of public property . . ." It concluded that "every exertion was used by officers to protect public property from loss or damage." Copy, *ibid.* A list of the "Cost of clothing Camp & Garrison Equipage appertaining to the 4th Regt of Infantry unavoidably lost or necessarily destroyed in crossing the Isthmus of Panama" puts the total value at $1349.76 3/4. *Ibid.*, Miscellaneous Records, Pre-Civil War Period.

1. Maj. Charles Stuart Tripler of N.Y.

To Julia Dent Grant

Steamer Columbia
Sept. 14th 1852

MY DEAREST JULIA;

We have left Benicia for our station at Fort Van Couver where we will arrive, probably, in about four days.[1] We are aboard of a nice little steamer that is perfectly sea-worthy, but from the present movements I know that I am bound to be sea

sick all the way up. I feel it already and would not write only that
there is a mail just going to the states. You know dearest Julia
that I will never allow a Mail to go without bearing a letter to
you?

I have had no letter from you since we left except one written
before you knew that we had left Governer's Island. One line
telling me that you was well and that our dear little ones were
well too would make me perfectly happy. I know dearest that
you have written often, but your letters going to San Diego
keeps them back half a month. I am in good health, as usual, and
see nothing in this country to induce sickness. From my little
experience I think it a peculiarly favored country. Of course I
have seen but a small portion of the country and cannot judge of
the whole, but from what I have seen the clima[te] is unequaled.
Up on the Stanislaus, where John is, it is very warm, at this
season, but there is no change from warm to cold, from rain to
dry &c. as there is with us, or with people who live up on the
lakes. Alltogether I am, so far, a Calafornian in taste, wanting
but one thing. That dearest is to have you and our little ones with
us. There is not a more pleasant country in the world, and where
I go it is said to be equal to anything, or any place, in this country.
Oregon I used to think I would prefer to Calafornia but now that
it has come to the pinch I would rather remain here. I only hope
that I will be as much pleased with Van Couver as I am with the
portion of Calafornia that I have visited. So much dearest for
Calafornia: we are now geting close to San Francisco where this
letter has to be mailed.

Mrs. Wallen, Mrs. Slaughter (a very nice lady by the way)
and Mrs. Collins[2] go with us. They are all sea-sick now however
and not visable. Mrs. Stevens[3] I have had the pleasure of seeing
frequently. She is very well and so are all the children. She was
quite anxious to get Maggy[4] to live with her, and as Getz only
has one year to serve I recommended her to go. Mrs. Stevens
proposed giving her seventy dollars per month but she says she
would prefer going with me, if you are comeing here, for ten
dollars.

Capt. McConnell and Mr. Russell[5] are both very well. Mr. Russell has a strong inclination to go into copartnership with Stevens in a Ranch, as termed here, a farm in the Atlantic States. At the present rate of vegitables one crop would make a farmer rich. Capt. Wallen has also had an offer of $600.00 per month, with two rooms and board, for himself & family, if he would stop in San Francisco and take charge of a Hotel. If he does it it will make me [a] Capt. My post however would not be [changed] by the promotion.

Remember me to all our friends, give my love to all all home and kiss our dear little ones a thousand times for their papa. When I get one line from you dearest saying that you are well and through your troubles I can write much better. Adieu dear dear Julia.

Your affectionate husband

U. S. G.

ALS, DLC-USG, postmarked "Steamship."

1. The 4th Inf. left Benicia Barracks on Sept. 14, 1852, and arrived at Columbia Barracks, Fort Vancouver, on Sept. 20, 1852.

2. Wives of Capt. Henry Davies Wallen, 2nd Lt. William Alloway Slaughter, and 2nd Lt. Joseph Benson Collins. For an anecdote about Slaughter, see *Memoirs*, I, 198–99.

3. Mr. and Mrs. Stevens of San Francisco, mentioned frequently in subsequent letters, have not been positively identified. Mrs. Stevens was probably the wife of Lt. Thomas H. Stevens, mentioned as stationed at Sackets Harbor in letter of June 16, 1851. This is, again probably, the T. H. Stevens referred to in *Calendar*, Jan. 5, 1854.

4. Margaret Getz, wife of a private soldier, had worked as a servant for the Grants.

5. Bvt. Capt. Thomas R. McConnell and 1st Lt. Edmund Russell of Pa., USMA 1846.

To Julia Dent Grant

On boar Steamer Columbia
Astoria Oregon
September 19th 1852

I have written you one letter from aboard this Steamer since we left Benicia and as she returns with a mail, the only one that will leave Oregon for two weeks, I write again. It is now 9 o'clock at night and in a few minuets we will be ~~at Colum~~ on our way for Columbia Barracks where we will arrive about breakfast to-morrow. As the Steamer only stops there long enough to land us there will be no time to give you any impressions that I may form of the place. There are however many passengers aboard who are well acquainted with the place and they all coincide in saying that it is as pleasant a place as there is in the country. The country is certainly delightful and very different from the same latitude in the Atlantic States. Here, I am told, ice scarsely ever forms to a greater thickness than one inch although we are about one degree North of Sacket Harbor.

Astoria—a place that we see on maps, and read about,—is a town made up of some thirty houses, (I did not count them) situated on the side of a hill covered with tall trees, looking like pines, with about two acres cleared to give way for the houses. There is nothing about the place to support it only that it is near the outlet of the Columbia river and they have a custom house, distributing post office for the Territory, and a few pilots for vessels coming into the mouth of the river. Boats anchoring in the stream (they have no wharf) gives occupation for a few boatmen to carry passengers ashore to see the town that they read about in their young days. So much for Astoria.—Our trip from San Francisco has been the roughest that I have ever experienced. All the passengers, and some of the officers of the boat, have been sea-sick. The wind blew for three days most terrifically, but now it is mild and we are in the river.

My dearest Julia had it not been for your situation you would have come with me. Seeing what you would have suffered I do not regret that you could not come along. I would give a great deel if you were here now, but I do not believe that you could have stoo[d] the trip at this season of the year with all the detintions consequent upon having troops along.

I have no doubt but I shall like Oregon very much. Evry one speaks well of the climate and the growing prospects of the country. It has timber and agricultural land, and the best market in the world for all they can produce. Evry article of produce can be raised here that can be in the states; and with much less labor, and finds a ready cash market at four times the value the same article would bring at home. Dearest I know you do not care about hearing this but would like to hear more about myself. Well! whilst we were in Benicia I devoted myself, as much as possible, to seeing Calafornia. I spent some days (as I told you before) with John, and was highly delighted with evry thing I saw. I afterwords spent a few days in San Francisco and must say that I consider that city the wonder of the world. It is a place of but a few years groth and contains a wealthy population of probably fifty thousand persons. It has been burned down three times and rebuilt each time better than before. The ground where the houses are build have either been filled in or els the hills dug away, and that too at an expense of not less than five dollars per day for labor.—After seeing San Francisco I spent my days galloping over the country in the neighborhood of our post, visiting Valijo,[1] the Capitol of the state, and looking at the resourses of the country.—The whole country from Benicia to the southern limits of the state, where not cultivated, abounds with wild oats, in a luxuriant groath, which only differs from our oats in becoming degenerate in the size of the grain, from not being replanted.

Dearest I could give you chapters upon what I have seen and thought upon our Pacific possessions, but I have not recieved a line from you since your confinement. I know that letters have been mailed to me regularly, but being directed to SanDiego we do not get them for a month after we would ~~did~~ had we known where we were going from the start. I expect however, by the mail which is now in San Francisco, that I shall get several.— Night-before-last I dreamed that I got home and found you, Fred. and a beautiful little girl, all asleep. Fred. woke up and we had a long conversation and he spoke as plainly as one of ten years old. Is my dream true, with the exception of my being there ?[2] Give my love to all at home and kiss our little ones for me.

Your affectionate Husband
ULYS.

a kiss for you

ALS, DLC-USG.

    1. Vallejo was the capital of California, 1851–53.
    2. The baby had been a boy, Ulysses S. Grant, Jr., born July 22, 1852.

To Julia Dent Grant

Columbia Bks. Fort Vancouver O. T.
October 7th 1852

MY DEAREST JULIA;

Another mail has arrived and not one word have I got from you. I have not heard a single word from you since about the 1st of July. I know though dearest that you have written often but your letters being directed to other parts of the country I do not get them. I am in hopes the next mail will bring me several letters. I am very anxious to hear from our little ones and from you dear dear Julia.

I am very much pleased with Vancouver. This is about the best and most populous portion of Oregon. Living is expensive but money can be made. I have made on one speculation fifteen hundred dollars since I have been here and I have evry confidence that I shall make more than five thousand within the year.

The population of Oregon is much less than I supposed. There is not over 15000 inhabitants in the whole territory

Emigrants are comeing in however very rapidly. The poor peo- ple have suffered very much this year. A great many widows have arrived penniless having lost their husbands on the road and spent all they had to get this far. They will now have a long winter to worry through and in a country where evrything is sold at exorbitant rates, and where no simpathy is shown.

I wish dearest that you were here. I think now that I shall be promoted this winter and when I am promoted I shall apply for orders to go to Washington to settle my accounts. If I am not promoted by spring I will resign my Quarter Master appoint- ment and make the application. This is supposing that your brother does not return this winter and bring you with him.

I have written a long letter home so that be where you may you will hear from me as soon as the mail can take a letter.—I have dreamed of you and our little ones two or three times lately. I always see you and them perfectly well. I wish I could know that my dream was true—

You cannot tell dearest how anxious I am to hear from you.

Did Lieut. Macfeely[1] give you $150 00 that I loaned him when he went back with Mrs. Gore? Have you seen poor Mrs. Gore since she went home? I have heard that she lost evry thing she had except just what she had on her back.

I expect dearest that you are in St. Louis enjoying yourself quite as well as though you were here. If I could only be there to spend the winter I should be too happy.—Tell Ellen that I got her letter at Benica and wrote a very brief reply. I shall write her a long letter by the next mail.

You will no doubt wonder what speculation I made? I will tell you I went into partnership with Elish Camp[2] and enabled him to buy, on credit, the house and a few goods where he keeps store. The business proved so profitable that I got $1500 00 to leave the concern. I was very foolish for taking it because my share of the profits would not have been less than three thousand per year.

Give my love to all at your house. Dont fail to write often and tell me all about our dear little ones. Fred. no doubt talks as plainly now as any body. Does he ever ask after his pa[?] Did you get the presents I sent you and him? I know you were pleased with them. I have a very handsom watch and chain that John gave me to send to you. I will send it by the first opportunity.

Is Fred. a good boy or has his aunt Ell learnt him to be bad? Pinch him for me. Kiss our little one for me. A thousand kisses for yourself dearest.

Adieu dear Julia until the next mail. I am in hopes then to have some letters from you to answer.

Good buy
ULYS.

ALS, DLC-USG. The post of Columbia Barracks was established May 15, 1849, on the Columbia River about 8 miles north of Portland, Ore. Territory. An AGO report of Nov. 15, 1852, lists 292 troops stationed there. *SED*, 32–2–1, pp. 62–63. A year later, the force had been reduced to 118 as troops were distributed to other Pacific coast posts. *Ibid.*, 33–1–1, pp. 122–3. An act of Congress, March 2, 1853, divided Oregon Territory into Oregon and Washington territories, placing Columbia Barracks in Washington. Orders of July 13, 1853, changed the name of Columbia Barracks to Fort Vancouver. Columbia Barracks, Post Returns, DNA, RG 94. See also Thomas M. Anderson, "Vancouver Barracks—Past and Present," *Journal of the Military Service Institution of the United States*, 35 (July–Oct., 1904), pp. 69–78, 267–79; "Vancouver Barracks," *Quartermaster Review*, 13 (May–June, 1934), pp. 18–21, 69–70.

1. 2nd Lt. Robert Macfeely. See letter of Aug. 9, 1852.
2. "Elish" Camp is almost certainly the "Elijah" Camp mentioned in letters of July 27, 1851, and Aug. 9, 1852.

To Julia Dent Grant

———

Fort Vancouver O. T.
October 26th 1852

MY DEAREST WIFE;

Another mail has arrived and not one word do I get from you either directly or indirectly. It makes me restless dearest, and much more so because I now know that I must wait over two weeks before I can possibly hear. I can write you nothing until

I hear from you and learn that you, and our dear little ones, are well. Just think, our youngest is at this moment probably over three months of age, and yet I have never heard a word from it, or you, in that time. I have my health perfectly and could enjoy myself here as well as at any place that I have ever been stationed at if only you were here. It is true that all my pay would not much more than pay the expenses of the table; yet I think, judging from what has taken place, that this expens could be born here better than the ordinary expenses in the Atlantic States. I have made something dearest for us, (including our children,) already, and have got the plans laid, and being carried out, by which I hope to make much more. I have been up to the Dalles of the Columbia, where the Immigrants generally first stop upon their arrival in Oregon, comeing by the overland route. I there made arrangements for the purchase of quite a number of oxen and cows, and for having them taken care of during the winter. If I should loose one fourth of my cattle I would then clear at least one hundred per cent, if I should loose all I would have the consolation of knowing that I was still better off than when I first come to this country. I have in addition to cattle some hogs from which I expect a large increase soon, and have also bought a horse upon which I have been offered and advance of more than one hundred dollars.

You have probably seen dearest Julia a publication reflecting upon the officers of the 4th Inf.y whilst crossing the Isthmus. You will soon see in the papers a very flat contradiction, with the actual facts given. It is stated that even Capt. Grant ran off, and left the men to take care of themselves. The facts are that the troops with the exception of a guard under the command of Lt. Withers,[1] and a large portion of the camp women, and Capt. Wallen's company, disembarked at Gorgona N. G.[2] whilst the rest were sent further up the river (Chagress) to Cruses. The next day after Capt. Wallen marched through to Panama, which left Mr. Withers and his guard, Dr. Tripler and myself at Cruses and all of us remained until I had got evry one started, (where they were unwell, on mules) or in litters) excepting one or two

who were so low with the cholera that they could not be carried.)
These persons were removed to to comfortable quarters, the
services of a Doctor employed, and arrangements made for their
transmission through to Panama as soon as they should recover
sufficiently. If I had time I would like to write several sheets
from which I would request extracts made by one of your
brothers for publication. But in consequence of having attended
an indignation meeting "of the officers of the Regiment," on the
subject³ that I have just been writing about, it is now after the
hour when the mail is to close. I can however send this by an
officer who is just starting for San Francisco who will see that it
goes by the steamer from there.

Give my love dearest to all your brothers, sisters, and our
acquaintances, giving my very best love to your pa & ma. Kiss
our dear little ones a thousand times for their pa, who is far
away from them, and retain for yourself love and many kisses.

Your affectionate husband bids you adieu dearest until the
next steamer arrives.

Adieu
ULYS.

ALS, DLC-USG.

1. 2nd Lt. John Withers of Miss., USMA 1849.
2. N.G. is Nueva Granada.
3. See July 21, Sept. 3, 1852.

To Bvt. Capt. Thomas R. McConnell

—————

Columbia Bks. Fort Vancouver O. T.
October 26th 1852.

CAPT.

Yesterday I made a requisition for Quarter Master's property which I deemed necessary to carry out the Commanding
Officers order requiring me to do the duties of post Qr. Master.

This morning having much writing to do preparitory for the Mail which leaves here on this date I sent the requisition to the Depot Qr. Master, by a sergeant, with *verval* instructions to get the articles called for, so far as the articles were alredy on hand, desiring to get into my possession the means of complying with the frequent requisitions made upon me for material necessary for repairs to Public buildings. After completing what I was engaged in I went to the office of the Depot Qr. Master and was surprised to find that my requisition had been enclosed to the Division Commander, probably, for his approval. As I had obtained the approval of the Commanding officer, to the very liberal requisition which I had made, on the assurance that I would draw upon it nothing but what was already on hand in the Department, save five barrels of lime, requested that it should be withdrawn from the Post Office and returned it to me. My request was not complied with. The Commanding officer had expressed to me, on signing my requisition, that he desired that the shops for mechanics, and the stable should be used by both Post, and Depot, Quarter Master so as to avoid the necessity of building new shops.

> I am Capt.
> Your Obt. Svt.
> U. S. GRANT
> Bvt. Capt. & R. Q. M. 4th Inf.y

To Brevet Capt. T. R. McConnell
Adj.t 4th Inf.y

ALS, DNA, RG 98, Pacific Division, Letters Received. This letter reflects a conflict in authority between USG and Capt. Thomas Lee Brent, of Va., USMA 1835. When Lt. Col. Benjamin L. E. Bonneville brought USG to Columbia Barracks, he believed that USG as regt. q. m. should replace Brent, who was assigned as post or depot q. m. Brent believed that since his rank as bvt. capt. antedated that of USG and his assignment as post q. m. was made on higher authority, he should continue. On Oct. 18, 1852, Brent wrote to USG. "Your requisition on me for Teams, Forage, &c, has this day been received. In reply I have the honor to state that I have been ordered by the Chief of my Department in the Pacific Division to act as Quarter Master of this post, and shall continue to do so until otherwise ordered by competent authority. I therefore decline acceeding to your request, as I deem it unnecessary, and as I believe myself perfectly competent to perform the duties of Asst Qtr Master, for this post, in addition to my other duties. The Commanding Officer has up to this time complied with any requests for extra duty men that I have made on him, and I have as yet received no official information that he will not continue to do so." Copy (made by USG), *ibid.*

On the same day Brent wrote to Bonneville. "By Paragraph 944 Gen. Regulations of the Army, 'All Junior Asst. Qr. Mrs. and other officers acting in the Department will consider themselves subordinate to and subject to the orders of the Principal Officers within their respective districts.' I therefore respectfully request that you order your Regimental Quarter Master to report to me for duty and instructions. By Paragraph 948 Same Regulations 'Quarter Master Sergeants will be placed under the Orders of the Officers of the Quarter Masters Department serving at the Post or with the Regiment to which they are respectively attached' Believing that the interests of the Public Service can be better served by a compliance with the above Regulations, I respectfully request that the Regtl. Qr. Master and Regtl. Qr. Master Sergt. of the 4th Infy. be ordered by you to report forthwith to me for duty in the Quarter Masters Department" *Ibid.*

On Oct. 19, 1852, Brent again wrote to Bonneville. "An informal requisition for Lumber and Tools for the purpose of making Bunks for 'Co E' 4th Infy. and signed by the Officer Comdg. the Company [USG] has just been received by me. By paragraph 974 Genl. Regulations of the Army, it is made the duty of the Officers of the Quarter Master's Dept. to perform the duty of directing the making of the Barrack furniture for Troops. I therefore respectfully request that such men as you may think proper to detail for that purpose be ordered to report to me for the purpose of finishing the Bunks for your Command, a portion of which have already been furnished—" *Ibid.*

On Oct. 20, 1852, Brent wrote to Bvt. Capt. Thomas Rush McConnell, Bonneville's adjt. "I have the honor to acknowledge the receipt from these Head Quarters of two orders of the 7th & 18th inst. The Colonel comdg. after having repeatedly in conversation denied his authority to give me any Order, has by these orders from his Head Quarters virtually ordered his Regimental Quarter Master to relieve me from the duties of Asst. Qr. Master at this Post; thus ordering his inferior and subordinate, as well as my own, to do that, which he is unable to do himself. With all due respect for the wishes of the Commanding Officer, I must decline acceeding thereto until I am ordered. I here again state that I am willing and ready cheerfully to obey any *Order* that the Commanding Officer of this Post shall give me in regard to my duties as Asst Qr. Master at this Post, but shall most respectfully decline complying with irregular and unauthorized demands on the Quarter Master's Department coming from what source they may. Having furnished to the Officers of the different Companies the Tools & Materials required to repair the Quarters, I request that should there be any surplus material it be returned to me, and also that as soon as the Quarters are finished that the tools issued to the men on daily duty employed for that purpose, be also returned to me." *Ibid.*

On Oct. 25, 1852, Bonneville attempted to explain the matter to Bvt. Maj. Edward D. Townsend at Pacific Division headquarters. "Some difference of opinion exists between Capt. Brent, a.q.m. and myself—The Captain is not born upon any return of this post; your remarks, in your office, to me respecting my *post* QrMaster, led me to infer that the Captain was exclusively under your orders. Your instructions, upon the Estimate of Captain Grant, L forwarded, dated the 28 ulto—confirmed me in this opinion; wherein you say 'he will be directed to furnish' &c To avoid the frequency of requisitions, I directed my Regimental QMaster to make one requisition—and embrace in it—every thing necessary to enable him to perform his duties at the post—getting wood, water, & police purposes,—together with such materials and tools, for fixing the quarters, tables, benches & bunks—Hence, Capt. B. remarks—: to let him have the use of his own explanations, I forward his four notes—If I could get these things in detail— Why not in gross?—I have carefully avoided giving this officer any orders—nor have I at this time—but the one to make the issue—I have no idea that it is your desire to separate me from my personal staff—to place it under a junior; nor do I suppose you wish me to communicate with my junior through his junior: but suppose it to be your wish that his depot and this post shall be separate and as distinct as those are at Benecia Although I suppose, Capt B.—will never have objection to any use I may wish to make of his stables, & shops all abundantly empty for both of our wants; Yet I would prefer the General to give his instructions—& no doubt be much more satisfactory—I wish the General to believe that I have always managed my posts with strict economy & of small expense & that I have now no disposition to increase them" *Ibid.*

Bonneville also endorsed USG's letter of Oct. 26, 1852. "Respecting the use of the shops, Capt. Grant knew at the time he received the requisition—that it meant—merely the priviledge of useing shops—in common with himself—I find under the Hospital a room of sufficient capacity to contain any tools &c I may require—I would not have the General believe that I would send my requisitions so irregularly as though the a. q. m. instead of doing so, directly. Forwarding explanation of Capt Grant Regt Q M to Division Hd Quarters—I have so far not had any thing done for myself—but only to put my men in comfortable quarters —& which I know is the Genls wish as well as mine—Most of the boards used are refuse, lumber—" See *Calendar* Sept. 28, 1852.

Brent continued as post q. m. until his transfer on May 1, 1853. As regt. q. m., USG was occupied chiefly with the outfitting of survey parties. When Brent left, USG handled his duties as well.

To Julia Dent Grant

Columbia Bks. Fort Vancouver O. T.
December 3d 1852

MY DEAR DEAR WIFE.

You can scarsely concieve how this Mails arrival has made me. It not only brought me a letter from you, but four letters, and two more from Clara written dearest at your request[.] I will not have time to answer your letters this time because the Mail closes in less than an hour. Now that I have got letters however I can prepare letter[s] before the arrival of the different

Mails and then add a Post Script informing of what I may have recieved.

Your letters, and Clara's too, said so much about dear little Fred. & Ulys. You have no idea how happy it made me feel. If I could hear Fred. talking it would do me a great deel of good. I know from the way he used to attempt to talk he must have a great deel to say. I am so glad too, dear Julia, to hear that our other little one is such a fine healthy boy! You must take good care of them and not let them grow rood[.] I have but a few minuets to write so I cannot say all I intended on this subject. Tell Fred. however that Mr. Brooke, a gentleman who I have long known, has presented him a pony which he will have just as soon as he gets here. I am glad to hear that Jenny[1] is with you in St. Louis, or rather at White Haven farm. How do your family like her? I know not otherwise than well. Jenny is so good and affectionate that no one could dislike her. Give her my love and tell her to write to Clara that I have recieved her two letters, but have no time to answer them this mail.

I am still very much pleased with this country if I could only have my family with me. Why did you not come with your brother? I think however it was better that you did not, for in crossing the Isthmus you would have run great danger of loosing Ulys.

Now about myself. I am in perfect health except I have suffered terribly of late from cramps. I have suffered so much that I walk like an old man of eighty. It is probably the effect of a terrible cold which I have scarsely recovered from. A week in the house will cure me and that I am going to take.

About pecuniary matters dear Julia I am better off than ever before, if I collect all that is due me, and there is about eighteen hundred dollars that there is but little doubt about. There is two hundred which I loaned a few weeks since which I do not expect to get. The person has already sacrificed his word, and as I had no note I may safely set it down as lost. I have got a farm of about one hundred acres, all cleared and enclosed, about one mile from here which I am going to cultivate in company with

Captains Brent Wallen & McConnell. I have leased it in my own name but there is four times as much of it as I could possibly buy seed for. We expect to rais some thirty acres of potatoes which may safely be put down at one dollars & fifty cents per bushel, and may be twice that, and the yeald in this country is tremendious   The ballance we will put oats in. The labor we all expect to assist in. It is necessary in this country that a person should help themselvs because it takes a great deel to live. I could not possibly keep house here for less than about one-hundred & fifty dollars per month aside from all expenses of clothing &c. Capt. McConnell & Wallen, the only officers here that you know are both well. Mc disired me particularly to remember him and Miss Kate to you Fred. & Ulys. Mrs. Wallen asks most particularly after you when ever she sees me.

Give my love to all at your house   Congratulate Fred. Dent for me and kiss his bride.[2] I must now close for I am after the hour for closing the Mail. Maggy and Getz are still with me, and for having such servants I am envied by evry body that comes to the house. You have no idea of the interest they both take in you and Fred. When I got these letters they fairly jumped with Joy.

Write to me often dearest. Kiss Fred. & Ulys a thousand times for me. Make them good boys. As many kisses for you dear wife.

Adieu. It will be a month I understand before another Mail leaves here.

> Your affectionate husband
> ULYS.

ALS, DLC-USG.

1. Virginia Grant, sister of USG.
2. Bvt. Capt. Frederick Tracy Dent had married Helen Louise Lynd.

To Julia Dent Grant

———

Columbia Bks. Fort Vancouver O. T.
December 19th 1852

My Dear Wife;

The Mail Steamer very unexpectedly arrived this morning before I had half my correspondence completed. It brings no Mail however to this point but leaves it at Astoria to be brought up by the river steamer.[1] As the Mail Steamer starts back before we will get the last Mail I cannot tell you whether I will recieve any letters or not; but I am very sure that there are letters for me.

I am, and have been, perfectly well in body since our arrival at Vancouver, but for the last few weeks I have suffered terribly from cramp in my feet and legs, and in one hand. You know I have always been subject to this affliction. I would recover from it entirely in a very short time if I could keep in the house and remain dry. My duties however have kept me out of doors a great deel, and as this is the rainy season I must necessarily suffer from wet and cold. I am now intending to spend one or two weeks indoors, on toast and tea, only going out once per day to see if the supply of wood is kept complete.

This is said by the old inhabitants of Origon to be a most terrible winter; the snow is now some ten inches in depth, and still snowing more, with a strong probability of much more falling. The Thermometer has been from Eigteen to twenty two degrees for several days. Ice has formed in the river to such an extent that it is extremly doubtful whether the Mail Steamer can get back here to take off the Mail by which I have been hoping to send this. You must know the Steamer comes here first, and then goes down the Columbia about four miles, to the mouth of the Willamett river, and up that some fifteen miles to Portland, the largest town in the Territory, though an insignificant little place of but a few hundred inhabitants. I do not know enough of this country to give you the account of it I would like to, having a desire to say nothing that is calculated to mislead others in their opinions of it, but this I can say; so far as I have seen it it opens the richest chances for poor persons who are willing, and able, to work, either in cuting wood, saw logs, raising vegitables, poultry or stock of any kind, of any place I have ever seen. Timber stands close to the banks of the river free for all. Wood is worth five dollars per cord for steamers. The soil produces almost double it does any place I have been before with the finest market in the world for it after it is raised. For instance beef gets fat without feeding and is worth at the door from seventy to one hundred dollars per head, chickens one dollar each, butter one dol[l]ar per pound, milk twenty five cents per quart, wh[e]at five dollars a bushel, oats two dollars, onions four dollars, potatoes two dollars and evry thing in the same proportion. You can see from this that mess bills amount to something to speak of. I could not mess alone for less than one hundred dollars per month, but by living as we do, five or six together it does not cost probably much over fifty.[2] I have nearly filled this sheet dear Julia without saying one word about our dear little ones about whom I think so much. If I could see Fred. and hear him talk, and see little Ulys. I could then be contented for a month provided their mother was with them. Learn them to be good boys and [to] think of their Pa. If your brother does not come out there is no telling when I am to see them and you. It cannot be a great while however because I would prefer sacrifising my commission and try something to continuing this seperation. My hope is to get promotion and then orders to go to washington to settle my accounts. If you, Fred. and Ulys. were only here I would n[o]t care to ever go back only to visit our f[r]iends. Remember me most affectionately to all of them. Kiss Fred. and Ulys. for their Pa and tell them to kiss their ma for me. Maggy and Getz enquire a greatdeel after you and Fred. They evidently think the world and all of him. I h[o]pe he is a favorite with his grandpa and all his Uncles and Aunts. I have no dought though the little rascal bothers them enough. When you write to me again dear Julia say a goodeal about Fred. and Ulys.

You dont kn[o]w what pleasure it gave me to read yours and Clara's account of them.

Has Jennie left yet ?[3] I suppose so however. How did they like her at your house ? Adieu dear dear wife; think of me and dream of me often. I but seldom dream myself but I think of you none the less often.

Your affectionate husband
ULYS. to his dear wife Julia.

ALS, DLC-USG.

1. Astoria was located on the Columbia River about ten miles from the mouth and Fort Vancouver eight miles north of Portland.
2. Three lines crossed out.
3. See preceding letter.

To Julia Dent Grant

Columbia Barracks O. T.
January ~~December~~ 3d 1853

I wrote you a letter two weeks ago upon the arrival of the Mail Steamer at this place and told you that I had no doubt but that I would find letters. I was disappointed.

The weather has been very cold here and what is most unusual, the Colum[bia] river has been frozen over. Captain Ingalls[1] and myself were the first to cross on it. It is now open however so you need not feel any alarm about my falling through. It either rains or snows here all the time at this place so I scarsely ever get a mile from home, and half the time do not go out of the house during the day. I am situated quite as comfortable as any body here, or in the Territory. The house I am living in is probably the best one in Oregon. Capt. Brent & Ingalls and their two clerks Mr. Bomford & myself live to gether and Maggy cooks for us and Getz assists about the house. Evry one says they are the best servants in the whole Territory. With Getz's pay, the sale of his rations, the wages we give and Maggy's washing, they get about 75 dollars per month. Living together as we do I suppose board, washing, and servant hire does not cost us over 61 dollars per month each, but alone it would require economy to get along inside of near twice that amount. For instance flour is 42 dollars per barrel and evry thing is proportionally dear. I expect to go to San Francisco in two or four weeks now, under orders to bring up public funds, and if I do I shall stay over one trip of the Steamer and go up and spend ten days with John and Wrenshall. You need not be atall surprised if my next letter should be from San Francisco.

I promised you to tell you all about Oregon, but I have seen so little of it that I know nothing that I have not told you. The country is very new but almost doubling its population yearly. The soil is generally very fertile but then there is but a very small proportion of it that can be cultivated.

My dearest I wish, if I am to be separated from you, and our little ones, that I could at least be where it did not take two months to get a letter. Just think, you write to me and tell me all Fred s pranks and how finely Ulys. is coming on all of which interests me exceedingly, but then I think what improvements must have taken place since the letter was written. I suppose that Ulys will be seting alone by the time you get this. Is Fred. very patronising towards him? I expect he wants to nurse him? The dear little dogs how much I wish I could see them. Is Fred. as fond of riding as he was in Bethel? How was Jennie pleased with her visit? and how were they all pleased with her? As a matter of course she had left before you will get this. Fred. and his bride no doubt have gone too. Does your Brother Lewis intend remaining in Missouri? or will he return to Calafornia? I have never recieved a line from your brother John since my arrival at Van-Couver although I wrote to him soon after we got here.

All the ladies here are quite well and the gentlemen also. Mrs. Wallen stays at home all the time and in fact she could not well do otherwise. She always enquires very particularly after you evry mail.

Give my love dearest Julia to your Pa & Ma and all the rest of the family. Tell Fred. to be a good boy and recollect his pa and mind evry thing his grand pa & ma tells him. Kiss him and Ulys for me and write a great deel about them. I will close here for the present hoping that before the Mail closes we will get the mail which has just come up and then I can let you know if I get anything.

Adieu dear wife
ULYS.

P. S. There is not a particle of hope of geting the Mail that come up in time to add anything to this   If the Mail should come in time to give me five minuets I will write you another letter if it is only to tell you whether or not I have heard from you. Do not fret dear Julia about me. I am perfectly well and have entirely recovered from those attacks of cramp which I had a few weeks since. They amounted to nothing except they were painful. Adieu again dear dear Julia.

Your affectionate husband
ULYS

ALS, DLC-USG.

1. Capt. Rufus Ingalls of Me., USMA 1843, served as asst. q. m. at Fort Vancouver, 1849–52.

To Julia Dent Grant

Columbia Barracks O. T.
January 4th 1853

DEAR WIFE;

The Mail has arrived and brought me a long letter from you in which you give me a long account of our dear little ones. How much I should like to see them! I had a long dream about Fred.

last night. I thought I was at home and playing with him. He talked so plain that he astonished me, then too his remarks were so sensible. I cannot recollect what I thought he said. Do you think ~~Fred.~~ Ulys. is going to be as smart as Fred.? I am glad to hear that all are well at your house. So Jennie has gone! and Fred. and his wife too! You do not say how they liked Jennie at your house, nor how she was pleased with her visit. I know though that it must have been satisfactory all round.

Capt. McConnell has just been reading me a portion of a long letter from his sister. She had just arrived at home. From New York to Charlston she went alone and as she expected to be very sea sick she shut herself up in her State room and did not come out the whole trip, but astonishing [*to say*] was not sick for an instant. She says that in the course of her travels she did not meet with any who she like half so well as you. She enquires particularly after Fred.

You enquire about my quarters! I have told you in the letter which will go by the same mail as this. The Plan is very much the same as yours only a little larger with higher sealings, and a piaza on thre sides, upstairs and down.[1] As I told you it is probably the best dwelling house in Oregon at present. But you must not think that the ballance of the quarters are like this; far from it. They are what are called temporary buildings having been put up in great haste with round and green logs, floors of rough green plank. They are very cold at present but they will be made comfortable next summer. I live where I do in consequence of being Commissary & Qr. Master.

I have written this in a very great hurry on account of having so many public papers to get into the office.

Kiss our little ones for their Pa. Write often to your affectionate husband

ULYS.

ALS, DLC-USG.

1. The house is now maintained as the Ulysses S. Grant Museum, 1106 East Evergreen Blvd., Vancouver, Wash.

To Charles M. Conrad

———

Columbia Bks. Fort Vancouver O. T.
January 4th 1852 [*1853*]

SIR:

I have just recieved your note of the 2d of November 1852, notifying me that I had been reported to the President as having failed to render within the period prescribed by law, my accounts for the Quarter ending the 30th of June 1852.

I would respectfully state that I left Governer's Island on the 30th of June, on a leave of absence for a few days, to attend to some business in Washington City before sailing for this coast. Returning I reached New York City about 11 o'Clock at night where I learned to my astonishment, for the first time, that the 4th Inf.y were to go aboard of the Steamer Ohio the next morning so as to be ready to sail by 2 o'Clock P. M. on the 5th. Otherwise my accounts would have been rendered within the time prescribed by law. As it is they were forwarded by the first mail after our arrival at our destination

I am Sir
Very Respectfully
over

To Hon. C. M. Conrad   Your Obt. Svt
Sec. of War   U. S. GRANT
Washington D. C.   Bvt Capt. & R. Q. M. 4th Infy

ALS, Mrs. Walter Love, Flint, Mich. Secretary of War Charles M. Conrad's letter to USG stated "Pursuant to the provisions of an Act approved January 31 1823, of which I hereto append an extract, you have this day been reported to the President as having failed to render within the period prescribed by law, your accounts for the quarter ending June 30 1852. On the receipt of this communication you will forthwith forward your accounts to the proper office for settlement, and address to this Department such explanation as you may desire to make, in order to relieve yourself from the penalty of the Act above cited." This was a form letter sent to eighteen other officers on the same day. Copy, DNA, RG 107, Letters Sent, Vol. 33. On March 22, 1853, Bvt. Maj. Gen. Thomas S. Jesup wrote USG. "The Secretary of War, has referred to this office your letter of January 4th 1853, in relation to the non-rendition of your accounts for the 2nd quarter 1852.

The accounts were received on the 20th December last, the fact communicated to the Secretary of War immediately, and your name dropped from the next Quarterly report, which was made on the 6th January last." Copy, *ibid.*, RG 92, Q. M. Letter Book.

To Dr. John S. Griffin

———

Columbia Barracks O. T.
January 5th 1852 [*1853*]

DR.
DEAR SIR:

Enclosed you will find the Certificate called for in your not of the 20th Ultimo. If it is not in such a form as to enable you to make use of it as a voucher please suggest what you want, consistent with the facts as set forth in my Certificate, and I will accomodate you with a greatdeel of pleasure.

I am Dr.
Very Respectfully
To Dr. J. S. Griffin   Your Obt. Svt.
Asst. Surg. U. S. A.   U S GRANT
Benicia Cal.   Bvt. Capt. & R. Q. M. 4th Inf.y

Certificate

———

I Certify, on honor, that six ounces of Quinine were borrowed from Dr Holdman Surgeon of board the steamer Golden Gate, for the use of the sick of the 4th Infantry on their passage from Panama to Benicia in the month of August 1852, this to be replaced on the arrival of the Troops at Benicia. This was borrowed on the recommendation of the Acting Surgeon serving with the troops, there being a great number of cases of fever on board, and being unable to find the Quinine belonging to the Army medical stores.

U. S. Grant
1st Lt. & R. Q. M. 4th Inf.[y]
Bvt. Capt. U. S. A.

ALS and DS, CU-B. Addressed to Asst. Surgeon John Strother Griffin of Ky.

To Julia Dent Grant

Columbia Bks. Fort Vancouver O. T.
Jan.y 29th 1853

My Dearest Wife;

There will be another Mail leaving here now very soon. Since I last wrote I have enjoyed excellent health and am larger than I have ever been before. I believe the usual effect of an Oregon climate is to make a person grow stout; at least I should judge so from the appearance of evry body that I see here and new before they came. The climate of Oregon is evidently delightful. Here we are North of 45° and though the oldest inhabitants say it has been about the most severe winter they have ever known here, yet it would surprize persons even as far south as St. Louis to be here now and witness our pleasant days. Farmers are ploughing and some sorts of vegitables have been growing all Winter, and will continue to grow. Such a thing as feeding cattle, except those that work is not dreamed of at any season. The farm that I have is a part of it already ploughed and I hope to have the whole of it finished in the course of a couple of weeks. All here are living very pleasantly only it requires very close watching to keep within our means. For instance; yesterday I was obliged to purchase some flour, for Government, and I could not get it under forty dollars per barrel; and that was about twelve dollars less than it could have been purchased for a week ago. All other articles, of food, are in about the same proportion.—There has been great suffering among the immigrants this year in consequence of the very high prices they have been compelled to pay for evrything they got, and then too from loosing their stock, and their all, in the mountains.

I have now written enough, for once, on these subjects dearest Julia; I will now notice your last sweet letter. It was one of the most interesting letters I have recieved, because it told me so much about our dear little ones: then too I got letters from Jennie and Orvil[1] in which our two boys are spoken of in just as high terms as a mother could speak of them. It made tears almost start in my eyes, with joy, to hear so much about them by one Mail. I only wish dearest that I could be there to look upon them now, and to see my dear wife again. Whilst speaking of seeing you and our two little boys let me tell you of the last plan I have hit upon for your geting out here. I am first for promotion to a [. . . . .] full Captaincy; Capt. Alden it is said intends to resign in a few months; (Brevet) Colonel Buchanan is near the head of Captains of Infantry and when either of these go I will get my promotion.[2] I will then have to give up my present position as Regimental Quarter Master and join my Company wherever it may be. I shall then apply for orders to go to Washington to settle my accounts as disbursing officer, and when I return bring you with me.

January 31st the Mail has just come in but brought no letter from you. I left this portion of my letter in order to answer anything that I might recieve from you. I know at so great a distance as we are seperated letters of different dates may arrive together, and then a Mail come without bringing anything. I however always feel much disappointed when I do not get letters from you. Write evry ten days and I will be almost sure to hear then by evry Mail.

Maggy and Gates have given me a little present for Fred. which I enclose with this. They appear to think a great deal of him and never fail to enquire, the first thing after the arrival of the Steamer (and before the Mail is opened) how you and Fred. are.

We are somewhat in hope that Col. Whistler will join us here. He writes that he is determined to come and asks for advice as to whether he had better bring his family with him. The advice will likely be (the Colonels letter was to the Adjutant) a short discription of this post; its conveniences & its inconveniencies. It is undoubtedly the best station in Oregon and the Colonel would not probably subject to a change for four or five years. The policy seems to be to transfer the enlisted men, when their time is near out, to some Regiment that has been but a short time in the country, and order the officers home to recruit new men. Give my love to all at home, kiss our little ones for me, and dream often of me. Dont fail to write as often as I told you.

Adieu dear dear wife
Your affectionate husband
ULYS.

ALS, DLC-USG.

1. Sister and brother of USG.
2. Capt. Bradford Ripley Alden resigned on Sept. 29, 1853; Capt. Robert Christie Buchanan (bvt. lt. col.) was promoted to maj. on Feb. 3, 1855. USG's promotion came through the death of Capt. William Wallace Smith Bliss (bvt. lt. col.) on Aug. 5, 1853.

To Julia Dent Grant

Columbia Barracks O. T.
February 15th 1853.

DEAR JULIA:

The Mail Steamer will be here to-day and I must fill up three pages for you, in advance, leaving the fourth to answer anything I may get from you. Since my last I have been very well. My opinion of Vancouver still remains unchanged. My hope is that I may be promoted to a company stationed at this post. The probabilities however are that I shall have to go to Humbolt

Bay. ~~Maj~~. Col. Buchanan[1] is there at present, I believe, establishing the post. There are no buildings at present. But you know when my promotion comes I intend applying for orders to go to Washington to settle my accounts.

We have had since the middle of Jan.y as pleasant weather as one could desire, this too at a place nearly two degrees North of Sackets Harbor. A great drawback to Oregon is that the land is so heavily timbered that it would take almost a life time to clear up a farm. People here dont however cultivate large farms as they do in the states. In this part but few cultivate more than from six to ten acres, and, where they are industrious and prudent, get rich at that. They will raise three or four acres of potatoes and usually get from 4 to 600 bushels per acre, and these generally bring $2.00 per bushel. On the ballance they can raise all other kinds of vegitables for their own use and to sell. Their bread they buy. Their cattle & hogs run out the year round and keep fat all the time.

16th of Feb.y

The mail is in and brought with her your long sweet letter of the 7th & 8th of December/52. You do not know how delighted I was to hear so much about our little boys. I am now so glad that you could not come along. As it is Fred. is a strong healthy boy. Had you come he no doubt would now be in his grave. I believe there was some twenty or more children of his age, and younger, come across the Isthmus with us. Out of that number seventeen died on the Isthmus and all the others contracted disease so that I believe there is not a single one left. Mrs. Wallen's little boy that she lost a few weeks ago, I believe, was the last survivor. You see now why I ~~was~~ am glad that you did not come.

If any one attempts to teaze you again about my making love to Spanish girls at Vancouver you can tell them that they must be desperately ignorant of the history of their own country not to know that there was probably never a Mexican or Spaniard in this part of Oregon.

Fred. I expect is a very good boy, at least if he has not been spoiled he must be, and does not give his ma much trouble. How I should like to have the little dog with me for a few days! Who does Ulys. look like? your family or mine? I hope he will grow up as good a boy as Fred. If Ulys. wont sleep of mornings I would keep him awake an hour or two past the usual time for a few nights. That would bring him too.—Your watch & chain are very pretty and I now have an opportunity of sending them to the states. You may look for them at "Wells & Fargo's American Express Company's Office, St. Louis," in about ten days after you get this. It requires repairs but they can be made in St. Louis. You speak of sending Mrs. Gore a present. I should like you to do so very much, and a handsome one too, but I do not want, unless it is absolutely necessary, to send you any money for some time yet. I am using evry dollar that I can raise[.] Potatoes for seed cost $2.00 per bushel and I shall plant 200 bushels, besides twenty acres of oats, and then raise a vegitable garden. I loaned $200 00 to an officer, who was going to San Francisco some two months since, on the solemn promise that he would return it by the next Mail. He has not paid and from what has transpired since I know he never will. I wish to gracious you had that. Has Capt. Calender[2] commenced paying you yet? if he has not I must, nothwithstanding my necessities here, send you money. ~~D~~ Mr. Camp owes me $1500 00[3] on a note that I hold against him, but it is not due for some time yet. If he lives and continues as prosperous as at present I would not give sixpence to have it secured. Do as you please with your money dearest Julia, I know you are always prudent as to expenditures.—Did you ever get a letter from Mrs. ~~Steven~~ Stevens? She has written to you and you must write to her whether you ever got hers or not. If you want the pearl handled knives you speak of buy them dearest. All the Gentlemen and ladies here are very well (Mrs. Wallen & Mrs. Collins are the only ladies,) Capt. McConnell, Wallen & Lt. Collins are the only gentlemen you know. Mrs. ~~Collins~~ Slaughter has gone to Steilacoom, on Pugets Sound to be stationed there.—Col. Whistler writes that he is very anxious to join, but I am sorry

to say that I very much fear he will not be permitted to do so.—
I think dearest your letters will come regularly now.—I was
disappointed in my trip to San Francisco. The Commissary there
thought it was not necessary for me to go after funds, but
directed me to draw drafts on him when ever I required money.
As the passage alone there & back is $150 00 it is not likely that
I shall see that city soon. Give my love to all at your house kiss
our dear little boys for thier papa. A thousand for yourself dear
Julia.

I forgot to say that I think you had better make a visit to
Bethel for three or four months this Summer coming. Dont you
think so? If you will write them the time you will start some one
will meet you.

                                                          ULYS.

ALS, DLC-USG.

    1. See preceding letter.
    2. See letter of June 28, 1852.
    3. See letter of Oct. 7, 1852.

To Julia Dent Grant

————

                                          Columbia Barracks, O. T.
                                               March 4th 1853

MY DEAR WIFE:
    I had the pleasure of reading a sweet letter from you and
Ellen last evening and was delighted to hear so much about our
dear little ones, and to hear too that you and them are so well
and are enjoying youselvs as much as you do. I got a letter from
father also in which he has a greatdeel to say about Fred. He says
that Fred. went with him to Georgetown and Felicity[1] and evry
body thought him a great boy.—Ellen says Ulys. looks like her
and bids fair to have her temper and wants to know if I am not
delighted. Tell her that the boy had better keep his temper to

himself when I get home. I am very tired and sore this evening.
You know that I am farming extensively and I work myself as
hard as any body. I have just finished puting in barley and I am
glad to say that I put in evry grain with my own hands. By the
end of the coming week myself and partners will have planted
twenty acres of potatoes and an acre of onions. In a week or two
more we will plant a few acres of corn. If I can only manage to
keep up until next fall I hope to be well enough off for the future.
At present however I am cramped all the time. I have a large
quantity of wood cut for which I had to pay and but little of it
will be sold for three months yet. I have been obliged to buy
horses, a wagon, harnass, farming utensils, garden seed &c.
I have too over two thousand dollars due me but little of which
will I get for six or eight months yet, and, I regret to say, some
of it never.

There is considerable excitement here just at this time in
consequence of the rumor of the discovery of gold high up on
the Columbia river and at the Grand Rondi[2] in this Territory.
If these rumors should prove true it will cause a great influx of
people to this part of Oregon. The fact is my dear wife if you
and our little boys were here I should not want to leave here
for some years to come. My fears now however are that I may
be promoted to some company away from here before I am
ready to go. I wish you could be here dearest to enjoy the fine
climate we have and the wild scenery. Since the middle of
January there has not been scarsely a day when an overcoat was
required, yet people who have been here the longest say that it
has been an unprecidented severe Winter.—The Mail which
brought your letter brought me a piece of unwelcom news. It
brought the orders for the Qr. Master here, Capt. Brent, to
proceed to Fort Hall,[3] and for me to perform the duties of that
office in addition to those of Commissary. This is a great
nusance because evry thing that is shipped to other posts, or to
this, have to be done by the quarter master here. All purchases
are made by him and all buildings are put up by him. It is not
like doing the same duty in the States because there communica-

tion from place to place is easy. Here I will be obliged to super-
intend, (with one clerk,) a blacksmith shop, Tin shop, sadlers
shop, Carpenter's shop and some two hundred pack and harnass
mules, all without additional compensation.

I recieved a long letter by this Mail from Charles Ford.[4] He
says that evry body who is any body, has left Sackets. Improvements however are going on. They have got their Rail Road
track laid and it has stimulated people there so evry body is as
busy as a bee. He says that he had a call from half the villege to
see and read my letter to which his is an answer.

Capt. Brent intends applying for permission to continue on
from Fort Hall to the United States, and if he gets it he will
probably return next Winter with Mrs. B. I think this might
prove a good opportunity for you to come on here. I will know
his arrangements however in time to let you know what to do.

Give my love to all at your house and kiss Fred. & Ulys for
me. I got a specimen of Freds. writing that his Aunt Nelly enclosed in your last letter you must not let Freds Grand pa spoil
him. Can Fred. say evry thing he wants too? and does he understand all that is said? Does he gisticulate like he used to do
before he could say many words? Whenever the mail arrives
Maggy always enquires most particularly after you and Fred.
but she never enquires after Ulys. How I would like to see the
dear little dogs. Tell Fred. that Mr. Brooke has given him a
pony that he can have to ride as soon as he gets here. Does Fred.
know his letters yet? If he was here I would learn him to read
before he was four years old. You know that he knew nearly all
his letters before he could pronounce many of them. What does
he call his Grandpa & ma? and his Uncles and Aunts? Adieu
dear dear wife. Dream of me often.

Your affectionate husband.
Ulys.

Dont forget to let me know as soon as you get your watch from
Wells & Fargo's Express office. I have forgotten whether or not
you ever told me if [y]ou got the presents I sent you from New

York City or not. Did you get them. Has Capt. Calender ever paid you anything on the note which you hold against him? It is time now that he commenced paying up. Adieu again dear Julia.

ALS, DLC-USG.

1. Felicity, Ohio, ten miles southwest of Georgetown.
2. Grand Ronde.
3. Fort Hall, Ore., located on the Snake River, in present-day Idaho.
4. Charles Ford was a lawyer at Sackets Harbor who shared USG's interest in horses. Later he became an agent for the United States Express Company in St. Louis when USG lived nearby, and their close friendship was maintained until Ford's death.

To George Gibbs

————

Portland, March 5th/53

Geo. Gibbs Esq.

Dear Sir:

Enclosed I send you a note from Col. Bonneville to Capt. Brent & Myself together with a number of points upon which Capt. Augur[1] (the Commander of the Company under orders for Fort Jones) wishes me to satisfy myself. Will you be kind enough to give me the benefit of your travels over the route that Capt. Augur will have to take.

All are well at Vancouver. We expected to see you upon the arrival of the Mail Steamer.—We have no news only that Ingalls is ordered to Camp Huma California, and Brent goes, as soon as practicable, to Fort Hall.[2]

Yours &c.

U. S. Grant

ALS, Bernard Gitlin, Detroit, Mich. George Gibbs was a lawyer and librarian of the New York Historical Society before going to Ore., in 1849. As an explorer, ethnologist, topographical engineer, and former gold-seeker in Ore., he was well-qualified to advise travellers. From Jan. through June, 1853, he was Collector of Customs at Astoria. Vernon Carstenson, ed., "Pacific Northwest Letters of George Gibbs," *Oregon Historical Quarterly*, LIV, 3 (Sept., 1953), 190–239.

1. Capt. Christopher Colon Augur of Mich., USMA 1843, was seeking the best route to Fort Jones on the Scott River, Calif.

2. Fort Yuma, Calif., was on the Colorado River, opposite the mouth of the Gila. For Fort Hall, see preceding letter.

To Julia Dent Grant

Columbia Barracks O. T.
March 19th 1853

My Dear Julia:

I have just recieved a long letter from you of the 20th of January from which I am happy to hear that you and our dear little boys, as well as all our friends, are quite well. How much I should like to see Fred. and Ulys.! I have no doubt but Fred. must have become very interesting by this time; and Ulysses too will soon be standing alone and attempting to talk. If there was any prospect of my being promoted to one of the companies at this place how much I would be delighted to have you here. There is not a more delightful place in the whole country and it has never been your fortune to witness any thing like such scenery. Evry body presents a perfect picture of health. I have grown out of my clothes entirely and am still geting larger. I take a great deel of exercise, and, I flatter myself, to some purpose. I have in the ground a field of barley evry grain of which I sewed with my own hands. The ground is already broken for twenty acres of potatoes, and a few acres for onions and other vegitables. I shall do all the ploughing myself all summer. You know besides my farming operation I have a large quantity of Steamboat wood cut for which I get $2 50 per cord more than it cost me to get it cut. It has to be howled but a short distance and that is done with my own private horses and wagon. Besides these speculations Capts. Wallen, McConnell and myself are starting two drays which we think will bring in from $10 to 15 dollars per day each.—If I am atal fortunate next fall will bring me in a good return which will make me easy for the future, for then I will never permit myself to get the least in debt.

I see that you must be geting near out of means. Has Capt. Calender not commenced sending you money on the note you hold against him? I think it was in March I told him to commence sending you fifty dollars evry alternate month. Be sure and let me know as soon as you get this and if necessary I will then send you a hundred or two dollars.

I am glad to hear that Fred. is growing up a good boy and that his Aunt Ellen is not learning him any mischief.

Do you intend going to Bethel this Summer? I think you had better make a visit there. If you go get Mrs. Gore to go with you. Maggy and Getz are still with me. They always enquire particularly after you and Fred. Maggy told me the other day that she and Getz had save four hundred and fifty dollars since they have been at Vancouver. Maggy gets twenty five dollars per month for cooking and two dollars per dozen for washing. Besides this there is Getz's pay and he sells his ration for twelve dollars per month and lives himself in the kitchen.

I am very sorry to hear that you have been suffering from weak eyes again! Take good care of them.

The money you got from Mr. Mackfeely was the hundred & fifty dollars left with the Quarter Master in New York.[1]—Have you got your watch yet? It must have reached Wells & Fargo's Express office befor this.

I see from your letter that you have been dreaming of me, but had me associated with wild horses. It is true that I have had the handsomest and probably most spirited horse in Oregon until lately, but I have sold him and have now two of the most sedate fellows you ever saw. Two besides Fred's poney I mean. By the way I must get Fred's poney up and ride him this Summer[.] Does Fred. talk any about his poney?

Mrs. Wallen and family are quite well. Capt. McConnell.

Mrs. Wallen sends you a great deel of love. She will be left entirely alone this summer so far as lady's society goes. The Company that Mr. Slaughter belongs too has gone to Puget's Sound. The one Collins belongs too starts soon for Scotts Valley, California. This is the Company that I belong too. I believe I told you that my promotion would in all probability take me to Humbolt Bay, California? I know nothing of the place except that I believe there are no quarters there.—You charge me to be cautious about riding out alone lest the Indians should get me. Those about here are the most harmless people you ever saw. It is really my opinin that the whole race would be harmless and peaceable if they were not put upon by the whites.

Give my love to all at home and continue to write often. Does Fred. know his letters? He will now soon be three years old and he ought to read by the time he is four. Kiss him and Ulys for me. A thousand kisses for yourself Dear Julia.

Your affectionate husband
ULYS.

P. S. I sent Mrs. Bailey the ring Mrs. Stevens sent her.

U.

ALS, DLC-USG.

    1. See letter of July 15, 1852.

To Julia Dent Grant

Columbia Barracks
Washington Territory
March 31st 1853

MY DEAREST WIFE;

The Mail has just arrived bringing me a very short and very unsatisfactory letter. You speak of not joining me on this coast in a manner that would indicate that you have been reflecting upon a dream which you say you have had until you really imagine that it is true. Do not write so any more dearest. It is hard enough for us to be seperated so far without borrowing immaginary troubles. You know that it was entirely out of the question for you to have come with me at the time I had to come. I am doing all I can to put up a penny not only to enable you and our dear little boys to get here comfortably, but to enable you to be comfortable after you do get here.

You ask why I do not live with the bachilors? I do: that is there are two "messes" and I am in one. Capt.s Brent & Ingalls, Mr. Bomford, Brooke and Eastman[1] are in the same mess that I am. If it is economy you think I should consult all I have to say is that my expenses are about twenty dollars per month less than if I was in the other. We all live and eat in the same house so that Maggy & Getz wash for us and wait upon us; and besides Maggy wastes nothing. The other "mess" is seperated from evry officer so that all expenses of servant hire &c. is surplus.

I am farming now in good earnest. All the ploughing and furrowing I do myself. There are two things that I have found out by working myself. One is that I can do as much, and do it better, than I can hire it done. The other is that by working my-self those that are hired do a third more than if left alone.

I was surprised to find that I could run as strait a furrow now as I could fifteen years ago and work all day quite as well. I never worked before with so much pleasure either, because now I feel sure that evry day will bring a large reward.

I believe I told you that I have to do that detestable Quarter Master business this Summer? I dislike it very much. Mr. Camp become very much dissatisfied here and sold out. He was making money[2] much faster than he will ever do again. Notwithstanding his bad luck having his store blown up he has cleared in the few months he has been here more than six thousand dollars, this without two thousand capital to start with.

Mrs. Wallen is quite well and so are all the officers. Capt. McConnell is here. Mr. Hunt is at Humbolt Bay, Russell[3] at Fort Reading Calafornia. All were well when last heard from.

Capt. Wallen met with a serious accident a few days since. He was riding in a wagon and the horse commenced kicking so to save himself he jumped out and fell throughing his right rist entirely out of joint. He will probably be lame in it all Summer.

You can tell your brother that we have had the news all the time that long beards were allowed, at least, on this coast. I have not shaved since I left Calafornia consequently my beard is several inches long. Why did you not tell me more about our dear little boys? I would like to hear some of Fred's sayings. I wish I could have him and his brother here. What does Fred. call Ulys.? What does the S stand for in Ulys.'s name? in mine you know it does not stand for anything! Give my love to all at your house. When you write again dearest write in better spirits.

Does Fred. and his Aunt Ellen get on harmoniously together? I expect she teases him. Cant you have your Daguerio-type taken with Fred. & Ulys. along? if you can send it by Adam's and Co['s] Express, to Portland, O. T. I presume you have recieved your watch ere this? I have no opportunity of buying any pretty presents here to send you.

Adieu dear dear wife. I shall hope to get a long sweet letter from you next Mail. Kiss our little boys for their pa. A thousand kisses for yourself dear wife.

Your affectionate husband.

ULYS.

ALS, DLC-USG.

1. C. A. Eastman was then employed as clerk by Capt. Thomas L. Brent. He was hired on May 1, 1853, at $150 monthly as clerk by USG. Report of Persons and Articles employed and hired at Columbia Barracks during the month of May, 1853. DNA, RG 92.

2. Two words crossed out.

3. 1st Lt. Lewis C. Hunt; 1st Lt. Edmund Russell of Pa., had been killed March 24, 1853, in an Indian skirmish at Red Bluffs, Calif.

To Julia Dent Grant

San Francisco, Cal.
May 20th 1853

DEAR WIFE,

I got here yesterday morning and astonishing to say was not atal sea sick by the way. I leave here again to-day for Knights Ferry where I shall have the pleasure of dining, with your brothers, to-morrow. I shall remain there about five or six days.

I have been trying to think what I could get pretty, that could be sent by mail, for Fred. and Ulys. but I can think of nothing.— I paid Mrs. Stevens a long call yesterday. Her and the children are all well. Mr. Stevens has been sick a good deal since they come out here. He is off from here now and probably will be absent most of the summer. Mrs. S. says she wrote you a very long letter when she first come out here but that she has never got a word in reply. Stevens is rich.

I saw young Dodge, Gladwin and Mrs. Gladwin, all of Sackets Harbor, yesterday. They are doing a good business here.

I have been ordered here as a witness on Lieut. Scott's[1] trial, but yesterday he sent in his resignation which will stop all proceedings against him.

I have but little to write you dear Julia only that I am still in the same robust health that I have been in ever since we come out here. Mrs. Stevens did not know me I have grown so stout, and so with several other persons. I am much more fleshy than I ever expected to be. Hard work, and the climate, agrees with me.—Kiss our little boys for me and tell them that their pa wanted to send them a present but he could find nothing to send. When you go to town you must get something for them and tell them that it was their pa sent it, or the money to buy it.

I send you with this a deed for the land located with my land warrant for you to sign before a Commissioner. Dont neglect to attend to this the first time you go to St. Louis and have it mailed to Preston Brady, Detroit, as soon as possible.—When

I get back from your Brothers I will write you a long letter, and another as soon as I get to Columbia Barracks. Give my love to all of them at home. You will get another letter from me by the same mail as takes this in which I have told you all the inconveniencies that the Ladies of the Regiment have had to undergo. —Tell Ellen and Emmy to write to me as well as yourself. Emmy I know will however. Dont neglect to write to Mrs. Stevens.

My dear wife it is very hard to be seperated from you so long but until I am better off it cannot be helped. If I can get together a few thousand dollars I shall most certainly go home however.

Kiss our dear little boys for me. A thousand kisses for yourself dear wife.

> Your affectionate husband
> ULYS.

ALS, DLC-USG.

1. On April 30, 1853, Bvt. Maj. Edward D. Townsend of Mass., USMA 1837, wrote to Lt. Col. B. L. E. Bonneville. "The General Commanding directs that you order Bvt. Capt. *U. S. Grant* to repair without delay to Benicia, with such evidence in relation to charges preferred against Lieut. *W. H. Scott*, 4th Infantry, as may be in his possession. The charges relate to the signing and transferring two sets of Pay accounts for the months of December, 1852, and January, 1853; and it is understood that Sutler Camp left said accounts with Capt. Grant. They will be required before the court. Major A J. Smith, Paymaster, has been ordered to Benicia for the same purpose." Copy, DNA, RG 98, Pacific Division, Letters Sent. Post Returns, Columbia Barracks, indicate that this order was received on May 14, 1853, and USG left the following day. On May 20, 1853, however, Townsend wrote to USG. "Lieut. *W. H. Scott*, 4th Infantry, having tendered his resignation, which will be forwarded, your services as witness before a General Court Martial in his case will not be required, and the commanding General directs that you return to your post accordingly." The same letter was sent to Maj. Albert J. Smith. Copy, DNA, RG 98, Pacific Division Letter Book. USG returned to Columbia Barracks on June 14, 1853.

To Julia Dent Grant

Columbia Barracks W. T.

June 15th 1853

I have just returned from Calafornia and found three long sweet letters from you; one of March, (no date) April 10th and 25th   In all of them you speak so highly of our dear little boys, as in fact do all the letters I get from my home. I got one from Jenny and Molly[1] in which they speak almost as much of them as you do. They say that father has gone to Galena and will stop to see Fred. That he thinks the country does not afford another like him.—When they wrote father had not yet returned and of course I heard nothing of the proposition to have me resign that you spoke of. I shall weigh the matter well before I act. If I could only remain here it would be hard to get me to leave the army. Whilst in Cal. I made such arrangements as would enable me to do a conciderable business, in a commission way, if I could but stay.

I have been quite unfortunate lately. The Columbia is now far over its banks, and ~~over all~~ has destroyed all the grain, onions, corn. and about half the potatoes upon which I had expended so much money and labor. The wood which I had on the bank of the river had all to be removed, at an expense, and will all have to be put back again at an expense.

You ask about Mr. Camp. Poor fellow he could not stand prosperity. He was making over $1000 00 per month and it put him beside himself. From being generous he grew parsimonious and finally so close that apparently he could not bear to let money go to keep up his stock of goods. He quit and went home with about $8000.00 decieving me as to the money he had and owing me about $800 00. I am going to make out his account and send it to Chas. Ford[2] for collection. I will some day tell you all the particulars of this transaction. I do not like to put it upon paper.

I got the lock of Ulys.s hair you send and kissed it. I dreamed of seeing you, Fred. and Ulys. night before last. I thought Fred.

& Ulys. were exactly alike, but not what Fred. was when I saw him last. They looked puny and not near so good looking as Fred. was. Did Fred. recognize his grandpa Grant? I sent you and the two boys presents from San Francisco   I hope you got them.

I told you in my letter from San Francisco that I am promoted![3] I go to Fort Reading in Calafornia. It is not probable however that I shall leave here befor October. I got a letter from Mr. Hunt but a short time since. He was quite well but hartily tired of Humboldt Bay, or rather with the commanding officer there.[4] In my other letters which you have not yet recieved I have answered all your questions about others of our Regiment.— Dr. Baily[5] was not at Governor's Island when I got there but had gone to Mackinac. I sent the thimble presented by Mrs. Stevens but never heard whether it was recieved or not.

I am very busy now being both Depot Qr. Master and Depot Commissary and having two expeditions to fit out for the great Pacific Rail Road Surveying party under Governor Stevens.[6] They require a large number of pack animals and many articles besides that have to be purchased, all of which has to be done by me.

I am very well dear Julia but ~~how~~ to write more about myself, as you so often request me to do, I do not know how.

Give my love to all at your house and kiss our dear little boys for me. Does Ulys. walk yet? From the progress he appears to be making I suppose he must. Continue dear Julia to write me as you do about the boys. I like to hear of Fred s sayings. If he talks as he used to try to do he must be very interesting.

People are waiting for me with a drove of horses so I must close. A thousand kisses for you dear dear Julia.

Adieu from your affectionate husband.
ULYS.

ALS, DLC-USG.

1. Virginia and Mary Grant, sisters of USG.
2. See letter of March 4, 1853.

3. USG had not written of his promotion and had apparently been mistaken about it. Capt. W. W. S. Bliss died on Aug. 5, 1853, and four days later Secretary of War Jefferson Davis sent USG a notice of promotion. He was then ordered to join Co. F at Fort Humboldt, Calif. Copy, DNA, RG 94, ACP 4754/1885.

4. 1st Lt. Lewis Cass Hunt was under the command of Bvt. Lt. Col. Robert Christie Buchanan, soon to command USG.

5. Dr. Joseph Howard Bailey of N.Y., asst. surgeon, U.S. Army.

6. Bvt. Maj. Isaac Ingalls Stevens of Mass., USMA 1839, resigned March 16, 1853, to accept an appointment as Governor of Washington Territory. He was then appointed director of the survey of a northern route for a Pacific railway. Several army officers were assigned to assist in preparing the survey, including Bvt. Capt. George Brinton McClellan of Pa., USMA 1846, who commanded an expedition outfitted by USG at Fort Vancouver.

To Julia Dent Grant

Columbia Bks. W. T.

June 28th 1853

By this Mail I recieved no letter from you, nor from any one at your house. Where Mails come but twice per month it does seem as though I might expect news from you and our dear little boys.

I cannot say that I have been atal well since my return from California. I have had a very sever cold and have been, necessarily, very busily engaged fitting out the expedition going out to meet Major Stevens of the Rail Road surveying party, and another party going into the Cascade range of mountains for the purpose of exploring are to be fitted out also.[1] I have purcased for them within a few days some two hundred horses besides other property and have still more to get. The present state of the Columbia makes transportation very difficult so I have to get Indians to pack, on their backs, all the provisions of one of these parties, over the portage at the Cascades, about forty five miles above here. The two companies of Infantry that come around Cape Horn have arrived, and with them, four families. Maj. Rains & lady & children, Mrs. Haller and two children, Mrs. Maloney and Mrs. Forsyth.[2] Forsyth was detained, on duty, at

San Francisco and very soon after leaving there Mrs. Forsyth, who was within a few weeks of her confinement, was taken sick and went into convulsions. By the time they arrived here she had had a great many[3] and was supposed to be beyond recovery. Soon after being got ashore however she was delivered of a child which had probably been dead for several days, and there is hopes of her recovery. As has been the fate of all the ladies who come out with us all these ladies are destined to the greates annoyance. Maj. Rains, and Hallers Co. goes to the Dalles. There are no quarters for them and as Maloney and Forsyth belong to the same co. they will all four families have to remain here while their husbands, though but ninety miles from them, will be more remote than if one was in Main and the other in Louisiana.— Maj. Larnard[4] and lady, I forgot to say have also arrived They go to Pugets Sound.

I will now speak of myself and affairs. Evry thing that I have undertaken, as a speculation, has proven profitable. I have though been unfortunate in some respects. I believe I explained in my last letter the result of the high waters! I have now had a chance of looking at matters and I find that we will have a crop of several thousand potatoes, and according to the opinion of old setlers they will bring from three to five dollars per bushel. This is in concequence of so many being drowned out. While in California I purchased a quantity of pork, its being low ther[e,] and knowing the price here, I made in partnership with another gentleman, about four hundred dollars upon it. I have still another lot to arrive and the article having risen we will clear about six hundred. Then another speculation which I have entered into is this. I made arrangements below for the sale of pigs and hogs. I have out now a man buying them and I am confident of clearing, for my share, a thousand dollars in the next four weeks. I told you in my last that if I could remain here that I would be able to do a handsom business in the Commission way! It is in this way. While in San Francisco a large business firm, from I have purchased flour &c. wanted me to watch the markets here, (they are very changeable) and when any article was, in my opinion, a speculation to inform them. They would furnish the capital, me make the sales and divide the profits. This dear Julia is the bright side. On the other hand I have lost from dishonesty of others, a number of hundreds of dollars which if you had would educate our dear little boys. The debt of eight hundred dollars against Camp I am going to sue for. You will be much surprized when I have an opportunity of explaining his whole conduct. He is I fear slightly deranged, and in that state the penuriousness, and dishonesty, of the whole family broke out. Enough. Give my love to all at your house, kiss our dear little ones for their Pa. I get a great many letters from my home now. They all say as much of Fred. & Ulys. as you do. I got a long letter from father this time. He has explained his whole business. The family will move to Covington, or Newport, Ky. and[5]

AL, DLC-USG.

1. See preceding letter.
2. Families of Maj. Gabriel James Rains, Bvt. Maj. Granville Owen Haller, Bvt. Capt. Maurice Maloney, and 2nd Lt. Benjamin D. Forsythe.
3. One word crossed out.
4. Bvt. Maj. Charles H. Larnard.
5. The remainder of the letter is lost. Jesse Grant moved to Covington, Ky.

To Julia Dent Grant

Columbia Bks. W. T.
July 13th 1853

My Dearest Julia;

It is about 12 o'clock at night, but as the Mail is to leave here early in the morning I must write to-night.—I got your long sweet letter giving an account of our dear little boys at the pic nic where Fred. started behind his Grand ma, but wanted her to ride behinde him before he got through. You know before he could talk he would always persist in having his hands in front of mine when driving. The loose end of the lines never satisfied him.

My dear Julia if you could see the letters they write from my home about our dear little boys it would make you as proud as it does me. I am sure there never was one of my own brothers or sisters who have been more thought of than Fred. & Ulys. In the long letter I got from father he speaks of him as something more than boys of his age. You understand though that I can make allowances for his prejudices either in favor or against; where prejudices are strong pred[il]ections are generally right, so I must conclude that Fred. & Ulys. are more than I ever dreamed they were. I dreamed of you last night but not of either of our dear little boys. I mearly saw you for a minuet without having an opportunity of speaking to you and you were gone.

My dear julia I have spoken of speculations so much that the subject is becoming painful, but yet I know you feel interested in what I am doing.—In a former letter I told you, for the first time, of the *downs* of all I had done. (Before I had never met with a *down*.) Since that I have made several hundreds in speculations of various sorts. In groceries which I do not sell, and which are not retailed. I have now a large quantity of pork on hand which is worth to-day ten dollars pr. barrel more than I gave for it at the very place where it was bought. All this will help to buy dresses for Fred. & Ulys. but what interests me most is to know how it is to let their pa see them wear them, and their ma put them on to advantage.

I wrote you that Scott was appointed Inspector General and that it would take me to Fort Reading.—It turns out that he has not been appointed so I must await my place either for Alden's resignation, or for Col. Buchanan's promotion.[1] The first would take me to Fort Jones, of which I have spoken, in former letters: the latter to a detestible place where the mails reach occationally. I should however have command of of the post, with double rations and two companies. Wallen is going to San Francisco before you recieve this letter with the intention of seting up a Dairy, Pigery, and market Garden, if practicable,. He will go on leave for a few months and then, if sucsessfull, strike out for him-self.

You ask how many children Laura[2] has? Before this you know. She has but two; Harry who is a healthy & smart boy, and Nancy who has always, until lately, been heathy.

My dear Julia I have said nothing about the pink leaves upon each of which you say you presed a sweet kiss. I cannot, in this, return the favor on flowers but you may rest assured that I will imprint them when we first meet upon your lips and those of our dear babes.

How can your pa & ma think that they are going to keep Fred. & Ulys always with them? I am growing impatient to see them myself.—Tell Fred. to say *Ugly Aunt Ell* I wont let you learn me anything.[3] so Fred. might say the same to his Uncle. If you cant go your self send him to his other Grandpa's for tuition for a few months.—Indeed dear Julia you must either go with the children or make a very good excuse. Thy want to see you so much. If you have not got means enough I have still some in N. Y. I shall never draw it so long as I remain in this country except in your favor. I hope you got the hundred which I sent you, and also the begining of what Calender was to send you![4] Give my love to all at your house. I got the pink leaves that you kissed. A thousand kisses for our little boys and yourself.

Adieu dear julia. the Steamer is in sight that is to take this.

Your affectionate husband
Ulys.

ALS, DLC-USG.

1. See letters of Jan. 29, June 15, 1853. Capt. Henry Lee Scott of N.C., USMA 1833, was not promoted until March 7, 1855.
2. Mrs. Henry Davies Wallen.
3. One line crossed out.
4. See letter of June 28, 1852.

Recommendation for Margaret Getz

———

Columbia Bks. W. T.

July 19th 1853

The bearer, Margaret Getz, has lived with me over two years, on the Atlantic and Pacific coast. I can recommend her most highly as a good family servant. She is a washer, ironer, plain cook and in evry way qualified to undertake the entire work of a small family.

Getz is a sober, industrious, and capable, man. He is a practicle gardner, a good man with horses, and no doubt would proove a good porter in a store.

U. S. GRANT

Bvt. Capt. & R. Q. M. 4th Inf.y

ADS, KHi.

To Maj. Osborn Cross

———

R. Q. Mrs. Office

Columbia Bks. W. T.

July 25th 1853

MAJ;

The constant, and unremiting, calls upon the time, both of myself and clerk, consequent upon the ~~time~~ fiting out of the expiditions connected with the Northern Pacific R. R. survey,[1] in addition to the current duties of the office, have prevented the making out, and forwarding, of the annual report called for, by you, at an earlier date; and obliges me to enter far less than I should have done into detail had I not feared that the delay of another mail would be too late to serve your purposes.

As I have only been on duty at this Post, as Post Qr. Mr., since the first of May last (my previous duties here, in the Q. M.

D, being merely nominal having neither funds nor stores in my charge) my Report can only embrace the operations of the Department here for the last two months of the past fical year.[2]

I enclose a plan of the post marked "A" and a statement of the public buildings marked "B".[3] With the exception of the shops, office & Qrs. in the immediate occupation of the Qr. Mr's Dept. & one cook house, the public buildings at this post are log buildings and most of them requiring repairs to make them comfortable.

By direction of the Com.g Genl. the Qrs. of the officers, and men, were chinked and daubed with mud, with a little lime to improve its consistency. The first heavy rains of winter swept this away and made new repairs necessary.

These Qrs. can only be made comfortable, permanently, by being ceiled inside in a manner similar to those of the Comd.g Officer & either weatherboarded, or at least chinked & daubed with mortar made of with plenty of lime & hair.

The Mechanics & Laborers employed have been one clerk, two herdsmen, one blacksmith and one carpenter & boatbuilder —and the amount in round number paid—$670 00

The transportation furnished has been for Capt. Brent's party, and "H" Co. hence to the Dalles at say a cost of $10 per man and twenty five tons of public property, between the same ponts, at an average cost of $60 00 per ton—with about twelve tons from Portland at $8 00 per ton.

The manner of transportation has been by steamer between Portland and this point, and between this point and the Cascades. Across the Cascade portage by R. R. & wagons; from the Cascades to the Dalles by boats & steamer, all private transportation.

The amt. of Lumber, Materials, Barley &c. is $2.342 00. The lumber was required for repairs &c. at this post; the materials & forage for the post & Depot.

The principle disbursments have been on account of other posts and expiditions fitted out at this point. The amount expended for the Dept. purposes of the post has been very small.

The soil on the borders of the river, where the banks are not precipitous, and the lands are level for some distance back, is exceedingly rich and productive, giving extraordinary yieald of oats, wheat and potatoes, but unfortunately subject to overflow during the June freshets. Farther back from the river the soil is of a more gravely or sandy nature, easily cultivated when once cleared, but far less productive than the bottom lands.

The country is heavily timbered, being, with the exception of the river bottom, occational plains, and now and then an occational clearing, almost entirely covered with a heavy growth of fir with here and there a cedar, and on the banks of the streams, groves of Oak, Cottonwood & Maple. The prevailing growth however is fir.

There are but few Indians in the vicinity of the post. These few are of the Clickitat tribe with occational passing visits from the Cowlitz and the Dalles, easily controlled and altogether to insignificant in prowess & numbers to need much care or attention, and even this poor remnant of a wonce powerful tribe is fast wasting away before those blessings of civilization "whisky and Small pox.

There are no outstanding debts of the Department, at this post, at the end of the fiscal year.

Very Respectfully
I am Maj.
Your Obt. Svt.
U. S. GRANT
Bvt. Capt. & R. Q. M. 4th Infy

To Maj. O. Cross
Chf. Q. M. Pacific Div.
San Francisco Cal.

ALS, CSmH. Maj. Osborn Cross of Md., USMA 1825.

1. For the survey expeditions see letters of June 15, 28, 1853.
2. USG began active q. m. duties after the transfer of Capt. Thomas Lee Brent.
3. No longer attached.

To Bvt. Maj. Gen. Thomas S. Jesup

Qr. Mr's Office
Fort Vancouver, W. T.
September 8th 1853

GEN.

Having resigned my appointment as Regimental Quarter Master, and having unsettle[d] accounts for years back, I would, most respectfully request orders to go to Washington for the purpose of setling my accounts.

I am particularly anxious to be present in Washington for the reason that I had public funds stolen from me during the Mexican War, and for which I have been petitioning Congress ever since, but without being able to get any action on my claim.[1]

At the same time I forward this I forward a similar claim to the Commissary General.

I am Gen.
Very Respectfully
Your Obt. Svt.

To Gen. T. S. Jesup
Qr. Mr. Gen. U.S.A.
Washington D. C.

U. S. GRANT
1st Lt. & R. Q. M. 4th Inf.y
Bvt. Capt. U.S.A.

ALS, Mrs. Walter Love, Flint, Mich. Favorably endorsed by Lt. Col. B. L. E. Bonneville. Bvt. Maj. Gen. Thomas S. Jesup replied on Dec. 2, 1853. "I recieved on the 31st of October, your letter dated the 8th of September, asking to be ordered to Washington City to settle your accounts. Before replying to your application, I have waited for the settlement of all the accounts which you have forwarded. To day I learn that your accounts to the 31st of March last have been settled at the Treasury leaving a balance due from you at that date of $753 93 Some portion of this it is understood, is made up of suspensions which can be readily obviated by written explanations. Your accounts for the 2d & 3d Quarters of the year, which should have been received here long ago, have not yet come to hand; you are required to forward them without delay—including the balance on the settlement of your first quarter's accounts, your accountability, as far as is known at this office is about forty thousand dollars. Most of the accounts from the Pacific Division are in for the 3d quarter of the year, while yours for for the 2nd quarter are still behind. There is no necessity for your presence at Washington to settle your accounts, you have only to forward them as you are bound to do by the laws and regulations, and they will be properly settled." Copy, DNA,

RG 92, Q. M. Letter Books. Docketing on the back of USG's letter indicates $37,977.90 advanced between May 14, 1853, and Sept. 15, 1853, yet to be accounted for.

1. For earlier petitions to Congress see July 1, 1852. Andrew Ellison of Ohio presented the petition again on Dec. 22, 1853, it was again tabled, and no action was taken until 1862. *House Journal*, 33–1, p. 129. The death of Capt. William Wallace Smith Bliss on Aug. 5, 1853, created a vacancy and USG's promotion to full capt. On Aug. 9, 1853, Secretary of War Jefferson Davis informed USG of his promotion and ordered "You will proceed, without delay, to join your company (F.) at Fort Humboldt, California." Copy, DNA, RG 94, ACP 4754/1885. The formal commission, however, was not signed by President Franklin Pierce until Feb. 9, 1854. It is reproduced in facsimile in William H. Allen, *The American Civil War Book and Grant Album* (Boston and New York, 1894). See letter of April 11, 1854.

To Bvt. Maj. Gen. George Gibson

Office of Com.y of Subs.
Fort Vancouver, W. T.
Sept. 8th 1853

GEN.

Being relieved as Asst. Com.y of Subs. I have the honor respectfully to request orders to repair to Washington for the purpose of setling my public accounts.

I am making a similar application to the Quartermaster General.

I am Gen.
Very Respectfully
Your Obt. Svt.
U. S. GRANT
1st Lt. & A. A. C. S. 4th Inf.y
Bvt. Capt. U. S. A.

To Bvt. Maj. Gen. Geo. Gibson
Com.y Gen. U. S. A.
Washington D. C.

ALS, Mrs. Walter Love, Flint, Mich. On Dec. 17, 1853, Col. Samuel Cooper of N.Y., AG, replied. "Your letter of September 8th, asking for orders to repair to this City for the purpose of settling your public accounts in the Subsistence Department, has been referred to this office by the Commissary General of Subsistence, with the endorsement that no necessity exists for your presence, in the settlement of said accounts." Copy, DNA, RG 94, Selected Letters Sent.

To Bvt. Maj. E. D. Townsend

———

San Francisco, Cal.
October 12th 1853

MAJ.

Finding that an application for orders to repair to Washington, D.C. to settling my accounts as a disbursing officer in the Quarter Master's & Commissary's Departments has not passed throug[h] Division Head Quarters I would respectfully submit the enclosed renewed application.

My former application was approved by Col. Bonneville, Comd.g 4th Inf.y.

I am Maj.
Very Respectfully
Your Obt. Svt.
U. S. GRANT
Capt. 4th Inf.y

To Maj. E. D. Townsend
Asst. Adj. Gen. P. D.
San Francisco, Cal.

ALS, DNA, RG 98, Pacific Division, Letters Received. The enclosure, addressed to Col. Samuel Cooper, was forwarded to Washington, D.C., on Oct. 14, 1853.

To Bvt. Maj. Gen. Thomas S. Jesup

Fort Vancouver, W. T.
Nov. 26 1853.

GENERAL:—

Herewith I have the honor to enclose copies of all contracts made by me on act. of the Qr. Mrs'. Dept. at this Post—

viz—

May.   7 1853 with Breck & Ogden for transpn of Troops & Stores
"   28   "   "   Van Bergen, Anderson & Co. "   "   " Stores
July   1   "   "   P. S. Ogden Chf T.H.B. Co. "   "   " Troops[1]
"   14   "   "   Van Bergen, Anderson & Co." "   "   "   "
Augt. 24   "   "   Allan, McKinley & Co.   "   "   " Stores

Most Respectfully
I am Genl.
Yr [Obt] Sevt
U. S. GRANT
Capt 4 Infy
Late R Q M

To Maj. Genl Thos S Jesup
Qr Mr. Genl. U S A
Washington D. C.

LS, DNA, RG 92, Consolidated Correspondence 350. Bvt. Maj. Gen. Thomas S. Jesup replied on Jan. 13, 1854. "Your letter of the 26th November last, enclosing a contract made by you, with Allan McKinley & Co—two with Van Bergen, Anderson & Co—one with Brick and Ogden and one with P. S Ogden, for the transportation of troops, has been received. It is perceived that some of those contracts were made as far back as May 1853. Such should have been forwarded to this office immediately—The law requires that all contracts, shall be sent to the second Comptroller for file, within 60 days after their date—This you will observe in future." Copy, *ibid.*, Q. M. Letter Books. The contracts sent by USG are in RG 217, Army Contracts.

1. Peter Skeen Ogden was chief factor of the Hudson's Bay Co.

To Julia Dent Grant

Fort Humboldt Cal.
Jan. 18th 1853 [*1854*]

My Dear Wife.

After a long and tedious voyage, from San-Francisco to this place,[1] I have arrived in safety. I cannot say much in favor of the place. It is about what I expected before my arrival. You know what my opinions of it were.[2] Imagine a place closed in by the sea having thrown up two tongues of land, closed in a bay that can be entered only with certain winds.[3]

In geting here, a distance of but a little more than 250 mile, we were two [*days*] in coming. There is no mail going but Mr. Hunt is just about starting for S. Francisco and I must avail myself of this occation of geting a letter to where it can be mailed.

Hunt is making application for promotion in a new Regiment, should any be raised this Winter, and any assistance that could be given by your father, or brother Lewis, in the way of writing to Col. Benton[4] he would gladly recieve, and, appreciate. In a few days I hope to have an opportunity of sending you a letter, and of having a steel pen instead of an old quil one, to write with.

Give my love to all at your house and kiss them for me. Our two dear little boys give a dozen extra for their Pa, in Calafornia.

Adieu dear wife
Ulys.

P. S. Mr. Hunt wants me to mention that his application is for a Captaincy. I hope that this matter will be attended to wishing him success.

U. S. G.

ALS, DLC-USG, postmarked Feb. 1, 1854.

1. USG arrived at Fort Humboldt on Jan. 5, 1854. His orders to join Co. F at Fort Humboldt were dated Oct. 11, 1853, but in the interval he was on detached service. Post Returns, Fort Humboldt, DNA, RG 94.

2. See letters of Feb. 15, March 19, June 15, 1853.

3. Fort Humboldt located at Bucksport near Eureka on Humboldt Bay.

4. Whether or not the Dents used their influence with Senator Thomas Hart Benton of Mo., 1st Lt. Lewis Cass Hunt was not promoted until May 23, 1855.

To Julia Dent Grant

———

Fort Humboldt,
Humboldt Bay, Cal.
February 2d 1853 [*1854*]

MY DEAR WIFE.

You do not know how forsaken I feel here! The place is good enough but I have interests at others which I cannot help thinking about day and night; then to it is a long time since I made application for orders to go on to Washington to settle my accounts but not a word in reply do I get.[1] Then I feel again as if I had been separated from you. and Fred. long enough and as to Ulys. I have never seen him. He must by this time be talking about as Fred. did when I saw him last. How very much I want to see all of you. I have made up my mind what Ulys. looks like and I am anxious to see if my presentiment[2] is correct. Does he advance rapidly? Tell me a great deel about him and Fred. and Freds pranks with his Grandpa. How does he get along with his Uncle Lewis?

I do nothing here but set in my room and read and occationally take a short ride on one of the public horses. There is game here such as ducks, geese &c. which some of the officers amuse themselvs by shooting but I have not entered into the sport.[3] Within eight or ten miles Deer and occationally Elk and black Bear are found. Further back the Grisley Bear are quite numerous. I do not know if I have told you what officers are at this post? Col. Buchanan, Hunt, Collins, Dr. Potts and Lt. Latimer[4] to join. Expected soon. Col. B expects promotion by evry Mail which, if he gets, will bring Montgomery,[5] and leave me in command of the post. Mrs. Collins is the only lady at the post. Dr. Potts however will have his wife here in a short time. The quarters are comfortable frame buildings, backed by a dense forest of immense trees. In front is the Bay. We are on a bluff which gives us one of the most commanding views that can be had from almost any point on the whole Bay. Besides having a view of the Bay itself we can look out to sea as far as the eye can extend. There are four villeges on the Bay. One at the outlet, Humbolt Point is the name, where there are probably not more than 50 inhabitants. What they depend upon for support I do'nt know. They are probably persons who supposed that it would be the point for a City and they would realize a California fortune by the rise of lots. Three miles up the Bay is Bucksport and this garrison Here geting out lumber is the occupation, and as it finds a ready market in San Francisco this is a flourishing little place of about 200. Three miles further up is Euricka with a population of about 50[0] with the same resourses. The mills in these two villeges have, for the last year, loaded an average of 19 vessels per month with lumber, and as they are building several additional mills they will load a greater number this year. Twelve miles further up, and at the head of the Bay, is Union, the larges and best built town of the whole. From there they pack provisions to the gold mines, and return with the dust. Taking all of these villeges together there are about enough ladies to get up a small sized Ball. There has been several of them this winter.

    I got one letter from you since I have been here but it was some three months old. I fear very much that I shall loose some before they get in the regular way of coming. There is no regular mail between here and San Francisco so the only way we have of geting letters off is to give them to some Captain of a vessel to mail them after he gets down. In the same way mails are recieved. This makes it very uncertain as to the time a letter may be on the way. Sometimes, owing to advers winds, vessels are 40 and even 60 days making the passage, while at others they make it in less than two days. So you need not be surprised if sometimes you would be a great while without a letter and then likely enough get three or four at once. I hope the next mail we get to have several from you. Be particular to pay postage on yours for otherwise they may refuse to deliver them at the San Francisco Post Office. I cant pay the postage here having no stamps and not being able to get them. I have sent below however for some.

I must finish by sending a great deel of love t[o] all of you, your Pa. Ma. brother and sisters[,] niece and nepews. I have not yet fulfilled my promise to Emmy ~~yet~~ to write her a long letter from Humboldt.

Kiss our little ones for me. A thousand kisses for yourself dear Julia.

> Your affectionate husband
> ULYS

ALS, DLC-USG.

1. See letters of Sept. 8, 1853, and the negative replies.
2. "presentiment" written over "judgement."
3. USG discusses his distaste for hunting in *Memoirs*, I, 75–76.
4. Bvt. Lt. Col. Robert Christie Buchanan, 1st Lt. Lewis Cass Hunt, 1st Lt. Joseph Benson Collins, Asst. Surgeon Richard Potts of Md., and Bvt. 2nd Lt. Alfred Eugene Latimer of S.C., USMA 1853. On Nov. 20, 1853, the AGO reported 118 troops stationed at Fort Humboldt, of which 99 were present for duty.
5. 1st Lt. Thomas Jefferson Montgomery.

To Bvt. Maj. Gen. Thomas S. Jesup

———

> Fort Humboldt, Humboldt Bay Cal.
> February 3rd 1854—

GEN—

Enclosed please find my Statement of allowances to officers for 2d & 3rd Qrs. 1853—Voucher No 1. 2. & 3. to abstract "B" 4th Qr. same year—

Mr. Eastman, who was my clerk, informs me that I have been reported for nonrendition of my accounts for 2d Qr. 1853—with-

in the time prescribed by law—They were mailed on the 1st &
2d of November, which owing to my absence was the earlyest
I could possibly get them off

I am Gen

Very Respectfully

Your Obt Svt

To Maj. Gen. T. S. Jesup   U. S. GRANT

Qr. Mr. Gen. U. S. A.   Capt. 4th Inf.y

Washington, D. C.   Late R. Q. M.

LS, DNA, RG 92, Consolidated Correspondence 350. On Oct. 31, 1853, Secretary of War Jefferson Davis wrote to USG. "Pursuant to the provisions of an
Act approved January 31, 1823, of which I hereto append an extract, you have this
day been reported to the President as having failed to render within the period
prescribed by law, your accounts for the quarter ending June 30 1853. On the
receipt of this communication, you will forthwith forward your accounts to the
proper office for settlement, and address to this Department such explanation as
you may desire to make, in order to relieve yourself from the penalty of the Act
above cited." An identical letter was sent to seven other officers. Copy, DNA,
RG 107, Letters Sent, Military Affairs. On Jan. 12, 1854, Bvt. Maj. Gen. Thomas
S. Jesup wrote to Davis. "I have the honor to report the reception of the money
and property accounts of Captain U. S. Grant, Regimental Quarter Master 4th
Infantry, for the 2d and 3d Quarters 1853. He was reported on the 5th instant
for the non-rendition of these accounts.—" Copy, *ibid.*, RG 92, Letters Sent,
Secretary of War.

To Bvt. Maj. E. D. Townsend

Fort Humboldt,

Humboldt Bay, Cal.

Feb. 3d 1854

MAJ.

When "F" Co. 4th Infantry left Benicia they left behind,
sick, one Edward Fling, a private in the Company. He is still
reported with the "Total" of the Comp.y as being detached, sick
at Benicia. I understand however that he was attached to one of

the Companies of the 2d Infantry and done duty with it after having recovered.

I would respectfully request, ~~that~~, if not practicable to send him to his Company, that he be transfered.

I am Maj.

Very Respectfully

Your Obt. Svt.

To Maj. E. D. Townsend   U. S. GRANT

A. A. G. Pac. Div.   Capt. 4th Inf.y

San Francisco, Cal.   Comd.g Co. "F"

ALS, DNA, RG 98, Pacific Division, Letters Received.

To Julia Dent Grant

———

Fort Humboldt

Humboldt Bay, Cal.

Feb. 6th 1854.

MY DEAR WIFE;

A mail come in this evening but brought me no news from you nor nothing in reply to my application for orders to go home. I cannot concieve what is the cause of the delay. The state of suspense that I am in is scarsely bearable. I think I have been from my family quite long enough and sometimes I feel as though I could almost[1] go home "nolens volens." I presume, under ordinary circumstances, Humboldt would be a good enough place but the suspense I am in would make paradice form a bad picture. There is but one thing to console; misery loves company and there are a number in just the same fix with myself, and, with other Regiments, some who have been seperated much longer from their families than I have been.

It has only been a few days since I wrote to you but it will not do to let an opportunity pass of geting a letter into the San Francisco Post Office, and there is a vessel to leave here to-morrow. It is not all the vessels that it will do to entrust letters with. A few that come take the trouble, and expense, of going to the Post Office in San Francisco and geting all the mail directed to this bay and bring it without any remuneration either from the Post Office Department, or from individuals.

I have been suffering for the last few days most terribly. I am certain that if you were to see me now you would not know me. That tooth I had set in in Wattertown (You remember how much I suffered at the time) has been giving me the same trouble over again. Last evening I had it drawn and it was much harder to get out than any other tooth would have been. My face is swolen until it is as round as an apple and so tender that I do not feel as if I could shave, so, looking at the glass, I think I could pass readily for a person of forty five. Otherwise I am very well.[2] You know what it is to suffer with teeth.

I am very much pleased with my company. All the men I have are old soldiers and very neat in their appearance. The contrast between them and the other company here is acknowledged as very great by the officers of the other company. The reason is that all my men[3] are old soldiers while the other were recruits when they come here. I have however less than one third of the complement allowed by law and all of them will be discharged about the same time. I wish their times were out now so that I could go on recruiting service if no other way.

My dear wife you do not tell me whether you are contented or not! I hope you enjoy yourself very much.—Has Capt. Calender[4] continued to send you money? Some three or four months since I bought two land warrants, one of which I want to send you but when I got to San Francisco I found that they were not negociable on account of not having on the transfer the Seal of the County Clerk. I sent them back to Vancouver to have this fixed and when I get them I will send you one. They are worth about forty dollars more there than I gave for them.

Do you think of going to Ohio this Spring? I hope you will go. They want to see you very much. Evry letter I get from home they speak of it.

In my letter written a few days ago I told you what officers we had here, the amusements &c. so I have nothing more on that head. Living here is extravigantly high besides being very poor. Col. Buchanan, the Dr. and myself live together at an expense of about $50 per month each including servant hire and washing. Mr. Hunt lives by himself[.] Give my love to all at home. Write me a great deel about our little boys. Tell me all their pranks. I suppose Ulys. ~~says~~ speaks a great many words distinctly? Kiss both of them for me.—I believe I told you that Mrs. Wallen had lost another child. I do not think Wallen will ever raise either of his children. Harry & Nan[n]y are large fat children but they do not look right and they are forever sick. If Wallen was out of the Army and had to pay his Doctor's bill it would amount to about as much as our entire living.—Kiss Fred. and Ulys. for their pa. A great many kisses for you dear wife.

> Your affectionate husband
> ULYS.

ALS, DLC-USG.

1. Two words crossed out.
2. USG was listed as "sick" in Fort Humboldt Post Returns for Feb., 1854.
3. Just before USG arrived, Bvt. Lt. Col. Buchanan reported the condition of Co. F: "*Discipline,* Improving; *Instruction,* Tolerable; *Military Appearance,* Fair; *Arms,* Good; *Accoutrements,* Good; *Clothing,* Good—an abundant supply on hand." Muster Roll, Co. F, 4th Inf. DNA, RG 94.
4. See letter of June 28, 1852.

To Julia Dent Grant

> Fort Humboldt
> Humboldt Bay, Cal.
> March 6th 1854.

MY DEAR WIFE;

I have only had one letter from you in three months and that had been a long time on the way so you may know how anxious I am to hear from you. I know there are letters for me in the Post

Office department, someplace, but when shall I get them. I sometimes get so anxious to see you, and our little boys, that I am
almost tempted to resign and trust to Providence, and my own
exertions, for a living where I can have you and them with me. It
would only require the certainty of a moderate competency to
make me take the step. Whenever I get to thinking upon the
subject however *poverty, poverty,* begins to stare me in the face
and then I think what would I do if you and our little ones should
want for the necessaries of life.

I could be contented if at Humboldt if it was possible to have
you here but it is not. You could not do without a servant and a
servant you could not have This is to bad is it not? But you never
complain of being lonesome so I infer that you are quite contented. I dreamed of you and our little boys the other night the first
time for a long time I thought you were at a party when I arrived and before paying any attention to my arrival you said you
must go you were engaged for that dance. Fred. and Ulys. did
not seem half so large as I expected to see them. If I should see
you it would not be as I dreamed, would it dearest? I know it
would not.

I am geting to be as great a hand for staying in the house now
as I used to be to run about. I have not been a hundred yards
from my door but once in the last two weeks. I get so tired and
out of patience with the lonliness of this place that I feel like
volunteering for the first service that offers. It is likely a party
will have to go from here for Cape Mendeceno in the course of
a week and if so I think I shall go.[1] I would be absent about two
weeks. In the Summer I will try and make an exkursion out into
the mines and in the fall another out on the immigrant trail. This
will help pass off so much of the time.

This seems to be a very healthy place; all here are enjoying
excellent health. The post has been occupied now for about
fourteen months, by two Companies, and I believe there has been
but two deaths. One by accidentally shooting himself and the
other by a limb from a tree falling on a man.

Wallen has made up his mind to resign.[2] Mrs. W. declared

she would not go back to Vancouver that if he went he would go without her. W. has gone into the Coal business.—Stevens is going ahead at a rapid stride. A recent decission of the Courts in a land case made him one hundred thousand dollars better off than before. Mrs. Stevens & husband intended to have gone home last January but S. could not find time to go. Mrs. S. will soon be confined again. You recollect what she said at Sackets Harbor?

Mr. Hunt has just recently returned from San Francisco. While there he met John looking well.—There is no news here only occationally a disater at sea. A few days since a steamer went down just inside the Columbia river bar; vessel with all on board except one lost. I am in a great hurry to get this ready for the Mail so I must bid you all good buy for the present. Give my love to your pa, ma, sisters and brother. Kiss our little boys for me. Talk to them a great deel about their pa. A thousand kisses for yourself dearest.

I have some land warrants one of which I want to send you to sell but I am afraid to trust it to the mail. I will send it by the first favorable opportunity. They are worth about $180.00 in N. York; I do not know what you will be able to get in St. Louis.

Adieu dear wife.
ULYS.

ALS, DLC-USG.

1. There is no record that USG did so.
2. Capt. Henry Davies Wallen remained in the army until he retired as col. in 1874.

To Bvt. Maj. E. D. Townsend

Fort Humboldt, Cal.
March 16th 1854

MAJ;

I would respectfully request that private John Wright of "F" Company, 4th Inf.y, who has been in confinement, at hard labor in charge of the Guard, since the 7th of April 1853, and charges forwarded to Head Quarters of the Division, be restored to duty on condition that he makes good the time lost by desertion and the expenses incured for his apprehension, or, brought to trial at as early a day as practicable.

Private Wright deserted from Benecia on the 3d of September 1852, was apprehended on the 4th of the same month and $30 00 paid. He was tried and punished by stopage of pay and confinement. On the 7th of April 1853 he deserted from Fort Humboldt, Cal. and was apprehended on the 7th and $30 00 paid for his apprehension. For this last offence he is now awaiting trial.

I am Maj.
Very Respectfully
Your Obt. Svt.
U. S. GRANT
Capt. 4th Inf.y
Comd.g Comp.y "F"

To Maj. E. D. Townsend
Asst. Adjt. Gen. U.S.A.
San Francisco, Cal.

ALS, DNA, RG 98, Pacific Division, Letters Received. Endorsed by Bvt. Lt. Col. Robert C. Buchanan the same day, "Respectfully forwarded. This man was tried, whipped, and confined at hard labour with a ball and chain on, for *four* months, and deserted a second time in less than 3 months after his release. I cannot recommend his release at this time." Bvt. Maj. Edward D. Townsend noted that the request of USG would be denied because the commanding officer of the post disagreed.

On March 27, Buchanan wrote to Townsend. "I have the honor to enclose a Certificate of Ordinary Disability, in the case of Pvt. John Wright, of "F" Comp. 4th Inf, and recommend that he be first pardoned in accordance with the recommendation of Capt. Grant as heretofore requested, and that afterwards he be discharged the service. When I forwarded Capt. Grant's application for this man's release a few days ago, I had not been informed that he was physically unable to perform the duties of a soldier, or I should then have approved it." A discharge without pardon was ordered on April 3, 1854. *Ibid.*

To Julia Dent Grant

———

Fort Humboldt
Humboldt Bay, Cal.
March 25th 1854

I have had just one solitary letter from you since I arrived at this place and that was written about October of last year. I cannot believe that you have neglected to write all this time but it does seem hard that I should not hear from you. I am afraid too that many of my letters do not reach you. The only way of mailing them is to give them to a Captain of a vessel to put them in the Post Office at San Francisco, which, if he does, they are all safe, but I have no doubt but that many times they never spend a second thought about letters entrusted to them.

April 3d After geting as far as I have done in this letter ~~as I have done~~ I was interupted by the entrance of some officers, from continuing for the evening and as the bar at the outlet of the bay was so rough as to prevent vessels from going out for some days I have not taken it up until now. There has been no vessel going out since. The irregularity of mails is an annoyance which can only be appreciated by those who suffer from it. We here however do not suffer from it so much as at two or three stations in this (by government) neglected country. It is very much to be feared that even this last place is to be abandoned for another in the interior where none, or but very poor quarters, will be found. The best we can expect is to go to fort Jones[1] where the buildings were hastily run up by the soldiers. They are just rough log penns, covered over, with places for a door & window but left without these luxuries as well as without floors. Mrs. Collins was there for two or three months where she says she had to live in one of these penns cooking, eating, sleeping and recciving calls from officers, all in but one of these small apartments. Here we are better off having each two comfortable rooms, plastered and with a brick chimney, to each. Mr. Hunt and myself live together and I think will be able to bring our mess bills down to a moderate rate.

How very anxious I am to get home once again. I do not feel as if it was possible to endure this separation much longer. But how do I know that you are thinking as much of me as I of you? I do not get letters to tell me so. But you write I am certain and some day I will get a big batch all at once. Just think; by the time you recieve this Ulys. will be narly two years old and no doubt talking as plainly as Fred. did his few words when I saw him last. Dear little boys what a comfort it would be to see and play with them a few hours evry day! I like to have you write me a great deel about them. Do write me long letters and dont put off writing until just as "Pa" or "Brother Lewis" are just going to town as you nearly always assign as an excuse for cuting your letters short. You told me to direct your letters to Sappington Post Office: why cant you finish those for me and mail at the same office? I have been wanting to send you a land warrant for some time as the best means of transmitting money; but I am afraid to entrust one to the Mail. As soon as the Pay Master makes his appearance however I will see if I cannot get a check on the East to send you.

Evrything to see or write about at Humboldt Bay can be taken in at a glance. I have not been a quarter of a mile from my room for about one week, and I am in excellent health[2] too. Except an occational ride of a few miles on horsback none of us go out at present, this not being game season.

Do you ever hear anything from Ohio? I have not had a letter from there written since last October.

I am enjoying good health but growing more lazy evry day for want of something to do. When the mountain streams dry up a little more however I will find something to do for if we do not move to the interior I, at least, have to go there with a party of men which will take up one month. This will be clear gain.

Give my love to all at your house. Kiss our dear little boys for their pa who thinks so much about them. I have to close dear julia for want of something more to write about. A thousand kisses for you dear wife. Write to me soon and tell me all about evry body at home.

Your affectionate husband
ULYS.

ALS, DLC-USG.

    1. Fort Jones was located on the Scott River, Calif.
    2. At the end of April, however, USG was reported "sick" in Fort Humboldt Post Return. DNA, RG 94.

To Col. Samuel Cooper

Fort Humboldt, Cal.
April 11th 1854

COL.
    I have the honor to acknowledge the receipt of my Commission as Captain in the 4th Infantry and my acceptance of the same.

I am Col.
Very Respectfully
Your Obt. Svt.
U. S. GRANT
Capt. 4th Inf.y

To Col. S. Cooper
Adj. Gen. U. S. A.
Washington, D. C.

ALS, DNA, RG 94, ACP 4754/1885.

To Col. S. Cooper

Fort Humboldt,
Humboldt Bay, Cal.
April 11th 1854.

COL.

I very respectfully tender my resignation of my commission as an officer of the Army, and request that it may take effect from the 31st July next.

I am Col.
Very Respectfully
To Col. S. Cooper   Your Obt. Svt.
Adj. Gen. U. S. A.   U. S. GRANT
Washington D. C.   Capt. 4th Inf.y

ALS, DNA, RG 94, ACP 4754/1885. The document is inconsistent with accounts that Bvt. Lt. Col. Robert C. Buchanan had previously held an undated resignation. Endorsements read,

Respectfully forwarded, with the recommendation that it be accepted.
ROBT. C. BUCHANAN
Bvt. Lt. Col. Capt. 4th Inf Commdg

Head Quarters, Detacht 4th Inf
Fort Humboldt, Cal. Apl 11th 1854

Hd. Qrs. Dept. of the Pacific
San Francisco, April 22/54.
Approved and respectfully forwarded.
JOHN E. WOOL
Major General

Head Qrs. of the Army N. Y. 26. May 1854.
Respectfully forwarded   By command of Maj. Gen. Scott.
IRVIN McDOWELL
Asst. Adjt. Genl.

It is respectfully recommended that Capt. Grant's resignation be accepted, to take effect as tendered *July 31, 1854.* The enclosed ~~within~~ paper, dated May 29th, shows the state of Capt. G's accounts with the Treasury.
A. G. Office,   S. COOPER
May 30/54.   Adj. Genl.

Accepted as tendered.

JEFFN DAVIS
Sec. of War

June 2d 1854

On May 29, AG Samuel Cooper issued a circular. "Capt. *U. S. Grant*, 4th Infantry, having tendered his resignation, to enable the Adjutant General to comply with the 42nd paragraph of the Regulations, you are desired to report, as early as practicable, whether the captain has any unsettled money or property accounts with your office." The replies were "Quartermaster General, Clothing accs. which will be immedly sent to Treasury. Subsistence Dept, No accounts recd since June 1853. Had then in his possession $2906.47. Sub. Funds and large quantities of stores. Ordnance Dept, ord return of Co. F 4th Infy—examd & found correct & will be sent to the 2nd Auditor for settlement immediately. Pay Dept, Nothing. 2d Auditor, cash a/cs closed . . MOODY—Has unexamined property accounts. G. CORING. 3d Auditor, Has Qr. Mr. a/cs now under examination— No uns. Subs. on file Bal on self 5 May 1854 $4361.70. 2d Comptroller, Sames as Auditors—F. PURRINGTON." LS, DNA, RG 94, ACP 4754/1885. USG was informed of the acceptance of his resignation by asst. AG W. G. Freeman, June 2, 1854. Because USG received a sixty day leave on May 9, 1854, and his resignation was to take effect on July 31, 1854, a question arose concerning pay for July. *Ibid*. USG resignation was announced through War Department Special Orders 87, June 3, 1854.

On June 5, 1854, Andrew Ellison of Georgetown, Ohio, Democratic member of the Thirty-Third Congress, wrote to Jefferson Davis. "I received a letter from Jesse R. Grant Esq—the father of Captain Ulysses Grant of the Army   Mr Jesse R Grant requests that I would ask to have Capt Grant ordered home on the recruiting service, as a favor, to obtain some rest and to see his friends and family If that cannot be permitted, then to allow him a six months leave of absence Capt Grant is in the Army on the Pacific   It is stated in one of the papers of this city that Capt Grant has resigned, if this be the fact, what I ask is not needed; but if it is not, I hope it may be found compatible with the service, to allow Capt Grant to come home on the recruiting service, or at least, to allow him a six month's leave of absence" ALS, *ibid*. Davis replied on June 7, 1854. "In reply to your letter of the 5 inst. requesting that Capt Ulysses S. Grant may be placed on the recruiting service or granted a leave of absence, I have the honor to inform you, that Captain Grant's resignation of his commission in the Army was accepted on the 2d inst." Copy, *ibid*., RG 107, Letters Sent, Military Affairs. On June 21, Jesse Grant wrote to Davis directly. "Your letter of the 7th inst announcing the acceptance of the resignation of my son Capt U. S. Grant, was recd a few days ago through Hon A. Ellison. That was the first intimation I had of his intention to resign   If it is consistant with your powers & the good of the servis I would be much gratifyed if you would reconsider & withdraw the acceptance of his resignation—and grant him a six months leave, that he may come home & see his family. I never wished him to leave the servis. I think after spending so much time to qualify himself for the Army, & spending so many years in the servis, he will be poorly qualifyed for the pursuits of privet life   He has been eleven years an officer, was in all the battles of Gen Taylor & Scott except Buenavista, never absent from his post during the Mexican war, & has never had a leave of six months—Would it then be asking too much for him, to have such a leave, that he may come home & make arangments for taking his family with him to his post I will remark that he has not seen his family for over two years, & has a son nearly two years old he has never seen. I suppose in his great anxiety to see his family he has been induced to quit the servis—Please write me & let me know the result of this request" ALS, *ibid.*, RG 94, ACP 4754/1885. Davis replied on June 28, 1854. "In reply to your letter of the 21 instant asking that the acceptance of the resignation of your son, Captain U. S. Grant may be withdrawn, and he be allowed six months leave of absence, I have to inform you that Capt. Grant tendered his resignation, but assigned no reasons why he desired to quit the service, and the motives which influenced him are not known to the Department. He only asked that his resignation should take effect on the 31 July next, and it was accepted accordingly on the 2d instant, and the same day announced to the Army. The acceptance is, therefore complete, and cannot be reconsidered." Copy, *ibid.*

To 1st Lt. Joseph B. Collins

Fort Humboldt,
Humboldt Bay, Cal.
April 11th 1854.

SIR;

I would respectfully request a leave of absence for *sixty days* with permission to apply for an extension until the 31st of July, 1854 at which date I have requested my resignation as an officer of the Army to take effect.

I am Sir
Very Respectfully
Your Obt. Svt.

To Lt. J. B. Collins   U. S. GRANT
Post Adj.t.   Capt. 4th Infy

ALS, DNA, RG 98, Pacific Division, Letters Received. 1st Lt. Joseph Benson Collins was adjt. for Fort Humboldt. The letter was endorsed by Bvt. Lt. Col. Buchanan on April 11, 1854. "Approved, and respectfully recommended that the application be granted. Capt. Grant has important papers and vouchers necessary to the settlement of his accounts, at Fort Vancouver, and wishes time to collect and arrange them."

Also on April 11, 1854, Buchanan wrote to Bvt. Maj. E. D. Townsend. "I have the honor to enclose the resignation of Capt. U. S. Grant 4th Inf., and recommend that it be accepted. I should feel much gratified if the General would grant the Captain's application for leave of absence, also enclosed." *Ibid.*

Buchanan again wrote Townsend on May 1, 1854. "Captain Grant is too unwell to travel just yet, but will be relieved to-day by Lt. Hunt in command of his Company, and will proceed to San Francisco by the first steamer, with orders to report in person to the Major General Commanding." *Ibid.* That same day Buchanan issued Orders No. 11, replacing USG in command of F Co. with 1st Lt. Lewis Cass Hunt. "After being properly relieved, Capt. Grant is authorized to proceed to San Francisco, Cal. where he will on his arrival, apply in person to the Major General Commanding, for such leave of absence, as he may desire." *Ibid.*

Before USG submitted his resignation, he and Capt. Henry M. Judah, then stationed at Fort Jones on the Scott River, Calif., had applied for an exchange of posts. USG was ordered to Fort Jones on June 10, 1854, although he had already left Calif. The order was later cancelled. Muster Rolls, Cos. E and F, 4th Inf., DNA, RG 94; Bvt. Maj. Edward D. Townsend to Bvt. Lt. Col. R. C. Buchanan, July 7, 1854; Bvt. Maj. Gen. John E. Wool to Col. Samuel Cooper, Oct. 19, 1854, Copies, DNA, RG 98, Pacific Division, Letters Sent.

To Julia Dent Grant

————

Fort Humboldt, Cal.
May 2d 1854

DEAR WIFE;

I do not propose writing you but a few lines. I have not yet recieved a letter from you and as I have a "leave of absence" and will be away from here in a few days do not expect to. After recieving this you may discontinue writing because before I could get a reply I shall be on my way home. You might write directing to the City of New York.

It will require my presence in Calafornia for some four or six weeks to make all my arrangements, public & private, before starting. I may have to go to Oregon before leaving; I will not go however unless I get an order to cover my transportation. On my way I shall spend a week or ten days with John Dent.— My love to all at home. Kiss our little boys for their pa. love to you dear Julia.

Your affectionate husbd.
ULYS.

ALS, DLC-USG.

To Bvt. Maj. Gen. Thomas S. Jesup

———

Fort Humboldt, Cal.
May 3, 1854.

GENERAL.

I have the honor to enclose, herewith, the Quarterly Return of Clothing, Camp and Garrison Equipage, appertaining to my Company, for part the 2d Quarter 1854.

	I am General,
	Very respectfully,
To Gen. Thos. S. Jesup,	Your Obt. Svt.
Quartermaster Genl. U. S. A.	U. S. GRANT
Washington, D. C.	Capt. F. Co. 4 Infy.

LS, ICarbS.

To Bvt. Maj. E. D. Townsend

———

Fort Humboldt,
Humboldt Bay, Cal.
May 7th 1854th

MAJ.

I would respectfully request a leave of absence for sixty days with permission to apply for an extension, of four months, at the Head Quarters of the Army.

	I am Maj.
	Very Respectfully
To Maj. E. D. Townsend	Your Obt. Svt.
Asst. Adjt. Gen. U.S.A.	U. S. GRANT
San Francisco, Cal.	Capt. 4th Inf.y

ALS, DNA, RG 98, Pacific Division, Letters Received. By Special Orders 43, May 9, 1854, USG received leave for sixty days and permission to apply for an extension to July 31, 1854. *Ibid.*, Special Orders.

To Jesse Root Grant

———

Sappington P. O.
St. Louis Co. Mo.
December 28th 1856.

DEAR FATHER:

Your's & Mary's letter inclosing Land Warrant was recieved a few days since. I will mail it in a few days.

Evry day I like farming better and I do not doubt but that
money is to be made at it. So far I have been laboring under
great disadvantages but now that I am on my place,[1] and shall
not have to build next summer I think I shall be able to do much
better. This year if I could have bought seed I should have made
out still better than I did. I wanted to plant sixty or seventy
bushels of potatoes, but I had not the money to buy them. I
planted twenty however and have sold 225 bushels and have
about 125 on hand, besides all that I have used. Next summer I
shall plant what is left of them and buy about fifty bushels of
choise seed besides. I have in some twenty five acres of wheat
that looks better, or did before the cold weather, than any in
the neighborhood. My intention is to raise about twenty acres
of Irish potatoes, on new ground, five acres of sweet potatoes,
about the same of early corn, five or six acres cabbage, beets,
cucumber pickles & mellons and keep a wagon going to market
evry day. This last year my place was not half tended because I
had but one span of horses, and one hand, and we had to do all
the work of the place, living at a distance too, all the hawling
for my building, and take wood to the city for the support of the
family. Since the 1st of April my teams have earned me about
fifty dollars per month independent of doing my own work.
This year I presume I shall be compelled to neglect my farm
some to make a living in the mean time, but by next year I hope
to be independent. If I had an opportunity of geting about
$500 00 for a year at 10 pr. cent I have no doubt but it would be
of great advantage to me.

Julia and the children are all very well. Mrs. Dent has been at the point of death for the last two weeks, but is now much better and will recover.

Mary makes no acknowledgement of having recieved a letter from me! Did she not get an answer to hers written shortly after you were here? I wrote in answer.

Some three weeks since I went into the Planter's House and saw registered "J. R. Grant, Ky." on the book. Making enquiry I found that J. R. G. had just taking the Pacific R. R. cars. I made shure it was you and that I should find you when I got home. Was it you?

Remember me to all at home. Tell Molly to write to me again. Write soon.

Yours Truly
U. S. Grant

To J. R. Grant, Esq.
Covington Ky.

P. S. In view of the Land Warrant having to go to such a distance, and likely, after reaching Washington Territory being obliged to pass through the hands of so many strangers, I have filled the assignment to J. R. Grant. It will be better for you to assign it again than that it should be endangered.

U. S. G.

ALS, NjR.

1. When USG resigned from the army in 1854 his family was reunited at White Haven, the home of the Dents, where USG began to farm an adjacent sixty acres given to Julia Grant by her father. In the spring of 1855 USG moved his family to Wish-ton-wish, the house built by Julia Grant's brother Lewis on another part of the Dent estate. USG was then clearing trees from his own land and preparing timbers for his own house, Hardscrabble, which was completed in the summer of 1856.

To *Jesse Root Grant*

Sappington P. O.
St. Louis Co. Mo.
Feb.y 7th 1857.

DEAR FATHER;

Spring is now approaching when farmers require not only to till the soil, but to have the wherewith to till it, and to seed it. For two years I have been compelled to farm without either of these facilities, confining my attention therefore principally to oats and corn: two crops which can never pay; for if they bear a high price it is because the farmer has raised scarsely enough for his own use. If ~~they are~~ abundent they will scarsely bear transportation. I want to vary the crop a little and also to have implements to cultivate with. To this end I am going to make the last appeal to you. I do this because, when I was in Ky. you voluntarily offered to give me a Thousand dollars, to commence with, and because there is no one els to whom I could, with the same propriety, apply. It is always usual for parents to give their children assistince in begining life (and I am only begining, though thirty five years of age, nearly) and what I ask is not much. I do not ask you to give me anything. But what I do ask is that you lend, or borrow for, me Five hundred dollars, for two years, with interest at 10 pr. cent payable anually, or semmi anually if you choose, and with this if I do not go on prosperously I shall ask no more from you. With this sum I can go on and cultivate my ground for marketing and raise no more grain than is necessary for my own use. I have now in the ground twenty five acres of wheat with the view of geting in that much meadow; but this ground ~~now~~ I shall not probably have for another year as it is not on my part of the place, and is for sale. I am geting some ten or twelve acres more cleared this winter which will turn off about 300 cords of wood that will be valuable next summer and winter; but the choping has to be paid for now.

The fact is, without means, it is useless for me to go on

farming, and I will have to do what Mr. Dent has given me permission to do; sell the farm and invest elswhere. For two years now I have been compelled to neglect my farm to go off and make a few dollars to buy any little necessaries, sugar, coffee, &c. or to pay hired men. As a proof of this I will state that since the 2d day of April last I have kept a strict account of evry load of wood taken to the City, or Coal Banks, by my team and it has amounted, up to Jan.y 1st, to a fraction over 48 dollars per month. Now do not understand from this that if I had what I ask for my exertions wood sease; but that they would directed to a more profitable end. I regard evry load of wood taken, when the services of both myself and team are required on the farm, is a direct loss of more than the value of the load.

My expenses for my family have been nothing scarsely for the last two years. Fifty dollars, I believe, would pay all that I have laid out for their clothing. I have worked hard and got but little and expect to go on in the same way until I am perfectly independent; and then too most likely.[1]

All of Mr. Dent's family, now here, and Julia are suffering from unusual colds. Dr. Sharp has purchased a house in Lincoln Co. this State and will move there soon; was to have gone several days ago, in fact, but recieving a Telegraphic Dispach a few days ago that his father was ~~about~~ very low he started immediately home, taking his wife[2] and child with him.—Mrs. Dent died on the 14th of Jan.y after an illness of about a month. This leaves Mr. Dent, and one daughter,[3] alone.

Julia wishes to be remembered. Please answer soon.

Yours Truly
U. S. GRANT.

ALS, NjR.

1. From the letter of Aug. 22, 1857, it is unclear whether or not USG received the loan.
2. Ellen Dent had married Dr. Alexander Sharp.
3. The remaining daughter was Emma.

To Mary Grant

———

St. Louis, Mo.
August 22nd, 1857.

DEAR SISTER:

Your letter was received on last Tuesday, the only day in the week on which we get mail, and this is the earliest opportunity I have had of posting a letter.

I am glad to hear that mother and Jennie intend making us a visit. I would advise them to come by the river if they prefer it. Write to me beforehand about the time you will start, and from Louisville again, what boat you will be on, direct to St. Louis, —not Sappington, P. O.—and I will meet you at the river or Planter's House, or wherever you direct.

We are all very well. Julia contemplates visiting St. Charles next Saturday to spend a few days. She has never been ten miles from home, except to come to the city, since her visit to Covington.

I have nothing in particular to write about. My hard work is now over for the season with a fair prospect of being remunerated in everything but the wheat. My wheat, which would have produced from four to five hundred bushels with a good winter, has yielded only seventy-five. My oats were good, and the corn, if not injured by frost this fall, will be the best I ever raised. My potato crop bids fair to yield fifteen hundred bushels or more. Sweet potatoes, melons and cabbages are the only other articles I am raising for market. In fact, the oats and corn I shall not sell.

I see I have written a part of this letter as if I intended to direct to one, and part as if to the other of you; but you will understand it, so it makes no difference.

Write to me soon and often. Julia wears black.[1] I had forgotten to answer that part of your letter.

Your affectionate Brother,
ULYSS.

P. S. Tell father that I have this moment seen Mr. Ford, just from Sacketts Harbor, who informs me that while there he enquired of Mr. Bagley about my business with Camp,[2] and learns from him that the account should be acted upon immediately. Camp is now at Governor's Island, N. Y., and intends sailing soon for Oregon. If he is stopped he may be induced to disgorge. Tell father to forward the account immediately.

U.

J. G. *Cramer*, pp. 3–4.

1. Her mother had died Jan. 14, 1857.
2. Charles Ford, a friend of USG in Sackets Harbor, moved to St. Louis as manager of the United States Express Co. Elijah Camp, also of Sackets Harbor, had still not repaid USG money he owed from a business venture on the Pacific Coast. See letter of June 15, 1853.

Pawn Ticket

ST. LOUIS, Dec 23rd *1857*

I THIS DAY CONSIGN TO J. S. FRELIGH, AT MY OWN RISK FROM LOSS OR DAMAGE BY THIEVES OR FIRE, TO SELL ON COMMISSION, PRICE NOT LIMITED, 1 Gold Hunting[1] Detached Lever & Gold chain ON WHICH SAID FRELIGH HAS ADVANCED Twenty two DOLLARS. AND I HEREBY FULLY AUTHORIZE AND EMPOWER SAID FRELIGH TO SELL AT PUBLIC OR PRIVATE SALE THE ABOVE MENTIONED PROPERTY TO PAY SAID ADVANCE—IF THE SAME IS NOT PAID TO SAID FRELIGH, OR THESE CONDITIONS RENEWED BY PAYING CHARGES, ON OR BEFORE Jan 23/58

U. S. GRANT

DS, IHi. On March 19, 1910, Louis H. Freligh, professor of music and organist of St. Mark's Lutheran Church, St. Louis, Mo., offered this document for sale to autograph dealer W. R. Benjamin. "I can attest to its authenticity, as I was present at the transaction, & saw him sign his name to the document. I am now 71½ years old, so as I was then less than 20, can very well remember it. Have refrained over 50 years from offering it for sale, because so many people consider it a disgrace to patronize 'mine uncle,' & I did not wish to give offense to the renowned general's family, by exposing the matter. If you don't want to buy the valuable paper, kindly keep ~~it quiet~~ quiet" *Ibid.*

1. "Watch" accidentally omitted.

To Mary Grant

——————

White Haven
March 21st 1858.

DEAR SISTER;

Your letter was recieved one week ago last teusday and I would have answered it by the next Mail but it so happened that there was not a sheet of paper about the house, and as Spring has now set in I do not leave the farm except in cases of urgent necessity. Fathers letter,[1] enclosing Mr. Bagley's, relative to the Camp business, was recieved one or two weeks earlier, and promptly answered. My reply was long, giving a detailed account of my whole transactions with Camp, and a copy of which father can have to peruse when he comes along this way next.

Julia and the children are all well and talk some of making you a visit next fall, but I hardly think they will go. But if any of you, except father, should visit us this Spring, or early Summer, Julia says that Fred. may go home with you to spend a few months. She says she would be afraid to let him travel with father alone for she has an idea that he is so absent minded that if he was to arive in Cincinnati at night he would be just as apt to walk out of the cars and be gone for an hour befor he would recollect that he had a child with him as not. I have no such fears however. Fred. does not read yet but he will, I think, in a few weeks. We have no school within a mile & a half and that is to far to send him in the winter season. I shall commence sending him soon however. In the mean time I have no doubt but he is learning faster at home. Little Ellen is growing very fast and talks now quite plainly. Jesse R. is growing very rapidly, is very healthy and they say, is the best looking child among the four.[2] I dont think however ~~that~~ there is much difference, in that respect, between them.

Emma Dent is talking of visiting her relations in Ohio and Penna. this Summer, and if she does she will stop a time with you. Any talk of any of us visiting you must not stop you from coming to see us. The whole family here are great for planning visits but poor in the execution of their plans. It may take two seasons yet before any of these visits are made, in the mean time we are anxious to see all of you. For my part I do not know when I shall ever be able to leave home long enough for a visit. I may possibly be able to go on a flying visit next fall. I am anxious to make one more visit home before I get old.

This Spring has opened finely for farming and I hope to do well but I shall wait until the crops are gathered before I make any predictions. I have now three negro men, two hired by the year and one of Mr. Dents, which, with my own help, I think, will enable me to do my farming pretty well, with assistance in harvest. I have however a large farm. I shall have about 20 acres of potatoes, 20 of corn 25 of oats 50 of wheat, 25 of meadow, some clover, Hungarian grass and other smaller products all of which require labor before they are got into market, and the money realized upon them. You are aware, I believe, that I have rented out my place and have taken Mr. Dents.[3] There is about 200 acres of ploughed land on it and I shall have, in a few weeks, about 250 acres of woods pasture fenced up besides. Only one side of it and a part of of another has to be fenced to take the whole of it in and the rails are all ready. I must close with the wish that some of you would visit us as early as possible. In your letter you ask when my note in Bank becomes due! The 17th of Apl. is the last day of grace when it must be paid and I dont see now that I shall have the money.

Give Julia's, the children's & my love to all at home and write soon.

Your Brother
ULYSSES.

ALS, ICarbS.

    1. See letter of Aug. 22, 1857.
    2. Ellen Grant was born at Wish-ton-wish on July 4, 1855, and Jesse Root
Grant at Hardscrabble on Feb. 6, 1858.
    3. Col. Frederick Dent had rented White Haven to USG and moved to his
town house at Fourth and Cerre in St. Louis with his daughter Emma.

To Col. John O'Fallon

OFFICE OF
BARNARD & Co.
51 WASHINGTON AV.
BETWEEN 2ND & 3D STRS.
ST. LOUIS. April 7th 1858

FIRM COMPOSED OF
WM D. W. BARNARD.
JAMES BARNARD.
COL.

    Please let W. D. W. Barnard, or agt. have your check for
the amount of Mr. Dent's note in the Bank of the State of Mo.
due Saturday the 10th inst. and oblige.

Your Obt. Svt.
U. S. GRANT

To Col. J. O'Falon
St. Louis, Mo.

ALS, O'Fallon collection, MoSHi.
    John O'Fallon, originally from Ky., had become wealthy in St. Louis banking
and real estate, had declined an appointment as Secretary of War in 1841, and
was widely known for his philanthropies. John O'Fallon's second wife was
a cousin of Col. Frederick Dent. Julia Grant had spent part of the winter of
1843–44 in the O'Fallon home and regarded their daughter, Caroline O'Fallon,
as one of her closest friends.
    William D. W. Barnard, a partner in the wholesale drug firm of Barnard &
Co. at 51 Washington Ave. in St. Louis, was a close friend of USG. Barnard's
wife, Eliza Shurlds, was a sister of the wife of George Dent, Mary Isabella
Shurlds. In 1864 USG wrote to Maj. Gen. William T. Sherman that "Mr.
Barnard has been a sincere friend of mine, when I wanted friends and when there
was no apparent possible chance of him ever deriving any benefit from it . . ."
Quoted in Barnard to USG, July 19, 1875, CSmH.

To Mary Grant

———

St. Louis, Mo.
Sept. 7th 1858.

Dear Sister;

Your letter was recieved in due time and I would have answered it immediately but that I had mailed a letter from Julia to Jennie[1] the morning of the receipt of yours. I thought then to wait for two or three weeks and by that time there was so much sickness in my family, and Freddy so dangerously ill, that I thought I would not write until his fate was decided. He come near being taken from us by the Billious, then Typhoid, fever, but he is now convelescing. Some seven of the of the negroes have been sick. Mrs. Sharp[2] is here on a visit and she and one of her childr[en] are sick, and Julia & I are both sick with chills and fever. If I had written to you earlier it would have been whilst Fred's case was a doubtful one and I did not want to distress you when it could have done no good to any one.—I have been thinking of paying you a visit this fall but I now think it extremely doubtful whether I shall be able to. Not being able to even attend to my hands, much less work myself, I am geting behind hand so that I shall have to stay here and attend to my business. Cant some of you come and pay us a visit? Jennie has not answered Julias letter yet. Did she recieve it? I was coming to the city the day it was written to hear a political speech and it was to late to get it in the P. O. so I gave it to a young man to put in the next morning. It is for this reason I ask the question. Write to me soon. I hope you have had none of the sickness we have been troubled with.

Your Brother
Ulysses.

To Mary F. Grant
Covington Ky

ALS, deCoppet Collection, NjP.

1. Jennie was USG's sister Virginia.
2. Ellen Dent Sharp was Julia Grant's sister.

To Jesse Root Grant

St. Louis,
Oct. 1st, 1858.

DEAR FATHER:

I arrived at home on Tuesday evening, and, it being my "chill" day, of course felt very badly. Julia had been much worse during my absence, but had improved again so that I found her about as when I left home. Fred. has improved steadily, and can now hear nearly as well as before his sickness. The rest of the family are tolerably well, with the exception of Mr. Dent whose health seems to be about as when I left. Mr. Dent and myself will make a sale this fall and get clear of all the stock on the place, and then rent out the cleared land and sell about four hundred acres of the north end of the place. As I explained to you, this will include my place. I shall plan to go to Covington towards Spring, and would prefer your offer to any one of mere salary that could be offered. I do not want any place for permanent stipulated pay, but want the prospect of one day doing business for myself. There is a pleasure in knowing that one's income depends somewhat upon his own exertions and business capacity, that cannot be felt when so much and no more is coming in, regardless of the success of the business engaged in or the manner in which it is done.

Mr. Dent thinks I had better take the boy he has given Julia along with me, and let him learn the farrier's business. He is a very smart, active boy, capable of making anything; but this matter I will leave entirely to you. I can leave him here and get about three dollars per month for him now, and more as he gets older. Give my love to all at home.

Yours truly,

To J. R. Grant, Esq., ULYSSES.
Covington, Ky.

J. G. Cramer, pp. 11–12.

To John F. Long

———

> Carondelet T. S.
> St. Louis Co. Mo.
> Oct. 16th 1858

MR. LONG;

DEAR SIR:

At Mr. Dent's request I called upon the County surveyor to come out here and run the line between your land and his. Teusday next is the day set for doing it and I give you the earlyest notice practicable. I would call upon you myself but I am going to the City this morning and shall not probably be back before dark.

> Yours Truly
> U. S. GRANT.

ALS, MoSHi. See letter of Oct. 1, 1858, for plans to sell part of White Haven. USG drafted a deed for Frederick Dent selling land to John Stewart for $800 on Nov. 1, 1858, and signed as witness on Nov. 9, 1858. DS, *ibid.* John F. Long, USG's neighbor at White Haven, became a lifelong friend.

To Jesse Root Grant

———

> St. Louis Mo.
> March 12th 1859.

DEAR FATHER;

It has now been over a month, I believe, since I wrote to you last although I expected to have written again the next week. I can hardly tell how the new business I am engaged in is going to sucseed but I believe it will be something more than a support.[1] If I find an opportunity next week I will send you some of our cards[2] which if you will distribute among such persons as may have business to attend to in this city, such as buying or selling property, collecting either rents or other liabilities, it may prove the means of giving us additional commissions. Mr. Benton was here for some time and used to call in to see me frequently. Whilst he was here I submitted to him some property for sale belonging to a Mr. Tucker. Since Mr. B's departure Mr Tucker has called several times and wants me to submit his propositions again and say that if he is disposed to buy, and pay conciderable cash, he will make his prices such as to secure to him a good investment. I enclose with this a list of the property, and prices, as first asked, one third cash, bal. one & two years. Please tell Mr. Benton if he feels like making any proposition for any part of this property to let me know and I will submit it and give him an answer.

We are living now in the lower part of the city, full two miles from my office. The house[3] is a comfortable little one just suited to my means. We have one spare room and also a spare bed in the childrens room so that we can accomodate any of our friends that are likely to come to see us. I want two of the girls, or all of them for that matter, to come and pay us a long visit soon.

Julia and the children are well. They will not make a visit to Ky. now. I was anxious to have them go before I rented but with four children she could not go without a servant and she was afraid that landing so often as she would have to do in free states she might have some trouble.[4]

Tell one of the girls to write soon.—Has Simp[5] gone South? —Are you going to the city to live?[6]

Yours Truly
U. S. Grant

To J. R. Grant, Esq,
Covington Ky

ALS, Warren Reeder, Hammond, Ind.

1. On Oct. 1, 1858, USG had written to his father of his expectation of working for him. Sometime between that letter and this, plans had fallen through. USG moved to St. Louis where he entered a real estate partnership with Julia Grant's cousin, Harry Boggs.

2. The cards read, "H. BOGGS. U. S. GRANT. BOGGS & GRANT,

GENERAL AGENTS, COLLECT RENTS. NEGOTIATE LOANS. BUY AND SELL REAL ESTATE, ETC., ETC. NO. 35 PINE STREET, Between Second and Third, SAINT LOUIS, MO."

3. It was located at Seventh and Lynch Streets.

4. The Supreme Court ruling in the Dred Scott case, March 6, 1857, upheld the right to travel with slaves. Adverse Northern reaction to the decision, however, made some slaveholders apprehensive about exercising their rights.

5. Samuel Simpson Grant, born Sept. 23, 1825, was employed at the leather store in Galena. His health declined due to tuberculosis, of which he died in Sept., 1861, and this may explain his trip to the South.

6. Jesse Grant spent the rest of his life in Covington, Ky.

Manumission of Slave

[*March 29, 1859*]

Know all persons by these presents, that I Ulysses S Grant of the City & County of St Louis in the State of Missouri, for divers good and valuable considerations me hereunto moving, do hereby emancipate and set free from Slavery my negro man William, sometimes called William Jones (Jones) *of Mullato complexion, aged about* thirty-five *years, and about* five feet seven inches *in height and being the same slave purchased by me of Frederick Dent—And I do hereby manumit, emancipate & set free said William from slavery forever*

In testimony Whereof I hereto set my hand & seal at St Louis this [29th] *day of March A D 1859*

Witnesses   U. S. GRANT (Seal)
J G McClellan
W. S. Hillyer

DS, MoSHi. At the foot of the document is a certification by Stephen Rice of the Saint Louis Circuit Court that the signature was genuine and that the document had been entered in the record of the court.

On March 21, 1858, USG wrote of employing "three negro men, two hired by the year and one of Mr. Dents . . ." When USG acquired William Jones is not known. At least two more slaves were owned by Julia Grant.

The witnesses, Josiah G. McClellan and William S. Hillyer, were partners in the St. Louis law firm of McClellan, Hillyer and Moody at 35 Pine Street.

USG and Harry Boggs had desk space in the firm's offices for their real estate business. USG appointed Hillyer his aide in Sept., 1861.

McClellan was born in 1824 in Wheeling, Va., and graduated from Williams College in 1847. After admission to the bar he moved to St. Louis in 1850. As chief clerk to Peter Ladue, assessor of St. Louis County, he learned about local real estate practice, and began practice with Hillyer and Moody in 1851.

To Board of County Commissioners

St. Louis, Aug. 15th 1859

Hon. County Commissioners,
St. Louis County
Mo.
Gentlemen;

I beg leave to submit myself as an applicant for the office of County Engineer, should the Office be rendered vacant, and at the same time to submit the names of a few Citizens who have been kind enough to recommend me for the Office. I have made no effort to get a large number of names, nor the names of persons with whom I am not personally acquainted.

I enclose herewith also a statement from Prof. J. J. Reynolds, who was a class mate of mine at West Point, as to qualifications.

Should your honorable body see proper to give me the appointment I pledge myself to give the Office my entire attention and shall hope to give general satisfaction.

Very Respectfully
Your Obt. Svt.
U. S. Grant

ALS, Andrew Joyner, Jr., Greensboro, N.C. Reynolds wrote, Aug. 1. "Captain U. S. Grant was a member of the class at the Mil Acady, West Point, which graduated in 1843—he always maintained a high standing and graduated with great credit, especially in mathematics, mechanics, & Engineering—From my personal knowledge of his capacity and acquirements as well as of his strict integrity and unremitting industry I consider him in an eminent degree qualified for the office of County Engineer." Joseph Jones Reynolds, then professor of mechanics and engineering at Washington University in St. Louis, had been appointed to USMA from Ind. to the class of 1843 and had resigned as 1st lt. on Feb. 28, 1857. He later served as maj. gen. of vols. during the Civil War. ADS, NN. Below his statement D. M. Frost wrote, "I was for three years in the Corps of Cadets at West Point with Captain Grant and afterwards served with him for some eight or nine years in the army and can fully endorse the foregoing statement of Prof. Reynolds." Daniel Marsh Frost of N.Y., USMA 1844, resigned as 1st lt. May 31, 1853. He then moved to St. Louis and organized D. M. Frost & Co., a fur-trading venture on the upper Missouri. He served four years, 1855–59, in the Mo. state senate as a Democrat. He was later brig. gen., C.S.A.

The endorsement on USG's letter read, "The undersigned take pleasure in recommending Capt U S Grant as a suitable person for the office of County Engineer of St Louis County August 1 1859

Thos. E. Tutt	N J. Eaton
Jno P Helfenstein	Taylor Blow
Frc Overstolz	T Grimsley
L. A. Benoist & Co	Saml B. Churchill
J. G. McClellan	Jas M Hughes
Chas. A. Pope	J. W. Mitchell
W. S. Hillyer	Lemuel G. Pardee
C. S. Purkitt	James C Moody
Wm. L. Pipkin	Felix Coste
J Addison Barret	Baman & Co.
K. MacKenzie	C. W. Ford
Daniel. M. Frost	A. S. Robinson
Robt. M. Renick	Geo M Moore
Robt. J. Hornsby	R. A Barnes
G. W. Fishback	Thomas Marshall
J McKnight	J O'Fallon
	John How
	John F. Darby
	Ed Walsh"

In a letter of Aug. 20, 1859, USG referred to the endorsers as "the very first citizens of this place, and members of all parties . . ." McClellan, Hillyer, and Moody were law partners in the office where USG had desk space. See March 29, 1859. For Charles W. Ford, see letter of Aug. 22, 1857. For John O'Fallon see letter of April 7, 1858. Dr. Charles A. Pope, professor of surgery at St. Louis Medical College and former president of the American Medical Association, was married to Caroline O'Fallon. George W. Fishback, part owner of the *Missouri Democrat*, was originally from Batavia, Ohio, and his sister was married to USG's friend, John W. Lowe. Possibly the support of some of the others came through a friendly disposition to the son-in-law of Frederick Dent.

To Jesse Root Grant

St. Louis,
Aug. 20th, 1859.

DEAR FATHER:

On last Wednesday I received your letter, and on the Monday before one from Mr. Burk, from both of which I much regretted to learn of Simpson's continued ill health.[1] I at once wrote to Orvil, whose arrival at Galena[2] I learned from Burk's letter, to urge Simpson to come by steamer to St. Louis and spend some time with me, and if it should prove necessary for anyone to accompany him, I would take him home. Cannot Jennie and Orvil's wife come this way when they start for Galena? We would like very much to see them.

I am not over sanguine of getting the appointment mentioned in my last letter. The Board of Commissioners, who make the appointment, are divided,—three free soilers to two opposed,— and although friends who are recommending me are the very first citizens of this place, and members of all parties, I fear they will make strictly party nominations for all the offices under their control. As to the professorship you speak of, that was filled some time ago. And were it not, I would stand no earthly chance. The Washington University, where the vacancy was to be filled, is one of the best endowed institutions in the United States, and all the professorships are sought after by persons whose early advantages were the same as mine, but who have been engaged in teaching all their mature years. Quimby,[3] who was the best mathematician in my class, and who was for several years an assistant at West Point, and for nine years a professor in an institution in New York, was an unsuccessful applicant. The appointment was given to the most distinguished man in his department in the country, and an author. His name is Shorano.[4] Since putting in my application for the appointment of County Engineer, I have learned that the place is not likely to be filled before February next. What I shall do will depend entirely upon what I can get to do. Our present business is entirely overdone in this city, at least a dozen new houses having started about the same time I commenced. I do not want to fly from one thing to another, nor would I, but I am compelled to make a living from the start for which I am willing to give all my time and all my energy.

Julia and the children are well and send love to you. On your way to Galena can you not come by here? Write to me soon.

                                                              ULYSSES.

J. G. Cramer, 16–18.

1. For Simpson Grant's health, see letter of March 12, 1859. W. T. Burke was the son-in-law of Ann Simpson Ross, sister of USG's mother. He and his brother-in-law Orlando Ross went to the leather store in Galena to learn the trade while working as clerks.

2. As Simpson Grant's health declined, more and more of the active management of the Galena store was assumed by Orvil Grant, born May 15, 1835, youngest of the Grant brothers.

3. Isaac Ferdinand Quinby of N.J., USMA 1843, had resigned as 1st lt. March 16, 1852 to teach at the University of Rochester.

4. William Chauvenet (1820–70), an astronomer and mathematician, had been a professor of mathematics in the navy since 1841 and had played a major role in the development of the U.S. Naval Academy. He rejected an offer from Yale in accepting an appointment to Washington University where he became chancellor in 1862. *DAB*, IV, 43–44.

To Jesse Root Grant

                                              St. Louis, Sept. 23d/59

DEAR FATHER:

I have waited for some time to write you the result of the action of the County Commissioners upon the appointment of a County Engineer. The question has at length been settled, and I am sorry to say, adversely to me. The two Democratic Commissioners voted for me and the freesoilers against me. What I shall now go at I have not determined but I hope something before a great while. Next month I get possession of my own house when my expenses will be reduced so much that a very moderate salary will support me. If I could get the $3000 note cashed which I got difference in the exchange of property, I could put up with the proceeds two houses that would pay me, at least, $40 pr. month rent.[1] The note has five years to run with interest notes given separately and payable annually.

We are looking for some of you here next week to go to the fair. I wrote to Simp. to come down and see me[2] but as I have had no answer from him, nor from Orvil to a letter written some time before, I do not know whether he will come or not. I should like very much to have some of you come and see us this fall.

Julia and the children are all very well. Fred. & Buck go to school every day. They never think of asking to stay at home.

You may judge from the result of the action of the County Commissioners that I am strongly identified with the Democratic party! Such is not the case. I never voted an out and out Democratic ticket in my life. I voted for Buch. for President to defeat Freemont but not because he was my first choice.[3] In all other elections I have universally selected the candidates that in my estimation, were the best fitted for the different offices and it never happens that such men are all arrayed on one side. The strongest friend I had in the Board of Comrs.[4] is a F. S. but opposition between parties is so strong that he would not vote for any one, no matter how friendly, unless at least one of his own party would go with him. The F. S. party felt themselves bound to provide for one of their own party who was defeated for the office of County Engineer; a Dutchman who came to the West as an Assistant Surveyor upon the publick lands and who has held an office ever since.[5] There is, I believe, but one paying office in the County held by an American unless you except the office of Sheriff which is held by a Frenchman who speaks broken English but was born here[6]

Write to me soon. Julia & the children join me in sending love to all of you.

Yours Truly
ULYSSES

Copy, MoSHi.

1. USG had traded Hardscrabble farm for a house and lot at Ninth and Barton Streets in St. Louis, receiving a note for $3000 representing the difference in value. The new owner of Hardscrabble was to pay off a $1500 mortgage on the St. Louis house, and secured the debt with a deed of trust on Hardscrabble. He was unable to pay, however, and USG sued, finally recovering the Hardscrabble farm in 1867. *Richardson*, p. 162.

2. See next letter for mention of Simpson's visit.

3. USG discussed his vote for James Buchanan in *Memoirs*, I, 214–15. Cf. John Russell Young, *Around the World with General Grant* (New York, 1879), II, 268.

4. The two Democratic members of the Board of County Commissioners were Col. Alton R. Easton and Judge Peregrine Tibbets. The Free-Soilers were John H. Lightner, Benjamin Farrar, and Dr. William Taussig. USG's friend among the Free-Soilers was probably Dr. Taussig, who later wrote *Personal Recollections of General Grant* (St. Louis, 1903).

5. "September 22, 1859. Ordered by the board, that C. E. Salomon be, and he is hereby appointed County Engineer; to hold until otherwise ordered by this board, at a salary of one hundred and sixty dollars per month." *Richardson*, p. 167. Charles E. Salomon later served in the Civil War as col. of the 5th Mo. Vols.

6. USG's reaction to his rejection and his brief membership in a Know-Nothing lodge are discussed in *Memoirs*, I, 212–13.

To Simpson Grant

St. Louis, Oct. 24th 1859

DEAR BROTHER;

I have been postponing writing to you hoping to make a return for your horse, but as yet I have recieved nothing for him. About two weeks ago a man spoke to me for him and said that he would try him the next day and if he suited give me $100 for him. I have not seen the man since but one week ago last Saturday he went to the stable and got the horse saddle and bridle since which I have seen neither man nor horse. From this I presume he must like him. The man, I understand, lives in Florisant, about twelve miles from the city.

My family are all well and living in our own house.[1] It is much more pleasant than where we lived when you were here and contains about as much room, practically. I am still unemployed but expect to have a place in the Custom House from the 1st of next month. My name has been forwarded for the appointment of Superintendent, which, if I do not get, will not probably be filled atal. In that case there is a vacant desk which I may get that pays $1200 pr. annum.[2] The other will be worth from $1500 to $1800 and will occupy but little time.

Remember me to all at home. There is a gentleman here who has lands in San Antonio de Bexar Co. Texas, that would like to get you, should you go there this Winter, to look after them. If you go, and will attend to his business, drop me a line and he will furnish me all the papers, and instructions, to forward to you.

Yours &c.

U. S. GRANT

P. S. The man that has your horse is Capt. Covington, a owner of a row of six thr[ee] story brick houses in this city and the probabilities are that he intends to give me an order on his agt. for the money on th[e] 1st of the month when the rents are paid. At all eve[nts] I imagine the horse is perfectly safe.

U. S. G.

ALS, deCoppet Collection, NjP.

    1. See preceding letter.
    2. USG received the lesser position but held it only one month.

To Hon. J. H. Lightner

———

St. Louis, Feb.y 13th 1860

HON. J. H. LIGHTNER:
PRES. BOARD COUNTY COMRS;
SIR:

Should the office of County Engineer be vacated by the will of your Hon. body I would respectfully renew the application made by me in August last for that appointment. I would also beg leave to refer to the application and recommendations then submitted, and now on file with your Board.

I am Sir

Respectfully Your Obt. Svt.

U. S. GRANT

ALS, MoSHi. See letter of Aug. 15, 1859. The board retained C. E. Salomon as county engineer.

To Julia Dent Grant

———

Covington Ky.

March 14th 1860.

DEAR JULIA:

I arrived here at ½ past 11 to day with a head ache and feeling bad generally. We were detained on the road last night by the train going to St. Louis Smashing up on the road ahead of us. The result was our train had to go back and ~~and~~ the passengers walk around the breakdown and get in another train and come on. This is why I arrived here so late and this caused me to miss seeing father for the next day or two. As I was walking up the Street home I saw him turn down another street not more than half a square ahead of me but I supposed he was just gowing down town for a few minuets and would be back home for dinner. But I found that he had gone over to the City to take the 12 m packet to go up the river and may not return before Friday evening. I shall have to remain until his return and as the river is in fine boating order I think I shall return that way, particularly if I can get started this week. Clara has gone to Bethel and will not return for a week or two.[1] Mother Jennie [&] Mary asked many questions about you and the children. They were quite disappointed that Fred. & Buck were not along. My head is nearly bursting with pain and I would not have written to you to-day but I wanted to make shure that my letter would be in St. Louis by Saturday now that it is not probable that I shall be there by that time.

Kiss the children for me. I should have written to John Dent before I left giving him instructions about what it was necessary for your father to have done in Washington to enable him to carry his Carondelet suit up.[2] Tell your father that I have not written to John on the subject and if he wishes it done he had better tell you what to write.

Again kiss the children for me and let them kiss you in return for their pa.

Your affectionate

DADO

P. S. I forgot to say that all here were well except Simp. I think he is about as he was last fall. He does not think there has been much improvement. I have not been through the house to see how things look though I have been here three or four hours. The dining room is the only one I have been in.

ALS, DLC-USG. The trip to Covington was probably connected with planning for USG's move from St. Louis to Galena. USG went to the J. R. Grant leather store in Galena as a clerk; accounts differ as to whether there was an agreement for an eventual partnership (See *Lewis*, 372–73). USG moved to Galena in the early spring of 1860.

1. Five words omitted.
2. In the course of dealing in land claims, Frederick Dent had acquired a Spanish grant for a considerable portion of Carondelet. He pressed his claim for many years without success. Walter B. Stevens, *Grant in Saint Louis* (St. Louis, 1916), pp. 12–13.

To Mr. Davis

————

Galena, August 7th 1860.

Mr. Davis;
Dear Sir:

When I left St. Louis you will remember you enquired of me if I had the Deed for that Carondelet property recorded. I told you that it had not been recorded and that the Deed had been left with Gibson. I feel anxious to know if you found it and if it has been recorded yet.

Since leaving St. Louis I have become pretty well inniciated into the Leather business and like it well. Our business here is prosperous and I have evry reason to hope, in a few years, to be entirely above the frowns of the world, pecuniarily.—I presume you had an exciting time of it in St. Louis Yesterday! I feel anxious to hear of Blairs defeat but as yet the Telegraph has brought us nothing Satisfactory. One rumor is that Barret is 45 ahead for the short term and Blair far ahead for the long. Another that Blair has gained in both; and still another that Barret is probably elected for both.[1] I cant help feeling more interest in the contest you have just gone through than I shall in the November election. The fact is I think the Democratic party want a little purifying and nothing will do it so effectually as a defeat. The only thing is I dont like to see a Republican beat the party. —How is Gibson now? Myself and family are all well and highly pleased with this place.

Yours Truly
U. S. Grant

P. S. Not being certain of your first name I shall have to send this through the Collector to whom please present my best respects. Please write to me soon.

ALS, MoSHi. Davis and Gibson may have been custom house employees when USG was there.

1. In the 1858 election contest for representative in Congress for the St. Louis district, Democrat John Richard Barret had opposed Francis P. Blair, Jr., who called his party the Free Democracy although he generally supported the Republicans. On the face of the returns Barret claimed victory by 426 votes. Charging fraud, Blair contested the election, and was finally awarded the seat. The 1860 campaign featured the same two candidates and even greater bitterness. Blair resigned his seat on June 25, 1860, to allow voters to elect a Representative for the remainder of his present term as well as a Representative to the next Congress. Blair won the long term by 1,486 votes but lost the short term by a slim margin. Blair was an open Republican by 1860 and served as maj. gen. of vols. under USG during the Civil War. He returned to the Democratic Party later, which nominated him for vice president in 1868. William Ernest Smith, *The Francis Preston Blair Family in Politics* (New York, 1933), I, 429–42, 489–96.

To Julia Dent Grant

Decora, Iowa
Dec. 31st/60

DEAR JULIA:

This is the day I had set for being at home, but various detentions, particularly the one at Prairie du Chien of four days has set us back considerably.[1] The weather has been very cold but I have not suffered any. We have had a fine snow up in these parts so that traveling in a buggy is out of the question. We have our buggy set up on runners and in that condition travel along finely and of course attract the attention of evry passer. Have you all kept well. I dreamed night before last that Jesse was sick. I hope in this case dreams may go by contraries.—To-morrow will be New Years day. I wish you all a happy New Year and wish I was at home with you. To-night, if we can get off, we want to go to West Union, twenty five miles from here. It will be sun down however before we can start and possibly we may not be able to get off to night atall. You may look for me home about the next Teusday after you recieve this.—I enclose a letter for Orvil which have sent to him at once.

Kiss all the children for me. I did not get a letter from you at Prairie du Chien. I shall enquire at the P. O. in West Union. I have not got anything to tell you about the trip until my return so wait patiently for

ULYS.

This will be my last letter.

ALS, DLC-USG.

1. "I travelled through the Northwest considerably during the winter of 1860–1. We had customers in all the little towns in south-west Wisconsin, south-east Minnesota and north-east Iowa." *Memoirs*, I, 222. J. R. Grant business papers in ICHi indicate that the firm was interested in real estate and other ventures in this territory and had leather stores in La Crosse and Prairie du Chien, Wis., and Cedar Rapids, Iowa.

Addressee Unknown

[*Dec., 1860*]

In my new employment I have become pretty conversant, and am much pleased with it. I hope to be a partner soon, and am sanguine that a competency at least can be made out of the business.

How do you all feel on the subject of Secession in St. Louis? The present troubles must affect business in your trade greatly. With us the the only difference experienced as yet is the difficulty of obtaining Southern exchange.

It is hard to realize that a State or States should commit so suicidal an act as to secede from the Union, though from all the reports, I have no doubt but that at least five of them will do it. And then, with the present granny of an executive, some foolish policy will doubtless be pursued which will give the seceding States the support and sympathy of the Southern States that don't go out. The farce now going on in southern Kansas is, I presume, about at an end, and the St. Louis volunteer General Frost at their head, covered all over with glory.[1] You will now have seven hundred men more in your midst, who will think themselves entitled to live on the public for all future time. You must provide office for them, or some of them may declare Missouri out of the Union. It does seem as if just a few men have produced all the present difficulty. I don't see why by the same rule a few hundred men could not carry Missouri out of the Union.

Richardson, pp. 175–76.

1. On Nov. 25, 1860, a brigade of Mo. militia left St. Louis under the command of Daniel M. Frost to protect western Mo. from a rumored invasion by Kan. Jayhawkers led by James Montgomery. *New York Times,* Nov. 26, 1860. The rumors proved exaggerated, however, and order was restored by U. S. troops commanded by Brig. Gen. William Selby Harney.

Calendar

1837, Nov. 13.   Bill headed Georgetown, Ohio, to Jesse R. Grant. "To extracting 1 tooth for Ulisses .50"—D, USG 3.

1837.   Resolutions presented by USG to the Philomathea Society at Maysville Seminary, Maysville, Ky. "H. U. Grant entered as a pupil the Maysville Seminary during the winter season of 1836 and 1837. . . . He was a member of the Philomathea Society, to which the juniors of the institution belonged. . . . I find in the records of the Philomathean that, 'in January, 1837, Lissant Cox, Ulysses Grant, Absalom Markland, Wilson G. Richardson and John P. Phister were appointed as the Executive committee for the ensuing month' . . . On another page of the Secretary's book I find that Mr. Grant submitted the following resolution: '*Resolved*, That it be considered out of order for any member to speak on the opposite side to which he belongs.' In February of the same year, 1837, the records show that 'Ulysses Grant and E. M. Richeson were appointed to declaim on the ensuing Friday.' At another meeting I find that 'Mr. Grant submitted the following resolution: *Resolved*, That any member who leaves his seat during debate, shall be fined not less than 6¼ cents.' "—W. W. Richeson, former teacher at Maysville Seminary, to W. M. Haldeman, Dec. 1, 1879, in *The Courier-Journal* (Louisville), Dec. 10, 1879. See *Garland*, pp. 18–19.

1839, FEB. 1.   Senator Thomas Morris to Secretary of War Joel Roberts Poinsett recommending USG for appointment to USMA— DNA, RG 107, Registers of Letters Received. On Feb. 5, 1839, Poinsett replied. "I have the honor to inform you that the district represented by the Hon. T. L Hamer will be entitled to a Cadet appointment in March next, and that his consent must be obtained before the appointment you solicit for U. S. Grant can be given."—Copy, *ibid.*, RG 94, Letters Sent, USMA.

1839, APRIL 24.   To Secretary of War Joel R. Poinsett accepting appointment of USG to USMA. DNA, RG 107, Register of Letters Received. On April 6, Jesse Grant had written to the Secretary of War giving permission for his son to accept the appointment—*Ibid.* On April 17, Capt. Frederic Augustus Smith of the engineers department replied, "I have the honor to inform you in answer to your letter of the 6th inst to the Secretary of War that the regulations of the War Department (see letter of appointment) require the acceptance by the person appointed a Cadet, as well as the assent of the Parent or Guardian: Your Son will therefore forward his acceptance as required, or decline the same, as may meet his views." Copy, *ibid.*, RG 94, Letters Sent, USMA.

1839, [SPRING?]. Poem supposedly written by USG for Mary King before his departure for USMA. Apparently not in USG's hand— ICarbS.

1839, MAY 26. Signature "U. H. Grant" in the register of Roe's Hotel, West Point, N.Y.—*Garland*, p. 31.

1839, MAY 29. Signature "Ulysses Hiram Grant" in adjutant record book of cadet arrivals—*Garland*, pp. 31–32.

1839, JUNE 4. USG to his mother—Major Penniman [Charles Wheeler Denison], *The Tanner-Boy: A Life of General U. S. Grant* (Boston, 1864), pp. 41–42. Probably spurious—See *USGA Newsletter*, II, 4 (July, 1965), 19–24.

1839, JUNE, to 1843, MAY. Account book kept by USG at USMA. Entries on 78 pages detailing sums spent for clothing, equipment, damages, subscriptions, and the services of the tailor, shoemaker, barber, and postmaster—CSmH.

[1839–1841]. USG to his father—Major Penniman [Charles Wheeler Denison], *The Tanner-Boy: A Life of General U. S. Grant* (Boston, 1864), pp. 43–45. Probably spurious—See *USGA Newsletter*, II, 4 (July, 1965), 19–24.

[1839–1841?]. "U. H. Grant Georgetown Ohio" written in the album of a USMA classmate. Facsimile—*The Century Magazine*, XXX, 6 (Oct., 1885), 939.

1840, DEC. 8. Jesse R. Grant to John W. Lowe. "I recd a letter from Cadet Ulysses dated 8th Nov. He says his prospects are more favorable than they have been since he has been at the Point—He says he has been transfered to the ~~second~~ first section in mathematics, &

thinks the report will show him about 9th or 10th in that branch. Since that I have recd the Oct report which places him 7 in mathematics 37 in French & the same in Drawing & English Grammar—This shows a raise of 9 in Mathematics, & 12 in French since the June examination —He says 'if you see Mr Lowe, tell him if I neglect to write to him, I will not forget to call & see him in July next.' We are all well, & would be glad to see you & Mrs Lowe here this winter. It would be a good sleigh ride—Come up the first good sleighing."—ALS, Dayton Public Library, Dayton, Ohio. See letter of June 26, 1846.

1843, [FALL?]. USG to Albert E. Church, Professor of Mathematics at USMA, asking appointment as his assistant. USG called the reply "entirely satisfactory."—*Memoirs*, I, 51.

1844, SEPT. 4. Three signatures as witness on a receipt for clothing issued to three sergeants of the 4th Inf.—IHi.

1844, OCT. 31. USG as commander of Co. A, 4th Inf., signed the muster roll—DS, DNA, RG 94.

1845, JAN. 1. To Col. George Bomford transmitting "a Return of Ordnance and Ordnance Stores pertaining to (.A) Company, 4th Infantry, for a part of the 4th quarter of 1844—also the necessary vouchers."—LS, DNA, RG 156, Letters Received. On Feb. 7, 1845, Lt. Col. George Talcott acknowledged receipt of the return and forwarded it to the Second Auditor's office—Copies, *ibid.*, Letters Sent (Miscellaneous).

1845, FEB. 21. Bvt. Maj. Gen. Thomas S. Jesup to USG. "Your Clothing Return for the 4th Qur. of last year has been received and examined at this Office, and sent to the Treasury for settlement"— Copy, DNA, RG 92, Letters Sent, Clothing. On May 26, 1845, the Second Auditor's office wrote USG that the clothing return was correct—*Ibid.*, RG 217, Second Auditor, Letters Sent, Property Division.

1845, MARCH 25. USG to Col. George Bomford, chief of ordnance, transmitting "a Return of Ordnance, and Ordnance Stores for Comp'y (A) 4th Inf'y, for a part of the 1st Quarter—commencing on the 1st, and ending on the 28. day of January, 1845 : also the necessary vouchers."—LS, DNA, RG 156, Letters Received. On May 12, 1845, Lt. Col. George Talcott acknowledged receipt of this return and forwarded it to the Second Auditor's office—Copies, *ibid.*, Letters Sent (Miscellaneous).

1845, MAY 16.   Col. Henry Stanton, asst. q. m. gen., to Second Auditor's office transmitting clothing returns, including one from USG for Co. A for part of 1st quarter, 1845—Copy, DNA, RG 92, Letters Sent, Clothing. On July 23, 1845, the Second Auditor's office wrote USG. "Clothing and Co. arms returns to first quarter of 1845 inclusive correct, and closed by receipt of Capt. Larnard."—*Ibid.*, RG 217, Second Auditor, Letters Sent, Property Division.

1845, JULY 10.   To Bvt. Brig. Gen. Nathan Towson, Paymaster General, requesting permission to have one month's account cashed in New York City—DNA, RG 99, Registers of Letters Received.

1845, OCT. 24.   USG to AGO requesting transfer to 4th Inf. Endorsed by Bvt. Brig. Gen. Zachary Taylor *et al.*, Parke-Bernet Sale 2254, Feb. 11, 1964. The letter was forwarded to Washington by Gen. Taylor on Oct. 24, 1845—DNA, RG 94, Mexican War, Army of Occupation, Letters Sent.

1846, AUG. 22.   To Col. George Bomford enclosing "an Invoice of the Ordnance & Ordnance Stores pertaining to (C) Co. 4th Inf.y"—ALS, DNA, RG 156, Letters Received.

1846, AUG. 26.   To Col. George Bomford enclosing "the return of Ordnance & Ordnance Stores, pertaining to Co. C 4th Inf.y ~~Voucher~~ also the necessary Voucher."—ALS, DNA, RG 156, Letters Received. On Oct. 1, 1846, Capt. William Maynadier acknowledged receipt of this return and forwarded it to the Second Auditor's office—Copies, *ibid.*, Letters Sent (Miscellaneous).

1846, SEPT. 30.   To Bvt. Maj. Gen. Thomas S. Jesup transmitting "a 'Semi-annual' and a Quarterly Return of Quarter Master's stores, a Return of Clothing, Camp and Garrison Equipage, and an Account Current of Expenditures on account of the Quartermaster's Dept. for the quarter ending the 30th of September 1846, with the required

Abstracts and vouchers."—ALS, DNA, RG 217, Third Auditor's Account 4006.

[1846, SEPT. 30]. "Quarterly Return of Quartermaster's stores, received and issued at Monterey, Mexico, in the quarter ending the 30th of September, 1846, by Lieut. U. S. Grant, 4th Inf. a. a. qm."—DS, OrHi.

1846, SEPT. 30. To Bvt. Maj. Gen. Thomas S. Jesup transmitting additional reports for Sept., 1846—DNA, RG 92, Registers of Letters Received.

[1846, SEPT. 30]. "Field Return of the Fourth Reg.t of Infantry for the Month of September 1846." Signed by USG as act. adjt.—DS, DNA, RG 94.

[1846, SEPT. 30]. "Return of the Fourth Regiment of Infantry Commanded by Colonel William Whistler for the Month of September 1846" Signed by USG as act. adjt.—DS, DNA, RG 94.

1846, OCT. 22. To Col. George Bomford enclosing "a Return, of Ordnance, and Ordnance Stores, for the late Lieut: & Adjt. C. Hoskins, 4th Infy, (Killed in action) for a part of the 3d Quarter, ending Sept 21st, 1846, with the necessary vouchers; also my receipt for the property 'remaining on hand to be accounted for.' "—LS, DNA, RG 156, Letters Received.

1846, OCT. 23. To Col. George Bomford enclosing "a Return of Ordnance, and Ordnance Stores, pertaining to the Non Com'd Staff & Band, 4th Infy, for a part of the 3d Quarter, ending Sept. 30th, 1846—Also the necessary vouchers."—LS, DNA, RG 156, Letters Received. On Dec. 1, 1846, Lt. Col. George Talcott acknowledged receipt of this return and the next day forwarded it to the Second Auditor's office—Copies, *ibid.*, Letters Sent (Miscellaneous).

1846, OCT. 28. Bvt. Maj. Charles H. Larnard to USG (then act. adjt.). "In consideration of the subsequent good conduct of private Byerly of "A" Comp 4th Inf., especially on the 21st Septr in action, I have the honor to reccommend the remission of the stoppage awarded him by sentence of Genl Court Martial July 9th 1846, amounting to twenty-five dollars."—ALS, DNA, RG 94, Mexican War, Letters Received.

1846, OCT. 29.   2nd Lt. Henry M. Judah to USG (then act. adjt.). "From the subsequent good conduct of Private C. Shadley of Co "C" 4th Infantry, I have the honor to recommend that his sentence as awarded by the General Court Martial instituted by order dated 'A O Jany 20th 1846' causing him to forfeit Five Dollars pr month for Eight successive months, be remitted, he not having as yet received the successive balances of one Dollar monthly. Private Shadley was for several years an orderly sergeant in the Regiment, and is from my own observation, and from the testimony of others, an attentive and faithful soldier."—ALS, DNA, RG 94, Mexican War, Letters Received.

1846, Nov. 1.   To Bvt. Maj. Gen. Thomas S. Jesup. Identical to letter of Sept. 6, 1846, printed in text with dates changed—Mrs. Walter Love, Flint, Mich.

1846, Nov. 3.   "Return of the Fourth Regiment of Infantry Commanded by Colonel William Whistler for the month of October 1846" Signed by USG as act. adjt.—DS (2 copies), DNA, RG 94.

1846, DEC. 1.   To Bvt. Maj. Gen. Thomas S. Jesup. Similar to letter of Sept. 6, 1846, printed in text—Mrs. Walter Love, Flint, Mich.

1846, DEC. 3.   "Return of the Fourth Regiment of Infantry Commanded by Colonel William Whistler for the Month of November 1846" Signed by USG as act. adjt.—DS (2 copies), DNA, RG 94.

1846, DEC. 31.   To Bvt. Maj. Gen. Thomas S. Jesup. Similar to letter of Sept. 6, 1846, printed in text—LS, DNA, RG 92, Letters Received.

[1846, DEC. 31].   "Return of Clothing, Camp and Garrison Equipage, received and issued at Monterey, Mexico, by Lieut. U. S. Grant, 4th Infantry, a. a. q. m. in the quarter ending on the 31st of December, 1846."—DS, OrHi.

[1846, DEC. 31].   "Abstract of articles issued on Special requisitions at Monterey, Mexico, in the quarter ending the 31st of December 1846, by Lieut U. S. Grant, 4th Infy a. a. q. m."—DS, OrHi.

1847, JAN. 3.   To Col. George Bomford transmitting ordnance return of the noncommissioned staff and band, 4th Inf., for 4th quarter, 1846—DNA, RG 156, Registers of Letters Received. On Feb. 10, 1847, Lt. Col. George Talcott acknowledged receipt of the return. On the preceding day he had forwarded it to the Second Auditor's office— Copies, *ibid.*, Letters Sent (Miscellaneous).

1847, JAN. 4.   "Return of the Fourth Regiment of Infantry Commanded by Colonel William Whistler for the Month of December 1846." USG signed as "Act. Adjutant."—DS, DNA, RG 94.

1847, MARCH 1.   To Bvt. Maj. Gen. Thomas S. Jesup, dated "On board Ship North Carolina Off Island of Lobos, Mexico." Similar to letter of Sept. 6, 1846, printed in text—Mrs. Walter Love, Flint, Mich.

1847, MARCH 3.   To Bvt. Brig. Gen. George Gibson transmitting provision return and vouchers for Feb., 1847—*ABPC* 1946, 623, and 1947, 533; DNA, RG 192, Registers of Letters Received.

1847, APRIL 1.   To Bvt. Maj. Gen. Thomas S. Jesup transmitting reports for March, 1847—DNA, RG 92, Registers of Letters Received.

1847, MAY 1.   To Bvt. Maj. Gen. Thomas S. Jesup transmitting returns and reports for 1st quarter, 1847—DNA, RG 92, Registers of Letters Received.

1847, MAY 1.   To Bvt. Maj. Gen. Thomas S. Jesup transmitting additional reports for April, 1847—DNA, RG 92, Registers of Letters Received.

1847, MAY 10.   To his parents—Major Penniman [Charles Wheeler Denison], *The Tanner-Boy: A Life of General U. S. Grant* (Boston, 1864), pp. 69–72. Probably spurious—See *USGA Newsletter*, II, 4 (July, 1965), 19–24.

1847, JUNE 1.   To Bvt. Maj. Gen. Thomas S. Jesup transmitting "a Muster-roll of a Non commissioned officer employed on extra duty under my direction, also, a Summary Statement for the month of May, 1847."—LS, DNA, RG 92, Consolidated Correspondence 859.

1847, JUNE 11.   Second Auditor's office to USG acknowledging receipt of clothing return "for the latter part of the 3d quarter 1846."—DNA, RG 217, Second Auditor, Letters Sent, Property Division.

1847, JUNE 12.   Second Auditor's office to USG. "Your clothing return for part of third quarter of 1846, has been received and examined is correct as stated by you, excepting that you have entered on your return from extra issues" 4 pr of flannel drawers, should have been from regular issues. It is closed by receipt of Lt. S. Smith dated 15th August at Camargo Mexico."—Copy, DNA, RG 217, Second Auditor, Letters Sent, Property Division.

1847, JUNE 20.   Second Auditor's office to USG acknowledging receipt of clothing return for 4th quarter, 1846—DNA, RG 217, Second Auditor, Letters Sent, Property Division.

1847, JUNE 23.   Second Auditor's office to USG acknowledging receipt of clothing returns for 3rd and 4th quarters, 1846—DNA, RG 217, Second Auditor, Letters Sent, Property Division.

1847, JUNE 23.   Second Auditor's office to USG. "Your return of clothing, camp and garrison equipage for the first part of the third quarter of 1846, made for the late Lt & adgt. C Hoskins, 4th Infy, has been received and is found correct. The receipt of Lt. Leslie Chase, dated 10th Nov. 1846, closes the clothing returns of said Hoskins."—Copy, DNA, RG 217, Second Auditor, Letters Sent, Property Division.

1847, [JUNE 30].   "Abstract of Purchases made on account of Subsistence of the Army in the Quarter ending on the 30th day of June 1847 by Lieut. U. S. Grant 4th Inf. A.A.C.S."—DS, OrHi.

1847, JULY 1.   To Bvt. Maj. Gen. Thomas S. Jesup transmitting reports for 2nd quarter, 1847, and additional documents for 1st quarter, 1847—DNA, RG 92, Registers of Letters Received.

1847, July 1. To Bvt. Maj. Gen. Thomas S. Jesup transmitting "a Muster Roll of Non commissioned officers employed on extra duty, under my direction, also, a Summary Statement, for the month of June, 1847."—LS, DNA, RG 92, Consolidated Correspondence 859.

1847, July 12. Second Auditor's office to USG acknowledging receipt of co. arms return for 4th quarter, 1846—DNA, RG 217, Second Auditor, Letters Sent, Property Division.

1847, July 14. Second Auditor's office to USG acknowledging receipt of co. arms returns for 3rd and 4th quarters, 1846—DNA, RG 217, Second Auditor, Letters Sent, Property Division.

1847, July 17. Peter Hagner, Third Auditor of the Treasury, to USG. "Your a/cs. for Disbursements at Monterey and Vera Cruz in 3d. and 4th qrs. 1846 and 1st qr. 1847 on a/c. Qr. Mrs. Dept. have been audited and reported to the Second Comptroller of the Treasury for his decision thereon, by whom they have been returned to this office, exhibiting a balance due from you to the United States of $156.06. and differing from your a/c current. $44.70 as the enclosed sheet of remarks will show. Vouchers 2 & 3 B. 3 qr. and 2 B. 4 qr. 1846. Suspended and herewith returned for corrections."—DNA, RG 217, Third Auditor, Miscellaneous Letters Sent. USG records as act. asst. q. m. for 3rd and 4th quarters, 1846, and 1st quarter, 1847—*ibid.*, Third Auditor's Account 4006.

1847, Aug. 1. To Col. George Bomford enclosing "the Ordnance Return, of the Non Com'd Staff & Band, 4th Infantry, for the 2nd Quarter of 1847."—L (accidentally unsigned), DNA, RG 156, Letters Received. On Dec. 20, 1847, Capt. William Maynadier wrote, "P.S. No return for the 1st qr. 1847, has yet been received.—neither your return nor letter of advice has your *signature*—As the return exhibits no receipts issues or expenditures of property, your signature may be dispensed with; if your next return properly signed, confirms this one." On Dec. 17, 1847, Lt. Col. George Talcott forwarded the return to the Second Auditor's office—Copies, *ibid.*, Letters Sent (Miscellaneous).

1847, Aug. 1.   To Bvt. Maj. Gen. Thomas S. Jesup transmitting "a Muster roll of Non commissioned officers & Privates employed on Extra Duty, and a Summary Statement for the month of July, 1847."—LS, DNA, RG 92, Consolidated Correspondence 859.

1847, Aug. 3.   To Bvt. Brig. Gen. George Gibson, from Puebla, Mexico, transmitting "Provision Return and Vouchers, and the Summary Statement for the month of July 1847."—LS, Taft School, Watertown, Conn.

1847, Aug. 31.   To Bvt. Maj. Gen. Thomas S. Jesup transmitting "the Summary Statement, and Musterroll pertaing to the 4th Infantry, for the month of August 1847"—LS, DNA, RG 92, Consolidated Correspondence 1102.

1847, Sept. 4.   To Bvt. Brig. Gen. George Gibson transmitting "Provision Returns and Vouchers and a Summary Statement for the Month of August 1847."—LS, DNA, RG 192, Letters Received.

1847, [Sept. 30].   "Abstract of Provisions Sold to Officers in the Month of September 1847 by Lieut U. S. Grant 4th Infantry A.A.C.S." —DS, OrHi.

1847, Oct. 3.   To Bvt. Brig. Gen. George Gibson transmitting "Account Current and Vouchers Provision Return and Summary Statement for the Quarter ending on the 30th day of September 1847."— LS, DNA, RG 192, Letters Received.

1847, Oct. 24.   To Bvt. Brig. Gen. George Gibson transmitting "account Current and vouchers for the 1st Quarter 1847, and Provision Return & vouchers for March 1847."—LS, Mrs. Walter Love, Flint, Mich.

1847, Oct. 24.   To Bvt. Brig. Gen. George Gibson transmitting provision return for April, 1847—DNA, RG 192, Registers of Letters Received.

1847, Oct. 24.   To Bvt. Brig. Gen. George Gibson transmitting "Provision Return & vouchers for May, 1847."—LS, Mrs. Walter Love, Flint, Mich.

1847, Oct. 24.   To Bvt. Brig. Gen. George Gibson transmitting "Account Current and Vouchers for the 2nd Quarter 1847, and also, my Provision Return & Vouchers for June, 1847."—LS, Taft School, Watertown, Conn. On Dec. 13, 1847, Gibson acknowledged receipt of accounts for 1st and 2nd quarters, 1847. "Lt. William Armstrong, in his last accounts forwarded to this office, charges you with 85$, 205$ and 30$ the first you take up on your Acct. Cur : 2d quarter but the two last named sums do not appear."—Copy, DNA, RG 192, Letters Sent. Gibson acknowledged receipt of provision returns, Feb.–June, 1847, on Dec. 21, 1847—*Ibid*.

1847, Oct. 24.   To Bvt. Maj. Gen. Thomas S. Jesup transmitting "Summary Statement and Muster Roll for July 1847."—LS, Mrs. Walter Love, Flint, Mich.

1847, Oct. 24.   To Bvt. Maj. Gen. Thomas S. Jesup transmitting "Summary Statement and Muster Roll for September 1847."—LS, Mrs. Walter Love, Flint, Mich.

1847, Oct. 30.   John M. McCalla, Second Auditor of the Treasury, to USG. "Your recruiting accounts for October, Nov.r & December 1846, and January, Feb.y, March and April 1847, have been examined and a balance of $181.—found due the U. States, agreeing with your Statement.—"—Copy, DNA, RG 217, Second Auditor, Letters Sent. USG took over the recruiting account of $202 of the 4th Inf. after 1st Lt. Charles Hoskins was killed at Monterey. During the seven months in his charge he paid $21 to a soldier who re-enlisted and enlisted two new soldiers—Records *ibid.*, Second Auditor's Account 5649. Recruiting records for May–Aug., 1847, *ibid.*, Account 6573. See letter of Sept. 1, 1848.

1847, Nov. 5.   To Bvt. Brig. Gen. George Gibson transmitting "Provision Return and Vouchers and a Summary Statement for the month of October 1847."—LS, Mrs. Walter Love, Flint, Mich.

1847, Nov. 28. To Col. George Bomford transmitting ordnance return of the 4th Inf. for 2nd and 3rd quarters, 1847—DNA, RG 156, Registers of Letters Received.

1847, Nov. 29. To Col. George Bomford transmitting ordnance return of the noncommissioned staff and band, 4th Inf., for 3rd quarter, 1847—DNA, RG 156, Registers of Letters Received.

1847, Dec. 5. To Bvt. Brig. Gen. George Gibson transmitting "Provision Return and Vouchers and a Summary Statement for the Month of November 1847."—LS, Mrs. Walter Love, Flint, Mich.

1848, Jan. 3. John M. McCalla, Second Auditor of the Treasury, to USG acknowledging receipt of co. arms return for 2nd quarter, 1847—DNA, RG 217, Second Auditor, Letters Sent, Property Division.

1848, Jan. 5. To Bvt. Brig. Gen. George Gibson, from Tacubaya, Mexico, transmitting "Account Current and Vouchers, Provision Return and a Summary Statement for the Quarter ending on the 31st December 1847."—LS, Mrs. Walter Love, Flint, Mich. Gibson acknowledged receipt of accounts for the 3rd and 4th quarter, 1847, in a letter of May 25, 1848—Copy, DNA, RG 192, Letters Sent.

1848, Jan. 7. Peter Hagner, Third Auditor of the Treasury, to USG. "Your letter dated Nov. 26, 1847, enclosing sundry vo.s suspended on a former settlement of your Qr. Mr's. a/cs, has been received & placed on file, to be acted on when your a/cs. are again taken up for adjustment."—Copy, DNA, RG 217, Third Auditor, Miscellaneous Letters Sent. See *Calendar*, July 17, 1847.

1848, Jan. 28. Capt. William Maynadier to USG acknowledging receipt of ordnance return for the non-commissioned staff and band, 4th Inf., for part of 3rd quarter, 1847, and return of stores on hand for 2nd and 3rd quarters, 1847. These returns had been forwarded to the Second Auditor's office by Lt. Col. George Talcott on Jan. 26, 1848—Copies, DNA, RG 156, Letters Sent (Miscellaneous).

1848, Jan. 30. To Bvt. Maj. Gen. Thomas S. Jesup transmitting reports for 3rd quarter, 1847—DNA, RG 92, Registers of Letters Received.

1848, JAN. 30.   To Bvt. Maj. Gen. Thomas S. Jesup transmitting reports for 4th quarter, 1847, "lost during his sickness" and duplicate reports for 3rd quarter, 1847—DNA, RG 92, Registers of Letters Received.

1848, FEB. 4.   To Bvt. Brig. Gen. George Gibson, from Tacubaya, Mexico, transmitting "Provision Return and Vouchers and a Summary Statement for the Month of January 1848."—LS, Mrs. Walter Love, Flint, Mich.

1848, FEB. 10.   Bvt. Brig. Gen. John Garland to Secretary of War William Learned Marcy, recommending USG and other officers for brevets—DNA, RG 107, Register of Letters Received.

1848, FEB. 28.   Jonathan D. Morris, Ohio Congressman, to President James K. Polk. "I take the directing you attention to the accompaying letter from J. R. Grant Esq of Ohio the Father of Lieutenant U Grant of the army   Some few weeks since I asked your attention to the claim of Lieutenant Grant and now repeat them by the above named letter." The letter of Jesse R. Grant was dated Feb. 21, 1848. "Your note of the 12th inst was recd by fridays Mail. Please accept my thanks for the interest you have taken in presenting the request of Lieut. Grant. I did not intend to trouble you any further on this subject, but learning through an Officer of the Army I saw in the city last week that there were several vacancies to fill in the Q. M. Department, & knowing that there were many applicants for promotion, whose claims would be pressed by their friends, and supposing that you would not be likely to have any other to present, I have concluded to trouble you with another letter on the subject. And request you if it would not be asking too much of you, to present the *claim* of Lieut Grant to the President personally, or in such other way as you may think best. I will ennumerate some of his *claims*. He has been in the south nearly four years, during which time he has not asked a leave of absence, or been absent from his post for a day. He has been nearly two years Q. M. of his Regiment, & was not necessarily required to incur the risk & danger of the 'Battle field' and yet you may see from the reports of Maj Lee who commands the 4th Infantry, that Ulysses has not only been in *every* battle fought by Taylor or Scott while he was with them, but he has taken an active, & conspicuous part in all of them. He was one of the Stormers at Chepultepec, & you may see in Gen Worths report of the 16th of Sept. *'especially* distinguish'. In addition to his claim for servises rendered you are probably aware that he possesses a goodeal of financial & business talent. If you cannot procure for him the appointment of Assistant Quarter master with the Brevet rank of Capt. I wish you would ask for him a six months leave, or get him ordered back to the States on the recruiting servis—For he is very anxious to visit home, & we all want to see him. As soon as you can learn the result of either of these applications, have the goodness to drop me a line."—Mrs. Walter Love, Flint, Mich. Morris' letter was referred by President Polk to Secretary of War William Learned Marcy who sent it to Bvt. Maj. Gen. Thomas S. Jesup—DNA, RG 92, Registers of Letters Received. Marcy also sent Jesup a letter from Morris, March 24, 1848, enclosing a letter recommending USG from G. S. Griffith, Bethel, Ohio, Jan. 18, 1848—*Ibid.*

1848, MARCH 2. To Bvt. Brig. Gen. George Gibson, from Tacubaya, Mexico, transmitting "Provision Return and Vouchers and An Summary Statement and Vouchers for the Month of February 1848." —LS, Mrs. Walter Love, Flint, Mich.

1848, MARCH 4. To Bvt. Maj. Gen. Thomas S. Jesup transmitting reports for Jan. and Feb., 1848—DNA, RG 92, Registers of Letters Received.

1848, MARCH 20. John M. McCalla, Second Auditor of the Treasury, to USG acknowledging receipt of ordnance stores returns for 2nd and 3rd quarters, 1847—DNA, RG 217, Second Auditor, Letters Sent, Property Division.

1848, MARCH 20. John M. McCalla, Second Auditor of the Treasury, to USG acknowledging receipt of co. arms return for part of 3rd quarter, 1847—DNA, RG 217, Second Auditor, Letters Sent, Property Division.

1848, APRIL 12. John M. McCalla, Second Auditor of the Treasury, to USG. "Your Clothing C. & G. Equipage Returns, for the 1st 2d & 3d Qr's, of 1847. are correct, with the following exception's on Return of 2d Qr. the Q. M. Gen. remarks, Vouchers. no. 1. Receipt Roll regular Isue, &c. no. 2. 'Extra Issue:, that Paragraph 1065 of Clothing regulations requires that the signatures of the soldiers on the receipt roll's shall be duly witnessed. This roll not *being witnessed*, is therefore not in conformity therewith.' In your Third Quarters returns you give yourself credit for 23 Canteen's & Straps on Lt. H Prince's receipt, dated City of Peubla Mexico July 10th 1847, when there is no such articles upon the face of his receipt. You will please send a Voucher for these articles."—Copy, DNA, RG 217, Second Auditor, Letters Sent, Property Division.

1848, MAY 1. John M. McCalla, Second Auditor of the Treasury, to USG. "Your Clo C. & G. Equipage return for 1st Qr. 1847. is correct. Except. 'Q. M. G. remarks' that Depositions setting forth circumstances of loss must be furnished"—Copy, DNA, RG 217, Letters Sent, Property Division.

1848, MAY 31. John M. McCalla, Second Auditor of the Treasury, to USG. "Your recruiting accounts for May & July 1847 have been adjusted and a balance found due the U. States of $173.—, differing from your Statement $10.—as will appear from the Statement of differences herewith enclosed."—Copy, DNA, RG 217, Second Auditor, Letters Sent.

1848, JUNE 2. To Bvt. Maj. Gen. George Gibson transmitting "Duplicates of my Provision Return and Vouchers for August 1847. My Account Current and Vouchers for the 3rd Quarter 1847. and Provision Return and Vouchers for September 1847."—LS, DNA, RG 192, Letters Received. On March 31, 1848, Gibson had written USG that provision returns for Aug. and Sept., 1847, were missing—Copy, *ibid.*, Letters Sent. On May 23, 1848, he stated that returns for July–Dec., 1847, were complete. This letter, however, addressed to USG, 4th Art., City of Mexico, was returned as a "Dead Letter."—*Ibid.*

1848, JUNE 3. John M. McCalla, Second Auditor of the Treasury, to USG, acknowledging receipt of equipage returns for clothing, C and

G for 2nd and 3rd quarters, 1847—DNA, RG 217, Second Auditor, Letters Sent, Property Division.

1848, [JUNE?]. To Bvt. Maj. Gen. George Gibson transmitting "Account Current and vouchers, for the 1st Quarter 1848 & my Provision Return and vouchers for March 1848." This undated letter was received in Washington, D.C., on Oct. 20, 1848—LS, DNA, RG 192, Letters Received.

1848, [JUNE?]. To Bvt. Maj. Gen. George Gibson transmitting "Summary Statement & Provision Return and vouchers for April 1848." This undated letter was received in Washington, D.C., on Oct. 20, 1848—LS, DNA, RG 192, Letters Received.

1848, [JUNE?]. To Bvt. Maj. Gen. George Gibson transmitting "Summary Statement, & Provision Return and vouchers, for May 1848." This undated letter was received in Washington, D.C., on Oct. 20, 1848—LS, DNA, RG 192, Letters Received. On Oct. 30, 1848, Gibson acknowledged receipt of provision returns, Jan.–July, 1848—*Ibid.*, Letters Sent.

1848, AUG. 1. John M. McCalla, Second Auditor of the Treasury, to USG. "Your Return of Clo. C. & G. Equipage for the 4th Qr. 1847. Except. Q. M. G. remarks you fail to furnish Vouchers No. 1. 2. 3 & 4."—Copy, DNA, RG 217, Second Auditor, Letters Sent, Property Division.

1848, AUG. 24. Bvt. Maj. Lorenzo Thomas to Secretary of War William L. Marcy. "In the list of brevets for Chapultepec, confirmed the 13th ultimo, is the following: 'First Lieutenant U. S. Grant, to be Captain by Brevet—' (to date from September 13, 1847.) At the battle of Chapultepec (Sept. 13, 1847,) Lieut. Grant was only a *2d Lieutenant*, his promotion to a 1st Lieutenantcy not having taken place till Sept. *16*, 1847. It is respectfully submitted whether the nomination to the grade of Captain was not the result of a misapprehension, and if so, that the commission be not issued. The necessary correction of grade can be made at the next session of the Senate." The letter was endorsed by A. Campbell, chief clerk of the War Department. "The nomination of Lt. Grant to a *Captaincy* being an error, the Adjutant General will not issue the commission to him until the mistake is corrected."—ALS, DNA, RG 107, Letters Received, Registered Series; copy, *ibid.*, RG 94, ACP Branch, Letters Sent, Nominations. See letter of March 30, 1849.

1848, Oct. 12.   To Bvt. Maj. Gen. George Gibson, from St. Louis, transmitting accounts and reporting loss of $1500 by robbery—DNA, RG 192, Registers of Letters Received.

1848, Nov. 20.   Bvt. Maj. Gen. William Jenkins Worth to Secretary of War William L. Marcy. "Notwithstanding the great pains taken to include in the list of brevet promotions all having claims to that high distinction several officers of my late Division who had been especially noticed on several occasions were, it is believed, accidentally omitted. Under these circumstances I beg permission to present the following list of officers, who in my judgement, have signally distinguished themselves . . . . 1st Lieut *Ulysses Grant* although on a staff which might excuse his absence was always present with regt. in battle evincing high courage and conduct."—ALS, DNA, RG 107, Letters Received, Registered Series.

1848, Dec. 11.   Secretary of War William L. Marcy to President James K. Polk. "The Brevet of *Captain*, conferred on Second Lieutenant Ulysses S. Grant, since promoted First Lieutenant of the Fourth Regiment of Infantry, and confirmed by the Senate on the 13th of July, 1848, 'for gallant and meritorious conduct in the battle of Chapultepec, September 13, 1847,' being the result of a misapprehension as to the grade held by that officer on the 13th of September, 1847, (he being then a Second Lieutenant,). I have to propose that the Brevet of Captain be cancelled and the Brevet, of First Lieutenant 'for gallant and meritorious services in the battle of Chapultepec September 13, 1847' —be conferred in lieu thereof.—" On the same day Polk wrote to the Senate of the United States. "I nominate Second Lieutenant *Ulysses S. Grant* (since promoted First Lieutenant.) of the Fourth Regiment of Infantry, to be First Lieutenant by brevet for gallant and meritorious services in the battle of Chapultepec, September 13, 1847—as proposed in the accompanying communication from the Secretary of War."— Copies, DNA, RG 94, ACP Branch, Letters Sent, Nominations. See letter of March 30, 1849.

1848, Dec. 15.   Report of a board of inspection, which included USG, on four soldiers recommended for discharge because of their health. Enclosed in a letter from Bvt. Col. Francis Lee to Bvt. Maj. Gen. Roger Jones, Dec. 21, 1848—DNA, RG 94, Letters Received.

1849, [Jan. 2?].   To Bvt. Maj. Gen. Thomas S. Jesup transmitting estimates of funds. Received by q. m. office on Jan. 8, 1849—DNA, RG 92, Registers of Letters Received.

1849, Jan. 5.   To Bvt. Maj. Gen. Thomas S. Jesup transmitting clothing accounts—DNA, RG 92, Registers of Letters Received.

1849, Jan. 10.   Bvt. Maj. Gen. Thomas S. Jesup to USG. "Your estimate of funds for the present month was received at this office under a blank envelope—a remittance has been required on it, in your favor, of $1.066, for the service of the Quarter Master's Department. It is proper to inform you that all papers transmitted to this office should be accompanied by a letter."—Copy, DNA, RG 92, Q. M. Letter Books. A copy of the requisition for $1,066 is dated Jan. 10, 1849—*Ibid.*, Requisitions for Remittances.

1849, Jan. 12.   To Bvt. Maj. Gen. Thomas S. Jesup transmitting abstracts for parts of 2nd and 3rd quarters, 1848. Referred to Auditor's Office on Jan. 19, 1849—DNA, RG 92, Registers of Letters Received.

1849, Jan. 13.   To Bvt. Maj. Gen. Thomas S. Jesup. "Herewith I have the honor of forwarding you Receipt for clothing recieved from Cap.t E. S. Faysoux Mil. Store keeper U. S. A." The officer was Edward Stevens Fayssoux—ALS and DS (receipt), DNA, RG 92, Letters Received, Clothing.

1849, Jan. 15.   To Bvt. Maj. Gen. Thomas S. Jesup. "Having to pay mileage to several officers traveling under orders I would respectfully request a printed copy of the distances between the various posts."— ALS, DNA, RG 92, Letters Received. Jesup replied on Jan. 24, 1849, "I have received your letter of the 15th instant and now send you a copy of 'Smith's New Travellers' Guide,' the distances laid down in which will govern, when they apply, in paying mileage to officers of the Army."—Copy, *ibid.*, Q. M. Letter Books.

1849, JAN. 16. To Bvt. Maj. Gen. George Gibson acknowledging receipt of funds—DNA, RG 192, Registers of Letters Received. On Jan. 8, Gibson had written, "The Treasurer of the United States has been this day requested to remit you Twelve Hundred dollars on account of Army Subsistence."—Copy, *ibid.*, Letters Sent.

1849, JAN. 16. Bvt. Maj. Gen. Thomas S. Jesup to USG. "I have required a remittance in your favor, of $1.235, on account of the appropriations for Barracks Quarters &c., that being the amount of Major D. H. Vinton's estimate for repairs at Sacketts Harbor."—Copy, DNA, RG 92, Q. M. Letter Books. A copy of the requisition for $1,235 is dated Jan. 16, 1849—*Ibid.*, Requisitions for Remittances.

1849, JAN. 16. Bvt. Col. Francis Lee to Bvt. Maj. Gen. Roger Jones. "I conceive it my duty to respectfully represent to the Adjt. Genl. to be refered to the Hon: Sect: of War—one or two incidents in the fight of our army on the 13th Sepr. 1847, at the taking of the City of Mexico, that seems to have been lost sight of which I consider as having eminently contributed to our success on that memorable day. On the retreat of the enemy from Chepultepec towards San. Cosme and Belien Garetas, he was closely & hotly pursued by our troops—that portion of the Mexican force that retreated by Gareta San. Cosme was pursued by Worth's Division, Garlands Brigade leading—. When the enemy got to their first battery, at the English Cemetery just where the Street turns leading up to Gareta San. Cosme,—they made a bold stand, and being reinforced by a large body of both Infantry and Cavalry, they deployed in most formidable array—they for a short time held our advance.—Annoying us very greatly, until by a most gallant manouver they were turned and driven. This gallant act, without any immediate orders, was performed by Capt. Horace Brook 2.d Artillery, now Bt Mjr Brook, and Lieut U. S. Grant 4.th Infantry. With a few men of their respective regiments, under the most galling fire, they by the front, turned the enemies right—and by a rush, and well directed fire, forced him to retreat in confusion: They were then joined by Lieut Gore (now Capt. Gore 4.th Infy.) and Lieut. Judah 4.th Infantry with a few more men, when they continued the pursuit, up the street—

driving the enemy before them, up to the very gate of the City, dislodging him from a second formidable battery, the first immediately in front of San Cosme, and opposite San. Cosme Church—. They nobly held their position here until they were recalled by order of Genl. Worth—by his A. D. Camp Lieut Pemberton. When it is recollected that all this occurred in the early part of the day, that these were the *first* and by far the most advanced successful demonstrations, then, on the city, they are certainly entitled to consideration, and reflect high credit on the conduct and gallantry of all the Officers and men concerned —they were not accomplished without much loss in killed & wounded, and I look on them as the most gallant acts of the day."—Copy, DNA RG 98, Letters Sent, Col. Lee.

1849, FEB. 2. John M. McCalla, Second Auditor of the Treasury, to USG. "Your Cash accounts of the 1st & 2d quarters 1848 for the apprehending of 4 deserters at Tucubayo, Mexico, amounting to $120.— are examined & adjusted—the amount is transfered to your Credit on the Books of the 3d Auditor's Office."—Copy, DNA, RG 217, Second Auditor, Letters Sent. The amount represented the $30 reward paid for the apprehension of each deserter. Records *ibid.*, Second Auditor's Account 7849.

1849, FEB. 2. To Bvt. Maj. Gen. Thomas S. Jesup transmitting reports for 4th quarter, 1848, and Dec., 1848—DNA, RG 92, Registers of Letters Received.

1849, FEB. 9. To Bvt. Maj. Gen. Thomas S. Jesup transmitting "Summary Statement for the month of January, 1849."—ALS, DNA, RG 92, Consolidated Correspondence 598. The statement is *ibid.*, 350.

1849, FEB. 14. To Bvt. Maj. Gen. George Gibson transmitting abstracts of provisions issued—DNA, RG 192, Registers of Letters Received. On Feb. 20, Gibson replied. "The Abstracts of provisions received with your letter of the 14 inst. are herewith returned. You will please cause to be made out a bill for the total number of complete rations receipted by the Contractor and transmit it to this Office accompanied by the enclosed Abstracts as vouchers."—Copy, *ibid.*, Letters Sent.

1849, FEB. 20. Bvt. Maj. Gen. George Gibson to USG. "As soon as navigation opens you will make requisitions on the Coms. of Subs. at New York for subs. Stores and make a contract for the supply of fresh Beef for your Post. Due notice will be given to the present Contractor that on receipt of these Stores from New York his contract will cease."—Copy, DNA, RG 192, Letters Sent.

1849, FEB. 22. To Bvt. Maj. Gen. Thomas S. Jesup transmitting "Muster Roll of men employed on Extra duty in the Quarter Master Department for the Month ending 31st of January, 1849." ALS, DNA, RG 92, Consolidated Correspondence 598.

1849, FEB. 23. To Bvt. Maj. Gen. Thomas S. Jesup requesting permission to extend the contract for wood from 300 to 500 cords since the contract was made before the arrival of the greater part of the command—DNA, RG 92, Registers of Letters Received. On March 6, 1849, Jesup replied to USG. "I have received your letter of the 23rd ultimo. You are authorized to extend the wood contract at your post, as proposed."—Copy, *ibid.*, Q. M. Letter Books.

1849, FEB. 25. Bvt. Maj. Gen. George Gibson to USG acknowledging receipt of accounts—Copy, DNA, RG 192, Letters Sent.

1849, FEB. 26. To Bvt. Maj. Gen. George Gibson transmitting accounts and discussing special contractor E. E. Camp—DNA, RG 192, Registers of Letters Received.

1849, MARCH 9. To Bvt. Maj. Gen. George Gibson transmitting abstract of issues of special contractor E. E. Camp—DNA, RG 192, Registers of Letters Received.

1849, MARCH 9. To Bvt. Maj. Gen. Thomas S. Jesup transmitting "Summary Statement for the month of February 1849, also Muster Rolls of men employed, at this Post, for the same month."—ALS, DNA, RG 92, Letters Received. The summary statement is *ibid.*, Consolidated Correspondence 350.

1849, MARCH 20. To Bvt. Maj. Gen. George Gibson discussing a draft in favor of special contractor E. E. Camp—DNA, RG 192, Registers of Letters Received.

1849, MARCH 31.   To Bvt. Maj. Gen. George Gibson transmitting abstract and bill of issues—DNA, RG 192, Registers of Letters Received.

1849, APRIL 2.   To Bvt. Brig. Gen. George Talcott, chief of ordnance, transmitting ordnance return of Co. I, 4th Inf., for 1st quarter, 1849—DNA, RG 156, Registers of Letters Received. On April 20, 1849, Capt. William Maynadier acknowledged receipt of the return and forwarded it to the Second Auditor's office—Copies, *ibid.*, Letters Sent (Miscellaneous). On April 28, 1849, Philip Clayton, Second Auditor of the Treasury, acknowledged receipt of this return—Copy, *ibid.*, RG 217, Second Auditor, Letters Sent, Property Division.

1849, APRIL 3.   To Bvt. Maj. Gen. George Gibson transmitting account current—DNA, RG 192, Registers of Letters Received. On April 11, 1849, Gibson replied, "Your account current 1st quarter 49. has been examined and transferred to the 3d Auditor for final settlement. The 84 cents communication of Whiskey paid to private Daly will not be admitted to your credit at the Treasury as the Man's Signature should have been obtained at the time he received the amount."—Copy, *ibid.*, Letters Sent.

1849, APRIL 3.   To Bvt. Maj. Gen. Thomas S. Jesup transmitting reports for 1st quarter, 1849, and March, 1849—DNA, RG 92, Registers of Letters Received.

1849, APRIL 4.   J. F. Polk, act. Second Auditor of the Treasury, to USG acknowledging receipt of return of camp equipage for the latter part of 4th quarter, 1848—DNA, RG 217, Second Auditor, Letters Sent, Property Division.

1849, APRIL 24.   Philip Clayton, Second Auditor of the Treasury, to USG. "Your Returns of Clothing Camp and Garrison Equipage for the 1st 2nd prt of 3d & prt of 4th Qrs. 1848, and with the exception of a few articles closed by receipts. Except, Q. M. G. remarks' upon vou. no. 15, 2nd Qr. & vou. no. 9, 3d Qrs Depositions must be furnished

setting forth the circumstances of the case as to the Damaged clothing
also—receipts must be furnished for vou. 10 & 11. 2nd Qr and vouchers
1. 2, 3, 4, & 5. 3d Qr. also. Certificate required for expended articles.
You also fail to furnish an Invoice in 4th Qrs. return for 52. Bed sacks"
—Copy, DNA, RG 217, Second Auditor, Letters Sent, Property Division.

1849, MAY 11.   To Bvt. Maj. Gen. George Gibson transmitting
summary statement for April, 1849—DNA, RG 192, Registers of
Letters Received.

1849, MAY 11.   To Bvt. Maj. Gen. Thomas S. Jesup transmitting
"Summary Statement for the Month of April 1849."—LS, DNA, RG
92, Q. M. Letters Received. The statement is *ibid.*, Consolidated Correspondence 350.

1849, MAY.   Report of a board of survey which condemned army
equipment, signed by USG as "President." *Richardson*, p. 130.

1849, JUNE 3.   To Bvt. Maj. Gen. George Gibson transmitting subsistence papers for May, 1849—DNA, RG 192, Registers of Letters
Received.

1849, JUNE 3.   To Bvt. Maj. Gen. Thomas S. Jesup transmitting
"Summary Statement for the Month of May 1849."—Detroit His-
torical Museum, Detroit, Mich. The statement is in DNA, RG 92,
Consolidated Correspondence 350.

1849, JUNE 11.   Philip Clayton, Second Auditor of the Treasury, to
USG acknowledging receipt of clothing, camp, and garrison equipage
returns for 1st quarter, 1849—DNA, RG 217, Second Auditor, Letters Sent, Property Division.

1849, JUNE 30.   To Bvt. Lt. Col. John Breckinridge Grayson, receipt
for subsistence stores—DS, Burton Historical Collection, MiD.

1849, [JUNE 30].   "Monthly Summary Statement of Funds Received and Disbursed . . ."—DS, DNA, RG 92, Consolidated Correspondence 350.

1849, JULY 6. To Bvt. Maj. Gen. George Gibson transmitting account current for 2nd quarter, 1849, and provision return for June, 1849—DNA, RG 192, Registers of Letters Received. On July 11, 1849, Gibson acknowledged receipt of accounts for 2nd quarter, 1849, and on July 21 acknowledged receipt of provision returns, April–June, 1849—Copies, *ibid.*, Letters Sent.

1849, JULY 7. To Bvt. Maj. Gen. Thomas S. Jesup transmitting reports for 2nd quarter, 1849; statement of allowances for 4th quarter, 1848; and summary statement for June, 1849—DNA, RG 92, Registers of Letters Received.

1849, JULY 27. To Bvt. Maj. Gen. Thomas S. Jesup explaining remarks made on his accounts for 2nd quarter, 1849, relating to the purchase of a filter—DNA, RG 92, Registers of Letters Received. On Aug. 7, 1849, Jesup replied to USG. "I have received your letter of the 27th ultimo in the relation to the purchase of 'water filters,' and have referred the same to the Third Auditor with the following endorsement, viz: The regulations secure the disbursing officers who obey the orders of their commanding officers and make the commanders accountable. The article is not one of military supply and the expenditure is inadmissible."—Copy, *ibid.*, Q. M. Letter Books. See *Calendar*, June 11, 1852.

1849, JULY 28. To Bvt. Col. Carlos A. Waite, superintendent of recruiting services for the western division, transmitting "the Descriptive Roll & other information as far as is known at this Post, of Pvt. Samuel Irish Company .C. 4th Infantry." Written by USG as act. adjt.—Copy, DNA, RG 98, 4th Inf., Letters Sent.

1849, JULY 31. Return of 4th Inf. for July, 1849, signed by USG as act. adjt. 1st Lt. Henry D. Wallen, regular adjt., had begun a seven days' leave on July 27, 1849—DS, DNA, RG 94.

1849, AUG. 1. To Bvt. Maj. Gen. Thomas S. Jesup transmitting "Summary Statement and Muster rolls for the Month of July 1849."— ALS, DNA, RG 92, Consolidated Correspondence 254. The statement is *ibid.* 350.

1849, Aug. 2. To Bvt. Maj. Gen. George Gibson transmitting provision return and summary statement for July, 1849—DNA, RG 192, Registers of Letters Received.

1849, Aug. 7. To Bvt. Capt. Henry M. Judah. "I am instructed to say that the Monthly & Casualty Return of Your Company have not yet been received. Having come in from all the Posts of the Regiment except Oswego, it is possible that Yours has been miscarried—" Written as act. adjt.—Copy, DNA, RG 98, 4th Inf., Letters Sent.

1849, Aug. 7. To Bvt. Capt. Ralph W. Kirkham, adjt. of the 6th Inf. "A deserter from the 6th Infantry by the Name of Reed, of Captain Lovel's Company "B" Your Regiment has been delivered up at this post—The Colonel Commanding directs me to request that his Descriptive Roll be sent to this post, with any information, concerning the prisoner, that You can give—" Written as act. adjt.—Copy, DNA, RG 98, 4th Inf., Letters Sent.

1849, Aug. 10. To Bvt. Capt. Henry M. Judah. "No descriptive Roll having been furnished to this office of Pvt. Patrick Parsons of F. Company 4th Infantry lately discharged by Order, I am directed by the Colonel Commanding to request that One be sent—" Written as act. adjt.—Copy, DNA, RG 98, 4th Inf., Letters Sent.

1849, Aug. 13. To 2nd Lt. John C. Bonnycastle. "Your application for leave of absence has been received and approved by the Colonel Commanding the Regiment & forwarded to Head Quarters of the Army—" Written as act. adjt.—Copy, DNA, RG 98, 4th Inf., Letters Sent.

1849, Aug. 18. Philip Clayton, Second Auditor of the Treasury, to USG. "Your 4th qtr, 1848, & the 1st qtr, 1849,—disbursements—, are examined & adjusted.—The amt $164.02, is transferred to your credit, on the Books of the 3d Auditor's Office.—For this Settlement, please see the third page of this letter."—Copy, DNA, RG 217, Second Auditor, Letters Sent. The $164.02 represented expenditures at Madison Barracks in the winter of 1848–49 for extra medicine and clothing, and for the apprehension of deserters—Records *ibid.*, Second Auditor's Account 8892.

1849, AUG. 20. To Bvt. Maj. Charles H. Larnard. "I am directed
by the Colonel commanding to say that You will have the Band of the
4th Infantry forwarded to this post by first opportunity—The Colonel
expresses his surprise that the Band should have been kept at Fort
Mackinac until this late date against his express and known will. After
giving Lt. Henry a leave of absence for the express purpose of accompanying the Band to Fort Mackinac (and to return with it as a
matter of course) the colonel commanding did not think it necessary
to give Major Larnard a positive order to have it returned by a certain
time, supposing that Major Larnard, in a case of this kind, would
consult the known wish of his commander without a positive order."
Written as act. adjt.—Copy, DNA, RG 98, 4th Inf., Letters Sent.

1849, SEPT. 3. To Bvt. Maj. Gen. Thomas S. Jesup transmitting
"Muster Rolls of extra duty men and Summary Statement for the
Month of August 1849."—ALS, Mrs. Walter Love, Flint, Mich. The
statement is in DNA, RG 92, Consolidated Correspondence 350.

1849, SEPT. 7. To Bvt. Maj. Gen. George Gibson transmitting subsistence papers for Aug., 1849—DNA, RG 192, Registers of Letters
Received. On Nov. 6, 1849, Gibson acknowledged receipt of provision
returns for July–Sept., 1849. Copy *ibid.*, Letters Sent.

1849, SEPT. 21. Receipt to Bvt. Lt. Col. J. B. Grayson for $275 of
government funds—ADS facsimile in *The U. S. Grant House in Detroit*,
Michigan Mutual Liability Company, n.d. A copy of this brochure is in
OHi.

1849, [SEPT. 30]. "Monthly Summary Statement."—DS (duplicate), DNA, RG 92, Consolidated Correspondence 350.

1849, OCT. 8. To Bvt. Maj. Gen. Thomas S. Jesup transmitting
reports for 3rd quarter, 1849, and Sept., 1849—DNA, RG 92, Registers of Letters Received.

1849, OCT. 13. "We the Constitutional Officers of the Aztec Club
Hereby make known that Lieut. U. S. Grant, 4th Infty was duly elected
Member of said Club in the City of Mexico, in accordance with the
provisions of the Constitution and is entitled to all the privileges of

such Membership." Certificate signed by Bvt. Lt. Col. John B. Grayson, President; Bvt. Col. Charles F. Smith, 1st Vice President; Bvt. Lt. Col. Robert C. Buchanan, 2nd Vice President; and Lt. M. L. Smith, Secretary. The Aztec Club was a social organization established by U.S. army officers in Mexico City on Oct. 13, 1847—William H. Allen, *The American Civil War Book and Grant Album* (Boston and New York, 1894).

1849, OCT. 22. To Bvt. Maj. Gen. George Gibson transmitting accounts for 3rd quarter, 1849—DNA, RG 192, Registers of Letters Received. Gibson acknowledged receipt of these accounts on Dec. 1, 1849—Copy, *ibid.*, Letters Sent.

1849, OCT. 31. Receipt to Bvt. Lt. Col. J. B. Grayson for subsistence stores—DS, Burton Historical Collection, MiD.

1849, Nov. 3. To Bvt. Maj. Gen. George Gibson transmitting abstracts and vouchers for Oct., 1849—DNA, RG 192, Registers of Letters Received.

1849, Nov. 3. To Bvt. Maj. Gen. Thomas S. Jesup transmitting "Summary Statement for the Month of October 1849."—LS, Mrs. Walter Love, Flint, Mich. The statement is in DNA, RG 92, Consolidated Correspondence 350.

1849, [Nov. 30]. "Monthly Summary Statement."—DS (duplicate), DNA, RG 92, Consolidated Correspondence 350.

1849, DEC. 3. To Bvt. Maj. Gen. Thomas S. Jesup transmitting reports for Nov., 1849—DNA, RG 92, Registers of Letters Received.

1849, DEC. 6. To Bvt. Maj. Gen. George Gibson transmitting provision return for Nov., 1849—DNA, RG 192, Registers of Letters Received.

1849, DEC. 13. To Bvt. Maj. Gen. Nathan Towson discussing the pay of a deceased soldier—DNA, RG 99, Registers of Letters Received. On Dec. 21, 1849, Towson replied. "Your letter in relation to amounts due Sergt Low, has this day been received and referred to the

Second Auditor in whose office the rolls of the 4th Infy. for July and August 1848 are filed."—Copy, *ibid.*, Letters Sent.

1849, Dec. 22. Philip Clayton, Second Auditor of the Treasury, to USG. "In answer to your letter of the 13″ Inst. addressed to the Paymaster General and by that office referred to this office, I have to state that the claim of *Sutler Perkins,* for Supplies of Tobacco in July and August 1848. amounting to $94.25 to Soldiers of the 4″ Inf.y cannot be allowed as the 11″ Section of the act making provision for an additional number of General officers, and for other purposes approved 3d March 1847. being all claims of this character arrising after that time."—Copy, DNA, RG 217, Second Auditor, Letters Sent, Claims.

1850, Jan. 26. To Bvt. Maj. Gen. George Gibson transmitting commissary papers for Dec., 1849, and accounts for 4th quarter, 1849—DNA, RG 192, Registers of Letters Received. On Feb. 2, 1850, Gibson acknowledged receipt of accounts for 4th quarter, 1849, and on Feb. 19, 1850, acknowledged receipt of provision returns for Oct.–Dec., 1849 —Copy, *ibid.*, Letters Sent.

1850, Feb. 1. To Bvt. Maj. Gen. Thomas S. Jesup transmitting reports for 4th quarter, 1849, and statements of allowances for 1st, 3rd, and 4th quarters, 1849—DNA, RG 92, Registers of Letters Received.

1850, Feb. 11. To Bvt. Maj. Gen. George Gibson transmitting subsistence papers for Jan., 1850—DNA, RG 192, Registers of Letters Received.

1850, Feb. 11. To Bvt. Maj. Gen. Thomas S. Jesup transmitting "Summary Statement for January 1850."—LS, Mrs. Walter Love, Flint, Mich.

1850, March 7. To Bvt. Maj. Gen. George Gibson transmitting subsistence papers for Feb., 1850—DNA, RG 192, Registers of Letters Received.

1850, March 7. To Bvt. Maj. Gen. Thomas S. Jesup transmitting

"Summary Statement for February 1850."—LS, Mrs. Walter Love, Flint, Mich.

1850, MARCH 16.   John S. Gallaher, Third Auditor of the Treasury, to USG. "Your a/c as actg asst. Comy. of Subs, during the years of 1847, 1848 & 1849, transmitted by the Comy Genl of Subsistence for adjustment has been examined and reported to the 2d. Compt. for his decision thereon, and returned to this office exhibiting a Balance due from you to the U. S. of Eleven hundred and thirty two dollars and seventy one cents, differing from your a/c in the sum of one hundred and eighteen dollars and eighty three cents arising from suspendid vouchers amounting to $73.48, items rejected as appertaining to the medical department $43.25. This sum disallowed 84 cents and over payments $1.26, an explanatory statement of which and eleven suspendid vouchers are enclosed—"—Copy, DNA, RG 217, Third Auditor, Miscellaneous Letters Sent. USG subsistence records for 1847–49 *ibid.*, Third Auditor's Account 8905. See letter of March 25, 1850.

1850, APRIL 8.   To Bvt. Maj. Gen. George Gibson transmitting subsistence papers for March, 1850, and accounts for 1st quarter, 1850—DNA, RG 192, Registers of Letters Received. Gibson replied on April 15, 1850. "You will please have the enclosed voucher completed by the signature of T. Fox to the receipt and return it to this Office as early as practicable."—Copy, *ibid.*, Letters Sent. On April 19, 1850, USG returned voucher No. 2, abstracts of purchases, 1st quarter, 1850—*Ibid.*, Registers of Letters Received. On April 24, Gibson acknowledged the accounts were in order, and on April 25 acknowledged receipt of provision returns for Jan.–March, 1850—Copy, *ibid.*, Letters Sent.

1850, APRIL 8.   Maj. Henry Lee Heiskell, surgeon, to USG. "Your communication of the 25th ultimo encloseing a statement of purchases made by you for the Hospital Department while Acting Assistant Commissary of Subsistence of the 4th Infantry has been received. In reply I have to inform you that the statement has been referred to the Second Auditor, and you will be credited with the amount of the purchases."—Copy, DNA, RG 112, Letters Sent.

1850, APRIL 15.   To Bvt. Maj. Gen. Thomas S. Jesup transmitting reports for 1st quarter, 1850—DNA, RG 92, Registers of Letters Received.

1850, APRIL 15.   W. Mechlin, act. Second Auditor of the Treasury, to USG. "Medical disbursements made by you in 1. 2. 3 & 4th quarters 1847, as per an extract from your vouchers, received 1st April 1850, from 3d Auditor's Office, amounting to $43.25, are adjusted, and the amount transferred to your credit on the Books of that office."—Copy, DNA, RG 217, Second Auditor, Letters Sent.

1850, MAY 6.   To Bvt. Maj. Gen. George Gibson transmitting subsistence papers for April, 1850—DNA, RG 192, Registers of Letters Received.

1850, MAY 7.   Frederick Dent to Bvt. Maj. Gen. Thomas S. Jesup. "My Son in Law, Lieut U. S. Grant of 4th Infy at Detroit Mich. enclosed to me a blank bond as regimental quarter master, with the request that I would execute the same, as surity for him—I regret to say that while on my way to the proper officer before whom it was to be executed I lost the blank & have now to request that you will cause another to be forwarded to me at St Louis, which I will execute & forward to Lieut Grant—I endeavored to obtain another from the Qr Mr at this place but was disappointed—I trust, therefore that the delay in returning to your office will be attributed to myself"—ALS, DNA, RG 92, Consolidated Correspondence 350.

1850, MAY 8.   To Bvt. Maj. Gen. George Gibson transmitting invoice for April return—DNA, RG 192, Registers of Letters Received.

1850, MAY 13.   To 2nd Lt. Benjamin D. Forsythe acknowledging "receipt of Twenty two Dollars for the Regimental fund for the Months of March & April 1850." USG was then act. regt. treasurer—Copy, DNA, RG 98, 4th Inf., Letters Sent.

1850, JUNE 5.   To Bvt. Maj. Gen. George Gibson transmitting subsistence papers for May, 1850—DNA, RG 192, Registers of Letters Received. On July 16, 1850, Gibson acknowledged receipt of provision returns for April–June, 1850—Copy, *ibid.*, Letters Sent.

1850, June 20. To Bvt. Maj. Gen. George Gibson discussing supplies for Detroit Barracks—DNA, RG 192, Registers of Letters Received. On June 25, 1850, Gibson replied. "Your letter of the 20 inst is received. Whatever provisions you may require over and above those to be delivered by Mr Newberry in October next, you will obtain from Lt Col Grayson C. S. at Detroit by making a requisition on him for them."—Copy, *ibid.*, Letters Sent.

1850, June 30. To Bvt. Maj. Gen. George Gibson transmitting accounts for 2nd quarter, 1850—DNA, RG 192, Registers of Letters Received. Gibson acknowledged receipt of these accounts on July 9, 1850. Copy, *ibid.*, Letters Sent.

1850, June 30. To Bvt. Maj. Gen. Thomas S. Jesup transmitting reports for 2nd quarter, 1850—DNA, RG 92, Registers of Letters Received.

1850, [June]. To Bvt. Maj. Gen. Thomas S. Jesup transmitting summary statement for May, 1850—DNA, RG 92, Registers of Letters Received.

1850, Nov. 6. To James L. Edwards, Commissioner of Pensions, requesting a land warrant on the basis of a sworn statement of service in the Mexican War which entitled him to bounty land under act of Congress of Sept. 28, 1850. The statement, sworn before George Clancy, Justice of the Peace in Wayne County, Mich., together with a certification by Silas A. Begg, Clerk of Wayne County, both dated Nov. 6, 1850, are in DNA, RG 15, Bounty Land Warrant Application File. Warrant 3514 for 160 acres was issued and sent on April 21, 1851—DNA, RG 49. On Oct. 21, 1852, the warrant was used at the land office at Sault Ste Marie to acquire the northeast quarter of section 20 in township 58 north of range 29 west—*Ibid.*

1850, Nov. 11. To Bvt. Maj. Gen. Thomas S. Jesup transmitting his oath of office—DNA, RG 92, Registers of Letters Received.

1850, Nov. 21–23. During the three day absence of Bvt. Capt. Thomas Rush McConnell of Ga., USMA 1846, adjt. of the 4th Inf., USG signed the daily report—DS, Burton Historical Collection, MiD.

1850, Nov. 23.   To Bvt. Maj. Granville O. Haller. "I am directed
by Colonel Whistler to return to you the inclosed proceedings of a
Regimental Court Martial convened at your post, they being informal,
not having the signature of the recorder."—Copy, DNA, RG 98, 4th
Inf., Letters Sent.

1850, Dec. 2.   To Bvt. Maj. Gen. George Gibson transmitting subsistence papers for Nov., 1850—DNA, RG 192, Registers of Letters
Received. On Feb. 18, 1851, Gibson acknowledged receipt of provision
returns for Oct. and Nov., 1850—Copy, *ibid.*, Letters Sent.

1850, Dec. 13.   To Bvt. Maj. Gen. Thomas S. Jesup transmitting
report for Nov., 1850—DNA, RG 92, Registers of Letters Received.

1851, Jan. 4.   To Bvt. Maj. Gen. George Gibson transmitting certificate of inspection—DNA, RG 192, Registers of Letters Received.

1851, Jan. 10.   To Bvt. Maj. Gen. George Gibson transmitting accounts for 3rd quarter, 1850—DNA, RG 192, Registers of Letters
Received.

1851, Jan. 11.   To Bvt. Maj. Gen. George Gibson transmitting accounts for 4th quarter, 1850—DNA, RG 192, Registers of Letters
Received. On Jan. 20, 1851, Gibson acknowledged receipt of accounts
for 3rd and 4th quarters, 1850—Copy, *ibid.*, Letters Sent.

1851, Jan. 11.   To Bvt. Maj. Gen. Thomas S. Jesup transmitting
report for 3rd quarter, 1850—DNA, RG 92, Registers of Letters Received.

1851, Jan. 17.   To Bvt. Maj. Gen. Thomas S. Jesup transmitting
reports for 4th quarter, 1850—DNA, RG 92, Registers of Letters Received.

1851, Jan. 31.   Receipt to Bvt. Lt. Col. John B. Grayson for subsistence stores—DS, Orville E. Babcock Papers, ICN.

1851, Feb. 2.   To Bvt. Maj. Gen. George Gibson transmitting subsistence papers for Jan., 1851—DNA, RG 192, Registers of Letters Received.

1851, March 2. To Bvt. Maj. Gen. George Gibson transmitting subsistence papers for Feb., 1851—DNA, RG 192, Registers of Letters Received. On May 23, 1851, Gibson acknowledged receipt of provision returns for Jan.–March, 1851—Copy, *ibid.*, Letters Sent.

1851, March 31. Receipt to Bvt. Lt. Col. John B. Grayson for commissary property—DS, ICHi.

1851, April 6. To Bvt. Maj. Gen. George Gibson transmitting accounts for 1st quarter, 1851—DNA, RG 192, Registers of Letters Received. On April 14, 1851, Gibson acknowledged receipt of these accounts—Copy, *ibid.*, Letters Sent.

1851, April 17. To Bvt. Maj. Gen. Thomas S. Jesup. "Herewith I inclose you the estimate of the act. Asst. Qr. Mr. at Fort Brady Michigan, for repairs to Hospital &c." Enclosed is a letter from Bvt. 2nd Lt. Robert Macfeely to Bvt. Maj. Ebenezer S. Sibley, Feb. 28, 1851—DNA, RG 92, Consolidated Correspondence, Fort Brady. See *Calendar*, April 28, 1851.

1851, April 22. Bvt. Maj. Gen. Thomas S. Jesup to USG. "I have received your letter of the 14th instant in regard to the lots, enclosed in the parade ground at Detroit Barracks, owned by Mr. Ingersoll. You will consult with the commanding officer and if these lots be absolutely necessary for public use you will make the best arrangements you can with Mr. Ingersol for them."—Copy, DNA, RG 92, Q. M. Letter Books.

1851, April 28. Bvt. Maj. Gen. Thomas S. Jesup to USG. "I have received your letter of the 17th instant transmitting the estimate of the Acting Assistant Quarter Master at Fort Brady, for repairs to the Hospital &c. Upon inquiry at the Adjutant General's Office I learn, that there is but one company at Fort Brady, and only two men reported sick, so that there cannot be much demand for Hospital accommodation, and, consequently, in the limited state of the appropriations the repairs estimated for the Hospital cannot be made. In regard to the store house all that the appropriations will admit of, are repairs to the roof, sufficient to protect the interior from the weather, which will be done and nothing more. As for the bake house, the Post Fund receiving all the profits from baking is the only one out of which its repairs should be made. This Department has never been called upon to estimate for any thing of the kind, and has therefore no money applicable to such purposes."—Copy, DNA, RG 92, Q. M. Letter Books.

1851, MAY 2. To Bvt. Maj. Gen. Thomas S. Jesup transmitting reports for April, 1851—DNA, RG 92, Registers of Letters Received.

1851, MAY 3. To Bvt. Maj. Gen. George Gibson transmitting subsistence papers for April, 1851—DNA, RG 192, Registers of Letters Received.

1851, MAY 13. Lt. Col. Charles Thomas of Pa., deputy q. m. g. to USG. "Your letter of the 2d instant has been received with its enclosed estimate of funds and summary statement. Capt. T. L. Brent, Asst. Quarter Master, has been assigned to duty at Detroit, and will be supplied with funds for the services of the Department at that station." —Copy, DNA, RG 92, Q. M. Letter Books.

1851, MAY 26. To Bvt. Maj. Gen. George Gibson (telegram) inquiring about provisions to be delivered by a contractor—DNA, RG 192, Registers of Letters Received. On May 27, 1851, Capt. Alexander Eakin Shiras of the office of Commissary Gen. of Subsistence replied to USG. "Your despatch of yesterday is received and I have replied in the same way but to be certain of your receiving my answer, I now repeat it as follows. 'Receive the Provisions and take them to Fort Gratiot for the use of the Troops going there.' " The last seventeen words were also telegraphed to USG—Copy, *ibid.*, Letters Sent.

1851, [MAY 31]. "Report of Persons and Articles employed and hired at Detroit Michigan during the month of May, 1851."—D (signature clipped), DNA, RG 92.

1851, JUNE 6. To Bvt. Maj. Gen. George Gibson transmitting subsistence papers for May, 1851—DNA, RG 192, Registers of Letters

Received. On Aug. 8, 1851, Gibson acknowledged receipt of provision returns for April–June, 1851—Copy, *ibid.*, Letters Sent.

1851, JUNE 7.   To Bvt. Maj. Gen. George Gibson transmitting receipt for stores received from a contractor—DNA, RG 192, Registers of Letters Received. On June 16, 1851, John S. Gallaher, Third Auditor of the Treasury, wrote to Gibson. "By the wording of the receipts of Mr Flagg in the enclosed account it would appear that the money has been paid by Lieut U. S. Grant. The whole papers are returned to you for reexamination, and the expression of your opinion thereon—"— Copy, *ibid.*, RG 217, Third Auditor, Miscellaneous Letters Sent. On June 17, 1851, Gibson wrote to USG at Fort Gratiot, Mich. "Payment on the account of Mr Saml. D. Flagg for deliveries to you at Detroit Mich : on the 3d inst has been refused at the Treasury in consequence of the Contractor having attached his receipt to the account, in which the amount appears to have been paid by you. You will as soon as possible inform this Office whether or not Mr Flagg was paid by you for the above delivery."—Copy, *ibid.*, RG 192, Letters Sent. On June 28, 1851, USG sent an explanation to Gibson which was referred to the office of the Third Auditor—*Ibid.*, Registers of Letters Received.

1851, JUNE 7.   To Bvt. Maj. Gen. Thomas S. Jesup transmitting reports for May, 1851—DNA, RG 92, Registers of Letters Received.

1851, JUNE 28.   To Bvt. Maj. Gen. Thomas S. Jesup transmitting estimates for July, 1851—DNA, RG 92, Registers of Letters Received.

1851, JULY 2.   To Bvt. Maj. Gen. George Gibson transmitting accounts for 2nd quarter, 1851—DNA, RG 192, Registers of Letters Received. On Sept. 22, 1851, Gibson acknowledged receipt of these accounts—Copy, *ibid.*, Letters Sent.

1851, JULY 2.   Notice soliciting sealed bids for supplying beef "of good, wholesome quality, necks and shanks to be excluded."— *Richardson*, p. 136.

1851, JULY 9.   Lt. Col. Charles Thomas to USG. "Your letter of the 28th ultimo has been received, with its enclosures, and a remittance has been required in your favor of $330, for the service of the Quarter

Master's Department."—Copy, DNA, RG 92, Q. M. Letter Books. A copy of the requisition for $330, dated July 9, 1851, is *ibid.*, Requisitions for Remittances.

1851, JULY 21.   John S. Gallaher, Third Auditor of the Treasury, to USG. "Your a/c as acting asst Comy. of Subs at Ditroit Bks Mich. for 1st 2d 3d & 4th qrs 1850. & 1st qr. 1851. having been duly audited and adjusted in this Office and in that of the 2nd Comptroller of the Treasury, a balance is found due by you to the U. S. of $910.54. differing from your a/c for same time in the sum of $45.35[.] The statement herewith will explain the difference."—Copy, DNA, RG 217, Third Auditor, Miscellaneous Letters Sent. See *Calendar*, March 16, 1850.

1851, AUG. 4.   To Bvt. Maj. Gen. Thomas S. Jesup. "In compliance with circular dated July 15th 1851, requiring a report of the improvements, repairs &c, for the last year, with the estimated cost, the amount of assignable public quarters, work shops, stables &c, I would respectfully submit the following. 2 Lieut L C Hunt having performed the duty of acting Asst. Qtr Master, at this post, for the last year, I submit his report of expenditures for that period."—LS, DNA, RG 92, Consolidated Correspondence 598.

1851, AUG. 5.   To Bvt. Maj. Gen. George Gibson transmitting subsistence papers for July, 1851—DNA, RG 192, Registers of Letters Received.

1851, AUG. 6.   To Bvt. Maj. Gen. Thomas S. Jesup transmitting reports for July, 1851, and requesting a copy of q. m. regulations— DNA, RG 92, Registers of Letters Received.

1851, AUG. 12.   To Bvt. Maj. Gen. George Gibson requesting authority to sell surplus pork—DNA, RG 192, Registers of Letters Received. On Aug. 15, 1851, Capt. Alexander Eakin Shiras replied to USG. "Your letter of the 12 inst. is received. You are authorised to sell the surplus Pork mentioned, either at public or private Sale as in your judgment will be most advantageous to the Government."— Copy, *ibid.*, Letters Sent.

1851, AUG. 15.   To Bvt. Maj. Gen. Thomas S. Jesup transmitting vouchers not forwarded with 2nd quarter reports—DNA, RG 92, Registers of Letters Received.

1851, AUG. 28.   To office of the Commissary General of Subsistence regarding stores needed in Oct.—DNA, RG 192, Registers of Letters Received. On Aug. 22, 1851, Capt. Alexander Eakin Shiras had written to USG. "On receipt of this please inform me what quantity of stores you will require in October to be delivered by Mr. Flagg under his Contract for Madison Barracks."—Copy, *ibid.*, Letters Sent. On Sept. 1, 1851, Capt. Shiras replied to USG. "Your letter of the 28 Ulto is received. I have this day notified the Contractor for Madison Barracks, Mr Flagg, that he could make his Oct delivery as follows.

32 Barrels of Pork   one-fourth less than the Contract.
62   ''   '' Flour
18 Bushels '' Beans   one-third less than the Contract.
433 Pounds '' Soap
164   ''   '' Candles
  7 Bushels '' Salt and
110 Gallons '' Vinegar.''
—Copy, DNA, RG 192, Letters Sent.

1851, [AUG.].   To Bvt. Maj. Gen. Thomas S. Jesup transmitting reports for 2nd quarter, 1851, and June, 1851—DNA, RG 92, Registers of Letters Received.

1851, SEPT. 1.   To Bvt. Maj. Gen. Thomas S. Jesup. "Herewith I inclose you my Summary Statement and other papers for the month of August 1851. I also inclose you the advertisement, and proposal, for furnishing wood for the use of this post."—ALS, DNA, RG 92, Consolidated Correspondence 956. See document of June 24, 1851.

1851, SEPT. 3.   To Bvt. Maj. Gen. George Gibson transmitting subsistence papers for Aug., 1851—DNA, RG 192, Registers of Letters Received.

1851, SEPT. 16.   Bvt. Maj. Oscar F. Winship for Bvt. Maj. Gen. John E. Wool issued Orders No. 22 assigning USG and seven others to a court-martial at Fort Ontario, N. Y., on Sept. 19—DS, DNA, RG 94, Eastern Division Orders. On Sept. 22, 1851, Winship issued Orders

No. 25, reporting the action of the court—*Ibid*. USG served as president of the court, which heard two cases. In the first, a private who pleaded not guilty of striking a sergeant was found guilty and sentenced to three months of hard labor with a ball and chain weighing eighteen pounds attached to his leg, and loss of six dollars of pay each month for three months. In the second case, a musician who had surrendered after 23 days of desertion was sentenced to four months of hard labor and loss of five dollars of pay each month for four months—DS, DNA, RG 153.

1851, SEPT. 22.   Lt. Col. Daniel Randall, deputy paymaster general, to USG. "Your letter of the 18th inst. is recd and I have to inform you that it appears from the books of this office that your a/c for the month of March 1848 was paid by Lt. Colonel Randall, Deputy Paymr Genl on the 31st of that month."—Copy, DNA, RG 99, Letters Sent.

1851, OCT. 1.   To Bvt. Maj. Gen. Thomas S. Jesup transmitting reports for Sept., 1851—DNA, RG 92, Registers of Letters Received.

1851, Oct. 6.   To Bvt. Maj. Gen. George Gibson transmitting subsistence papers for Sept., 1851, and accounts for 3rd quarter, 1851—DNA, RG 192, Registers of Letters Received. On Oct. 14, 1851, Gibson acknowledged receipt of the accounts and on Oct. 20, 1851, acknowledged receipt of provision returns for July–Sept., 1851. Gibson added to his letter of Oct. 14: "Commutation at the rate of 75¢ being prohibited except in particular cases by Genl Orders No 25 and as there is no authority found in the Subs Regulations for such commutation to men employed in pursuit of deserters, all such payments will be charged to the officer under whose order they are made."—Copies *ibid*., Letters Sent.

1851, OCT. 7–Oct. 19.   Morning reports signed by USG—Burton Historical Collection, MiD.

1851, Oct. 14.   To Bvt. Maj. Gen. George Gibson transmitting certificate of inspection—DNA, RG 192, Registers of Letters Received.

1851, Oct. 23.   To Bvt. Maj. Gen. George Gibson answering Gibson's letter of Oct. 18—DNA, RG 192, Registers of Letters Received. Gibson had written: "You will please inform this Office under what circumstances, the October delivery of Mr Flagg was received deficient in the Articles of *Pork* and *Beans*." Gibson also requested an explanation of S. D. Flagg, Buffalo, N. Y., that same day—Copy, *ibid.*, Letters Sent. See *Calendar*, Aug. 28, 1851.

1851, Nov. 1. To Bvt. Maj. Gen. Thomas S. Jesup transmitting reports for Oct., 1851—DNA, RG 92, Registers of Letters Received.

1851, Nov. 3. To Bvt. Maj. Gen. George Gibson transmitting subsistence papers for Oct., 1851—DNA, RG 192, Registers of Letters Received.

1851, Nov. 3. John S. Gallaher, Third Auditor of the Treasury, to Samuel D. Flagg. "The Treasurer of the U. S.s will remit you the Sum. of $346.63, being the amt. of your a/c for sundry Provisions furnished under your contract with the commissary General of Subsistence to Bvt Capt. U. S. Grant, A.A.C.S, Madison Bks, N. Y, Oct.r 13, 1851. for which sum when received, you will please forward your receipt to this office."—Copy, DNA, RG 217, Third Auditor, Miscellaneous Letters Sent.

1851, Nov. 17. To Bvt. Maj. Gen. George Gibson transmitting beef contract—DNA, RG 192, Registers of Letters Received. On Nov. 21, 1851, Gibson replied. "The fresh Beef Contract made by you with H. McKee is approved."—Copy, *ibid.*, Letters Sent.

1851, Nov. 22. Bvt. Maj. Oscar F. Winship for Bvt. Maj. Gen. John E. Wool issued Orders No. 37 assigning USG and seven others to a court-martial at Fort Niagara, N. Y., on Nov. 27, 1851—DS, DNA, RG 94, Eastern Division Orders. The court heard the case of a sergeant who pleaded guilty to striking one of his men with a spade. He was sentenced to be reduced to the ranks, but the punishment was remitted by Gen. Wool on recommendation of the court. The other case was that of the private who had been struck while struggling with the sergeant on the way to the guardhouse. The court found him guilty and sentenced him to fourteen days solitary confinement on bread and water, hard labor for two months, and loss of five dollars pay each month for two months. Gen. Wool later remitted the two months of hard labor—DS, DNA, RG 153.

1851, Dec. 3.   To Bvt. Maj. Gen. Thomas S. Jesup transmitting reports for Nov., 1851—DNA, RG 92, Registers of Letters Received.

1851, Dec. 5.   To Bvt. Maj. Gen. George Gibson transmitting subsistence papers for Nov., 1851—DNA, RG 192, Registers of Letters Received. On Dec. 11, 1851, Gibson wrote to USG. "In glancing over your November Return, it is observed that you have quite a large surplus of Flour Beans and Salt on hand as compared with your issues of those items. Your particular attention is called to seeing that no unnecessary accumulation of any of the items composing the ration occurs in future. This can be done by your carefully examing the quantity of each item on hand at the time of each delivery of the Contractor, & giving this Office timely notice of what reduction is necessary in the next subsequent delivery of the Contractor. Should any reduction be deemed by you as necessary under the 1st delivery of the next Contract for Madison Barracks which takes place on the 1st June 1852, inform me of it in time to give Sixty days notice to the Contractor of the reduction. Attached is a printed slip showing the quantity to be delivered on the 1st June 1852."—Copy, *ibid.*, Letters Sent. On Jan. 27, 1852, Gibson acknowledged receipt of provision returns for Oct.–Dec., 1851—Copy, *ibid.*

1852, Jan. 5.   To Bvt. Maj. Gen. Thomas S. Jesup transmitting reports for Dec., 1851—DNA, RG 92, Registers of Letters Received.

1852, Jan. 9.   To Bvt. Maj. Gen. George Gibson transmitting accounts for 4th quarter, 1851—DNA, RG 192, Registers of Letters Received. On Jan. 17, 1852, Gibson acknowledged receipt of these accounts—Copy, *ibid.*, Letters Sent.

1852, Jan. 12.   To Bvt. Maj. Gen. George Gibson requesting funds —DNA, RG 192, Registers of Letters Received. On Jan. 17, 1852, Gibson replied. "The Treasurer of the United States has been this day requested to remit you Five hundred and fifty dollars on account of Army Subsistence."—Copy, *ibid.*, Letters Sent.

1852, JAN. 18.   To Bvt. Maj. Gen. Thomas S. Jesup transmitting reports for 4th quarter, 1851, and Dec., 1851—DNA, RG 92, Registers of Letters Received.

1852, JAN. 26.   Bvt. Maj. Gen. Thomas S. Jesup to USG. "Your letter of the 18th instant. has, together with its enclosures, been received. The Mackinac boats, if condemned by a Board of Survey, can be broken up or sold and dropped from your returns. The Wagon and Sleigh can also be sold."—Copy, DNA, RG 92, Q. M. Letter Books.

1852, JAN. 30.   To Bvt. Maj. Gen. Thomas S. Jesup transmitting voucher not sent previous quarter—DNA, RG 92, Registers of Letters Received.

1852, FEB. 1.   To Bvt. Maj. Gen. Thomas S. Jesup transmitting reports for Jan., 1852—DNA, RG 92, Registers of Letters Received.

1852, FEB. 2.   To Bvt. Maj. Gen. Thomas S. Jesup transmitting certificate of the judge advocate concerning the services of Bvt. Capt. Thomas R. McConnell and 2nd Lt. Lewis C. Hunt. The matter was referred to the office of the 3rd auditor on March 10, 1852—DNA, RG 92, Registers of Letters Received.

1852, FEB. 7.   To Bvt. Maj. Gen. George Gibson transmitting subsistence papers for Jan., 1852—DNA, RG 192, Registers of Letters Received.

1852, FEB. 13.   To Bvt. Maj. Gen. Thomas S. Jesup. "Herewith I have the honor to enclose to you the several bids for furnishing wood for the coming year at this post, together with the contract entered into with Elish Parrish, subject to your approval."—ALS, DNA, RG 92, Consolidated Correspondence 956. Acknowledged by Jesup, Feb. 18.—Copy, *ibid*., Q. M. Letter Books.

1852, FEB. 22.   To Bvt. Maj. Gen. George Gibson discussing fund for the army asylum—DNA, RG 192, Registers of Letters Received.

1852, FEB. 25.   To 2nd Lt. William A. Slaughter. "The Colonel commanding the Regiment directs me to call your attention to Regimental Orders No. 59, of 1851, requiring accounts current of the company funds of the Regiment to be forwarded *Quarterly* to this office. Your account current with the fund of company "C" 4th Infantry, for the Quarter ending December 31st, 1851, has not been received." Written as act. adjt.—Copy, DNA, RG 98, 4th Inf., Letters Sent.

1852, FEB. 25.   To Bvt. Maj. Charles H. Larnard. "Your account current with the fund of Company "A" 4th Infantry, for the *Quarter* ending December 31st 1851, has not been received at this office. Please forward it as soon as possible." Written as act. adjt.—Copy, DNA, RG 98, 4th Inf., Letters Sent.

1852, FEB. 28.   To Bvt. Maj. Gen. George Gibson transmitting receipt for twenty barrels of pork—DNA, RG 192, Registers of Letters Received.

1852, MARCH 4.   "Return of the Fourth Regiment of Infantry, (Colonel William Whistler, commanding,) for the month or January, 1852." Signed by USG as act. adjt.—DS, DNA, RG 98, 4th Inf.

1852, MARCH 5.   To Bvt. Lt. Col. Robert C. Buchanan. "Your letter of the 19th Ultimo is received. I am directed, by the Colonel Commanding, to reply that we are much in want of the Musician you have enlisted, and would like to get him at as early a day as possible." Written as act. adjt.—Copy, DNA, RG 98, 4th Inf., Letters Sent.

1852, MARCH 8.   To Bvt. Maj. Gen. George Gibson transmitting abstracts and summary statements for Feb., 1852—DNA, RG 192, Registers of Letters Received. On May 25, 1852, Gibson acknowledged receipt of provision returns for Jan.–March, 1852. Copy, *ibid.*, Letters Sent.

1852, MARCH 9.   To Bvt. 2nd Lt. Francis H. Bates. "Your letter of the 1st instant, enclosing *Six* dollars to the Regimental Fund, for the months of January and February, 1852, has been received." Written as act. adjt.—Copy, DNA, RG 98, 4th Inf., Letters Sent.

1852, MARCH 12.   To 2nd Lt. Edmund Underwood. "A man calling himself John M. Crane gave himself up to the guard *here* last night—saying that he was a deserter from "F" Company, 4th Regiment U. S. Infantry." Written as act. adjt.—Copy, DNA, RG 98, 4th Inf., Letters Sent.

1852, MARCH 21. To Capt. Henry D. Wallen. "I am directed by Colonel Whistler to say that the Regimental Court-Martial, asked for in your letter of the 15th instant, cannot be ordered at present: There not being a sufficient number of Officers at your post to constitute the Court, and a General Court having been applied for at this post, renders it impracticable." Written as act. adjt.—Copy, DNA, RG 98, 4th Inf., Letters Sent.

1852, MARCH 22. Bvt. Maj. Oscar F. Winship for Bvt. Maj. Gen. John E. Wool issued Orders No. 10 assigning USG and seven others to a court martial at Madison Barracks, N. Y., on March 26, 1852—DS, DNA, RG 94, Eastern Division Orders. The court found three privates guilty of desertion—DNA, RG 153.

1852, [MARCH 31]. "Abstract of Fuel issued to the troops of Madison Barracks . . ."—DS, OrHi.

1852, APRIL 1. To Col. Henry Knox Craig, chief of ordnance. "I herewith enclose a Return of Ordnance and Ordnance stores, for the 1st Quarter of 1852." Written as act. adjt.—Copy, DNA, RG 98, 4th Inf., Letters Sent.

1852, APRIL 1. "Return of the Fourth Regiment of Infantry, (Colonel William Whistler, Commanding,) for the month of February, 1852." Signed by USG as act. adjt.—DS, DNA, RG 98, 4th Inf.

1852, APRIL 5. To Bvt. Maj. Gen. Thomas S. Jesup transmitting "the monthly papers pertaining to the quarter masters department, at this post, for March 1852"—LS, DNA, RG 92, Letters Received.

1852, APRIL 12. To Col. Henry K. Craig transmitting ordnance return of noncommissioned staff and band for part of 1st quarter, 1852—DNA, RG 156, Registers of Letters Received. On April 26,

1852, Craig acknowledged receipt of the return and forwarded it to the Second Auditor's office—*Ibid.*, Letters Sent (Miscellaneous).

1852, APRIL 14. To Bvt. Maj. Gen. George Gibson discussing June deliveries and his need for funds—DNA, RG 192, Registers of Letters Received. On April 19, 1852, Gibson replied. "The Treasurer of the United States has been this day requested to remit you Four hundred dollars on account of Army Subsistence. I have written to Mr Buell relative to his June delivery."—Copy, *ibid.*, Letters Sent. USG probably enclosed accounts for 1st quarter, 1852, with his letter, for on April 19, 1852, Gibson acknowledged them—*Ibid.* On April 30, 1852, Gibson again wrote to USG. "Mr. Buell has consented to dispense with Beans in June delivery, and Pork and Flour have each been reduced one-third under said delivery and it will be as follows—

28 Barrels of Pork
42   ″   ″ Flour
No Beans
438 Pounds of Soap
164   ″   ″ Candles
7 Bushels ″ Salt and
110 Gallons ″ Vinegar."
—*Ibid.*

1852, APRIL 14. To Bvt. Maj. Benjamin Alvord. "I am directed by Colonel Whistler to return you the enclosed Casualty return to be made out on paper of proper size, and folded as required in Regimental Orders No. 78, of 1850." Written as act. adjt.—DNA, RG 98, 4th Inf., Letters Sent.

1852, APRIL 14. To 2nd Lt. William A. Slaughter. "I am directed by the Colonel commanding to call your attention to paragraph II of Regimental Orders No. 78, of 1850—which Order you never comply with in folding your company returns. Your account current with the Company fund is returned for correction as marked in red ink." Written as act. adjt.—Copy, DNA, RG 98, 4th Inf., Letters Sent.

1852, APRIL 18–MAY 7. USG as act. adjt. signed the morning reports at Sackets Harbor—DS, CSmH.

1852, May 4.   To Bvt. Maj. Gen. Thomas S. Jesup transmitting "papers, pertaining to the Quarter Master's Department, for the month of April 1852. I also enclose Voucher No 6 Abstract B 4th Quarter 1851, to take the place of the voucher already furnished which is incorrect."—ALS, DNA, RG 92, Letters Received.

1852, May 8.   To Bvt. Maj. Gen. George Gibson transmitting certificate of inspection—DNA, RG 192, Registers of Letters Received.

1852, May 9.   To Bvt. Maj. Gen. George Gibson transmitting subsistence papers for April, 1852—DNA, RG 192, Registers of Letters Received.

1852, May 15.   "Return of the Fourth Regiment of Infantry, (Colonel William Whistler Commanding,) for the month of March, 1852." Signed by USG as act. adjt.—DS, DNA, RG 98, 4th Inf.

1852, May 15.   "Return of the Fourth Regiment of Infantry, (Colonel William Whistler Commanding,) for the month of April, 1852." Signed by USG as act. adjt.—DS, DNA, RG 98, 4th Inf.

1852, May 25.   John S. Gallaher, Third Auditor of the Treasury to Samuel D. Flagg. "The Treasurer of the U. States will remit to you the sum of $368. being the amount of your a/c. for sundry provisions delivered under your contract with the Commissary Genl of Subs, to Bvt Capt. U S. Grant, at Madison Bks, N Y, on the 26th of Feby. & May 8th 1852, for which sum when recd you will please forward your receipt to this office."—Copy, DNA, RG 217, Third Auditor, Miscellaneous Letters Sent.

1852, May 26.   To Bvt. Maj. Gen. George Gibson discussing disposal of subsistence stores and his need of funds. DNA, RG 192, Registers of Letters Received. On May 29, 1852, Capt. Alexander E. Shiras replied. "Bvt Lt Col Jno B. Grayson C. S. has been charged with the arrangement of the Stores left at Madison Barracks by the movement of the Troops from that Post. The Treasurer of the United States has been requested to remit you $1500, Subsistence funds." On May 31, 1852, Shiras wrote, "I have this day with the Consent of the Contractor Mr I. S. Buell annulled his Contract for Madison Barracks.

Consequently no deliveries will be made by Mr. Buell at said Barracks."—Copies, *ibid.*, Letters Sent.

1852, JUNE 3.   Col. William Whistler to Bvt. Maj. Gen. Roger Jones enclosing USG accounts of the post fund of Madison Barracks and the regt. fund, 4th Inf., for part of Feb. and March and April, 1852—Copy, DNA, RG 98, 4th Inf., Letters Sent.

1852, JUNE 8.   To Bvt. Maj. Gen. Thomas S. Jesup transmitting "the monthly papers, pertaining to the Quarter Master's Department at this post, for the month of May, 1852."—LS, DNA, RG 92, Letters Received.

1852, JUNE 10.   John S. Gallaher, Third Auditor of the Treasury, to USG. "Your A/c. as Asst. Qr. Mr. for the years 1847. 1848. 1849. & 1850. & for 1. 2, & 3d qrs 1851. having been examined & adjusted in this office, & reported to the 2nd Comptroller of the Treasury, has been returned with the following result, Viz; A balance is found due U. S. of $2.026.45. differing from the balance rendered in his last A/c. current by $785.01. an explanation of which is given in the enclosed statement of difference. The suspended vouchers are herewith returned."—Copy, DNA, RG 217, Third Auditor, Miscellaneous Letters Sent.

1852, JUNE 10.   John S. Gallaher, Third Auditor of the Treasury, to Philip Clayton, Second Auditor of the Treasury. "The following vouchers from the A/c. of Capt. U. S. Grant a.q.m. in & at Madison Bks, N. Y, are respectfully referred to you, Viz; vou 2, $5.00 Abst "A" 3d qr. 1847. part voucher 15, $2.81 abst "A" 1st qr. 1849. & part of vou. 0, $4.50 Abst "A" 2d qr 1851."—Copy, DNA, RG 217, Third Auditor, Miscellaneous Letters Sent.

1852, JUNE 11.   John S. Gallaher, Third Auditor of the Treasury, to Col. William Whistler. "In the settlement of the a/c. of Capt. U. S. Grant, a.q.m. at Detroit for the 2nd qr, 1849. Vouch 1. Abst "A." 2d qr. 1849, for $5.50. cost of one Filter was disallowed on remarks of Qr. Mr. Genl. that 'the article is not one of military supply. & the expenditure is inadmissible,' as it was paid on your order, the amt. has been admitted to the credit of Capt Grant, & charged to you pr paragraph of Regulations No 1028.—"—Copy, DNA, RG 217, Third Auditor, Miscellaneous Letters Sent. See *Calendar*, July 27, 1849.

1852, JUNE 19. To Bvt. Maj. Gen. George Gibson transmitting subsistence papers for May, 1852—DNA, RG 192, Registers of Letters Received.

1852, JUNE 29. To Bvt. Maj. Gen. George Gibson discussing payment for stores for Plattsburgh Barracks—DNA, RG 192, Registers of Letters Received. On July 2, 1852, Gibson replied. "You will please turn over to Lt. W. H. Scott, 4 Infantry such Subsistence funds as may be requisite to pay the debts of the Department contracted by him, & enable him to close his accounts."—Copy, *ibid.*, Letters Sent.

1852, SEPT. 3. Along with Bvt. Maj. Benjamin Alvord and Asst. Surgeon Charles Henry Crane, USG signed the report of a board of officers at Benicia assigned to inspect the bark *Anita* and the schooner *Sierra Nevada*. The vessels had been assigned to carry troops to Columbia Barracks, but the officers reported them unsatisfactory—DS, DNA, RG 98, Pacific Division, Letters Received.

1852, SEPT. 21. Receipt to 1st Lt. Theodore Talbot for subsistence property received at Columbia Barracks—ICarbS.

1852, SEPT. 25. Bvt. Capt. Thomas R. McConnell to USG. "I am directed by the commanding officer of the post to call upon you for a report of what contracts made by the Subsistence Dept. are still in force at this post, stating the purposes and length of time for which they were made."—Copy, DNA, RG 98, 4th Inf., Letters Sent.

1852, SEPT. 26. Bvt. Capt. Thomas R. McConnell to USG. "The commanding officer of the post directs me to say to you that he wishes you to make a Contract for the delivery of fresh beef to the troops for six months."—Copy, DNA, RG 98, 4th Inf., Letters Sent.

1852, SEPT. 28. Bvt. Maj. E. D. Townsend to Lt. Col. B. L. E. Bonneville. "Your letter of the 21 instant with the enclosed report from Bvt Capt *Grant* has been submitted to the General Commanding— Captain Grant's report has been referred to Major Cross, Chief Quartrmaster, with instructions to direct the Asst QrMaster at Columbia Barracks to provide such materials as can be had from the use of the saw mills with the labor of the troops—The General directs that the repairs to the Barracks be made by the troops not on 'Extra duty'— Nails will be furnished and if absolutely necessary, a small quantity of lime, not to make mortar for chinking but to improve the consistency of the mud as ordinarily used in log buildings—Stoves will be furnished in place of building chimneys."—Copy, DNA, RG 94, Pacific Division Letter Book.

1852, SEPT. 29. To Col. Henry K. Craig transmitting ordnance return of the noncommissioned staff and band, 4th Inf., for part of 2nd quarter, 1852—DNA, RG 156, Registers of Letters Received. On Jan. 7, 1853, Craig acknowledged receipt of the return and forwarded it to the Second Auditor's office—*Ibid.*, Letters Sent (Miscellaneous).

1852, OCT. 5. To Bvt. Maj. Gen. George Gibson transmitting accounts for 2nd quarter, 1852, and subsistence papers for June, 1852— DNA, RG 192, Registers of Letters Received.

1852, OCT. 5. To Bvt. Maj. Gen. Thomas S. Jesup transmitting accounts for 2nd quarter, 1852, and reports for June, 1852—DNA, RG 92, Registers of Letters Received.

1852, OCT. 6. Lt. Col. Benjamin L. E. Bonneville to Col. Samuel Cooper enclosing "the Account Current of Bvt. Capt U. S. Grant, with the Regimental Fund of the 4th Infantry for the month of May, 1852." Also forwarding a letter of USG transmitting account of the post fund, Madison Barracks, for May, 1852—Copy, DNA, RG 98, 4th Inf., Letters Sent.

1852, OCT. 15. To Bvt. Maj. Gen. George Gibson transmitting subsistence papers for July–Sept., 1852, and accounts for 3rd quarter, 1852—DNA, RG 192, Registers of Letters Received. On Dec. 30, 1852, Gibson acknowledged receipt of provision returns for April– Sept., 1852, and on Jan. 15, 1853, acknowledged receipt of accounts for 2nd and 3rd quarters, 1852—Copies, *ibid.*, Letters Sent.

1852, Oct. 21. To Bvt. Maj. Gen. George Gibson transmitting beef contract—DNA, RG 192, Registers of Letters Received. On Nov. 29, 1852, Gibson replied. "The fresh beef Contract made by you with Mr. John Switzler is approved."—Copy, *ibid.*, Letters Sent.

1852, Nov. 1.   To Bvt. Maj. Gen. Thomas S. Jesup transmitting "a Semi Annual return for the half year ending on the 30th June 1852, and Quarterly Statement of allowances paid to officers and furnished in kind for the quarter ending at the same time. Voucher No 6 Abstract "B" 2d Quarter, 1852, I will forward to your office as soon as I receive Lieut Russells certificate."—LS, DNA, RG 92, Letters Received.

1852, Nov. 2.   John S. Gallaher, Third Auditor of the Treasury, to USG. "The Comsy Genl. of Subs having transmitted to this office your a/cs as Acting Asst Commissary of Subsistence for the 2nd 3rd & 4th qrs 1851. & 1. qr 1852. at Detroit Bks Michn & Madison Bks N. Y, the same have been audited & sent to the 2nd Comptroller of the Treasury, for his decision thereon, and having been returned, exhibit a balance due from you to the u. States, of \$2.178.40. Differing from the balance in your a/c, current, of March 31st 1852. in the sum of \$1.945.35. An explanation of which you will find in the statement of differences herewith, enclosed."—Copy, DNA, RG 217, Third Auditor, Miscellaneous Letters Sent.

1852, Nov. 5.   To Bvt. Maj. Gen. George Gibson transmitting subsistence papers for Oct., 1852—DNA, RG 192, Registers of Letters Received.

1852, Nov. 5.   To Bvt. Maj. Gen. Thomas S. Jesup transmitting "my Summary Statement and Muster Roll of men on extra duty, for the month of October 1852."—LS, DNA, RG 92, Letters Received.

1852, Dec. 5.   To Bvt. Maj. Gen. George Gibson transmitting subsistence papers for Nov., 1852—DNA, RG 192, Registers of Letters Received.

1852, Dec. 20.   To Bvt. Maj. Gen. Thomas S. Jesup transmitting "a Muster roll and Summary Statement for the month of November, 1852."—LS, DNA, RG 92, Letters Received.

1853, Jan. 4.   To Bvt. Maj. Gen. George Gibson transmitting subsistence papers for Dec., 1852—DNA, RG 192, Registers of Letters Received. On March 22, 1853, Gibson acknowledged receipt of provision returns for Oct.–Dec., 1852. "The following errors appear in your Dec. Return . . . . Which errors you will please correct."—Copy, *ibid.*, Letters Sent.

1853, Jan. 4.   To Bvt. Maj. Gen. Thomas S. Jesup transmitting "my Summary Statement for the month of December 1852."—ALS, DNA, RG 92, Letters Received.

1853, Jan. 8.   To Bvt. Maj. Gen. Thomas S. Jesup transmitting accounts for 4th quarter, 1852—DNA, RG 92, Registers of Letters Received.

1853, Jan. 10.   To Bvt. Maj. Gen. George Gibson transmitting accounts for 4th quarter, 1852—DNA, RG 192, Registers of Letters Received. On April 29, 1853, Gibson acknowledged receipt of these accounts—Copy, *ibid.*, Letters Sent.

1853, Jan. 10.   Return of farm operations for fourth quarter, 1852—DNA, RG 94, Index to Letters Received.

1853, Feb. 5.   To Bvt. Maj. Gen. Thomas S. Jesup transmitting "a Summary Statement for the month of January 1853."—LS, DNA, RG 92, Letters Received.

1853, Feb. 9.   Bvt. Capt. Thomas R. McConnell to Col. Henry K. Craig enclosing duplicate of ordnance return of noncommissioned staff and band of USG for part of 2nd quarter, 1852—Copy, DNA, RG 98, 4th Inf., Letters Sent.

1853, Feb. 17.   To Bvt. Maj. Gen. George Gibson transmitting subsistence papers for Jan., 1853—DNA, RG 192, Registers of Letters Received.

1853, March 5.   To Bvt. Maj. Gen. Thomas S. Jesup transmitting report for Feb., 1853—DNA, RG 92, Registers of Letters Received.

1853, MARCH 5. To Bvt. Maj. Gen. Thomas S. Jesup transmitting duplicate vouchers. The matter was referred to the office of the 3rd auditor on July 8, 1853—DNA, RG 92, Registers of Letters Received.

1853, MARCH 13. To Bvt. Maj. Gen. George Gibson transmitting subsistence papers for Feb., 1853—DNA, RG 192, Registers of Letters Received. On June 23, 1853, Capt. Alexander Eakin Shiras acknowledged receipt of provision returns for Jan.–March, 1853. "The following errors appear in your returns . . . . Which errors you will please correct."—Copy, *ibid.*, Letters Sent.

1853, APRIL 3. To Bvt. Maj. Gen. Thomas S. Jesup transmitting accounts for March, 1853—DNA, RG 92, Registers of Letters Received.

1853, APRIL 30. To Bvt. Maj. Gen. George Gibson transmitting accounts for 1st quarter, 1853—DNA, RG 192, Registers of Letters Received. On Oct. 24, 1853, Gibson acknowledged receipt of these accounts—Copy, *ibid.*, Letters Sent.

1853, APRIL 30. Proceedings of the council of administration of Columbia Barracks—DS, DNA, RG 98, Columbia Barracks.

1853, [APRIL]. To Bvt. Maj. Gen. Thomas S. Jesup transmitting property accounts for 1st quarter, 1853—DNA, RG 92, Registers of Letters Received.

1853, MAY 14. To Bvt. Maj. Gen. George Gibson transmitting subsistence papers for April, 1853—DNA, RG 192, Registers of Letters Received.

1853, [MAY 31]. "Report of Persons and Articles employed and hired at Columbia Barracks W. T. during the month of May 1853."—DS, DNA, RG 92.

1853, [MAY 31]. "Report of Stores received for transportation and distribution at Columbia Barracks, W. T. by Bvt. Capt. U. S. Grant, R. Q. M. 4 Inf. during the Month of May, 1853."—DS, DNA, RG 92, Letters Received, Clothing.

1853, JUNE 1. To Bvt. Maj. Gen. Thomas S. Jesup transmitting report for April, 1853—DNA, RG 92, Registers of Letters Received.

1853, JUNE 1. Return of farm property—DNA, RG 94, Index to Letters Received.

1853, JUNE 13. Henry H. Hall to Bvt. Maj. Gen. Nathan Towson enclosing a draft for $50 of Maj. A. J. Smith in favor of USG—ALS, DNA, RG 99, Letters Received.

1853, JUNE 15. To Bvt. Maj. Gen. Thomas S. Jesup transmitting reports for May, 1853—DNA, RG 92, Registers of Letters Received.

1853, JUNE 29. To Bvt. Maj. Gen. George Gibson transmitting subsistence papers for May, 1853—DNA, RG 192, Registers of Letters Received. On Nov. 18, 1853, Gibson acknowledged receipt of provision returns for April–June, 1853. "The following error appears in your June Return . . . which Error you will please correct."—Copy, *ibid.*, Letters Sent.

1853, [JUNE 30]. "Report of Persons and Articles employed and hired at Columbia Barracks during the month of June 1853."—DS, DNA, RG 92.

1853, [JUNE 30]. "Report of Stores received for transportation and distribution at Columbia Barracks, W. T. by Bvt. Capt. U. S. Grant, R. Q. M. 4 Inf. during the Month of June, 1853."—DS, DNA, RG 92, Letters Received, Clothing.

1853, JUNE. Proceedings of the council of administration of Columbia Barracks—DS, DNA, RG 98, Columbia Barracks.

1853, JULY 1. USG contract with S. W. Coe, owner of the steamer *Cascade*, specifying transportation of men and supplies from the portage of the Cascades to the Dalles of the Columbia at a cost of $5 per man and $20 per ton of supplies—DS, Jesse Jay Ricks Collection, IHi.

1853, JULY 8. Bvt. Maj. Gen. Thomas S. Jesup to USG. "I have received your letter of April 24, with its enclosures, relative to your accounts for the 2 & 3d Qrs. 1852, and have referred it to the 3d Auditor, endorsed as satisfactory; the Secretary of War having allowed the 1st item ($20) of voucher 4. 3d. Qr. '52. for attendance on sick soldier, as a charge against the Medical Department."—Copy, DNA, RG 92, Q. M. Letter Books. On June 25, 1853, Jesup had endorsed the voucher in transmitting it to Secretary of War Jefferson Davis. "The first item on this voucher was objected to when Captain Grant's accounts were examined at this office—it seems to me to be a proper charge against the Medical Department; but, on being referred to the Surgeon General's office, Doctor Heiskill (the Surgeon General not being in) stated that he knew of no appropriation applicable to the payment of accounts for taking care of sick soldiers—that it was the duty of enlisted men, and consequently no estimate had been contemplated by the Medical Department, nor appropriation made, with a view to the hiring of such service. The great extent of our territories, and the necessity of taking troops through the most sickly climates, render additional measures necessary for the care and accommodation of troops, and particularly of the sick. I respectfully ask that the Secretary of War direct what appropriation should be charged with the expenditure."—Copy, *ibid.*, Letters Sent, Secretary of War; *ibid.*, RG 107, Registers of Letters Received. Returned by Davis to Jesup on July 6 endorsed "Charge Medical & Hospital Department $20."— *Ibid.*, Orders and Endorsements, Vol. 4; *ibid.*, RG 92, Decision Book. On July 14, 1853, F. Burt, Third Auditor of the Treasury, wrote to Philip Clayton, Second Auditor of the Treasury. "I transmit, herewith, an extract from a Voucher, of the a/cs of Bvt Capt U. S. Grant 4th Infty. a.a.q.m. amounting to Twenty Dollars, which you will please cause to be settled and the amount to be transferred to his credit on the books of this office.—"—Copy, *ibid.*, RG 217, Third Auditor, Miscellaneous Letters Sent. On July 7, 1854, F. Burt wrote to Philip Clayton. "Enclosed is Vou 4. ab. "B," 3d qr 1852 of the a/c of Bv't Captain U. S. Grant which is respectfully referred to your office to be charged to the appropriation as mentioned by the Sec'y of War."—Copy, *ibid.* On July 8, 1854, Philip Clayton, Second Auditor of the Treasury, replied to Burt. "On the sett: of the a/c of Bt. *Capt. U. S. Grant*, A.A.Q.M. on the 20 Sept. 1853, in this Office the sum of $708.64 was found due him and transferred to his credit on the Books of your Office. The sum of $20.—paid for taking care of Private *Silas Simpson* of Co. H. 4 Inf was embraced in said sett: upon an extract received from your Office on the 15 July 1853. As your letter of the 7 inst. refers solely to this item, I herewith respectfully return Vo. No. 4. Abstract B. 3.d quarter 1852, as the credit has already been given to Bt. Capt. Grant."—Copy, *ibid.*, Second Auditor, Letters Sent.

1853, July 13.   To Bvt. Maj. Gen. Thomas S. Jesup transmitting reports for June, 1853—DNA, RG 92, Registers of Letters Received.

1853, July 16.   Second Auditor's office to Secretary of War Jefferson Davis enclosing voucher of USG for $3.50 for black crape—Copy, DNA, RG 217, Second Auditor, Letters Sent; *ibid.*, RG 107, Register of Letters Received. Returned by Davis, July 26, 1853, endorsed "charge army contingencies."—*Ibid.*, Orders and Endorsements, Vol. 4.

1853, [July 31].   "Report of Persons and Articles employed and hired at Columbia Barracks during the month of July 1853."—D (signature clipped), DNA, RG 92.

1853, [July 31].   "Report of Stores received for transportation and distribution at Columbia Barracks, W. T. by Bvt. Capt. U. S. Grant, R. Q. M. 4 Inf. during the Month of July, 1853."—DS, DNA, RG 92, Letters Received, Clothing.

1853, Aug. 28.   To Bvt. Maj. Gen. Thomas S. Jesup transmitting reports for July, 1853—DNA, RG 92, Registers of Letters Received.

1853, [Aug. 31].   "Report of Persons and Articles employed and hired at Fort Vancouver during the month of August 1853."—DS, DNA, RG 92.

1853, [Aug. 31].   "Report of Stores Received for transportation and distribution at Ft Vancouver, W. T. by Bvt. Capt. U. S. Grant, R. Q. M. 4 Inf. during the Month of Aug., 1853."—DS, DNA, RG 92, Letters Received, Clothing.

1853, Aug.   Notation in court docket that a suit of Adams and Co. against USG has been dropped—Washington County Court House, Hillsboro, Ore.

1853, SEPT. 6. To Bvt. Maj. Gen. Thomas S. Jesup transmitting "the following monthly papers for Augt. last—Viz: Monthly Summary Statement, Report of Persons & Articles, Report of Extra duty men, Report of Stores, Report of Animals foraged & Return of Animals, &c.—"—LS, DNA, RG 92, Letters Received.

1853, SEPT. 8. To AG Samuel Cooper asking permission to go to Washington, D. C., to settle his accounts—DNA, RG 94, Index to Letters Received.

1853, SEPT. 9. Lt. Col. B. L. E. Bonneville to Bvt. Maj. Gen. Thomas S. Jesup transmitting proceedings of a board of survey held Sept. 5 to inspect clothing received by USG from Capt. R. E. Clary, act. q. m. at Benicia—LS, DNA, RG 92, Consolidated Correspondence 350.

1853, SEPT. 13. F. Burt, Third Auditor of the Treasury, to Secretary of the Treasury James Guthrie. "I have the honor to transmit herewith a Requisition No 1928 for $700. in favor of Br Capt U. S. Grant—and request that the amount may be covered into the Treasury by your Warrent to come to the credit of said Grant on the Books of this office on account of Military Contributions in Mexico"—Copy, DNA, RG 217, Third Auditor, Miscellaneous Letters Sent.

1853, SEPT. 14. F. Burt, Third Auditor of the Treasury, to USG. "Your accounts for disbursments at Madison Barracks N. Y. during the 4 qr 1851 and 1 & 2. qr 1852 have been audited and reported to the second Comptroller of the Treasury for his decision thereon, by whom they have been returned to this office showing a balance due from you to the U States of $1566.78 and differing from your account Current of 2 qr 1852 in the Sum of $564.42 as set forth in the enclosed sheet of remarks The suspended vouchers are herewith returned to you for correction"—Copy, DNA, RG 217, Third Auditor, Miscellaneous Letters Sent.

1853, SEPT. 15. To Bvt. Maj. Gen. George Gibson transmitting accounts for 2nd quarter, 1853—DNA, RG 192, Registers of Letters Received. On Oct. 31, 1853, Gibson wrote to USG. "On examination of your account current for the 2nd quarter 1853 it is perceived you make a payment of $50 for cashing a Draft, which amount you will take up on your next account current, as the same will not be passed to your credit at the Treasury."—Copy, *ibid.*, Letters Sent. On March 10, 1854, Gibson again acknowledged receipt of accounts for 2nd quarter, 1853, apparently a revised version—*Ibid.*

1853, SEPT. 20.   Philip Clayton, Second Auditor of the Treasury, to USG. "Your a/c.s for disbursements as A.A.Q.M. in 3d qr. 1847; 1. qr. 1849 2d & 3d qrs 1851. and 1st & 3d qrs 1852, have been examined and adjusted and the sum of $708.64 found due you which has been transferred to your credit on the Books of the Office of the 3d Aud.r"—Copy DNA, RG 217, Second Auditor, Letters Sent.

1853, SEPT. 26.   F. Burt, Third Auditor of the Treasury, to Bvt. Maj. Gen. George Gibson. "I herewith enclose Voucher No 6 abst. Contingencies 4th qr. 1852. belonging to the a/cs. of Bt. Capt. U. S. Grant, 4th Infty—a.a.c.s. with the request that you will approve the same."—Copy, DNA, RG 217, Third Auditor, Miscellaneous Letters Sent.

1853, SEPT. 30.   F. Burt, Third Auditor of the Treasury, to USG. "The Comry. General of Subs. having transmitted your a/cs as a. a. Comry at Madison Bks & Fort Columbus N. Y, and Columbia Bks O. T, in the 2. 3. & 4th qrs 1852, to this office, the same have been audited & sent to the 2nd Comptroller of the Treasury, for his decision thereon, by whom they have been returned exhibiting a balance due the U. States, from you, of *Three thousand seven hundred and fifty five dollars and eighty six cents*, differing from your own a/c. Current in the sum of *$538.39*, arising thus: on a former settlement *disallowed* $2.10. amt of Reqn credited on a/c. of Qr. Mr. Depmt. $43.25. on present settlement, ref.d to 2nd Aud[r] $8. susp.d $8. amt. of farm culture not properly accounted for, $477.74. deduct error in sales to officers 70 cts The statement herewith, with susp.d vouchers, will explain the above. Your attention is called to error in provision Return.—"—Copy, DNA, RG 217, Third Auditor, Miscellaneous Letters Sent.

1853, [SEPT. 30].   "Report of Persons and Articles employed and hired at Fort Vancouver, W. T. during the month of September 1853." With notation that responsibility had been transferred to Capt. Thomas L. Brent—DS, DNA, RG 92.

1853, [SEPT. 30].   "Report of Stores received for Transportation and distribution at Columbia Barracks, W. T. in the month of September, 1853, by Bvt Captain U. S. Grant, Regimental Quartermaster, U. S. Army."—D (signature clipped), DNA, RG 92, Letters Received, Clothing.

1853, Nov. 1.   To Bvt. Maj. Gen. Thomas S. Jesup transmitting reports for 2nd quarter, 1853—DNA, RG 92, Registers of Letters Received.

1853, Nov. 2.   To Bvt. Maj. Gen. Thomas S. Jesup transmitting additional reports for 2nd quarter, 1853—DNA, RG 92, Registers of Letters Received.

1853, Nov. 4.   To Bvt. Maj. Gen. Thomas S. Jesup transmitting "the triplicate of Camp & Garrison Equipag[e] & Clothing Return reqd. by Genl. Orders No. 14—"—LS (and DS return), DNA, RG 92. See *Calendar*, Jan. 20, 1854.

1853, Nov. 5.   To Bvt. Maj. Gen. Thomas S. Jesup transmitting duplicate account for 2nd quarter, 1853—DNA, RG 92, Registers of Letters Received.

1853, Nov. 13.   To Bvt. Maj. Gen. Thomas S. Jesup transmitting abstract of disbursements made and articles furnished during the 2nd and 3rd quarters, 1853, for the northern Pacific railroad survey and expedition—DNA, RG 92, Registers of Letters Received.

1853, Nov. 26.   To Bvt. Maj. Gen. Thomas S. Jesup transmitting reports for Sept., 1853—DNA, RG 92, Registers of Letters Received.

1853, Nov. 26.   To Bvt. Maj. Gen. Thomas S. Jesup transmitting accounts for 3rd quarter, 1853—DNA, RG 92, Registers of Letters Received.

1853, Nov. 26.   To Bvt. Maj. Gen. Thomas S. Jesup transmitting reports for Oct., 1853—DNA, RG 92, Registers of Letters Received.

1853, Nov. 26.   USG voucher for $150.00 for transportation for himself to San Francisco on Sept. 24 and return to Fort Vancouver on Oct. 30, 1853—ADS, DNA, RG 92, Consolidated Correspondence 350.

1853, Nov. 26. USG voucher for payment to Henry E. Helting of $200 for copying public papers, to enable USG to close his accounts and transfer to Fort Humboldt—DS, DNA, RG 92, Consolidated Correspondence 350.

1853, Nov. 26. Certification of payment to J. D. Van Bergen of the Steamer *Fashion* of $4.40 for carrying q. m. supplies from Portland to Fort Vancouver—DS, DNA, RG 92, Consolidated Correspondence 350.

1853, Dec. 15. F. Burt, Third Auditor of the Treasury, to USG. "Your A/cs. as R. Qr. Mr. at Columbia Bks O. T. in 3d & 4th qrs 1852 & 1st qr. 1853. have been examined and adjusted at this office, & revised by the 2nd Comptroller of the Treasury, the result of which is a balance found due from you to the U. States of $625.92. differing in the sum of $20.44 from your last account current, (in which you acknowledge a balance due the U. S. of $605.48.) The difference is fully explained by the enclosed statement. The suspended Vouchers, owing to the distance, & the uncertainty of their reaching you, are retained in this office. You will, therefore, please correct the duplicates in your possession."—Copy, DNA, RG 217, Third Auditor, Miscellaneous Letters Sent.

1853. Certification that five pounds of sperm candles were needed for USG's office work. Approved by Lt. Col. Benjamin L. E. Bonneville—Listed in Charles Hamilton catalogue, Aug., 1962.

1853. USG signature on a petition requesting legislative assembly of Oregon "to authorise the Commissioner's Court of [Clackamas] county to establish a Ferry a cross the Willamette River at the termination of the Road lately laid out and opened from Vancouver to Portland . . ." Oregon State Archives, Portland.

1854, Jan. 5. Receipt by T. H. Stevens, San Francisco. "Received of Isaac M. Hale his promissory notes for $8750. bearing interest at the rate of two per cent per month in which U. S. Grant has an interest amounting to $1750—which amount with interest as collected is subject to his order—"—Copy in letter of March 3, 1863, from Julia Dent Grant to Capt. T. H. Stevens. "I enclose you copy of a receipt given me by my husband some years ago. I have never trouble[d] you on the subject before because I supposed you were unable to pay it. But now I am informed that you have been successful in business and are able to pay it, I would earnestly request that you would do so. We need the money very much—I am trying to save money to purchase a home for myself and children that we can have some place to live in and feel at home while this war is raging and to which my husband can come when peace is restored. Mr Grant has not been prosperous in business and has nothing to rely on except his pay which may be stopped at an early day by the ending of the war—My Dear Sir, let me urge you to do me an act of justice and settle this matter of so many years standing. You can send me a draft to care of J. R. Grant Covington, Kentucky or advise me by letter when you can pay it—P. S. I do not expect the interest stated—you can pay the amount with such interest as you think right, or you can send me the amount without interest"—ALS, Dr. Victor Turner, Newark, Ohio.

More information concerning this debt and others is contained in a letter from Z. Holt, San Francisco, to USG, Oct. 17, 1865. "Enclosed you find D. S. Laceys note Dated San Francisco May 12, 1854, to the order of H D. Wallen for $356.^{20}/$_{100}$ intrest at 3% pr Mo till paid—Hiram Thorns note dated 'Town of Clinton, Jany 4th 1854 to your order for $600—at 2% in pr mo till paid—Likewise your acct. current to Lt Derby for $279.^{66} with your order for Same—I handed Capt. J. C. Dent when laving here Lt. Stevens Recipt to you for $1750—I gave to Mr Eastman Capt. Wallens note which I think was paid or some settlement made to your satisfaction—Lacey Died a few years since verry poor—Hiram Thorn removed from Clinton a few years since—A Gentleman tells me to day they are neighbours. That he is verry poor 'and of no acct at that—' Should have reported before this but from the knowledge I had of your ocupation the last four years—"—ALS, USG 3.

1854, JAN. 14. C. A. Eastman, q. m. clerk at Fort Vancouver, Wash. Terr., to Bvt. Maj. Gen. Thomas S. Jesup transmitting a receipt for the steamer *Montgomery* to be filed with USG accounts for 3rd quarter, 1853—DNA, RG 92, Registers of Letters Received.

1854, JAN. 20.   Lt. Col. Charles Thomas, deputy q. m. gen., to USG. "Your letter of the 4th of November last, with the *triplicate* of your Return of Clothing & Equipage for the 2d qur of 1853, has been received; but the Return itself, with the Vouchers appertaining to it, has not reached this Office—You are requested to furnish another at your earliest convenience. Your Return for the 3d qur of 1853 closed by receipt of Capt Brent, was received on the 13th instant—"—Copy, DNA, RG 92, Letters Sent, Clothing. On Jan. 27, 1854, Bvt. Maj. Gen. Thomas S. Jesup wrote to USG. "Your Return of Clothing and Camp and Garrison Equipage as Regimental Quartermaster 4th Infy, for the 2d qur 1853, together with the Vouchers appertaining thereto, has been received. It will be unnecessary for you to forward the Return and papers for the 2d quarter, which you were requested to do by letter from this Office, on the 20th Inst."—*Ibid.* Also on Jan. 27, 1854, Jesup transmitted the returns to the Second Auditor's office—*Ibid.*

1854, JAN. 27.   Col. Samuel Cooper to Bvt. Maj. Gen. George Gibson, transmitting accounts in regard to farm culture, including a report from USG covering the last quarter of 1852 and the first quarter of 1853—DNA, RG 94, Selected Letters Sent. The report has not been found.

1854, FEB. 6.   Philip Clayton, Second Auditor of the Treasury, to F. Burt, Third Auditor of the Treasury. "I herewith respectfully enclose voucher 1. 3.d quarter 1852. of the a/c of *Capt. U. S. Grant* A.A.C.S. for $8.—which was received from you on the 1st of October 1853 in order that you may furnish me with the requirements of the Surg. Gen.l endorsed thereon, if the same be on file with the a/cs of Cap. U. S. Grant."—Copy, DNA, RG 217, Second Auditor, Letters Sent.

1854, FEB. 18.   By Orders No. 6 of Bvt. Lt. Col. Robert C. Buchanan, USG was appointed to a board of survey to report upon the condition of subsistence stores—Copy, DNA, RG 98, Pacific Division, Letters Received.

1854, FEB. 20.   By Orders No. 7 of Bvt. Lt. Col. Robert C. Buchanan, USG was appointed to a board of survey to report upon the condition of q. m. stores—Copy, DNA, RG 98, Pacific Division, Letters Received.

1854, M<small>ARCH</small> 11. Bvt. Maj. Gen. Thomas S. Jesup to USG. "Upon examining the accounts of Lieut: R Saxton a. a. q. m. to the North P. R. R. Survey, it is perceived that he transferred to you, pr your receipt of July 12, 1853, $6,300—which is not credited in your accounts for that period. You will credit this amount in your next account current, and explain why it was not done at the proper time."—Copy, DNA, RG 92, Q. M. Letter Books.

1854, M<small>ARCH</small> 15. To Bvt. Maj. Gen. George Gibson explaining nonrendition of his accounts. The letter was referred to the Secretary of War—DNA, RG 192, Registers of Letters Received.

1854, A<small>PRIL</small> 1. To Col. Henry K. Craig transmitting ordnance return for Co. F, 4th Inf., for 1st quarter, 1854—DNA, RG 156, Registers of Letters Received. On May 29, 1854, Capt. William Maynadier, Ordnance Department, acknowledged receipt of this return—Copy, *ibid.*, Letters Sent.

1854, A<small>PRIL</small> 23. C. A. Eastman, q. m. clerk at Fort Vancouver, Wash. Terr., to Bvt. Maj. Gen. Thomas S. Jesup enclosing nine vouchers and sub-vouchers necessary to complete USG accounts for 2nd and 3rd quarters, 1853. The matter was referred to the office of the 3rd auditor on June 13, 1854—DNA, RG 92, Registers of Letters Received.

1854, M<small>AY</small> 3. To Col. Henry K. Craig transmitting ordnance return for Co. F, 4th Inf., for part of 2nd quarter, 1854—DNA, RG 156, Registers of Letters Received. On June 15, 1854, Capt. William Maynadier acknowledged receipt of the return and forwarded it to the Second Auditor's office. The letter addressed to USG was returned as a dead letter on Nov. 18, 1854—Copies, *ibid.*, Letters Sent (Miscellaneous).

1854, M<small>AY</small> 8. F. Burt, Third Auditor of the Treasury, to USG. "The Commy. Genl of Subsistence having transmitted your a/cs as A.A.C.S. at Columbia Bks O. T. in 1st & 2nd qrs. 1853 to this office, the same have been audited and sent to the 2nd Comptroller for his decision thereon, by whom they have been returned exhibiting a balance due the U. States, from you, of $4.361.90, differing from your own a/c in the sum of $103.97 arising thus: disallowed $96.67 Susp.d $8. deduct error in your favor 70 cents. The accompanying statement will fully explain the above. Your attention is called to provision difference." —Copy, DNA, Third Auditor, Letters Sent, Collection Division.

1854, MAY 20. F. Burt, Third Auditor of the Treasury, to Secretary of War Jefferson Davis. "I have the honor, herewith, to enclose a voucher for the payment, in June 1853, by Bt. Capt. U. S. Grant, for a skiff lost in crossing the Columbia river in the pursuit of deserter. As pay for damages to or loss of private property is not deemed chargeable to the appropriations of the Qr. Master's Depmt, it is referred to the Secretary of War for his decision as to the appropriation to which it should be charged   As Capt Grant is now out of service, and his account now under examination, I respectfully request that the Voucher may be returned as ~~soon~~ early as convenient.—"—Copy, DNA, RG 217, Third Auditor, Letters Sent, Collection Division; *ibid.*, RG 107, Registers of Letters Received. Returned by Davis on May 30 endorsed "Charge transportation of troops and supplies."—*Ibid.*, Orders and Endorsements, Vol. 4.

1854, JUNE 1. F. Burt, Third Auditor of the Treasury, to Philip Clayton, Second Auditor of the Treasury. "Herewith enclosed are extracts from Vouchers 42 & 64. Ab "A" 3d qr. 1853. of the a/c. of Bt Capt: U. S. Grant, which are respectfully referred to your office for settlement.—"—Copy, DNA, RG 217, Third Auditor, Letters Sent, Collection Division. See *Calendar*, June 5, 1854.

1854, JUNE 5. Philip Clayton, Second Auditor of the Treasury, to F. Burt, Third Auditor of the Treasury. "I respectfully return an extract from Voucher No. 42. Abstract A. 3.d qr. 1853 of the A/c of *Capt. U. S. Grant*, R. Q. M. which you referred to this office on the 1.st inst. in order that the object for which the purchase of Black Crape, may be stated, if the same be on file in his accounts in your Office."— Copy, DNA, RG 217, Second Auditor, Letters Sent. See *Calendar*, June 7, 1854.

1854, JUNE 6. Philip Clayton, Second Auditor of the Treasury, to

F. Burt, Third Auditor of the Treasury. "In reply to your enquiry relative to the A/c.s of *U. S. Grant* Bt. Capt. I have to inform you, that his Cash A/c.s are closed, but his property a/c.s are unclosed."—Copy, DNA, RG 217, Second Auditor, Letters Sent.

1854, June 7.   Philip Clayton, Second Auditor of the Treasury, to Secretary of War Jefferson Davis. "I herewith respectfully submit for consideration, at your earliest convenience an extract from Voucher No. 42. Abstract A. 3.d quarter 1853. of the account of *Capt. U. S. Grant.* Regimental Quartermaster being a payment of $1.87 to the Hudson Bay Co. for 1½ yards of Blk: Crape."—Copy, DNA, RG 217, Second Auditor, Letters Sent. On July 27, 1854, Davis returned Clayton's letter, endorsed "Charge army Contingencies $1.87."— DNA, RG 107, Orders and Endorsements, Vol. 4.

1854, [June 30].   "Return of clothing . . . for quarter ending 30 June 1854."—Listed in Kingston Galleries, catalogue 19.

1854, July 5.   John Livingston to USG. "Your name has been proposed as a suitable one to occupy a place in our 'Portraits & Memoirs of Eminent Americans now living' several volumes of which has already been published. This great work has been recieved with much favor everywhere and contains some of the highest names in the country. including President Pierce & his cabinet with several prominent Army officers. Our portraits are engraved on steel by the first artists, and are true and life like, possessing greater value to the subjects and their friends than the most costly painting. You are respectfully solicited to occupy a place in the pages of this work. Should your compliance afford us the opportunity of giving to the world a true and permanent record of your life & features, please send us your likeness (a good daguerreotype of the same size as our portrait of Maj. Gen. Towson, herewith sent) to be handed over to our engravers. Please cause to be sent also a memoir of yourself—such facts as will enable me to prepare it; and I will not forget to say they should be fully and accurately given. I hope you will send both the Daguerreotype and memoir at your earliest convenience, as we have a volume in progress, and desire to avoid delay."—LS, USG 3. John Livingston, *Portraits of Eminent Americans Now Living: With Biographical and Historical Memoirs of their Lives and Actions* (New York, 1853–54) appeared in four volumes and a revised and consolidated edition appeared in 1854. USG is not included, and the letter would probably have come too late in any case since it was originally sent to Fort Vancouver.

1854, AUG. 17.   Philip Clayton, Second Auditor of the Treasury, to W. H. S. Taylor, act. Third Auditor of the Treasury. "Herewith I enclose extracts from vouchers 2 & 4. Abstract N. Third quarter 1853 of the account of Captain *U. S. Grant*, late Regimental Quartermaster amounting to $34.—which were excluded in the settlement of his accounts in this office."—Copy, DNA, RG 217, Second Auditor, Letters Sent.

1854, AUG. 19.   Philip Clayton, Second Auditor of the Treasury, to W. H. S. Taylor, act. Third Auditor of the Treasury. "On the settlement of the account of Capt. *U. S. Grant* late 4 Infantry, and Regimental Quartermaster, for the second and third quarters 1853, the sum of $1.802.82 has been found due him which will be transferred to his credit on the Books of your Office."—Copy, DNA, RG 217, Second Auditor, Letters Sent.

1854, SEPT. 26.   Robert J. Atkinson, Third Auditor of the Treasury, to USG. "Your a/c. as asst Qr Mr during the 2 & 3d qr.s 1853, has been examined & adjusted in this office & reported to the 2nd Comptroller of the Treasury, the result of which settlement is a balance found due from you to the U. S. of $9.787.84. differing in the sum of $37.312.67. from your own a/c. Current last rendered, in which you claim a balance due you of $27.524.83. This difference is fully explained by the enclosed statement & suspended vouchers to which your early attention is respectfully requested."—Copy, DNA, RG 217, Third Auditor, Miscellaneous Letters Sent.

1855, MAY 22.   USG as an appraiser (with Thaddeus Lovejoy and James L. Kennerly) of the estate of Richard Wells, prepared and signed two inventories covering real and personal property. He also witnessed the document in which the widow, Martha Wells, requested possession of one of the three slaves as her share of that portion of the estate.—Probate Court, City of St. Louis, Mo.

1855, JUNE 11.   USG receipt to William Musick, executor of the estate of Richard Wells, for one dollar "for services as Commissioner in assigning the Widow her Dower in the Slaves belonging to said Deceased."—DS, Probate Court, City of St. Louis, Mo.

1855, JUNE 19. Robert J. Atkinson, Third Auditor of the Treasury, to USG. "On the settlement of your Subs a/c, you were informed by letter from this office under date of May 8, 1854 addressed to you at Fort Humboldt Cala enclosing a statement of difference: that the balance due the U. States from you on said a/c was $4.361.90, subsequently you have been credited the sum of $150 turned over to A. V. Kautz per his acknowledgement of Sept 23/53 and by that of Lt. Withers under date of Sept 30, 1853 a further credit of $1.201.46 reducing your indebtedness on Subs a/c to $3.010.44 By letter dated Sept 26 1854 retained in this Office your address not being then known, the balance ascertained to be due from you on the settlement of your Qr Mr a/cs, was $9.787.84 differing from your own a/c in the sum of $37.312.67, as is now fully explained by the enclosed statement & suspended vouchers. It is necessary that your a/cs should be promptley closed as you are now out of service & I have to request that the suspended vouchers may be returned with such corrections & explanations as you may desire to submit when your a/c will be again audited & you advised of the result"—Copy, DNA, RG 217, Third Auditor, Letters Sent, Collection Division.

1855, SEPT. 1. William H. S. Taylor, act. Third Auditor of the Treasury, to USG. "By letter from this office of June 19" last you were advised that you stood charged on the Books of this office on a/c. of subsistence with the sum of $9.787.84. It being necissary that your a/c should be promptly closed, unless you can satisfactorily show that you have disbursed said sums in the public service, you will please pay it into the Treasury or to some disbursing officer of Gov.t entitled to receive the same and forward the evidence of such payment to this office and thereby ~~close~~ avoid the expense of a suit."—Copy, DNA, RG 217, Third Auditor, Letters Sent, Collection Division. This letter was sent to USG "Care of J. R Grant, Bethell Clermont Co. Ohio." On Oct. 6, 1855, Robert J. Atkinson wrote directly to Jesse R. Grant. "On the 19th June last, a letter from this office was addressed to U. S. Grant at Bethel, Clermont Co. Ohio, to Your care—will you please inform me

by return of mail if Mr. Grant has received the above named communication."—*Ibid.*

1856, JULY 5.   Robert J. Atkinson, Third Auditor of the Treasury, to
USG. "I have again to call your attention to the necessity of forwarding
the Suspended Vouchers, returned to you, with such corrections and
explanations as will be deemed by this office sufficient to allow them to
pass to your credit."—Copy, DNA, RG 217, Third Auditor, Letters
Sent, Collection Division.

1856, DEC. 19.   Robert J. Atkinson, Third Auditor of the Treasury,
to USG. "I will thank you to inform me why the long delay in transmitting your suspended vouchers, corrected, to this office. This matter
is of no little importance and must receive your prompt attention"—
Copy, DNA, RG 217, Third Auditor, Letters Sent, Collection Division. A statement prepared by the Third Auditor's office, July 29,
1857, showed a balance due from USG of $8,427.06.—DLC-Elihu
B. Washburne.

1860, APRIL 11, to 1861, APRIL 10.   Bills-of-lading prepared by USG
for the J. R. Grant store records in Galena—ICHi.

1860, SEPT. 12.   Two receipts to Smith Ellison for leather goods—
DS, Allyn K. Ford, Minneapolis, Minn.

1861, FEB. 25.   Receipt to Nack and Weiderholdt for payment for
leather goods—DS, Galena Historical Society, Galena, Ill.

1861, MARCH 8.   Receipt to W. W. Venable for payment for leather
goods—DS (facsimile), IHi.

Index

All letters written by USG of which the text was available for use in this volume are indexed under the names of the recipients. The dates of these letters are included in the index as an indication of the existence of text. Abbreviations used in the index are explained on pp. xxxiv–xxxvi.